Praise For L

"If there is a Mozart of Interviewers, Larry Grobel is that individual ... If the Interview as an art form emerges as a predominant prose genre in the 21st century, it will be the result of interviewers like Larry who manage to be both invisible and yet subtly dominating. In Larry's case, the Mozartian metaphor has a twofold meaning: the interviewer's apparent ease of execution and the consistently high quality of the work."

–Joyce Carol Oates

"As an interviewer Larry's all the things Joyce Carol Oates has said he is: prepared, adaptable, and graced with the intelligence needed to shoot the breeze and elicit intriguing responses from uncommonly gifted and often uncommonly suspicious subjects."

–Robert Towne

"I have come to know Larry Grobel very well. I have learned to appreciate his manner, his style, over the years. Some of which is shocking. But you accept it because it's Larry. He persists but never with guile. He has a genuine interest in people, which is why he's such a good writer. Still, I'm trying to figure out why it's so easy to talk to him, to confide in him. That's his talent, I guess."

–Al Pacino

"Larry Grobel's writing is quite marvelous. He would have to be regarded as the most intelligent interviewer in the United States."

–J.P. Donleavy

"In his quiet, conversational way, Larry gets people to talk about things they'd rather not talk about."

–Elmore Leonard

"Larry Grobel's interviews are informative and insightful without being pandering or intrusive. You get the sense at all times of intelligence at work—the interviewee's and Grobel's—both inspired by the encounter."

–David Duchovny

"There are few interviewers that you actually want to talk to. Larry Grobel is at the top of my list. [His work is] smart, witty, and a whole lot of fun. There are passages in his books that will leave you stunned."

–Dylan McDermott

"I would recommend Larry Grobel as a therapist to just about anybody."

–Montel Williams

"A legend among journalists, Grobel's penchant for landing the impossible subjects has earned him respect among his peers."

–*Writer's Digest*

"I think I could read Lawrence Grobel forever.... His previous books, *Above the Line: Conversations About the Movies, Conversations with Capote, The Hustons, Conversations with Brando,* and *Talking With Michener*, are textbook studies in the nimble, alchemical art of interviewing someone–listening well, asking improper questions when necessary, and transforming the somewhat artificial setup of an interview into intriguing dialogue. ... Grobel deserves a chunk of your reading time; he's able to take you in directions you didn't think you'd be heading."

–*Austin Chronicle*

"On top of being a great interviewer, Grobel must be the world's most fascinating dinner guest, having traveled the world, talked to the most famous people of our time, all while he worked at his art."

–Blake Snyder, *Movieweb.com*

"Lawrence Grobel is the Interviewer's Interviewer."

–*Playboy*

Books by Lawrence Grobel

Fiction
Begin Again Finnegan
Catch a Fallen Star
The Black Eyes of Akbah
Commando Ex

Memoir
You Show Me Yours

Poetry
Madonna Paints a Mustache & Other Celebrity Happenings

Non-fiction
You, Talking to Me
Meryl Streep
Barbra Streisand
Conversations with Ava Gardner
Marilyn & Me (for Lawrence Schiller)
Signing In: 50 Celebrity Profiles
"I Want You in My Movie!" The Making of Al Pacino's WildeSalome
Yoga? No! Shmoga!
Icons: 15 Celebrity Profiles
Al Pacino: In Conversation with Lawrence Grobel
Conversations with Robert Evans
The Art of the Interview: Lessons from a Master of the Craft
Climbing Higher (with Montel Williams)
Endangered Species: Writers Talk About Their Craft, Their Vision, Their Lives
Above the Line: Conversations About the Movies
Conversations with Michener

The Hustons
Conversations with Brando
Conversations with Capote

www.lawrencegrobel.com

You, Talking To Me

■ ■ ■

Lessons I Learned Along the Celebrity Trail

Lawrence Grobel

FIRST EDITION
HMH Press
contact@lawrencegrobel.com

For Mika and Adrian
(& Ella and Ethan),
who have a lot to learn

Lawrence Grobel: The freshman who called you by your last name and was the catalyst for your being fired, was burned in effigy outside President Brand's home; flyers of him were printed with the words "Wanted: Dead." He and his two brothers withdrew from the university and they've left the state. How concerned were you about any of this?

BOB KNIGHT: I have not followed what direction their lives have taken.

Grobel: Didn't the boy's stepfather say that he didn't think that you should be fired over this incident?

KNIGHT: [*BANGS the center of his car's steering wheel with his fist. His rage is sudden, frightening, and unexpected.*] JESUS CHRIST! THIS IS BULLSHIT! I'M NOT HERE FOR A FUCKING INQUISITION! AND IF THAT'S WHAT THIS IS THEN GET THE FUCK OUT AND HITCHHIKE BACK HOME! THE FUCKING STEPFATHER WAS A FUCKING GODDAMN FUCKING ASSHOLE FROM THE WORD GODDAMN GO! HE FUCKING LIED AND HE LIED AND HE LIED! *JESUS CHRIST!* I MEAN THIS IS MY FUCKING LIFE HERE THAT WE'RE TALKING ABOUT! MY FUCKING *HEART* WAS RIPPED OUT BY THIS GODDAMN BULLSHIT!

Grobel: OK...

KNIGHT: OK MY *ASS!* IT ISN'T FUCKING OK! GODDAMN IT, I DON'T NEED THIS SHIT! I'LL DROP YOU OFF IN FUCKING DAYTON AND YOU CAN GET HOME.

Grobel: Please coach...

KNIGHT: THIS IS FUCKING BULLSHIT! I DON'T WANT TO HEAR ANOTHER FUCKING WORD!

—*Playboy* Interview, March 2001

Contents

Introduction

When comedian/curmudgeon Marc Maron asked me to be a guest on his WTF podcast, I knew he was skeptical but curious about how I did what I did. I wasn't a comedian or an actor, but I had interviewed a lot of them. Maron being Maron—neurotic, insecure, jealous, yet funny, and always in search of answers—he wanted to hear my stories and find out whether I was sane or slightly insane, like himself. I figured he wanted to hear the inside scoop behind the scenes of some of my interviews with hard-to-get celebrities, but I didn't expect that the question he would keep returning to was "OK, so what have you learned from talking to these people?" I deflected any answer the first time he asked, and the second, third and fourth times as well, because I had begun working on this book, and I didn't want to jinx it by talking about it. I know it frustrated him that I was being evasive, but I just wasn't ready to say what I had learned, even though I had given it a lot of thought.

I first started thinking about this when I was asked by the National Scholastic Press Association to speak at their annual convention in 2011. The organizers wanted me to talk about what I'd learned from interviewing. I came up with a number of lessons that I thought might work. After I spoke, some of the young journalists asked if I might expand on the lessons I presented.

A few months later I gave a similar lecture to a different group of people at Rancho la Puerta, a popular health spa in Tecate, Mexico. They weren't writers or journalists, so I was interested to see if I could hold their interest. The scheduled hour wound up as a three-hour conversation. These people—doctors, lawyers, executives, musicians, scientists and social workers—were fascinated that interviews could result in such a diverse number of life lessons. These were people who went to The Ranch to work on themselves, and learning lessons was a way to self-improvement. One of the people, a psychologist, suggested that I consider writing a book. Another added, "It's inspirational, it's educational, and it's about celebrities. How can you *not* write a book?"

My initial answer was that I had already written a book about interviewing (*The Art of the Interview*), and I wasn't really sure the world needed a second book about the subject from the same author. But then, when I got home, I realized these lessons would approach it from a completely different angle.

In *The Art of the Interview*, I was looking outward: how to prepare, how to write questions, how to segue from one subject to another, how, basically, to propel conversation. I summed up the skills I thought made for a good interview: One must be able to converse like a talk show host, think like a writer, understand subtext like a psychiatrist, hear like a musician, select the best parts like a book editor, and piece them all together dramatically like a playwright. My aim was to demonstrate these skills and help potential interviewers along their way.

I wrote that book when I was teaching the subject at UCLA and didn't have a text that mirrored my experiences. I wasn't thinking about the inward journey of interviewing, what

I personally took away from talking to a motley crew of talented people. But talking to people is something we all do, not just journalists. Everyone asks questions, and everyone seeks answers. It's what propels movies, television and social media. People talking to people; people trying to understand other people. What are we taking away from all this talk? What do we learn?

I began looking at the long list of people I've interviewed over the years and thought about what I had learned from each of them. I made notes. Being with Henry Fonda taught me something different from being with Richard Feynman. Joyce Carol Oates was unlike Saul Bellow, who was very different from Truman Capote. One by one I discovered that almost everyone I interviewed at any depth taught me something.

I shouldn't have been surprised. I remembered when Marlon Brando asked me how I could keep interviewing actors and I answered that I learned something new from each one, because people, even self-centered actors, are all individuals with their own unique stories.

The Lessons in *You, Talking to Me* aren't written as a text, but more as a personal memoir. Some of my conversations were amusing and some were harrowing. Robert De Niro called me a Judas; Patty Hearst said she wanted to shoot me; Bob Knight threatened to throw me out of his car; Pavarotti told me I had gotten him in a lot of trouble; Alec Baldwin woke me at 5:00 a.m. to complain that I had screwed him; Dolly Parton stopped speaking to me after I mentioned the name Charlie Manson. Most every famous person said or did something to me that made me see them or me differently. And that, in essence, is a lesson.

Over the years I've appeared on radio and television to talk about people I've interviewed. When Mel Gibson and

Charlie Sheen were in the news for their outlandish behaviors respectively, I was on CNN and the *E! True Hollywood Story*. When Bob Knight was fired from his coaching job at Indiana, I spent a week on sports radio shows describing his psychotic behavior towards me. When Gov. Jesse Ventura spoke to me for *Playboy*, he talked about organized religion being a sham and a crutch for weak-minded people. I wound up talking to dozens of TV hosts, including Matt Lauer on the *Today Show*, Geraldo Rivera on his show, and Brian Wilson on CSPAN. I've done a half hour with Charlie Rose talking about John Huston. When Marlon Brando died, I was on TV and radio discussing what he had said during the ten days I spent with him on his island in Tahiti. When the Blu-Ray edition of *Scarface* was released, I wrote the liner notes and was interviewed by a half dozen magazines regarding Al Pacino.

Lessons are best when they're shared. I hope to continue learning new ones, but here's what I've learned so far.

Expect The Unexpected

1. ALLOW FOR IT

My first celebrity interview was with **Mae West**, and it's one I've never forgotten. Mae was a living legend when my *Newsday* editor gave me the assignment. He had no idea how to get to her but figured that as I had moved from New York to Los Angeles, I should be able to figure it out.

When he mentioned her name, my initial reaction was to ask if she was still alive. Mae West had been a huge star in the 1930s and '40s, the Madonna/Amy Winehouse/Lady Gaga/ Miley Cyrus of her day. At one time Hollywood's highest paid star, her films are credited with saving Paramount Pictures from bankruptcy. She was more sexual innuendo than titty flasher; she wrote her own material for stage and films; she was once put in jail for being too sexy on stage; she plucked a young Cary Grant out of obscurity and made him a star; she subjugated the repressive W.C. Fields; and her double entendre one-liners have passed the test of time. Who isn't familiar with: "Why don't you come up and see me sometime?" delivered with all the nuance of a professional cockteaser. Or, "Is that a gun in your pocket or are you just glad to see me?" purred to one of her pursuers. She was more quoted than Will Rogers, much the way Rodney Dangerfield was after his Tonight Show appearances with Johnny Carson. In movies like *She Done Him Wrong, I'm No Angel*, and *My Little Chickadee,* we heard such lines as: "You only live once, but if you do it right, once is enough." "When I'm good I'm very good; when I'm bad, I'm better." "A hard man is good to find." "I speak two languages: Body and English." "Sex is emotion in motion." "It's not the men in my life that count, it's the life in my men." "To err is human, but it feels divine."

Her voice was so recognizable that some impressionists made their livings imitating her. And even at 77 she was camp enough to play Leticia Van Allen in Gore Vidal's *Myra Breckinridge* (which also starred John Huston, Raquel Welch and Farrah Fawcett). I was invited to her apartment on Rossmore Avenue in Hollywood when she was 80. I was so nervous that I prepared as many questions as I could imagine, and made sure my tape recorder was new and the batteries fresh. I spotted a florist near her apartment building and got the bright idea of bringing her flowers. Once inside her place, the first thing I noticed was the white marble statue of her on top of the piano. Her muscleman/bodyguard/boyfriend was in the living room and we sat in chairs waiting for her entrance.

"Are those for me?" she said as she glided into the room. "How nice." Her intonation reminded me of her throwaway line in *I'm No Angel*: "Beulah, peel me a grape." She was obviously a woman used to receiving flowers.

She wasn't very tall but with her high heels and high hair we were almost equal in height. She was wearing a white brocaded dress and was full figured, still well built for an aging legend. I took out my notes and tape recorder and placed them on the coffee table. Mae sat down slowly on her couch, looked at my machine, and with a swipe of her hand said, "No, you can't use that. Put it away."

I couldn't record our conversation? How else could I be accurate? Weren't all interviews recorded? Didn't stars worry about being misquoted?

"I don't understand," I stammered.

"I allowed a reporter to use one once and he turned it into a recording that he subsequently tried to market. I don't want that to happen again."

"I would never do that," I protested. "And I can put that in writing if you like."

"What I would like," she said, "is for you to put it away."

I wasn't prepared for this curveball. This was my first celebrity interview and I was being told that I would have to rely on my memory and whatever notes I could scribble as we talked. Luckily I had a pad with me, but I certainly hadn't expected to use it as a replacement for my tape recorder. But I had no choice. She may have been 80, but she was still Mae West. I wish I could have appropriated one of her lines to help me out, like "When I'm taking notes I'm good, but when I'm tape recording, I'm even better." But I didn't have my wits about me. I only had my yellow pad and my pen.

It could have been a disaster if she had been a rapid talker, but Mae West spoke slowly, and I was able to get her words down. When she forgot something, her muscleman/ bodyguard/boyfriend would prompt her and she would pick up where she left off, nice and slow. About an hour and a half into our conversation I had to go to the bathroom, but I feared she might see that as a termination of the interview. Unfortunately, I couldn't count on her own bathroom needs, because she was like a camel, not needing to relieve herself for the entire three hours we talked. She told me that her secret was simple;

that she regulated herself by taking an enema twice a day. She had done it all her adult life, starting in vaudeville when she had to wear corsets on stage and never had enough time between acts to get them off and back on. She told me a lot of other things as well, and I was grateful that the interview went as well as it did. My editor was pleased and asked me to continue doing them. But without that pad of paper and pen, I would have been lost, and perhaps never gone on with what would become my lifetime career. I always used a tape recorder after that, but for my first legend I managed to meet the unexpected head on. A good lesson to learn when just starting out.

2. BE DISTINCTIVE. GO BEYOND WHAT EVERYONE KNOWS

Mae West prepared me for the unexpected, but no one could have prepared me for **Elliott Gould**. He was in a class all by himself, and forty-three years later, I haven't changed that opinion. His star had already waned from when he appeared on the cover of *Time* in 1970, three years earlier, and it had to do with (a) drugs (b) losing Barbra Streisand and (c) not being ready when director Ingmar Bergman singled him out as the first American actor to star in one of his films. He went from being the number one box-office attraction after appearing in *M*A*S*H, The Long Goodbye*, and *Bob & Carol & Ted & Alice* to scaring his director (Anthony Harvey) and costar (Kim Darby) on the set of a film called *A Glimpse of Tiger*. That led to his becoming uninsurable for major studio films for a few years. Plus, his marriage to Streisand went sour when their roles reversed and she became the biggest star after *Funny Girl*, and she subsequently wound up saving him from lawsuits after his behavior closed down *A Glimpse of Tiger*. Then his behavior was further altered after David Carradine introduced him to LSD, which opened his mind a little too much. Whether he spoke in a Joycean stream-of-consciousness manner before he dropped acid I cannot know, because I met him after that.

He was renting a house in Beverly Hills and wasn't there when I arrived in the evening. His publicist let me in and stayed with me for an hour before he had to leave. He didn't think it a problem that I should wait alone in the house for Elliott to return. I thought that was strange but plunked down on a couch and went over my questions. When Gould finally got home he seemed ready to go. He was instantly recognizable, tall with curly hair and fire in his eyes. He asked me if I wanted some soup, turned on the television, and didn't react to my mentioning that we had Brooklyn in common. I asked if we could turn off the TV, since it would make recording him difficult and he obliged, only to put on a Marvin Gaye record instead. "That's not going to work either," I said, and tried to ease into his backstory by asking him about having done Bosco chocolate commercials as a kid.

"Information," he answered. It was the same response he had given me when I started with Brooklyn.

I tried again, asking him about learning to tap dance at an early age.

"Information," he repeated a third time.

The interview was going nowhere fast. I knew my opening questions were from his bio and things I had read while preparing to talk to him, but I thought that it was a way to warm up and get us comfortable together. But Gould had a different mindset. Why go over things everyone already knew?

"Your real name is Goldstein," I said. "How'd it become Gould?"

"Sometimes I'm Elliott Goldstein, sometimes I'm Elliott Gould. It's the same person. More information."

I figured Elliott was stoned and was just going to continue going around in circles, and that wasn't going to make for good copy, so I suggested that perhaps this wasn't the right time for doing this interview. I said I could come back on another day. But that wasn't how Gould saw it. "We're talking, man," he said. "You just got to come up with better questions."

By "better questions" he meant questions that he hadn't answered a dozen times before, questions that piqued his interest. He didn't want to be bored; he wanted to be stimulated. Why do an interview if it's just the same thing over and over again? Bosco commercials, tap dancing, Brooklyn, Barbra, name change, and so on.

'Let's keep going," he said. "You sure you don't want soup?"

"Sure," I said. "Let's have soup."

I left a few hours later and returned the next day, and the next, and have been talking to Elliott ever since. He's become a friend, an outcome I never would have anticipated, given that first hour we met. But he taught me an important lesson when he kept repeating that one word, "Information." Be distinctive. Go beyond. Don't give up. And by not dismissing me when I was ready to call it quits, he made me a better journalist.

3. WHEN YOU SAVE SOMEONE FROM GETTING HIS HEAD SMASHED, HE'LL RESPOND WITH KINDNESS

Like Gould, **Sylvester Stallone** kept his distance when we began our cable TV interview on the front lawn of the Playboy Mansion. Stallone was still coming to grips with stardom and what happened between us was something neither of us could have predicted.

His face had been damaged at birth when the doctor used forceps to bring him out of his mother's womb; consequently, he spoke with a Lower Eastside-accented gruffness out of one side of his mouth. In spite of that, he had big dreams but, before *Rocky,* he was just a bit player. He knew the way to becoming a star was to have the right project, and the only way for him to find such a project would be to write it himself. His *Rocky* script hit a nerve in Hollywood and he was offered a lot of money for it. But when he insisted on starring in it as well, the bids dropped drastically. He didn't care; he knew fortune would follow fame and the only way to become famous was to succeed as Rocky Balboa. It worked. After two *Rocky* sequels, he took on the Vietnam War in *First Blood*, a smart move because the character of Rambo was physical, but not very verbal. That's when I met him, promoting this second great character.

Though it was a hot summer day, Stallone was dressed in a pinstripe suit, looking very dapper and somewhat out of place. The sun was so strong in midday that a huge canvas screen had to be erected behind him to defuse the brightness. The screen was supported by two heavy 12-foot iron poles. There were workers on each side of the screen holding those poles upright, and all went well for the first thirty minutes until the cameramen had to change reels. Stallone and I got up from our director chairs to stretch and get some water.

I went over to talk to him, just to maintain any rapport we were beginning to have, but he was busy on the phone and wasn't looking to make small talk. Finally, when we were ready to roll we both sat back down, clipped on our small microphones, had our faces patted down by the makeup woman, and got ready to resume our interview. But just as Stallone got settled, I noticed that the worker assigned to hold one of the poles behind him was not there. The steel pole had been planted a few inches into the ground, so it stood by itself for a few minutes, but when the other worker gripped his pole, it tugged on the one behind Stallone and it started to fall.

I saw this happen almost in slow motion. The pole was coming down directly behind Stallone's head, and in another ten seconds he would have been crushed. I reacted instinctively and immediately, jumping forward to catch it. Stallone thought I had somehow lost my mind and was leaping to attack him, because he curled into a fighter's crouch and was about to punch me in the gut, just as I managed to reach above his head and grab the pole.

"Holy geez," he said when he looked up and saw what had happened. "Good reflexes. Thanks, man, you saved me. Wudda been some lawsuit."

"Only if you survived," I joked.

My mic broke when I jumped up, so while the crew was finding me another, Stallone became more talkative. We shared some personal stories and, once we resumed rolling, we picked up where we had left off, and he answered my questions in a much more invigorating manner, elaborating on self-deprecating stories that he had never revealed in previous interviews. Everyone was pleased with the result and I came away with this story, how I literally saved Sylvester Stallone's life. Or, at the very least, from some serious head injury. And he paid it off with stories no one had heard before.

4. MAKE THE BEST OF AN AWKWARD SITUATION

Sometimes the unexpected doesn't happen during an interview, but before it even begins.

When I wanted to take my skills to another level, a step above the 3000-word newspaper magazine interview, I conceived a plan to burrow my way into the Interview pantheon—i.e., the *Playboy* Interview. The challenge was to figure out how to convince the editors there that I was worthy of a shot. I was young and didn't have an agent, but I was ambitious. So I thought if I interviewed **Hugh Hefner**, the head honcho himself, and did a good job (no soft or easygoing piece, something hard-hitting yet fair), I might get favorable attention by the magazine's editors. I wasn't exactly sure how this might work, but I suggested Hefner as a subject to my *Newsday* editor and he liked the idea. So did *Playboy's* publicist, and it didn't take long to set up a time for me to see the boss at his Holmby Hills mansion.

A few days before the scheduled event I found out that the photographer I had used on previous assignments was unavailable. But I knew the brother of a friend of mine was a photographer and looking for work, and he would jump at the opportunity to photograph Hefner and, like me, somehow work his way into the Playboy Empire. Though I had never worked with him before, all that was needed for this shoot was a smiling headshot of the man who gave us the Centerfold and forever changed the masturbatory habits of young American boys.

The Playboy Mansion was one of those bucket-list places one hopes to see, like Disneyland, the Eiffel Tower, and the Taj Mahal. It's the only private home in Los Angeles that has a registered zoo and has a permit to set off fireworks on the 4th of July. There's a tennis court where pro tennis players come to practice, a game room featuring archival pinball machines, a pool table, two guest rooms with waterbeds, a separate building that houses human bunnies, a well-stocked koi pond, caged exotic birds and small mammals, and a curvaceous swimming pool that leads to a private Jacuzzi grotto. If those faux grotto rock walls could talk, there would be quite a lot of fantasy fulfillment to relate.

When I arrived and met Grayden, the photographer, we stood in the foyer near the dual staircases that led to Hefner's bedroom and discussed how we wanted to do this. I thought that he should set up his tripod and be ready to shoot but not begin until Hefner and I were at least fifteen minutes into our conversation. I was hoping he could get his shot quickly, then leave as quietly as possible. We were brought to Hef's study and Grayden started to unpack his equipment. "Oh shit," I heard him mumble.

"What's the problem?" I asked.

"I forgot the film."

"You what?" I couldn't believe what he just said. How could a photographer forget film? That would be like me forgetting batteries for my tape recorder.

"I thought I put my bag of film in, but I must have left it at home."

"Where do you live?" I asked.

"A half hour away."

"Too far. We're supposed to start in ten minutes."

"Maybe they have film here. After all, it *is* Playboy," he said.

"We can ask," I said, already disheartened.

We asked the publicist who was waiting to introduce us, and he asked a secretary who asked someone in the kitchen. There was no film. Grayden would have to get in his car and drive into nearby Westwood and buy some film.

Just as he walked out the door, Hefner came down the stairs and we shook hands. I told him that we could get started and that the photographer would come in twenty minutes to shoot while we talked. "No, let's get the photographs out of the way first," Hefner said. "Then we won't have any distractions. Is he ready?"

Well, I thought, so much for my impressing this guy and landing a shot at the magazine. "He...uh...actually...well, he discovered that his film was dated and ran out to get some more. He should be back any minute. Perhaps you could show me around before we begin?"

Yikes, did I actually say that? Was I asking Hugh Hefner to give me a tour of his fabled mansion? He didn't know my work, or me, and the publicist had said he had only allotted an hour for our interview, including the photographs. But I got lucky; Hefner was game, and we went out to the beautifully land-scaped backyard, where we walked among the flamingoes and peacocks, fed the koi, and stopped by Teri, a wooly mon-key, chained to a stake in the lawn near the monkey cages. Hefner told me how he had always loved animals and enjoyed bringing so many to his estate. As he talked, Teri wrapped one hand around my ankle and held tight. I felt like I had been snagged by a miniature gorilla. When Hefner started to walk toward the cages, I couldn't follow. I tried my best to get the little ape to unlock her grip, but she showed me who the real boss was. I thought of kicking her with my other foot, but knew that would get me thrown out of the mansion even before we started taping.

"Uh, Hef," I stammered, "I think we have a situation here."

Hefner turned around and walked back to where I stood with his favorite pet. "She likes to do that to people," he said. "She'll let go when you stop resisting."

"Well," I said with a laugh, "this is a first for me."

The monkey eventually let go of my ankle and we contin-ued the tour. Hefner even took me up to his bedroom to show me his rotating circular bed and the Monopoly game he had specially made, featuring likenesses of him and his friends as the moving pieces, with the money displaying the famous

Hefner face. By the time Grayden returned, Hef and I had somehow bonded and once the pictures were taken, we went on to have a seven-hour long conversation, and I returned the next day to continue for another hour.

When the piece was published, Hefner was pleased with the photo they chose and liked our interview so much that he decided to distribute it at the annual Advertiser's Lunch at the Playboy Club in Century City. I was invited to that lunch and was introduced to Arthur Kretchmer, the Editorial Director of the magazine. "Nice job with Hef," he said. I thanked him and showed him some clips of other people I had interviewed for *Newsday*, saying I'd like to do some interviews for *Playboy*. He told me to call the editor in charge of that section. And that's how I became a *Playboy* interviewer.

Had Grayden not forgotten his film, I never would have had that private time with Hefner, and I doubt that he would have given me more than that scheduled hour. But Fate, in the guise of an absentminded photographer, stepped in and I managed to make the best of what had been a very awkward situation.

5. IF THEY MISTAKE YOU FOR SOMEONE ELSE, LET IT RIDE

I faced another awkward moment when **Bette Midler** mistook me for a hotel worker. Midler was the very picture of a diva when I walked into her suite in the fall of 1991, when she was promoting her latest film, *For the Boys*. She was in boss-mode, giving instructions to her assistants and including me as someone who could get her something to eat and drink. I've always been a big Bette Midler fan and when I put out my hand to greet her, she looked puzzled. "I think you've mistaken me," I said. "Who are you?" she asked. I told her and she walked into her bedroom to talk to her husband, the performance artist and commodities broker Martin von Haselberg. I didn't hear what they talked about, but I suspected she was complaining about not being told of the time of my arrival. When she came out, she apologized for mistaking me for a hotel employee and I laughed and said I could use a steady job. Then we got down to business.

She let me know that she didn't read anything about herself because she had a thin skin when it came to criticism. She told me that if I quoted something negative about her she'd have to throw me out. "I try not to let that into my life," she said. "I'm too sensitive. I made up my mind a long time ago—if you're gonna read the good you gotta read the bad, too. And since I had no tolerance *at all* for even one bad word, even a suggestion, it became impossible for me to read not only reviews, but also any interview that I had ever given. I don't read any of it."

Midler was so convinced of her talent that she decided early on to become a legend. "I wanted to be a phenomenon," she said. "I didn't want to be just a schlepper." Success, to her, was a game. "It's like everybody's playing and playing to win. So you're constantly jockeying for position."

The character she created, the flamboyant Divine Miss M, came to her only after someone took her to see Marlene Dietrich on stage in 1966. "I had no idea who she was," she said. "I'm watching this woman with her hairdo and this long white fur coat. She sashays across the stage and drops the coat, and this crowd is going *crazy!* People are screaming! Their faces are turning red. They're crying. And I'm thinking, 'What the fuck is going on here?' She does this whole show and *I didn't get it.*"

What she did get was a new understanding of stardom. She began seeing all of Dietrich's movies. "I'd never seen so much gauze, so much glue, so many eyelashes, and so many sequins. It started out neat and then got bizarre. But it was so beautiful. I was totally enchanted by it. I had no idea that any of this was going on."

When I tried to get her to talk about her life before stardom, when she felt beaten down by "this cheese-bomb American crappola dream," she became defensive. "Am I on trial?" she asked.

"No, you're just being interviewed," I said.

"Because I feel like I'm on trial."

Though I felt the tension between us, I found her to answer honestly and directly when she stopped feeling like she was being closely examined. She had nothing good to say about Bruce Springsteen, who wouldn't sign off on her recording "Pink Cadillac," and she refused to talk about Madonna. "I have nothing to say about her," she said. "I have no opinion about Madonna. I can't say anything without sounding like a jerk. You can't talk the truth, and I don't want to lie. I don't want to slander the girl. It's nobody's business what I think of Madonna. I certainly couldn't put her in the vast cosmic picture."

I wouldn't have known she had such distaste for Madonna if she hadn't called me at 11:00 p.m. that night to ask me not to include what she had said about being funnier than Madonna. I told her that we hadn't talked about Madonna. "We didn't?" she asked.

And that's when I asked her why Madonna was on her mind and she gave me the "I have nothing to say" answer.

"Be kind," she whispered on the phone. "We had a nice day."

We did. She mistook me for the help at the hotel, and when she later called she tried to go off the record about something she hadn't put on the record. When you're The Divine Miss M, confusion, like success, is just part of the game when you're struggling to stay a phenomenon and not become a schlepper.

6. WHEN YOU DON'T KNOW, DON'T SHOW...LET THEM EXPLAIN

Charlie Sheen also went off the record to ask me about something I knew nothing about, which was one of those unexpected gifts coughed up by a careless star.

As much as I pride myself on preparation, I'm aware that there is also a lot that I don't know about a person I'm going to interview. The research I do informs me on the main points of a person's life, and allows me to bring up topics that can set the stage for extensive elaboration during the course of the conversation. If I know how many times someone has been married, I can try to have the blanks filled about the times in-between those marriages. If I knew everything I needed to know to write a profile, I wouldn't need to do the interview.

That being said, Charlie Sheen gave me a lesson in the art of faking-like-I-know-about-something-when-I-didn't.

This happened when he was still a movie star to be reckoned with, before he started on *Two and a Half Men*, and subsequently went ballistic and lost his job on that show, resulting in his touring the country attempting to do stand-up before audiences who bought his WINNING! T-shirts and then booed him when he had nothing entertaining to say. And it was definitely before his father and brothers sought to have an intervention with him to get him back to Planet Earth. This was the Sheen of *Platoon* and *Wall Street*, of *Young Guns*, *Major League* and *Hot Shots* when I met him at his house in Malibu. He was living the high life, enjoying his fame, driving flashy cars, dating beautiful women, and doing the drugs that kept the rollercoaster going but didn't yet throw him into rehab. He was young, handsome, and wealthy, and seemed to have the rock-and-rolling Hollywood scene in the palms of his hands. I was there to ask him about how he got caught using stolen credit cards as a teenager; how he got thrown off his high school baseball team for failing a class; how he once attacked a teacher and got thrown out of school; and how he dealt with his father's heart attack in the Philippines during the filming of *Apocalypse Now*! And, of course, about the films he starred in.

I wasn't there to ask him about his girlfriend getting shot by his gun in the house where we were talking—*because I didn't know about it.* And—sonofabitch!—he didn't know I didn't know! That's how I managed to dodge that bullet of ignorance. Because I should have known about it. If it happened, and it was out there in the ether, a good reporter would have heard about it. And surely would have addressed it. But it was just one of those juicy bits that I had missed, and Charlie saved my ass by bringing it up first.

About an hour into our interview he stopped to ask me a question. "How do we talk about what happened in my house without me going into too much detail, since it's still under police investigation?"

What?? I practically threw up in my mouth when he asked this. *What had happened in his house? What were the police investigating?* If I admitted to not knowing what he was referring to, he would have said something like, 'Oh, okay, let's continue then.' And I would have been sitting there thinking, 'What? How? When? Who?'

Instead, I did what came naturally to me. That is, I acted like I knew all about it. "The best way to handle that, Charlie," I said as matter-of-factly as I could muster, knowing this was a gambler's bluff on my part, "is to just lay it out the way it actually happened, so all the tabloid reporting can't distort the truth."

"You think so, huh?" he asked.

"I know so. If you don't talk about it, then the rumors will become facts and you don't want that. Who needs to have to deal with having to correct the record every time you do an interview from now on? All you have to do is set the record straight now, right here with me, once and for all."

"Yeah, maybe you're right," he said. "Why don't you ask me questions about it and I'll answer them."

"Great," I said, still in the dark. "Why don't you tell me what happened in your house that led to the police beginning an investigation?" I had no idea what had happened, so I really couldn't ask any leading questions, other than this general one, which is what he had just told me. But it worked.

"I was downstairs in the bathroom one morning and my girlfriend Kelly was upstairs," he began. (Kelly was Kelly Preston.) "She went to move my pants off the scale and my gun fell out of the back pocket, hit the linoleum floor and discharged a round that, thank God, didn't hit her directly. But it hit the toilet next to her, and she got hit with the porcelain shrapnel and lead from the bullet itself."

Holy shit! Charlie Sheen's girlfriend, who would later become John Travolta's wife, got injured from the gun Sheen kept in the back pocket of his pants! This was surely a gift. Thank you, Charlie, I thought. Thank you, thank you, *thank you.* And now, let's continue.

Why did he carry a loaded gun? I wondered.

"With Rebecca Schaeffer being murdered at her own door one night by a lunatic, with John Lennon, with the continual threat of crazy people towards celebrity, I've been carrying a weapon for quite some time because I felt that if shit ever went down I'd want to return some fire."

What kind of gun did he carry? I mused.

"A little .22 Mag and five-shot revolver."

"How serious was Kelly's wound?"

"When I rushed upstairs she was in her underwear, holding her wrist and bleeding from several places."

"What did you do?"

"I picked up the phone in a panic, and I didn't know whether to call 411 or 911. It was terrifying. The paramedics came and the police had to come because it was a shooting incident."

"Did they think you shot her?"

"No, they didn't haul me away for shooting her, but she was taken to the hospital and got stitches in her wrist and calf."

"Do you still have the gun?"

"No. The police held it for 72 hours and then gave it back. I threw it in the ocean because it had a vibe about it that was not healthy."

"What did you learn from this incident?"

"It was a turning point in my philosophy of arming myself in the streets. I'm studying hand-to-hand now instead of carrying a weapon."

"Do you still have weapons in the house?"

"Yes. In the times we live and the profession we work in I feel it necessary to keep armed. If some lunatic wants to come and do some damage, he's going to walk into an arsenal and I'll have a bead on him."

The questions were endless, and all because he had opened it up himself. Had he not asked me how to handle this incident, I would never have asked him any of this, and the interview would not have been nearly as good as it was. I didn't know anything about it, but I hid my ignorance when he brought it up. I just rolled with it and let him explain.

7. A LIE CAN BE AS TELLING AS A TRUTH

The performance artist **Paul McCarthy** had a very different mindset than the TV and movies stars I had been interviewing. My unexpected moment with him came about after he had told me about an incident in his life that never happened.

In the Dec. 12, 2011 issue of *Newsweek*, there was an article called "Why Does Art Cost So Effing Much?" It dealt with the Art Basel in Miami Beach. The double page photo the editors chose was of some people standing around a five-foot pink sculpture of Bashful, one of the Disney Seven Dwarfs. It had a penis hanging from its chest and a bunch of penises laying on the ground and wrapped around its legs. The caption read that it was by Paul McCarthy and was one of three that had sold for $950,000 each. McCarthy's Tomato Head sculpture—a life size sticklike figure with a giant tomato head and a long hose-like penis—had previously sold at auction for $5 million. In an outdoor exhibit in Paris in 2014 vandals destroyed his 30-foot inflated sculpture of a butt plug (which he called a "tree") and McCarthy made international news when the president of France apologized to him.

The price of McCarthy's work caught my attention because I knew him in the 1970s and '80s when he was a struggling performance artist, doing things to his body that made me wince. He would stuff twenty raw hotdogs in his mouth, put on a woman's black slip, shave his body hair using mustard and ketchup as shaving cream, and do things that were repulsive to many, but perversely attractive to me. I thought that he was my opposite. I would never do the things he did, privately or publicly, and yet I felt the need to understand him and his art. So I got to know him and to write about him. I even hired him to build a room in my house and bought the one piece of art he had framed. I couldn't pay him much, but at the time anything helped. But by 1985 I had lost touch with Paul and, though I knew he had become a recognized artist, I had no idea he had become so successful.

It was through him that I had met another performance artist named Barbara Smith, who once appeared in a San Francisco gallery allowing only one person at a time into her space, where she lay nude on a mattress surrounded by all kinds of food and fruits with a tape loop repeating the words "Feed me." I wanted to know her, too, and when she rented a gallery in L.A. in 1975 to hold an auction where people could bid on bits of her time, I wound up buying her for a week. I was the sole bidder for that one.

One of the things I wanted to do with Smith was learn more about performance artists, and so we invited a dozen of them to my apartment. Paul McCarthy was among them. By then I had gotten to know Paul and his family. One of the pieces he had described to me was the week he spent in his car parked outside his studio in Pasadena. He said that he never left the car during that time. He ate, slept, defecated, and ignored the passersby. I got the eating and sleeping, but the defecations got me. How on earth could he have lived with his own waste for an entire week in such a small space?

When the artists came to my apartment I played devil's advocate, challenging them about their work and its value. Was it really art? What was it accomplishing? How could they support themselves on work so ephemeral, which lasted only as long as it took to do it? At one point I asked Paul to talk about what he did in the car for a week and why did he do it?

"Let's pass on that one for now," McCarthy said. Then he whispered to me, "Can I talk to you in the kitchen?"

We went to the other room and he said, "You know that car piece you were asking about? I never did it."

I was stunned. I had written about some of his other work and asked if he had done those.

"Yes," he said.

"So why did you tell me about living in your car for a week?"

"I knew you liked stories, so I gave you a story."

"Was that part of your art?" I asked. "Had I written about it would it have existed, even if you never did it?"

"Sort of," McCarthy said. "But I didn't think about that when I told you. I just wanted to give you a story."

I was impressed. Paul had seen through me. He knew what I wanted to hear—good stories to tickle the imagination—so he made one up. He nailed me! I wasn't upset. It's rare that one is so understood. And it made me think about the nature of art. (Some years later when I was interviewing Nick Nolte, Nolte extolled on the virtue of lying. "I happen to think that the lie is the truth," he said. "I haven't been able to find anybody who tells the truth. There is mythologizing in everybody's life.") Paul's lie was as revealing about me as all the real stories he told me about his work. He made me realize that I could be "had" with a good story, and that I really had to fact check anything I wrote about, to make sure it had actually happened. That made me a better reporter. He also gave me his gift of imagination. And he made me think that a good lie can enhance the truth about anyone.

8. WHEN DEALING WITH AN EXHIBITIONIST, WARN THE AGENT BEFORE THE MEETING

Rodney Dangerfield left nothing to the imagination when it came to the unexpected.

Of all the comedians who performed on the late night talk shows over the years the one I most looked forward to was Dangerfield. He threw out one-liners faster than a great pitcher throws a fastball, and they were so well honed that they almost always hit their mark, which was my funny bone. Rodney never failed to make me laugh. He was probably more quoted at the next day's water coolers than any of T.S. Eliot's or Bob Dylan's best lines.

"When I was born the doctor smacked my *mother.*" "My parents took me to a child psychiatrist. The kid didn't help me at all." "My ol' man was dumb. He worked in a bank. They caught him stealing pens." "If it wasn't for pickpockets, I'd have no sex life at all." "Last week I found a guy's wallet.... inside was a picture of my two kids."

Who could suppress a laugh when you heard lines like these for the first time? When Al Pacino saw that Rodney was appearing in Las Vegas, he booked two plane tickets so we could fly up and see him, then fly back to L.A. after the show. We sat in the back of the theater and laughed our asses off. Nothing like laughter to make you feel life's worth living.

For Rodney, though, life wasn't a joke. He suffered from severe depression until he finally found a doctor who prescribed the antidepressant drug that worked for him. He was 75 when he began to feel what "normal" felt like. When I interviewed him for *Parade* magazine, he didn't shy away from speaking about how tough his life had been. He started doing stand-up when he was 18, earning $12 a week. As a singing waiter in Brooklyn he made $20 a week. He quit show business at 28 and became an aluminum siding salesman. When he was 40, with a wife, two kids, and $20,000 in debt, he changed his name from Jack Roy to Rodney Dangerfield and returned to doing stand-up. He made a lot of people laugh. But he rarely laughed himself. Not even the marijuana he constantly smoked helped his outlook.

"I have a down head," he told me, "and there's nothing you can do about it. People think comedians are happy people, but it's the reverse."

When he tried to reconcile with his father, who was never there for him, he asked him on his deathbed what the secret to life was and his father said, "It's all bullshit."

Because he was open about his depression, New York Times Books got in touch with him and suggested he write a book about it, like William Styron's *Darkness Visible*. Rodney asked if I wanted to write it with him, so I spent a few weeks at his Westwood apartment getting the details of his dark and disturbing life. But I also got more than I bargained for when I realized that Rodney was an exhibitionist. My first glimpse at his private parts happened when he asked if I wanted soup (what is it with Jewish guys and soup?) and then brought the pot to the table and poured me a bowl as I sat staring at what hung out from the front of his opened robe.

He was very casual about his nudity. He'd smoke his dope pipe, eat his soup, and let it all hang out. I later heard stories of him showing his stuff on airplanes and in his dressing room when people stopped by to say hello. It didn't appear to me that he was showing off as much as he just didn't give a fuck. He apparently liked to let his balls air out.

As we progressed with the book, I asked if he had a literary agent and he said he didn't, so I offered to introduce him to mine and see if he'd want to use her to make his deal with the Times. But before I brought my agent to his apartment, I told her that she shouldn't look shocked if he came out with his dick exposed. Sure enough, when he joined us in his living room, he was wearing his opened robe, with nothing underneath. He sat down, spread-eagled, and gave her a full view of his junk. I'm glad that I had prepared her because she didn't bat an eye. This was business as usual for the funniest man I knew, who was also the most depressed person I had ever dealt with.

In the end, Rodney couldn't bring himself to release a book about his miserable life. "I have kids," he said. "They don't know these stories. They won't be comfortable reading about them for the first time." I understood. Why should a comedian who got superstars to fly to Las Vegas to see him perform write a down book just because he had a down head? Better to remember him as the man who got no respect, and made his living telling you why.

9. BE PREPARED TO SWIM

Jean-Claude Van Damme was a different sort of exhibitionist. But he had a body worthy of exhibiting. I just didn't expect to see him stripped to a tiny Speedo on our first meeting.

Van Damme's career might be compared to the bullish/ bearish ups and downs of the stock market. He was down, he was up, and he was down again. I got to him when he was up, a strong Muy Thai kicking bull with a Belgian Horatio Alger backstory.

He was born Jean-Claude Van Varenberg in Berchem-Sainte Agathe, just outside of Brussels. He wasn't much of an academic student, but he studied ballet and karate when he was eleven. He began developing his body, and while still in his teens he won the Mr. Belgium bodybuilding crown, and the European middleweight black-belt karate championship. He married at 18, opened a gym in Brussels, and became a personal trainer. But his ambition was bigger than this, and when he was offered a job playing a soldier in a Rutger Hauer movie, he jumped at it. The movies became his way towards achieving fame and fortune. He left his wife and went to Hong Kong to break into the martial arts film industry. When that didn't work, he went to Los Angeles. He was 20 years old, had no money, and didn't speak English, but that didn't hold him back. He worked as a bouncer, an aerobics instructor, a limo driver, a pizza deliveryman, and a carpet layer. He found another woman to marry and divorce, changed his last name from Van Varenberg to Van Damme, had 8x10 glossy head-shots made, and stuck them under the windshield wipers of luxury cars parked in Beverly Hills, hoping to be discovered. Van Damme knew that he had the strength and flexibility to be an action star, but it took six years before he caught the attention of a producer who could help him. Cannon Pictures' Menacham Golan was leaving a restaurant when Van Damme approached, told him he was a martial artist who could be the next Bruce Lee or Sylvester Stallone, and demonstrated with a high sweeping kick that nearly took Golan's head off. Golan wiped the perspiration from his brow and told him to come to his office the next day. Van Damme arrived at noon and waited until 6:00 p.m. before Golan finally listened to his pitch—which consisted of his taking off his shirt to show off his muscles and doing a full split balanced between two chairs. Golan wound up giving him a contract for the movie *Bloodsport*. It was made in Hong Kong, because it was cheaper there than in the U.S. and because Van Damme didn't have a green card or work permit to do it in the U.S. It was shelved for nineteen months, but when it was finally released, Van Damme no longer had to drive a limo or deliver a pizza. He became a legitimate action hero. He made low-budget films like *Cyborg, Kickboxer,* and *Lionheart*, and then larger budget films like *Universal Soldier, Hard Target*, and *Nowhere to Run.* By the time I caught up with him, he was under contract to earn $3 million for *Time Cop* and $6 million for *Street Fighter.*

It was 110 degrees in Chatsworth in the San Fernando Valley when I went to Van Damme's home. He was floating on an inflated raft in his swimming pool and invited me to join him. I don't usually travel with a bathing suit, so I stripped down to my underwear, and carefully got on a second raft. I placed my tape recorder on my chest, turned it on, and we began our interview.

"Do people think you have a tough job?" he asked me.

"Do you think this is easy?" I replied.

"Could be worse if there were waves," he laughed.

"That's why I have a second tape recorder in my bag. I believe in being prepared."

"Maybe that's something you can teach me," he said. "I'm only 33, too young for such an in-depth interview, don't you think?"

"I think you've come a long way from the streets of Brussels," I said. "Did you always know this was going to happen for you?"

"I believed in my dream," he said as he floated by, puffing on a Cuban cigar and flexing his muscles. "I pushed every day to make it happen. If you saw me when I was young, I came a long way. I was not born this way. I became. I changed. I came to America without the language, without the permit, and I became a movie star. People call me lucky, they say I was in the right place at the right time. You have to make it happen, pal. You have to push hard, because it pays off. When you know who you are in life, you can go so high. I really believe so."

Van Damme would later struggle with booze and drugs, he would marry and divorce a few more times, and he would wind up making films that went straight to DVDs. In July 2016 he walked out of a TV interview in Australia because he overheard some of the crew behind the camera comment on how he was sweating. He blamed it on the banal questions he was struggling to answer. "Sorry guys, I cannot do this any more. I'm trying to do something different. I'm 55 years old now; I've got a different view of life. The questions are boring. I start to sweat. I cannot do this."

He had soared pretty high in the nineties, but what goes up eventually comes down. That's an obvious lesson to learn. But the real lesson I learned from The Muscles from Brussels happened that first day in his swimming pool. You've got to be prepared for anything when it's 110 degrees in the shade, so make sure your underwear is clean, and know how to swim.

10. IF THEY OFFER TO LASSO YOU, GO FOR IT
The same holds true when the person you're interviewing offers to lasso you from behind.

Though he has appeared in over thirty films, including *Stand By Me, A Few Good Men, A Time to Kill, Young Guns*, and *The Three Musketeers*, what made **Kiefer Sutherland** a household name was when he brought Jack Bauer to life in the TV series *24*. He was the right wing answer to why we need to torture the terrorists who want to destroy us. When a nuclear bomb is about to go off or a deadly virus is going to be released and you only have 24 hours to make sure that doesn't happen, who you gonna call? Not the Ghostbusters. America needs Jack Bauer to be like the Wolverine, prepared to go for the jugular.

With Donald Sutherland as his father, Kiefer had large footprints to follow. When he was born in London on December 21, 1966, his father bestowed seven names on him: Kiefer William Frederick Dempsey George Rufus Sutherland. Is it any wonder that he grew up a feisty kid whose parents separated when he was four? He dropped out of high school in Toronto before his sixteenth birthday and lived like a fugitive, sleeping in parks or at different friends' homes, until his father agreed to help him out, provided that he would re-enroll in school. He agreed, but he also auditioned for and landed the lead in an acclaimed Canadian film, *The Bay Boy*. That signaled the end of any formal schooling. By 1986 he was living in Los Angeles with Robert Downey Jr. and Sarah Jessica Parker, and acting in *At Close Range*, with Sean Penn and Christopher Walken, and in *Stand By Me*, as a small-town bully. Other films followed, and then he decided to take a break from acting to compete in rodeos; he won his first competition in Phoenix. He lived on a Montana ranch for six years and then owned a 500-head cattle ranch in central California.

I was expected to talk to him about his highly rated TV show, and with the world going to hell in a hand basket there was plenty to discuss. But I had read about an incident that happened when he and Woody Harrelson were filming *The Cowboy Way* in 1994 that caught my attention. He and Woody were hanging out on set between shots when the script girl walked by carrying a clipboard in one hand and a cup of coffee in the other. Kiefer had learned to use a lasso during the making of *Young Guns*, when he was twenty. He happened to have one in his hands when this young woman passed them and he said to Woody, "Watch this." He wanted to show off his skill by skipping the rope from the ground to her foot as she walked, stopping her forward progress. But instead of catching one foot he encircled both her feet. "Before I could let go, the knot went down, and she went down," he said. She was shocked, of course. And Kiefer was embarrassed. But the crew thought it funny and the star was given a pass, as stars usually are on movie sets. I wanted to know if he was truly sorry, or was he actually proud of his prowess with a lasso.

"I had learned roping well enough to be on the cusp of knowing that if I pushed it a little further I could really do it," he said. "When I was practicing I would rope everything. I'd sit in my hotel and rope the chair by the desk. When I was living on the cattle ranch I had to make a decision: Did I want to raise cattle or be an actor? I asked myself what more could I find out that I didn't know already? I could ride well, handle cattle, castrate a calf, use a rope."

I was skeptical that he could actually lasso someone the way he did that script girl, by throwing the knotted rope to the ground behind her feet as she walked. It seemed to be something only a skilled rope artist might accomplish, and I wondered if Kiefer had simply been lucky to have captured the woman in that way, even if he caught both her feet instead of just one.

"I knew I could do it," he said. "But I guess I wasn't good enough to get just one leg, so I needed more practice. But I could probably do it eight times out of ten."

"Sounds like bullshit to me," I needled.

"Want me to try on you?" he said.

"You want to lasso me?" I asked.

"Why not? I've got a few ropes in the trunk of my car."

"Sure," I said. "Let's go outside."

After Kiefer got one of his lariats, he instructed me to walk in front of him at my regular pace and not look back. The street in front of my house was sloped, and I got about twenty yards before I heard the snap on the ground behind me and felt the pull of the rope on my left ankle. I was impressed.

"You want to learn how to do it?" he asked.

"Would probably take all day," I said.

"Well, I'll leave you the lasso," he said. "You can practice with it. And think of me when your wife walks away from you. You can surprise her."

He didn't shout "Hi-ho Silver" when he got into his car to drive away, but he did have a big shit-eating grin on his face. I, too, was smiling. I had met my first real cowboy who also happened to be the kind of actor who didn't need a stunt man when it came to the tricky stuff. America will always need a Jack Bauer.

11. SOME STARS WILL GET
THEIR HANDS DIRTY

I once had a shit-eating grin on my face when I drove away from **Robin Williams** seventeen years before his suicide on August 11, 2014 shocked the world. That such a manic, hilarious, life-of-the-party type guy suffered from depression and the onset of dementia was difficult to grasp. I will always remember what he did with a silk scarf when he was interviewed at the Actor's Studio. Or how he turned into a giant chimpanzee jumping on chairs and tables as Billy Crystal fed him imaginary treats to calm him on *The Tonight Show.* Or his hilarious rap on the absurdities of golf on his HBO Special. And, of course, there was his other side: the serious actor in films like *Dead Poets Society, Good Will Hunting, The Fisher King, Mrs. Doubtfire, Awakenings, Insomnia,* and *One Hour Photo.*

I interviewed him for *Playboy* in 1997 and *Rolling Stone* in 2002. He told me that he never read his interviews because he felt it was like two lepers doing a tango. He described an interview "like jerking off in a wind tunnel. Whoosh!—it blows back in your face!" But that didn't keep him from doing riffs on almost every topic I brought up because he just couldn't help himself. His mind was like a Whirling Dervish, in constant motion, making leaps and connections that didn't seem probable or possible.

Terry Gilliam worked with him on two films (*The Adventures of Baron Munchausen*, where Robin appeared as a giant-headed man in the moon, and *The Fisher King). Gilliam, who knew something about comedy as a founding member of

Monty Python, described him as "having the ability to go from manic to mad to tender and vulnerable. He's the most unique mind on the planet. There's nobody like him out there." Oliver Sacks, the neurologist who wrote *Awakenings*, thought that the way Robin's unconscious and preconscious mind worked was a form of genius.

Williams had just completed playing Peter Pan in Steven Spielberg's *Hook* when we first met at a home he was renting in Bel-Air. I thought it might be fun to get him going by asking what other actors could have played the role. He said that Michael Jackson had worked with Spielberg on it for a while. "If anybody is Peter Pan, he has the credentials. He could play it up the wazoo. If you wanted to get a punk Peter Pan, Gary Oldman would be great. Who else? Tom Cruise, if you want a kind of *Top Pan*. John Candy once did it, where he played Divine playing Peter Pan."

"How about Linda Hunt?" I asked

"Whoa," Robin laughed. "The European directors' versions. Now we're getting into interesting casting. Gerard Depardieu as Pan." Then he began: [*French accent*] "Luk out, everybudy, luk up here, I'm flying. I have happy thoughts. And then I have sad thoughts. It's the sad thoughts that keep me on the ground for a brief moment. Then I fly again."

"What about Steven Seagal?" I challenged.

[*Tough–guy whisper*] "Yeah, right, I'm, uh...are you Hook? [*Grabs an imaginary arm, snaps it, becomes Hook screaming in pain. Then back to Seagal's voice*] Look at you now, you've got two hooks, no waiting."

"Robert De Niro?"

[*Becomes De Niro's character in Taxi Driver*] "What? You want me to fly? *You want me to fly?* Excuse me? I have happy thoughts. I have happy thoughts. You want me to fly? Right.

Lost Boys. Right." [*Changes to De Niro as Jake La Motta*] "*Raging Pan.* 'Scuse me. Scuse me. What? I'm supposed to fly? Pardon me. Yeah, kiss...my tights. Scuse me. I'm flyin'. Can't you see? I'm off the ground. I'm flyin.'"

"How about *Pacino Pan*?" I continued.

[*Turns into Al Pacino's character from And Justice for All*] "I'm outta order, you're outta order, I'm flying, I got my happy thought. I'm outta dust, you're outta dust, you're old, you're wrinkled, go."

"How about Bette Davis as Wendy?"

[*As Davis*] "Get over here. Shut up! Get over here, you little creep. But you are. You're a fairy!"

It didn't take much to loosen him up, but once you unleashed his subconscious, it didn't stay light and bright for long. "Want to know the dark side of Peter Pan?" he asked. "Look at the Khmer Rouge. That's the most frightening army in the whole world, because it was an army of twelve-year-olds, and they committed most of the atrocities, they were the ones who could get rid of people with no compunction. It's the perfect age for an army—eleven- and twelve-year-olds—because they have all that rage, all the power of pubescence, and they don't give a shit about anything."

Since what we knew about the atrocities of war reached most Americans through television, Robin had a lot to say about that as well.

"Watch the way people watch TV; it's hypnotic. Just sit back and you've got cable and ninety-five choices and you don't really care much about anything else. Eventually, you don't know about history, you can't remember if there really was a Civil War, and eventually people get slaves again. You can have a President who basically reads cue cards and it seems OK, because he's just like the guy on the series with the family with the little black child and it seems all right, because he's kind, and when he's angry, it's TV angry, where you get kind of angry but you don't go 'Fuck off!' You basically get where your eyes dim and the world seems all right and you kind of tighten up so much that your sphincter doesn't open. Then people at home can be TV pissed and they can go to a TV war and watch it. We basically fought a war, watched it on the TV set, and you can buy the tapes, sucking on the glass teat."

Though Robin was having a successful career doing stand-up and movies, he was well aware of the nature of the film business. He was still bitter about how Warner Bros. used him as bait to get Jack Nicholson to agree to play The Joker in the first *Batman* movie. (Williams was asked, he said yes, they took his response to Nicholson, and then said sorry to Williams when Nicholson agreed.) And he remembered how a film called *Jack the Bear* was developed for him and then given to Danny DeVito.

"I don't want to harbor hatred or anger," he said. "I just have to keep working. Otherwise, how do you separate yourself from not wanting to go and buy an automatic weapon, kick down the studio doors and say, 'I'm coming'? The bottom line in Hollywood is that they'll smile at you, but they're thinking, 'You prick, you scumbag, I hope you choke on your own shit! Why don't you gag on your own genitals?' That's why stand-up is great. It really helps to defuse that."

But because his stand-up routines took on serious subjects, those on both sides of the political spectrum often attacked him. "I've taken a lot of shit," he said, "but how do you not offend anyone? These born-again Christians were shooting down AIDS research money at a time when it could take out the species. Finally, you just say fuck it; I have to do what I do. I've got the born-again Christians after my ass because I defend gays, and gays are mad at me because I do effeminate characters. You can't keep modifying or you're like a chameleon in front of a mirror."

The pro-lifers also went after him for his being pro-choice when it came to a woman's right to have an abortion.

"Here's what bothers me more than anything about those who believe in the right to life. They don't support the second part of the process, when they have all these children. Amend 'right to life' to 'right to a decent life.' They don't support the education; they don't support the health care. If you are going to have a society where it's mandatory to have a child, let's make this child's life wonderful. I don't want to deny life to anybody, but sometimes you have to choose—and it's a horrible choice, I'm not denying that. To deny people that choice forces them into the other dilemma, and then you raise children who are not loved and who go through a living hell of not being wanted, or are tossed off and live in homes or institutions, or who grow up numb."

The *Rolling Stone* piece we did five years later was entitled "Don't Laugh. Here's the Dark Side of Robin Williams," because it had to do with the movie he was promoting, *One Hour Photo*, where he portrayed a quiet nut job who developed pictures at a mall and kept copies for himself. Since the character Sy he played was both creepy and scary, I asked Robin if he had a scary side.

"Have you ever really scared anyone?" I asked.

"I've done violent things to things, where I destroyed an object rather than cause harm to a person," he said. "And that's been frightening—to myself, too. I've shattered things. It's learning to find outlets for that. Most animals have a defense mechanism. Comedy is mine. It's my offense and defense."

And he carried that through even as we spoke. When I asked if he could change one thing about his first sexual experience, he said, "The length." If he could pick his pall-bearers, they would be "The Supreme Court." Yet he tempered that with a highly intellectual yearning. If he could be successful in any other field, he said it would be Quantum Mechanics, and the brain he would most like to have was Einstein's.

These comments made me think back to how I ended the *Playboy* interview in '97 by asking him how he balanced his life with his work, and if he had any fears of losing that balance.

"Recently," he said, "Jerzy Kosinski killed himself; supposedly, the reason was that he just didn't want to become a vegetable, he didn't want to lose his sharpness. There's that fear—if I felt like I was becoming not just dull but a rock, that I still couldn't spark, still fire off or talk about things, if I'd start to worry or got too afraid to say something. As long as you still keep taking the chances and you're not afraid to play Peter Pan. ...What if it fails? 'I don't care, I'm having a great fucking time.' If I stop trying, I'd get afraid."

We know what happened when Robin reached the point where he outgrew Peter Pan, and where he stopped trying. But of all the things I remember when I was with him, what brings me to the lesson I learned occurred after we concluded our first interview. Robin walked me to my car in the driveway and cracked a joke about the diminutive size of my Fiat 124 sports car. When it wouldn't start, he laughed, then apologized for making fun of it. I said I'd call my wife to come to help me jumpstart the battery, but Robin insisted we try to push the car down the slope of the driveway, to see if it kicked in.

"Are you sure you want to do that?" I asked

"Yeah, yeah, you just pop it into gear when we're halfway down and step on the gas."

"And then I'll call my wife," I joked.

Robin got behind the car and began to push. I watched him through the rearview mirror. His face turned red, he was giving it everything he had. I hit the clutch, put it in first gear, stepped on the gas, and got it going.

"You see," Robin shouted. "Didn't have to bother your wife. Just let her know how much time you saved her. Maybe you'll get lucky tonight."

I raised my arm and waved goodbye, wondering how many other stars I'd interviewed would have done what he just did. I couldn't come up with any. It was an act of kindness I just never expected.

12. A CASUAL REMARK MIGHT MAKE *YOU A* STAR!

Of all the unexpected moments I've had to finesse, the one that brought me the most public attention is one neither the subject nor I saw coming.

When **Jesse Ventura** was elected Minnesota governor as a Reform party candidate in 1998, he proved every pollster wrong. Eighteen years before Donald Trump, it was Ventura who had been a national joke before the election and a politician to watch after it was over. I went to see him a few months after he became governor for a wide-ranging conversation about how serving in the Navy SEALs and then becoming a pink boa-wearing professional wrestler prepared him to govern a state.

We discussed what he wanted to accomplish while in office and, with his popularity reaching a very favorable 70%, the question he was most frequently asked was whether he would consider a run for the presidency. His fellow governor, Republican Bob Taft from Ohio, believed Ventura was "bringing more national attention to governors than we've ever had before." Senator John McCain admired him for "telling the truth and having some rational ideas." People liked the way he stripped away the typical politician's avoidance of saying anything controversial and just said whatever was on his mind. Prostitution? Legalize it. Weed? Smoke it. Who killed JFK? It was definitely a conspiracy. Favorite rocker? Johnny Lang.

The governor was a loose cannon. And most appealing about him was that he showed no fear or hesitation. He was a man of action and reaction. He had a SEAL mentality. You go forward, you don't look back, and you cover your tracks. He wrote a book—or had someone ghostwrite it for him— and became the subject of other books, including a Garrison Keillor satire that got under his skin. You didn't want to make him your enemy, and both Democrats and Republicans in Minnesota treaded carefully around him.

Should he have agreed to a *Playboy* interview so early in his governorship? He didn't see why not. He was a fan of the magazine. And he felt he could handle any questions I put forth. So batten down the hatches and full speed ahead!

When I challenged him on handgun control, he called me a "liberal weenie" for not believing every house should be equipped with weapons of destruction. His own definition of gun control was "Being able to stand at 25 meters and put two rounds in the same hole." He had no problem with gays serving in the military, but opposed gay marriage because the dictionary defined marriage as between a man and a woman. (This was still sixteen years before the Supreme Court would change that definition.) He wasn't lenient toward prisoners with a life sentence getting paroled in seven years. "Life should be life." But he was lenient toward drug crimes and prostitution. "That's consensual crime. That's crime against yourself. We shouldn't even prosecute them."

This talk led him to relate how he and his wife once walked around the heart of the red-light district in Amsterdam, seeing busloads of senior citizens enjoying the drugs, pornography, and open prostitution. He brought the observation back home, saying "We give a false portrayal of freedom in the U.S. We're not free. If we were, we'd allow people their actual freedom. Prohibiting something doesn't make it go away. Prostitution is criminal, and bad things happen because it's run illegally by dirtbags who are criminals. If it were legal, then the girls could have health checks, unions, benefits, anything any other worker gets, and it would be far better."

I reminded him that what he was saying wasn't a very popular position among America's lawmakers. And that's when he said: "No, and it's because of religion. Organized religion is a sham and a crutch for weak-minded people who need strength in numbers. It tells people to go out and stick their noses in other people's business. I live by the Golden Rule: Treat others as you'd want them to treat you. The religious right wants to tell people how to live."

Now, that might seem innocuous enough in a general sense but, because of a lull in the serious news when the interview was published in November 1999, that remark exploded in the media. It didn't hurt that he also said that overweight people were too weak to push away from the dinner table; that the Tailhook Navy sexual harassment scandal was "much ado about nothing"; that it was our own military-industrial complex that killed President Kennedy; and that if he were reincarnated he'd like to return as a 38DD bra. But it was the remark about organized religion that galvanized the media and brought TV news trucks to my door at 6:00 a.m.

It came as a complete surprise. Neither the governor nor *Playboy* nor I imagined that anything he said in that interview was going to be so controversial. The governor wound up on the cover of the next issue of *Newsweek* and I led off NBC's *Today Show* with Matt Lauer, followed by other television interviews with Geraldo Rivera, C-SPAN's Brian Lamb, MSNBC, and mentioned on ABC and NBC *Evening News*. The radio talk shows from around the country wanted to ask me about the interview and *Playboy* even decided to run my outtakes, the material I had edited out of the first interview, as an unprecedented second full interview a few months later. When the governor was asked on one of the nightly news programs about his explosive remarks, he quoted me saying that it really was much ado about nothing, "And I think you should listen to Larry Grobel, because he's right."

It was truly crazy. I had never experienced anything like it. I had been on a lot of TV shows after my Brando interview had come out, and I was put on the cover of *Writer's Digest* after the Streisand interview, but nothing as frenzied as this had ever happened to me before.

The governor's offhand remark hadn't even been spurred by one of my questions, yet resulted in this sudden burst of recognition. And that's how I learned that a casual remark by a powerful or popular figure could shine a light not only on him, but on his interrogator as well.

And that was completely and totally unexpected!

Don't Lose Control

13. NEVER SURRENDER

It's tough enough to strike up conversations at a social gathering full of unfamiliar people, but imagine when you're about to interview someone for the first time, whom you've researched and prepared hundreds of questions, many of them intimate. It's a rare interviewer who can knock on a door, not knowing what to expect on the other side, and be relaxed and cool. What if the person is in a bad mood? What if the subject feels forced by a publicist or publisher into doing this and would rather be somewhere else? What if he or she was one of the biggest stars in the world, and had never given an in-depth interview before, so all your background research was only based on what you've seen on screen and brief snippets in magazines? It can often feel like trial by fire, where you learn how good a chameleon you can be, but what it often boils down to is who's in charge. And that means knowing how to take control.

Control is a trigger word. **Barbra Streisand** told me she hated the word because it had "negative implications." Her critics called her a control freak, but she preferred to call it artistic responsibility. "If you mean that I am completely dedicated and care deeply about carrying out a total vision of a project—yes, that's true."

It took me months to get her to say that because she tried very hard to take artistic responsibility over our interview, which I refused to allow. And she wasn't the only one. I've dealt with dozens of people who felt the way Streisand did when it came to being interviewed and have come to the same conclusion each and every time.

Let me start with Barbra. When I met her in 1976, she was the biggest female star on the planet, having won Grammies for her music, Emmys for her TV specials, and a Tony and an Oscar for her Broadway and film performances in *Funny Girl*, respectively. But Al Pacino and Sharon Stone also challenged me from the start; Betty Friedan took umbrage in the middle of our talk; Robert De Niro was defiant throughout the seven times we met; and Marlon Brando, Bob Knight, and Vincent Bugliosi did their best to wrest control—or insist on their "artistic responsibilities," if you will—just when I thought I could get away unscathed.

Streisand was my first *Playboy* assignment. I had been trying to get to her for *Newsday* for months with no success. When the editor at *Playboy* also expressed an interest, I had stronger ammunition to impress her publicist.

It wasn't till many months later that I got the call saying she wanted to see me. It caught me by surprise; I wasn't prepared to interview her, but I should have known better. Streisand was a supremely cautious woman and had wanted to check me out before making any commitment. So I appeared at the designated time at the studio where she was putting the finishing touches on *A Star is Born*, and waited an hour for her to appear. When she did, she was all business, wanting to know why she was viewed as such a thorn among journalists. I didn't want to lump myself among those who had been pricked by her in the past, but I couldn't resist reminding her of her regular mistreatment of the media, and expressing my own frustration as well. She listened to what I had to say, and then invited me to watch a screening of her movie. I sat next to her for two hours, just the two of us, and when it was over, she asked my opinion. Rather than answer her with an honest appraisal, I skirted the issue by saying "You're gonna make a lot of money." She took that as a positive response, and told me to call her publicist to arrange for a time to interview her. But having spent over a year getting to this point, I didn't want to go back to dealing with her publicist. I asked her for her phone number so I could call her directly to make a time. She hesitated for what seemed like five minutes before she tore a small piece of paper from her notepad and wrote her number on it.

Victory! Or so you would think. But it was foolish to seem triumphant with Streisand. She was a force like no other. She could be funny and friendly, or angry, bordering on belligerent, depending on her mood at any given moment, often the result of recent media reports or her crew's ability to meet her expectations. It took even more months for her to give me a date, allowing me time to research and prepare for her. When I finally made it into her house in Holmby Hills, coincidently close to the Playboy Mansion, she casually handed me a legal document to sign. Her lawyer had drawn it up and it basically said that she would retain all control over the tapes and the transcript and in the end, if she decided she didn't like what she read, she could kill it.

This was the biggest crossroads of my career. I had worked hard for years getting to this point, and now I was going to do my first *Playboy* interview. It meant a lot to me, even more than I could have imagined at the time. I could have signed the document, not tell my editor, make the interview something Streisand would be pleased with, and move on. But my instinct told me that this was a huge red flag. If I signed it I would no longer be an independent journalist; I would be more like a freelance secretary to Barbra Streisand. I couldn't do it.

She insisted.

I resisted.

She told me everyone who talks to her signs something like it.

I told her she was cutting off my balls.

She yelled at me.

I (gulp) yelled back.

We were at an impasse. One of us had to blink.

It wasn't me.

I was 29 years old in 1976 and I had never realized I would have the courage to stare down the biggest star in the world. I didn't know that I could hold my ground when her lawyer called, then her manager, and then her boyfriend, all insisting that I sign the document. I was actually willing to give up the most important assignment of my life up to that time and walk out with my pride and dignity intact, but most likely without any further *Playboy* assignments. So when Streisand told her lawyer and manager and boyfriend that I had refused to sign and that she was going to go ahead anyway, I learned something about myself that day. I learned not to surrender control when dealing with a star's demands. That mantra would keep me on my toes over and over again.

14. SILENCE ISN'T ALWAYS GOLDEN

The success of the Streisand interview led to my being asked to tackle an even more reclusive subject: **Marlon Brando**. If Streisand was a crossroads for me, Brando was my Rubicon. This would be my Point of No Return as an interviewer. I knew it as soon as I got the assignment.

There was no question that Brando was considered the Holy Grail among actors. I've never talked to an actor who didn't genuflect when his name came up. Some worshipped the way he turned his craft on its head with his early films; others were in awe of the way he defied authority, including the producers, agents, and heads of studios that could make or break lesser talent. Brando behaved like he just didn't give a shit about anything, and, in a profession where people were obsessed with their personal appearance or public image his nonchalance was refreshing. Even his desire to get away from it all by buying an island in Tahiti was seen as an act of admirable defiance. So when I was tapped to go to that island and spend as much time alone with him as it took to get him to open up, I knew the stakes, and what it would mean if I succeeded.

I didn't know what to expect when I got off the small private plane that landed on the unpaved airstrip on Tetioroa, but I certainly didn't expect Brando to be standing there to welcome me or to grab my suitcase and escort me to my bungalow. And I didn't expect him to sit down in one of the two canvas backed chairs and start talking to me about the island before I even got settled. I don't think he expected that I would gift him with a tin box of chocolate chip cookies. He said he'd give them to the children, and then devoured them himself before he left me to unpack.

But his initial hospitality and openness was not a harbinger of things to come. Over the next three days I was hoping to capture what he had to say on tape, but he insisted that we get to know each other first. His idea of getting to know each other precluded my work as a journalist. Had I gone there as a visitor I would have been far more relaxed and uninhibited sharing meals, taking walks, playing chess, going into the bay on his catamaran, and just shooting the shit with the man who brought Stanley Kowalski, Terry Malloy and Don Corleone to life. But I had a purpose and that purpose was thwarted every time I pulled out my tape recorder; I was on edge and he knew it. In fact, he was toying with me, wondering how long I was going to stay, telling me that most people who came to see him on business got antsy after a few days of his being non-cooperative, and he enjoyed watching them squirm. "Add me to the list," I said, which got a big laugh out of him. It wasn't hard to make him laugh; he loved puns and wordplay. (When he told me that the Japanese film *Ugetsu* was a favorite of his, I responded "Ugetsu when you're rich and famous," which cracked him up.) It was his island, his rules, and visitors were bit players in his movie.

Perhaps the most profound thing he said was on our third day together. We were sitting quietly in the sand with our backs against his bungalow, looking out at the coral reef and the vast blue horizon of sea and sky. "Conversation keeps people away from one another," he said. "People don't feel assaulted by conversation so much as silence. People have to make conversation in order to fill up this void. Void is terrifying to most people. What you're really having in silence is a full and more meaningful conversation."

I think he was probably right about this, but if he was trying to tell me something, I wasn't listening. I hadn't flown to the middle of the Pacific Ocean to communicate in silence with the world's greatest actor and most visible activist when it came to Native American rights. I was there to talk, to ask questions, and to seek answers. Once I didn't take his bait, I turned things around. Instead of spending our days in meaningful silences I stopped asking for permission to turn on my tape recorder and just did it. And though he had instructed me before I had arrived that he didn't want to talk about acting, I found ways to get his thoughts on the subject. It wasn't easy, especially when it came to trying to get him to speak about some of his most iconic moments on film, like the scene in which he sat in the backseat of a car with his older brother (played by Rod Steiger), in *On the Waterfront*, and delivered his famous "cudda been a contendah" line. I just had to find some way around his reluctance. He kept insisting that he wasn't special, that everyone was an actor in life no matter what one's profession. That gave me an opening to protest his modesty, suggesting that few other actors, if any, could have pulled off that particular scene any more effectively than he had.

"Yeah," Brando said, "but there are some scenes, some parts, that are actor-proof. If you don't get in the way of a part it plays by itself."

But did he know that scene was actor-proof when he did it?

"No, at the time I didn't know," he said. Now it was getting interesting. He was actually talking about a scene most Brando fans would be familiar with.

We began talking about the way Elia Kazan directed and how he allowed his actors to be spontaneous. And then he said, "As it was written, they had this guy pulling a gun on his brother. I said, that's not believable—I don't believe one brother's going to shoot the other. There was no indication in the script that they had that kind of relationship—it's just not believable; it's incredible. So I did it as if he wouldn't believe it, and that was incorporated into the scene. So there is room for improvisation. Some directors, they don't want you to improvise anything—very insecure, or they're hysterically meticulous about things. And some directors want you to improvise all the time."

We were on a roll. Marlon Brando was talking about the subject he had specifically directed me not to bring up. It was fascinating to hear his thoughts and I pushed further, asking him about his refusal to memorize lines.

"Do you have a bad memory, or is it that you feel remembering lines affects the spontaneity of your performance?" I asked.

"If you know what you're going to say," he answered, "if you watch somebody's face when they're talking, they don't know what kind of expression is going to be on their face. You can see people search for words, for ideas, reaching for a concept, a feeling, whatever. If the words are there in the actor's mind ... OH, YOU GOT ME! [*Laughing*] YOU GOT ME RIGHT IN THE BUSH. I'm talking about acting, aren't I?"

And so it went, tit for tat. I'd ask, he'd deflect, I'd try again, he'd give a little before changing the subject, I'd go with his flow until I glimpsed an opening and return to getting him to talk about his real expertise right down to his core. It was a challenging ten days with Brando on his island, just the two of us. It almost felt like we were going into battle each day, only we had to use our wits, make each other laugh, pick up signals when to push forward and when to recede. Once I inserted myself in our conversations and didn't allow him to dictate what we could talk about, I was able to get him to open up, and left the island with a better understanding of how silence isn't as golden as actual communication.

15. SOMETIMES YOUR SUBJECT IS
MORE NERVOUS THAN YOU ARE

When I got the assignment to interview **Al Pacino,** I had seen all of his movies up until then and had nothing but admiration for what he did in his first five films: *Panic in Needle Park, Serpico, Dog Day Afternoon,* and *The Godfather 1 & 2.* What a superb actor! He seemed to fill the entire screen; it was hard to take your eyes off him. He was The Real Deal. *And Justice for All….* was about to come out and he was in the middle of filming *Cruising* when I flew to New York, hoping the magic interplay that happened with Brando could happen again with Al Pacino.

Pacino was reluctant to do any interview, but if he had to—and the studio was insisting that he had to—then he wanted to do it with "The Guy Who Did Brando." He actually said that. He loved Brando and couldn't believe his own luck when he got to play his son and successor in *The Godfather.* Since Brando was notorious when it came to dealing with journalists, Pacino figured if Brando had let me in, then he could as well.

But Pacino was no Brando. Pacino was a guy from the Bronx who grew up in the projects, was abandoned by his father when he was a kid, lost his mother before she had a chance to see him in the movies, dropped out of high school, and was fearful that if he opened up in conversation, he might reveal himself in a way that would lessen his mystique. He certainly had that mystique going for him, because nobody really knew who he was, where he came from, or what he thought about. Nobody knew that for those first five pictures his memory was fogged by the excessive use of alcohol. He wasn't drunk when he acted, but he got drunk at the end of each day. The pressure of stardom was something he hadn't been prepared for. He had no problem getting into the characters he played, but he had a lot of problems just being himself.

Having survived Streisand and Brando, I felt confident that I could get Pacino to talk, but when I tried to read about him and discovered how little there was, I started getting nervous. My confidence comes from preparation. When there isn't that much out there besides the movies themselves, then you have to rely on chemistry. If you click with your subject, talk flows. If the subject is reluctant, reticent, shy, and non-verbal, then you've got trouble. Pacino was reluctant, reticent and shy, but thankfully, not nonverbal. It just took a while for us to dance to the same tune.

Our relationship, which would go on to become a thirty-year friendship, was determined in the first five minutes of our meeting. He was living in an apartment near Central Park on the East side of Manhattan, and I picked up on his reclusive-ness when I saw that the name under the buzzer to his apartment said "C. Bergen." It had once been Candice Bergen's apartment and Pacino never changed the name. When I got off the elevator on his floor, he opened the door, looked at me with a jittery smile, and turned pale when I put my bag down and took out my tape recorder.

"Ah, can you put that away?" he asked. "It's a little early, don't you think?"

Having let Brando dictate when I could start taping, I knew that I would never let that happen again. I could see in Pacino's eyes that he was far more nervous than I was, and that calmed me down considerably. "Why don't I just turn it on and let whatever happens between us happen," I said.

He could have said no. He could have insisted, like Mae West once had, that I couldn't record at all. But it happened so fast, just as I walked into his place, before we even sat down or had a drink or made small talk, that it took him by surprise and threw him off his guard. I had reverted back to the days when, as a teenager, I sold encyclopedias and knocked on strange doors trying to get invited inside. When I did, I often asked if I could take a chair from their kitchen because of my "sore" back and, by doing so, I was able to change the décor of their living room. It put me in control psychologically. With Pacino, I was going against his wishes in his apartment and he had only a moment to make a decision. If he had decided I could not turn on my tape recorder, I doubt if we would have continued the camaraderie after our marathon interview was over.

"Uh, okay, I guess you know what you're doing," Pacino yielded.

We walked into his small living room and he sat on his worn out green felt couch and I sat on a shabby rattan chair that had a hole in the center and I laughed at the squalor of his place. He was a huge movie star, making millions of dollars for his films, and he lived in a smaller place than I did in L.A. He had moldy yogurt cups on the coffee table and half-eaten cookies on top of his old refrigerator. He was like a deer caught in the headlights when I turned on my machine and started asking about his life. But I grew up in Brooklyn and he in the Bronx and we were in this bizarre situation and could both laugh about it. And it all happened because his insecurities and nervousness allowed me to relax. Once he sensed that he could trust me, he was also able to loosen up. We wound up talking for weeks, and then months, and when the interview was done he said that it felt like therapy for him and that he couldn't imagine we would just shut down and go our separate ways. I told him to tell me that *after* he read what was printed, and if he still wanted to talk, I was game.

As it turned out, so was he.

16. CONTROL THE ENVIRONMENT
AS BEST YOU CAN

It didn't feel like therapy for **Sharon Stone** when I was late for our lunch at the Delancey Street Restaurant in the Embarcadero in San Francisco. I couldn't help it; my Southwest flight from Los Angeles was delayed. I had called her publicist to let her know.

"Sharon likes to eat at noon," I was coldly told.

"Well, I'll let the airline know," I said, "and see if they can fix whatever problem is causing the delay." I mean, really, what was I supposed to do about it? Her publicist clearly didn't have a sense of humor (they rarely do). I got to the restaurant around 1:30 p.m. Sharon wasn't there.

I wasn't surprised. I didn't expect her to be waiting for me. Her husband, Phil Bronstein, the executive editor of the *San Francisco Examiner*, was there having lunch with his lawyer. When I saw him I wondered if his wife had expected us to join them—a nightmare scenario for any journalist. I took advantage of her being late by going to the maître d' and asking if there was another, private room where I might eat with Ms. Stone. I explained that we were going to do an interview and that she had chosen this particular restaurant, so it would be mentioned in my story, but that I needed some place quiet to record our conversation. The restaurant was full at that time and the combined chatter of the diners would have made any recording done in that room close to unintelligible.

With the help of a twenty dollar bill, the maître d' showed me to a room usually reserved for private parties. It was off the main dining area and had a long table. I thought it was perfect, and asked if it was possible to get some cushions for the hardwood chairs to make us more comfortable. He obliged and I returned to the bar to wait for her.

I didn't have to wait long. She came in and assessed the room like the movie star she was. As heads turned her way, she strolled over to where her husband was sitting, kissed his cheek, and gave his lawyer her hand to shake. I walked over to them and introduced myself. "I see you managed to get here," she noted sarcastically.

"Yes, I did my best to fix the plane. Sorry about that."

She introduced me to her husband and then we stood there awkwardly. I still didn't know if she planned to join them, but Sharon pointed to a reserved table in the middle of the restaurant and said, "We'll sit there." Right smack in the center of all the chatter, with the clinking of glasses, the abrasive sounds of silverware on plates, and the hum of conversations.

I leaned forward and whispered in her ear. "Sharon, I got us a private room. It'll be quiet."

"I don't want to eat in a private room," she said. "I want to eat over there. That's where I always eat."

"It's pretty noisy," I said. "It will be hard to tape."

"Your problem, not mine," she said.

"It wouldn't have been my problem if I had chosen the venue," I said.

"Over there," she repeated, doggedly.

We were still standing at her husband's table and I was thinking that he must understand my dilemma, being a journalist himself. But he also understood his wife's need to be the focus of attention, so he probably found these introductory moments amusing.

I took a chance. I leaned forward again and whispered, "Follow me," and turned my back on her to walk towards the private room. I happened to see through the corner of my eye as Sharon stood looking at me walking away and then rotate her finger around her ear, indicating to her husband and lawyer that I was crazy. I held my breath as I continued walking. Very reluctantly she followed.

When we got to the other room she saw the cushions on the chairs and my two tape recorders already on the long table. She wasn't happy that I had made all these arrangements. She had wanted to be in control, and be buffered by what she must have considered to be her adoring fans. Now we were all alone, just the two of us, and it might as well have been at her home—a one-on-one situation that, by choosing a restaurant venue, she had apparently hoped to avoid.

"I prepared a good deal for you," I said, in an effort to mollify her. "I've done interviews in restaurants and they don't really work out. Besides the noise, there's the distraction of people coming to say hello or asking for your autograph. I realize that can be flattering, but it interrupts the flow and energy of the interview. And since this is going to be a cover story, I hope you can understand."

Whether she understood or not, she didn't suddenly warm up and start talking. It took nearly an hour to get her to do that. I wasted dozens of questions, getting only one word or one sentence replies, until she finally came to see that I really had prepared. We wound up talking until 5:00 p.m., when the maître d' came to say they were closing for the next hour. I walked Sharon out and waited with her until her cab arrived and we actually hugged goodbye.

I doubt if there would have been any hugging had we sat at her usual table. I was lucky to have gotten to the restaurant before her, lucky there was another room, lucky that for twenty bucks the maître d' was willing to let us use it. But it wasn't luck that got her to follow me to that room. It was my sheer conviction that convinced her that I knew what was best for both of us.

17. KEEP THE CAMERAS ROLLING
(& MAKE SURE THERE'S FILM!)

I felt the same way about **Betty Friedan** when she made three attempts to walk out on our interview.

In 1963, Betty Friedan's *The Feminine Mystique* served as a wake-up call to women to take themselves seriously, get out of the housewife role, and be competitive with men in the workplace and creative fields. Friedan was calling for nothing less than a woman's movement to affect social change. Though its significance wasn't as apparent in the beginning, women soon began to rally behind the idea of feminism. Friedan became a leading figure, outspoken and confrontational. She also had her detractors among women who preferred the housewife role, chief among them a conservative activist named Phyllis Schlafly, who spoke against the idea of feminism, saying it was "doomed to failure because it is based on an attempt to repeal and restructure human nature."

Twenty years after she wrote *The Feminine Mystique,* Friedan wrote *The Second Stage,* a book Erica Jong considered "a new direction for feminism." It was Friedan's attempt to answer new questions for women: How can we live the equality we have won? How can women with successful careers combine work, marriage, and children into satisfying lives? How can men liberate themselves from their own rigidified sex roles?

I thought we should do a cable TV interview with her for the Playboy Channel, and she agreed. I knew Friedan was an articulate fighter and I expected her to say a few choice words about the company I was representing, so I was prepared for sparks to fly.

What I wasn't prepared for was the inefficiency of the crew we hired in New York. Playboy had felt it was cheaper to use a local freelance cameraman and director than to bring their own team and equipment from Los Angeles, but in the end, we paid dearly.

Betty Friedan arrived at our suite at the Drake Hotel on time, and we didn't waste much time before the cameras began to roll. I asked her to put the Woman's Movement in historical perspective and estimate how much she felt her first book changed the course of history. "It has changed history," she said. "There's no question about it. I've had historians and political scientists tell me that it has had a deeper, more widespread change in society than any other movement or phenomenon in modern times. My role is that I articulated what had been unconscious and I did take responsibility for organizing and giving some leadership to the Movement."

Off to a good start, I thought. I brought up some of the statistics in her *Second Stage* book, like how 71% of divorced women were working, as compared to 78% of divorced men, but the women weren't on an equal pay level as the men. She gave a long answer and I started to ask another question when the director interrupted us to say there was a technical glitch and asked if we could repeat the question and answer. This didn't go over well with Friedan. "We're starting all over again?" she asked.

"No, no, that would be ridiculous," I said. "We're just going to continue." I had 160 prepared questions; I figured we could lose the first two. I asked her if women over thirty felt more pressure and frustration than women under thirty. She answered citing psychiatrists and epidemiologists, focusing on the fact that no matter the age, it was healthier for all women to have control of their lives and not feel helpless and stuck in bad marriages. I brought up the one famous question Sigmund Freud could never figure out: What do women want?

"He couldn't figure that out because he was a man of his culture, of his time, who had no way of seeing women as people," she responded. "He saw women through the eyes of a feminine mystique. You only have to read his letters to his wife while he was courting her and after they were married. She was a hausfrau, a child, something less than fully human. Furthermore, women weren't supposed to have any real wishes or choices of their own. Marriage and children—that was the justification for a woman's existence."

"OK," I said. "For today, can you answer that question in less than half an hour?

I smiled when I asked this, but I was trying to steer her towards shorter answers, since this was television, not print, and I knew long answers would have to be cut down. But Friedan didn't appreciate being told to keep it short and stood up from the couch and said, "Well, I can leave right now."

She caught me off guard. We'd only been talking for ten minutes and we lost her opening comments and now I had offended her. "No, no, no," I said, "I'm sorry. I didn't mean to insult you. I was joking. Take as long as you like."

"This wasn't one of my great wishes to do this for Playboy," she said, pointing out how it demeaned women with the image of the Playboy Bunny and the Centerfold. "You've got to do intelligent interviews like this if you want to sell your wares to women, who are people just like men."

"Getting back to what women want...." I coaxed.

"Women want to be themselves, to have a good life, to make some mark in life, to love, to have adventure, to express what's in them, to have security. The complexity of a woman's desires is no different than men having a complex range of desires and wishes."

We went back and forth for another twenty minutes. I brought up Norman Mailer's remark that he was "the last man in America to understand that the Woman's Movement was serious." She waved her hand and said the Movement was never going away, though she felt the struggle was in danger. "There is unfinished business," she said. "Certain rights which we won in the first stage are in danger now. The Equal Rights Amendment, which should have passed in 1982, won't get passed this century, but it will happen." She blamed the Republican Party and President Reagan for keeping that amendment from being ratified. When I asked her why, she started to answer, but the issue was still a ticking time bomb for her and she stood up for a second time and began to remove her microphone.

"I don't want to do this interview," she said. She walked away from the couch again and once again I pleaded with her to continue. "I don't have the patience for this," she said. "It isn't going to do me enough good."

I somehow got her back on the couch and we continued to talk. I was thinking that in just this first half hour we had two dramatic moments where she got up to leave, and that would make for good television.

As our interview continued, I asked her about her early life, the battles she had with her parents, how she felt when she became a mother and wife, how she came to write *The Feminine Mystique*, and how women basically lived their lives as a lie. We discussed the phrase "Anatomy is destiny" and whether she viewed men as the enemy. I asked her about Germaine Greer's remark that "Women have very little idea of how much men hate them," then brought up Gore Vidal's comment that "Men do hate women...and dream of torture, murder, flight." I made her laugh when I quoted Natalie Wood saying,

"The only time a woman really succeeds in changing a man is when he's a baby." And she nodded in approval when I mentioned Simone de Beauvoir saying, "No one is born a woman." But when I got to quoting some of the anti-feminists like Phyllis Schlafly and Marabel Morgan things got testy again. "You've called Schlafly a 'traitor to her sex' and she's said that you and your followers 'hate homemakers.' Your organization, NOW, defends homosexual rights as human rights. Schlafly's Eagle Forum uses 'Lesbian' as a swear word. Will the two sides ever come together?" I then quoted a few of Schlafly's more inflammatory remarks, like "We cannot reduce women to equality. Equality is a step down for most women." And, "The liberals will learn that lesbian privileges and child care and the ERA and abortion are anti-family goals, and not what the American people want."

The rage ignited in Friedan's eyes. She couldn't stand Phyllis Schlafly and barely sat still when I mentioned her name. "She beat a dead horse," she said. "And she's....wrong!" She jumped up off the couch for the third time, tore off her mic, and shouted, "That's it! That's it! I don't need this interview! I don't want to do this anymore!" She moved away from the camera, but then turned back and said, "Phyllis Schlafly is a liar. She has taken full advantage of equal rights. She has gone to law school, which would never have taken a middle-aged woman like herself if it hadn't been for the movement of equality. And yet she denies the reality of the law. She talks about polls, but she doesn't talk about the polls that show that most Americans do want control of their own bodies in the matter of abortion. Most Americans do believe in equality. Phyllis Schlafly tries to make it seem like equality is a matter of losing privacy in bathrooms, which is a lie; it has nothing to do with that. You know she was a member of the John Birch Society;

she was on the payroll of McCarthy; she was an agent of the extreme reactionary right wing in this country long before she discovered she was a woman. So don't go there. Get away from Phyllis Schlafly."

I knew what I was witnessing would make great TV and, when her rant was finished, she agreed to sit down once again so I could finish up my questions. By this time it was 5:00 p.m. and the director took me aside to say that his crew was only contracted until five. I hadn't yet asked Friedan how she thought she'd be remembered, and I knew I needed that for an ending, so I instructed the director to put another reel of film in the camera and we'd cover the overtime. Friedan knew exactly how she wanted to be remembered and I knew that I had my ending.

At least, I thought I knew. After I walked her to a taxi and returned to the suite I asked the cameraman if he caught all of her attempts to leave and that wonderful rant about Phyllis Schlafly. No, he told me, he never moved the camera off its tripod. So when she stood up, he was filming an empty couch. I couldn't believe that he wasn't professional enough to lift the camera and follow Friedan. But at least I had that all-important ending.

"No," the director said. "I told the cameraman not to load any more film."

"Why the hell not?" I asked.

"It was past five, and I didn't know whether Playboy would honor overtime charges, since it wasn't in our contract."

"It was just fifteen more minutes. Goddamnit!"

I fumed all the way back to L.A. and when I saw what we had and what we missed, I fumed some more. I don't think I was ever as angry about losing material as I was about this. Though I had managed to maintain control with Friedan by keeping her from walking out on me, I hadn't given thought to losing control of the interview itself to a recalcitrant director and cameraman. And that's something I vowed would never happen again.

18. NEVER LOSE SIGHT OF WHY YOU'RE THERE

But when it came to recalcitrance, **Robert De Niro** stands in a place of (dis)honor all alone. *Playboy* wanted him for their January 1989 35th anniversary issue. It was going to be the only new piece, with all the other articles reprints of past issues, so it was a big deal. De Niro was the hook to bring attention to the magazine's anniversary. The publishing world knew that De Niro rarely gave interviews. He just didn't like to talk about what he did, who he was or where he came from. He also didn't like to proffer his opinions about other people, the entertainment business, sports, or world events. That left nothing to talk about. Which is why he didn't do interviews.

But he was also under pressure from the indie production companies Kings Road and Sandollar-Schaeffer to help promote his latest movie, *Jacknife*, costarring Kathy Bates and Ed Harris. No film company liked to pay a star millions of dollars and then have him refuse to go on TV or do high profile magazine interviews. So when push came to shove, De Niro got pushed into doing an interview with me. But he went into it very reluctantly. He probably knew that *Jacknife* was one of his minor films, much like his next two pictures would be (*We're No Angels*; *Stanley & Iris*), so he wasn't exactly jacked up to talk about them. *Goodfellas* was a year away, and that one was with his favorite director, Marty Scorsese, but he certainly wouldn't want to make the mistake of talking about that one before it was finished.

When we met at the Chateau Marmont Hotel in West Hollywood, I saw the same uncertainty in his eyes that I had seen in Al Pacino's ten years earlier. When we started to talk, I sensed the same reluctance I had felt when I was with Robert Mitchum four years earlier. The Pacino interview had turned out well, and Mitchum's had been a disaster. De Niro could flip or flop, depending on how I played it. I wanted to put him at ease, but I also wanted him to understand that what we were committing to was an interview, not a ten-minute meet-and-greet that actors do on publicity junkets. I eased into our conversation with compliments, telling him how, when I first saw him in *Mean Streets*, I was sure that he wasn't an actor, but some quirky guy Scorsese had known from the streets of New York. I had nothing but admiration for De Niro's work, and I knew that he was considered among the greatest actors in American cinema. That's why it surprised me to see him hop up every fifteen minutes of the first hour we had together to go to the bathroom and come back rubbing his nose. I figured he was doing cocaine, but I wasn't sure. Unless a person returns with some white powder remnants around his nose or upper lip, it's probably best to assume he has a weak bladder. And even if there is a trace of white, it could be from a powdered donut he was secretly eating.

We didn't tape anything that evening, just talked. Or I just talked and De Niro spoke in half sentences. But he agreed to do the interview on his home territory in New York. I left before I said anything that might make him change his mind, and a few weeks later I waited for him in my room at the Drake Hotel on 56th Street in Manhattan.

De Niro was to meet me there at 9:00 a.m. He arrived eight hours late, at 5:00 p.m. I wasn't pleased. He acted as if he hadn't kept me waiting, made no apology, and couldn't wait to leave soon after he arrived. We taped for an hour and he suggested we continue at a diner he frequented in Tribeca the next morning. I got there on time; he arrived an hour later. We talked for another hour and he said he had to leave for an appointment. We scheduled another meeting the next day in another location.

This is how I interviewed De Niro. In bits and pieces. Never more than ninety minutes in one sitting. It was annoying and frustrating, having to start and stop this way. I understood that it was his way of controlling the conversation and making sure we never got too deep into any particular subject. But I was determined to get as much as I could out of him, and then write the interview depicting him as the White Rabbit, always late for a very important date that was never our interview.

De Niro wasn't happy with that depiction and let me know it when I saw him some months after it was published. He even accused me of being a "Judas" because he felt I had betrayed him. But I stood my ground with him and said that I had done nothing of the kind. He knew what we were doing and he had willfully chosen to lose sight of why we were together. I had not. One of us had to stay focused, especially when the other was determined to play the saboteur.

19. KNOW HOW TO DEFUSE A POTENTIALLY THREATENING SITUATION. AND KEEP ENOUGH CASH IN CASE YOU'RE THROWN OUT OF THE CAR ONTO A DESERTED HIGHWAY IN OHIO

A dozen times over the seven days with De Niro he reached over to turn off the tape recorder to say something he didn't want recorded, but at least he didn't ask for the tapes when we finished so he could destroy them, as **Bob Knight** had in 2000. I met with Knight two months after he had been fired from coaching the Indiana University basketball team for violating their "Zero Tolerance Policy" when it came to infractions. That was, far and away, the most dramatic interview I've ever done. It was also the most violent, the most confrontational, the most fearful, the most threatening, and the most frightening. I had never gone face-to-face with someone whose face turned blood red in anger, whose head swelled to twice its normal size, and who wanted to do to me what Homer Simpson was always doing to his son Bart whenever he lost it. I truly believed that Knight would have liked to strangle me.

It was not, by any stretch of the imagination, a "normal" interview. It didn't even take place in a house or a restaurant, but in a car. For six of the twelve hours we were in that car, Knight drove and I sat in the passenger seat. For the other six, Knight's colleague, coach and pro scout Don Donoher, drove, Knight sat up front, and I sat in the back. It didn't matter if I sat next to Knight or behind him, when he got angry he just blew up and went after me, both verbally and physically. When he was driving, he wanted to throw me out on the highway and let me hitchhike back to my motel. When Donoher was driving, he told him to pull over so I could get out and find my way back to my motel. His anger was nothing if not consistent. And considering that Knight was a husky 6'5," he used his height and weight to intimidate those he looked down upon. Those he looked down upon the most were journalists.

Knight had a history of public flare-ups that made him a media darling; much the way Donald Trump became so beloved by both the liberal and conservative pundits for his free-swinging approach to politics. The media is attracted to train wrecks. When Knight was coaching, he couldn't contain himself if he disagreed with a referee's call or a player's poor judgment or a drunken heckler. He once threw a chair across the gym floor during a game. When his team played a Russian team, he protested what he felt was wrong in the first half by not allowing his players to play the second half. He once fired a starter's pistol at a reporter. Another time, he picked up a drunken fan and dropped him into a garbage can. He held up used toilet paper in the locker room during half time to show his players what he thought of their performance. He put his large hands around a player's neck during practice. He even head-butted his own son during a game! If he hadn't been the second winningest coach in the history of college basketball, he would have been booted out of coaching long ago. But that was the rub. Knight was a damn good coach.

He just wasn't a very good man.

From his behavior, shown over and over again on sports channels and written about in every article about him, it was evident that Knight needed a coach of his own, someone who understood how to calm enraged beasts. Or maybe he needed some strong drugs to mellow him out and reduce his stress. He even might have needed someone his size to beat the crap out of him. But it seemed the only way to put him in his place was to threaten him with expulsion if he continued to behave so outrageously. And when a 19-year-old freshman called him by his last name, Knight stepped over the line one time too many. He put his hand on the kid. He didn't choke him. He didn't punch him. He just let him know he wanted to be treated with respect. You didn't call a man like him by his last name without prefacing it with "Coach" or "Mr."

The student told his stepfather about it. The stepfather had a radio show and told his listeners. The incident—quite minor in the list of Knight infractions—blew up and the university had no choice but to enforce it's Zero Tolerance Policy.

After coaching at Indiana for 29 years, with a win-loss record of 659-242, Knight was given the boot.

Two months later, I appeared on his doorstep. He knew I was coming and thought that we could drive six hours to Akron, Ohio, to see his son coach at the university there. I've held a tape recorder in a car for short distances but never for six hours. And never with a man as volatile as Bob Knight.

The craziness started right away when he surpassed the speed limit on the highway and was pulled over by a cop. Knight didn't seem fazed. From the way he sat back and smiled, I sensed he'd been pulled over routinely. When the officer recognized him, as all officers do when they pull him over (he would later tell me), he asked for his autograph and wished him luck. No ticket, no warning. Just a thrill to actually meet the legendary coach. Once we were driving again I tried to be chummy and ask him about the incident that got him fired. Big mistake!

Knight wasn't ready to talk about it rationally. He was still pissed off about it and he let me know. First, by banging his fist against the steering wheel so hard it made a thumping sound, like we had hit an animal crossing the highway. Then, by yelling at me for bringing it up. And finally, by screaming that he should throw me out of the car. When I tried to apologize for getting into the subject so early, he just barked at me, "Don't. Say. Another. Fucking. Word!"

I didn't. At least not until he stopped hyperventilating and resumed talking. I sat quietly as he gave his side of the story. From his point of view, he had done nothing to deserve losing his job. He felt this freshman and his stepfather had set him up. We continued on our way to Ohio, as I cautiously asked him all the easy questions that I felt wouldn't trigger an angry response. We picked up Don Donoher once we crossed over from Indiana to Ohio and I continued to ask softball questions. Once at the university, we watched Knight's son coach, then we all went out for dinner, and began our drive back to Bloomington around 9:00 p.m. That's when the second explosion occurred.

This time it was Knight who told me to ask him more questions, as Donoher drove. I prefaced what I was about to ask by saying that all my easy questions were asked and I only had the tougher ones left. I told him that I had a list of things he allegedly did and I would like to have him comment on them, one by one. If he didn't want to talk about any of them, he could just say "Pass," and I'd move on. Knight gave me the go-ahead. I asked about the chair-throwing incident. He answered and then pointed out that other coaches did what he did in anger, but they weren't thrown up on ESPN as raging lunatics all the time. So my next question, just the second one, was, "So why you, Coach?" And that was it. That seemingly innocuous question threw him into a worse rage than the one on our drive up. He picked up the tape recorder I had put between him and Donoher in the front seat, and flung it past my head behind me. Then he asked me to give him the tapes I had recorded. When I refused, he shouted his demand. When I refused again, he yelled at Donoher to pull over so he could grab my tapes and throw me out of the car. When Donoher didn't listen to him, he got up on his knees, turned back towards me, and tried to wrestle my bag with the tapes from me. I wouldn't let go. He punched me. I still held on. By then I was shouting at him, "You're making a mistake, Coach. You're making a mistake!"

I knew if I survived this ordeal I had a good story to write. But how to survive it?

When we reached the Ohio/Indiana border, Donoher pulled into a parking lot where he had left his car to join us.

Donoher was so concerned about what had just happened that he offered to drive me the three hours back to Bloomington. I said no, I'd find a cab and get back myself. I had around $200 cash and thought that might be enough, if I could get a cab. Where we were was pretty isolated. But Knight spoke up. He said he'd drive me back. Donoher suggested that I stay in the back seat, which I did. But as soon as he left, Knight said, "I'll take you, but I'll be goddamned if I'll be your chauffeur. Get in the front."

And here is where my lesson comes in. I didn't know how to defuse this ticking time bomb that was Bob Knight. He was just so off the charts when it came to decent human behavior. He was really a raving lunatic who just happened to be the most famous man in Indiana. He had so much built-in anger and he was spewing it all at me. I knew enough to leave my tape recorder and tapes in the back seat as I got in the front and looked at him. He didn't look at me, just straight ahead. I stuck my hand out and said, "Take my hand, Coach." He didn't respond. I said it again. He sneered. I said it a third time, pushing my hand at him. Finally, he took it and we held hands tightly. I wasn't going to let go until I had my say.

"Look, Coach, I'm sorry about all of this. I didn't fly all the way out here to piss you off and have you yell at me. I'm not comfortable with the way this has gone down, but we have three more hours on the road together and I'd like us to get back in one piece. I'm not out to "get you" in this interview. I'm just trying to give you the chance to correct the record. There's been so much written about you, so much negativity, that I thought you should have this opportunity to put your side out. That was my intention. It hasn't worked. But let's just get back without argument or incident and I'll leave in the morning. I'm really sorry it's come to this."

All this time I'm squeezing his giant hand and looking him in the eye and being as sincere as I can be. And Knight responded. Something in him clicked and he just started to open up about how the university had ripped his heart out, and how much coaching had meant to him. It was pure interview gold. I got my tape recorder from the back and let him unload his despair and anguish and frustration for the next three hours.

The interview was published in March 2001 and got a tremendous reaction. I was asked to be on dozens of sports radio shows. I wound up putting that interview, along with my comments, as an appendix in my *Art of the Interview* book, to demonstrate how to deconstruct an interview as a three-act play. By refusing to give in to his demands I somehow was able to defuse a potentially threatening situation.

Knight was a big time bully with a hair trigger temper, and perhaps my confidence had something to do with the fact that I had enough cash in my wallet to pay for a taxi back to Bloomington. But bullies come in different forms, which I learned when I encountered Vincent Bugliosi.

20. DON'T BE BULLIED

After the 'Not Guilty' verdict gave O.J. Simpson his freedom, former prosecutor **Vincent Bugliosi** was so outraged that he wrote a book called *Outrage*, outlining the five reasons why Simpson got away with murder. And then he cut that down to two: "The jury could hardly have been any worse, and neither could the prosecution." Bugliosi achieved his fame as the prosecutor who put Charlie Manson and his "Family" in prison for life. He ran unsuccessfully for public office twice (for L.A. District Attorney and for California Attorney General) and then turned to writing and commentating. His *Outrage* brought him back into the limelight, as radio and TV news and talk shows booked him to give voice to the indignation he felt compelled to detail in his book. I was given the task to interview him for *Playboy*. Not only did I read *Outrage*, but also *Helter Skelter*, the book he coauthored about the Manson trial that became a huge bestseller (seven million copies and counting). I also read *The Phoenix Solution*, which was a proposal on how America could win its war on drugs; and two books he coauthored: *Till Death Do Us Part*, and *And the Sea Will Tell*. Bugliosi's strong opinions and complete conviction that he knew what he was talking about made him a formidable public figure. What I would soon find out was that it also made him a bully.

I met with Bugliosi at his house in the San Fernando Valley for a week, beginning on Oct. 24, 1996. I knew my questions would have to be sharp, especially since I didn't have any legal training and Bugliosi, as a prosecutor, won 105 of 106 felony trials, including 21 consecutive murder convictions. Lawyers like Alan Dershowitz, Harry Weiss, and Gerry Spence all gave him high praise. Dershowitz considered him "as good a prosecutor as there ever was." Weiss said he'd seen all the great trial lawyers of the past thirty years "and none of them are in Vince's class." Spence went up against him in a televised "docu-trial" of Lee Harvey Oswald, and after Bugliosi "proved" that Oswald acted alone in the killing of President John F. Kennedy, Spence said, "No other lawyer in America could have done what Vince did in this case."

During the 30 hours we taped, we covered a lot of territory. The Simpson trial was the main focus, but you couldn't talk to Bugliosi without going into the Manson trial, the war on drugs, terrorism, gun control, politics, the Kennedy assassination, and his personal life. He was a tenacious competitor who thrived on challenges. In high school he won the Minnesota state tennis championship; at UCLA Law School he was the president of his graduating class. And he wasn't afraid to take a stand against art and culture. "Things such as opera, ballet, sculpture, paintings depress me," he told me. "I have no appreciation of art. Art is motionless, it's not representative of life. Life is motion and energy, so when I look at sculptures or paintings it's depressing."

I found Bugliosi to be amusing when he wasn't being outraged, especially when it came to describing his marriage. "Marriage, the family, it's an organization, a unit," he said. "And like any other unit, someone has to be in charge. If people don't agree that the man should be in charge then the question is, do they want the woman to be in charge? I believe in complete equality between men and women in every area except marriage. In marriage the woman has to take the subordinate role, not because man is superior, but because every unit has to have a leader, and the man is the more natural leader." To Bugliosi, the woman's role was in the home. But when I asked him to describe his wife Gail, he said she did the cooking, the social planning, the decorating, and the bill-paying. "She takes care of everything," he said.

My initial impression after our first session was that he looked like Robert Duvall and had a world-weariness about him. His living room and kitchen were in disarray from work being done. After he offered me coffee, Bugliosi wasn't sure how to work the new stove and said all he was good at was boiling water. His phone kept ringing as editors and TV producers called asking if he'd like to cover the Simpson civil trial for them. Someone from *Dateline* called and wanted to send a limo to bring him to their studio, and a movie producer called wanting to option the novel he wrote with Bill Stadium.

In an attempt at some kind of twisted modesty, he said that he couldn't understand how he could be the only one who saw things the way he did. He was straightforward about not wanting to comment on other O.J. books, just his own, and admitted to understanding why some people considered him arrogant and egotistic. The coffee wasn't worthy of a compliment, but the conversation was feisty and I looked forward to each of the following four days.

On Jan 20, 1997, well after I had finished editing the 450 pages of transcript, Bugliosi called me to make sure that I didn't overlook the fact that he was the only commentator who had spoken out against the way the Simpson prosecution blew its case and that he hoped I would mention in my introduction to our interview how his book had helped change the mind of the American people. I responded by saying that it would all be duly noted and he said he just was making the call because he didn't want me to overlook his significance. I joked that I was sure after the interview appeared I would hear from him about every misplaced comma.

Ten days later it was no longer a joking matter. I heard from my editor, who said that after a proofreader called Bugliosi to check on some facts, Bugliosi exploded, claiming he didn't say what I had him saying. He used his friendship with Hugh Hefner to bully the proofreader (and possibly the executive editor) into sending him the galleys of our interview. This is a journalistic no-no because it can only lead to a Pandora's Box of protest from the subject being interviewed. And sure enough, Bugliosi responded as if I had shot him in both knees, his elbows, and then his heart. He railed to my editor that he was being misquoted, that much of what he had to say about so many topics had been edited down or out, and that he wanted to correct all of his responses. The Managing Editor of *Playboy* said that Vince was upset about what he said concerning Prosecutor Marcia Clark's knowing whether there was one or two gloves at the crime scene; and what he had to say about the police lying; and how his comments about how the drug war could be won were reduced to a few paragraphs.

I reassured the editors that everything I had him saying he had actually said. It was all on tape and I stood by what I had given them. I actually got angry even having to deal with this—Bugliosi should never have seen the galleys, and he certainly had no right to edit his own interview. His behavior was immature and thin-skinned. He reminded me of a crybaby. If he didn't get his way, he wanted to take his bat and ball and go home. "Why not just drop the interview altogether and use my Saul Bellow one instead?" I suggested, knowing of course that they wouldn't do that. O.J. was still in the news and thus more timely (if not more permanent) than Bellow.

The *Playboy* editors weren't the only ones having to listen to Bugliosi's tirades. He left a number of messages on my answering machine letting me know that I hadn't done my homework, that I blew what could have been a forceful presentation of his thoughts, and that he wasn't Marlon Brando (whom I had once interviewed for *Playboy*, and, though Bugliosi didn't know this, who had also complained about the end result). His messages made him sound like a crazy person. And he made a point of letting me know that he was going over all the editors' heads and contacting Hefner, which he did. And, to Hef's credit (more than any of the editors'), Hef said that he was willing to give up his friendship with Vince to publish the interview the way I had edited it.

Up until this point I still hadn't seen what Bugliosi had actually done with the galleys he was sent. So I went to the Playboy offices in Beverly Hills on Feb. 4, 1997 and took a look. And that's when I saw how Bugliosi transformed the seventeen galley pages into a work of art.

Each galley proof page consists of a single column of 1000 words, so this interview came to approximately 17,000 words. Bugliosi didn't like any of them! When I saw what he had done, I was impressed. He didn't just want to change a word or a line or a sentence or a paragraph, he wanted to change it *all*–INCLUDING my questions, which he rewrote as well! To me, it was worthy of framing. There was my interview, and on top of it were his "corrections," additions, and edits. It felt so alive, it almost had a pulse. And it also felt so very wrong that I couldn't take it seriously, though Bugliosi had taken it very seriously. Just looking at all the giant X's he made in what must have been anger and frustration through each paragraph, how he then boxed them in dark squares and wrote his new responses in the small spaces between each line, with his new questions in the margins. This was a man who wanted his voice heard in a very specific way. And if he wasn't able to articulate his answers to his own satisfaction the first time around, he wanted to make sure they came across just the way he wanted them this time.

Here's an example of a question I didn't ask, but which he thought should have been, with his accompanying answer:

> PLAYBOY: In *Outrage*, you go off on quite a few philosophical tangents, discussing things like the morality of lying under certain circumstances, the question of God's existence, mankind's being caught up in, as you say, "the music, not the lyrics, of human events." Do you view yourself as a philosopher of sorts?
> BUGLIOSI: [Smiles] No. Philosophers are people who are much more interested in the questions they ask

than the answers they seek. I'm much too pragmatic and result-oriented to be a philosopher.

Now, what's interesting about this is that I never thought of Bugliosi as a philosopher, so I would never have come up with such a question. Obviously, Vince did think of himself that way, so he wanted it posed, and then he could humbly make the distinction. What's amusing is that the question is better than the answer, which contradicts his answering "No" according to his own definition in the answer he supplied. Bugliosi also must have liked how mankind seemed caught up in "the music, not the lyrics, of human events" to have quoted himself in his own question. But my favorite part of this exchange is his bracketed "[Smiles]." Not only has he taken over the part of the interviewer, he's also making sure his humility is duly noted.

Here's one more example of a question he wrote and his response:

PLAYBOY: There was constant talk during the criminal trial that if there was a hung jury, [District Attorney] Garcetti was going to appoint you as a special prosecutor for the retrial. Would you have accepted that assignment?

BUGLIOSI: In the first place, the likelihood of that happening would have been one out of a hundred. It would have hurt the esprit of the deputies in the office for Garcetti to appoint someone outside the office. But if he had asked me, of course I would have accepted. I would have dropped everything I was doing and started working on the case 7 days a week around the clock. It would have been no different than the other cases I had prosecuted, meaning I would have all the DA's office providing me with whatever assistance I needed.

Again, I didn't ask such a question because (a) the criminal trial was over and (b) I wasn't aware of the "constant talk" Bugliosi mentioned. But his answer is interesting, because it implies that he believed he could have won the case, and his book details why. But since it was the book we were there to talk about, we got all of his reasoning in the interview without adding this to our conversation.

Of course, I could not accept all the work he had put into this. In fact, I didn't even read all of what he reworked because it didn't matter. If *Playboy* published his version, then it was no longer my interview; it was Bugliosi interviewing Bugliosi. Which might have been all right if we lived in Poland, where journalists are obligated to show their transcripts to their subjects, but it isn't the way it's done here. "You have a choice," I said to my editor. "You can publish it as I edited it, or you can publish it as Bugliosi changed it. If you use my edit, then keep my name on it. If you use his, then remove my byline and replace it with his."

The interview appeared under my name in the April 1997 issue of *Playboy* and, though I was sure Bugliosi wasn't pleased, he stopped leaving messages on my answering machine. The lesson I learned from this was: Don't be bullied. When you know you are in the right, don't allow anyone to push you into compromising your ethics or your convictions. Maintain control of your work, and if the editor chooses to drastically alter it, then insist it not be credited as your work.

But there's also another lesson I learned from Vincent Bugliosi.

About fifteen years after our interview appeared I was invited by Hefner to attend his Sunday Movie Night at the Mansion. It was an open invitation, meaning once invited, you were on the list and could attend every week. The movies are always new releases and before the movie there is a buffet dinner. At one of these Sundays my wife and I were at a table when Vincent and his wife Gail sat down opposite us. I was talking to my wife when I saw the color drain from her face. Her eyes jiggled toward Vince, who was looking down at his plate. Uh-oh, I thought. This could be embarrassing.

Knowing how Bugliosi never shied from a verbal fight, I had to think fast. Did I want to greet him and remind him of our time together fifteen years earlier? Would he start shouting at me for not including all he wanted to say in his edit of our interview? I could just hear him asking me why I left out his mentioning the Posse Comitatus Act of 1878, concerning the law that prohibits the U.S. armed forces from directing their efforts against U.S. dissident groups. That was one of the phrases he repeatedly insisted I put back in the interview, and one which I stubbornly left out because I knew it would slow down any reader wanting to hear more about Manson, Simpson, Oswald or Kennedy. So, to avoid any possible scene at the Mansion, I looked at my wife, rocked my head, picked up my plate and we walked to another table in a different room. Once settled, I started to laugh. "We're in hiding," I said.

The next Sunday Vince and Gail had come again and this time we sat with them and had a nice, peaceful conversation. I didn't bring up our interview and I wasn't sure if Vince recognized me. Over the next four years we became friends, often talking about our writing projects, commiserating on how publishers don't properly know how to promote books. I had a copy of Vince's 1500 page magnum opus, *Reclaiming History: The Assassination of President Kennedy*, which he finally had published in 2007, and which he graciously signed and inscribed for me, and I gave him a copy of one of my books. But we never talked about the *Playboy* interview. We learned to enjoy each other's company and looked forward to sitting together whenever we both were there. During those years Bugliosi suffered some serious illnesses, one in which he had gone into a coma and was thought dead, but he had survived and came to the Sunday dinners and movies for months afterwards. We talked about what had happened to him and, though I thought he should walk with a cane, Gail said he was just too stubborn and proud to use one.

I grew very fond of Vince, almost felt like he was a wise, cranky uncle who was smarter than most and couldn't suffer fools easily. He was 80 years old when he died in June 2015 and the news bummed me out. I felt like I had lost a friend. Which is so contrary to the way I had felt about him in 1996.

I've subsequently run into most of the people I'm writing about in this book and while the main lesson to be learned is not to lose control of the interview, I've also learned that even when you encounter animosity or belligerence, time heals.

Be True To Yourself

21. IF WE DON'T BECOME OURSELVES,
THEN WE'RE NOTHING

When you deal with the very famous, it's easy to be seduced. I was lucky, early on, that I got to know two men who weren't famous–the musician Ted Harris and the bird artist Arthur Singer. Each had a healthy belief in himself, and some of what they said rubbed off on me, giving me the courage to remain true to myself when celebrities came into my life.

When the U.S. Bicentennial was approaching, I was aware of a libretto for an opera about George Washington that William Carlos Williams had written for the 1939–40 New York World's Fair. No one had composed the music for it then, but I heard there was an eccentric composer named **Theodore Harris** who had discovered it in 1959 and found that "the words sang" to him. He was so sure he could put those words to music that he spent months in his Brooklyn apartment doing just that.

I thought this was a great American story and so did the *New York Times* when I approached them and they gave me the assignment. I went to see Harris at his small apartment on

Avenue Z, near Ocean Parkway in the Sheepshead section of Brooklyn, and knew instantly that this piano teacher and composer would become one of my most memorable characters. His gray hair was long, his fingers were in constant motion, and his eyes sparkled. He showed me a closet full of his compositions: sonatas, sonatinas, etudes, fugues, operas. It didn't depress him that most of them were unpublished and never played because he had a very healthy, and very rare, outlook on life. "I had a nervous breakdown when I was a year old," he said. "Since then, it's only been up."

I asked him about what happened with the opera. He said when he finished a rough draft of the music for the first act, he found out where the Pulitzer Prize-winning poet Williams lived in Rutherford, New Jersey and sent him a note, along with a recording of a children's opera, *Bumpo the Ballerina*, which he had composed. When Williams didn't respond, Harris decided to drive to his home with his wife and approach him face to face. Once they found his house, Harris told his wife to wait in the car and he went and knocked on Williams' door.

"I'm Ted Harris," he said when the poet answered. "I sent you a letter about your opera and a record of mine."

"Yes," Williams said, "I got it. But that record... I guess it's about the best you could have done with it."

Harris managed to get inside Williams' house and saw the record near the record player. "You played it?" he asked.

"Yes, see," Williams said and put the record on.

"It was awful," Harris recalled. "He was playing it as a 33 rpm and it was a 45. So I adjusted it and he heard it the way it was supposed to sound."

"That's pretty good," Williams said. "Much better."

"So's my music for your libretto," Harris said with confidence. He sat down at Williams' piano and started playing the scene about Benedict Arnold, singing Williams' words in his craggy voice.

"I like that," Williams said enthusiastically. "Do it, do it, young man, do it!"

Harris returned to his Brooklyn apartment and spent the next two years writing the opera, modernizing it with an Irish jig, a ballet, some 12-tone music, and conferring with Williams by phone or in person every Monday. "We used to go walking in the street," Harris recalled. "He could barely walk, because he had had three strokes. He'd spit all the time."

In 1973, ten years after Williams died, Harris received a letter from the New York Bicentennial Corporation stating that they were interested in the opera. Harris wasn't sure how they knew about him but suspected they may have seen mention of him as the composer of the music for *The First President* in the New Directions paperback of Williams's plays, *Many Loves and Other Plays*. Harris didn't get excited by the letter because he had been through such letters concerning his work before, and most of the time nothing happened. "Had it been 13 years ago, when I wrote it, I would have been flying," he said. "What would be more logical than an opera about George Washington for 1976? It's this country's first grand opera and it's fitting for New York to introduce it to the world."

He said that when he was working on *The First President* Bach, Beethoven, Mozart, Chopin, Stravinsky, Schoenberg, and Alban Berg influenced him. "Because we are all someone else," he said. "We don't exactly impersonate...we add something of our own. But you have to work on what has happened before you.

"When I first started playing jazz I had to impersonate Fats Waller, 'Fatha' Hines, Teddy Wilson. You know, how are you going to get to yourself? But if we don't become ourselves, then we're nothing. Bach became himself, and yet you can look at Bach and see Palestrina. *The First President* is an original opera that stands right there as me. I wrote the music for that opera."

When I got in touch with someone at the New York Bicentennial Corporation, I was told that they had no funding; they just acted as brokers between good projects and possible performances. I told this to Ted Harris and he shrugged. "Somebody's going to play it," he said. "If not now, then later. In the beginning of my career I'd get discouraged for maybe three weeks. Then it got down to two weeks. Now it's down to about 15 minutes. Because I figure they're all not worth it. These guys who say what goes on and what doesn't aren't big enough to beat me. Who are they? They're guys who all day long are doing their deals. I don't have time for that. You've seen my closet—it's full of my work. You just do it, like life. I mean, you get up in the morning, you've made it. You couldn't be sure you were going to get up. Now you have to make the whole day. Which is difficult. But if you have your work...."

The U.S. government wound up commissioning a European to compose an opera in honor of our bicentennial, but in 1979 *The First President* was performed at Kean College in New Jersey. Harris wasn't bitter at the government's decision. He didn't have time for stupidity.

When Lin-Manuel Miranda's rap musical *Hamilton* became a Broadway sensation and wound up winning eleven Tony Awards in 2016, I couldn't help but think how prescient both William Carlos Williams and Ted Harris were. It wasn't until over a half century later that the time was right for a musical work about our Founding Fathers to find its way into our culture. But Harris felt the words "sang" to him. I still remember him sitting at his piano, banging out the score for the betrayal scene of Benedict Arnold, singing the name of our country's most infamous traitor in his rough, off-key voice.

Harris was ahead of his time, but good ideas will eventually find their way into the light. And that's what I learned from this unheralded but wise man. Do the work. Become yourself. Don't let the bastards beat you down.

22. SHLOCK CAN BE ART IF
YOU BELIEVE IT

After two years barely managing to cover my expenses freelancing in New York I decided that if I was going to keep the bastards from my door, why not do it where the sun was always shining? So I moved to Los Angeles in 1974.

Sometime that year I came across a full page ad in the *L.A. Times* that showed a man in a leopard print bathing suit, looking like Tarzan, offering his how-to-make-millions through mail order seminars. I laughed with some friends at his picture and we speculated that he had most likely hired a model to pose and in real life he probably looked more like Woody Allen. I thought there might be the makings of an article about a contemporary snake-oil salesman and found an editor who agreed with me. So I went to see **E. Joseph Cossman** and got educated in the fine art of selling anything, as long as you believed in it.

As we were relaxing in the Jacuzzi in his home in Palm Springs, he explained his pitch. "I'm the only one in this country who tells people how to get off their butts and turn their talents into something they can own." He looked very much like the guy in his ad. "I'm touching a nerve no one else in this country is touching."

Cossman charged individuals $200 an hour to pick his brain or $65 to hear him speak at sold-out auditoriums. He had earned the right to tell others how to bootstrap their way to fortune by doing it over and over again himself. After the Second World War, Cossman got a job at a steel mill in Pittsburgh, but during his free time he wrote letters to companies all over the world offering his services as a middleman for any product they might need. After hundreds of rejections, one South American company sent him a $180,000 letter of credit for 30,000 cases of laundry soap. He had no idea how to make that happen, but after spending $810 in phone calls he managed to locate the soap. He then had to put up a $5,000 guarantee to the owner of a fleet of trucks to pick it up in Alabama and deliver it to the New York shipyard. In the end, he pocketed $25,000, which was the most meaningful fistful of dollars he would ever earn, because it showed him it could be done.

He left his job at the steel mill and became a traveling soap salesman. Then a Swedish businessman wrote him for a soap quotation. With his reply, Cossman threw in a few balloons for the man's children. The man sent back a $10,000 order—for balloons.

"Once you show people that they can do something," Cossman said, "it's incredible how they repeat."

He was a repeater not in what he promoted but in the way he was able to jump onto whatever product happened to be going his way and jump off again just as easily. He slid out of the soap business and into balloons, packaging them in bags of fourteen, with instructions on how to twist them into animal shapes, and selling them as "five animals to a package." They were the beginning of his mail order career.

"If you don't have a profession, you drift into an occupation," he said as we sat under the stars sipping wine in our bathing suits. "If you happen to drift into something you like, you become successful at it." Cossman drifted into mail order in its heyday. Radio and television were more available, magazines flourished, ads were cheap, and the mechanisms of larger companies to instantly co-opt mail order ideas were not yet set up.

After the balloons, Cossman read an article in *Reader's Digest* titled, "Relax, It's Later Than You Think," which warned of dying from overexertion. It convinced him to abandon smoky Pittsburgh for someplace healthier, like Southern California. It also gave him the idea for his next mail order item, the perfect novelty gift for businesspeople who overexerted themselves: a tombstone paperweight which read: RELAX, IT'S LATER THAN YOU THINK.

For the next twenty years, Cossman located products that were dead or hibernating and gave them new life, grossing $25 million along the way. He didn't invent a single product from scratch, but he had this uncanny ability to change unprofitable items like plastic containers designed for food stamp booklets into a very profitable pair of bookend planters, simply by adding the soil and plants. When someone showed him a plastic toy octopus that, powered by baking soda, zigged around under water, Cossman bought the rights and presented the very latest in fishing lures. After the Davy Crockett craze died, manufacturers were left with warehouses full of corncob pipes. Cossman picked them up at three for a penny and promoted them as a novelty Smoking Breaker to *give up* smoking; all he did was cap the stems with rubber baby-bottle nipples. He discovered the rubber-shrunken head at a trade fair, marketed by a guy who put them together in his garage. Cossman bought him out and sold two million of them as "the perfect gift for the man who has everything." He did the same with the Ant Farm. There were fifty competitors in the field, but Cossman cornered the market by replacing the glass with plastic and getting rid of the ants. Dealers were then able to order in bulk and stock them on shelves, without having to worry about keeping the ants alive or wondering what to do if the glass broke. The ants were shipped separately in a vial. Schools, hospitals and toy and hobby shops bought the Cossman Ant Farm, which was named the Educational Toy of the Year by a trade journal. He even created a battle between different species of ants at the 1964 World's Fair that received full-page coverage in the New York press.

Ants. Toy Balloons, Shrunken heads. Cossman understood that the business of America was more than just business; it was promotion and gimmickry. It was taking a W. C. Fields maxim—Never Give a Sucker an Even Break—printing it on a poster and daring people to pay two dollars for it. And after finding success with hundreds of such products, Cossman revealed his magic formula in a book, *How I Made $1,000,000 in Mail Order*. "In the United States," he proclaimed, "if you just sell the product, you die. You've got to sell the dream."

You also had to believe in both the product and the dream, as I learned when I challenged Cossman in that Jacuzzi, accusing him of making his fortune by selling schlock.

"That's not true," he said, hopping out of the tub to get a few toy soldiers that were on a shelf in his living room. "These sold in comic books, a hundred for a dollar. Sold cowboys and Indians the same way. Take a close look at this; see all the detail that went into the mold. There's nothing schlocky about them. They're miniature works of art."

And right then I realized that Cossman saw things differently than I did. I drove out to write an article about a schlock-meister, a con man, a guy who hired a model to pose as him.

After a few hours he had me convinced that it didn't matter what I thought about him or what he sold; he saw himself as both an artist of persuasion and a champion of the arts. He was true to that vision. And that's how he was able to sail through life—promoting his dream by making you feel it's yours.

23. WALK AWAY: GET A RETURN

My dream was to be able to choose what I wanted to write about and live a life unburdened by bosses. The freelance life appealed to me, and being paid to talk to people seemed a pretty good way to make a living. But sometimes there are circumstances that call for decisions that can be surprising, especially if it means walking away from an interview before it even begins. This happened to me twice, but for entirely different reasons. In both instances, I trusted my instincts and remained true to myself.

The first time was with **Cher** and started with **Tina Turner**.

When I was in the Peace Corps, living in Accra, Ghana, there was an all-night soul and rock concert in Black Star Square on March 6, 1971. Tens of thousands of Ghanaians attended. It was called Soul to Soul, and featured an array of American and African R&B, soul, rock and jazz musicians. Soul Brother No. 2, Wilson Pickett, headlined (Soul Brother No. 1, James Brown, couldn't make it). It also featured Roberta Flack, Santana, The Staple Singers, Les McCann and Eddie Harris, The Voices of East Harlem, and Ike and Tina Turner. The show lasted fourteen hours and was over at 6:45 a.m. (There was a film made and is available on DVD.) I was there, and while the crowd was enthusiastic for all of the artists, the act that brought down the house was Ike and Tina Turner performing "Proud Mary."

So imagine my surprise when I went to interview Cher at CBS in 1975, and sat in the same waiting room as Tina

Turner, who was there to see about appearing on Cher's variety show. Talk about having a ready icebreaker!

"You were there?" Tina asked.

"I was," I said, hoping to get to know her a bit while we waited. "You guys knocked it out of the park."

"Well, isn't that something," she said and drifted into a nervous silence after I mentioned that I was there to interview Cher. Tina Turner wasn't having the career that Cher was, and I think she was a bit embarrassed to be there, waiting to see whether she'd be asked on Cher's show. I saw how she was on edge, and even the mention of that dazzling performance in Ghana couldn't get more than "Isn't that something" out of her. When Cher came out to greet her, they acted like old friends (and maybe they were), and I waited another twenty minutes before it was my turn to talk to Cher.

"I saw Ike and Tina in Ghana four years ago," I said when I walked in. "Terrific show."

"They're not doing so well," Cher said with a weak smile. She probably didn't mean to say that. I now assume Tina must have been talking about her problems with her drug-addicted and abusive husband. It was a year before they would split up, but I didn't know any of that at the time. As I reached into my bag to take out my tape recorder and questions, her phone rang. Cher picked it up and five minutes later she was in tears.

"What happened?" I asked.

"I was supposed to see a little girl who had leukemia and said she wanted to meet me. I've been so busy lately I kept putting it off, though I got her a doll and was going to give it to her when I found the time. They just told me the girl died."

Cher was visibly upset. Tears made her mascara blacken her cheeks and once she composed herself she looked at me with a sad face, waiting for me to start asking her questions. Instead I said, "Would you rather we do this at another time?"

"Do you mind?" she asked, clearly grateful for the offer.

Of course I minded, since it had taken months for her to fit me into her schedule, and who knew if I would get another chance once I walked out. But I didn't think it appropriate to interview her then. So I packed up my equipment and she said her publicist would call me. I had my doubts about that, but a few days later I got the call. Cher wanted to do the interview at her Egyptian-styled palatial home in Malibu. Instead of the hour she had set aside in her CBS dressing room, she said we could talk as long as I liked. It was a generous payback. And a very rewarding interview.

It is my natural instinct to be sensitive to others, even if it means losing work. In this case, the return exceeded my expectations.

24. KEEPING YOUR DIGNITY MIGHT MEAN LOSING THE JOB

The other person I walked out on was **Robert Mitchum**, whose chilling performances in *The Night of the Hunter* and *Cape Fear* in the mid-fifties and early sixties should have tipped me off that he might be a son of a bitch in real life as well. I hated losing the assignment, but I would have hated myself more had I hung around.

Playboy had been trying to land Robert Mitchum for decades. He fit all the criteria for a perfect subject: he was a huge star, he'd been thrown in the slammer for smoking marijuana, he was a sex magnet for beautiful women, he had a rogue's reputation, he liked to get into bar fights, and he seemed not to give a shit about anything. Especially being interviewed in any kind of depth. So year after year the editors made their request and were repeatedly turned down, until finally they stopped trying. Mitchum just wasn't going to talk.

But then, one day, I got a call from his publicist, who also wanted Mitchum to sit for an interview. He was filming *That Championship Season* and his publicist suggested that I go to the set and meet him. There would be no actual interview, just a chance to get to know each other and see where that might lead. I had nothing to lose, so I went over to the lot where they were shooting and, when the crew broke for lunch, I followed Mitchum to his trailer and introduced myself. He didn't respond. He didn't even look at me. He just started eating his lunch. He didn't offer me anything. He behaved like I wasn't even there.

His silence denied me a chance at an opening for conversation. Well, I thought, we weren't going to get to know each other by avoiding eye or voice contact, so I started talking. He didn't respond to small talk, so I tried dropping some names of people I had interviewed, like Marlon Brando, Henry Fonda, Al Pacino, and George C. Scott. I thought they might pique his curiosity. But their names passed over him like a slow breeze. He never looked up, just chewed on his sandwich, waiting to be called back on set.

What to do?

I brought up the idea of our doing an interview, which was the reason I was in his trailer, and he winced, as if I had mentioned something distasteful. I picked up on that and said, "I'm guessing you don't much care for being interviewed." He mumbled something I couldn't make out, sort of the way a bear might growl before making a move.

"I can understand," I said, hoping to form some sort of connection. "A lot of people are reluctant at first, until they see it isn't as painful as they thought."

"Grrrrrrrr," grunted the bear.

Desperate times call for desperate measures, and I found myself making him an offer I had never made to anyone before. "Look," I began, "seeing how you feel about this, what if we try for an hour, and if after that hour you don't like my questions or don't feel like answering any more of them, I'll give you the tape, give you my word that I will not write anything about you, and walk away."

"That's the problem," he finally spoke.

"What is?"

"It's that first hour."

Screw this guy, I thought. Here I was making him an offer any sane curmudgeon might be thankful for, allowing him the option to do the interview to satisfy the studio higher-ups who wanted the publicity and to pull the plug on the interview at the same time, and he was behaving like….he didn't give a shit. It wasn't an act. That was Mitchum.

"I don't know what else to say," I said. "I'm just here doing my job."

"That's what Eichmann said," the grizzled star said.

"Excuse me?" I said, not sure I heard the reference correctly.

"That's what Eichmann said. Just doing his job."

"And you're comparing doing a *Playboy* interview with what Adolph Eichmann did to the Jews?"

"Same thing," Mitchum said. He wasn't being ironic or sarcastic. Just unbelievably ornery.

I was stunned, and for a brief moment I couldn't even speak. Then I had only one move and that was to stand up and say, "Your publicist knows how to reach me if you change your mind." I didn't bother to shake his hand, which still held a piece of his sandwich. I didn't smile in a friendly manner. And

I didn't call him any names or walk out in a huff. I just turned toward the door and left.

By the time I got to my car I felt depressed, as if I had been hit below the belt, and I wasn't able to catch my breath. What a truly lousy thing to say, I thought, wondering what I might have done differently to alter the outcome. My editor was not going to be happy to hear that I had failed to land this reclusive, recalcitrant star. But I wasn't really sure that I was the right guy for the job. With that doubt in my head, I left to meet with Al Pacino at Anna Strasberg's house. He knew I was meeting with Mitchum that afternoon, and asked how it went. I was pretty glum and said, "Not that well." I told him what Mitchum had said and Pacino was furious. "Who the fuck does he think he is?" Al raged. "You've been with Brando, you've interviewed Linus Pauling. Fuck him, he doesn't deserve you."

It felt good to see Pacino react that way and, as I thought about it, I realized that I had done all that I could without resorting to groveling. But with a man with such a twisted view of life, I doubt that groveling would have worked anyway. I lost that job, but not my dignity. And in the long run of any profession, that's the best way to go.

25. DON'T BE SWAYED BY THE PROMISE OF FRIENDSHIP

I also walked away from another potential interview subject against my better instincts, and am not sure to this day if it was the right thing to do.

A few years after my daughter was born in 1980, my *Playboy* editor called to say that they had a subject they'd like me to consider. From the way he worded it, I wondered who it might be. Most of the time he would call and say, "Are you sitting down? We got Brando." Or, "Good news, Hef's agreed to put Goldie on the cover." Or, "You win, let's do Saul Bellow." But this time he sounded cautious.

"We've got a good chance at **Charlie Manson**," he said. "But I don't want you to answer right away; I want you to take the weekend to think about it." He knew that I lived in the Hollywood Hills, not far from where Manson had once lived. "There are still a lot of his followers out there," he warned me, "and if word gets out that you're seeing him, you might be subjected to various attempts to get to him through you."

Manson lived in San Quentin State Prison ever since his arrest and conviction in 1971 for being the ringleader of his "Family,"—a cadre of young men and women who followed his orders to jumpstart a "revolution." Their plan included taking the lives of seven people, including film director Roman Polanski's wife, actress Sharon Tate in 1969, ending the Sixties in horrific fashion. He had a self-inflicted swastika carved into his forehead and a name that rivaled John Wilkes Booth and Lee Harvey Oswald in infamy.

Since I was married and had a small child, I had more than myself to worry about. I told my editor that I would let him know my answer in a few days. I then called friends and associates who had written about Manson to see what they thought about the assignment. Most of the men I spoke to thought it was a great journalistic opportunity and I should do it. Most of the women thought I should pass.

The more I thought about it, the more I was drawn to the assignment—even after I found out that a producer I knew who had been in touch with Manson had had his mailbox blown up by one of Manson's followers. I think I wanted the thrill of coming face-to-face with such an evil figure, and trying to get to his very core. After all, this was my job, and interviewing Charlie Manson would be an ultimate test of my journalistic skills.

I was leaning toward accepting the assignment when the phone rang late Saturday night. "Hi, guy, howya doin'? I was just thinkin' about you and thought I'd call." It was **Dolly Parton**. I had interviewed Dolly for *Playboy* four years earlier, in 1978, and we had become friends. We'd see each other whenever she came to Los Angeles and had some free time, sometimes taking a drive out to the beach, sometimes meeting for lunch. She had a terrific personality, very much like her public persona, and was one of the most creative talents in show business. Everyone liked Dolly, and when you were around her you just felt uplifted. I was proud to call her my friend and felt lucky that I had been given the assignment that brought us together. I hadn't talked to her for a while, and suddenly, out of the blue, she was checking in. I started to tell her about the possible Manson assignment and the decision I was wrestling with when she very abruptly and very curtly cut me off.

"I don't know what this is worth to you," she said sternly, "but I want to tell you what I think about it. The man is pure evil. He's the devil. His kind rubs off on anybody who meets him. If you see him, if you even talk to him, if... have you talked to him yet?"

"Not yet," I said. "My editor just asked me to consider it."

"Well, consider this then," she said. "If you so much as talk to him—*even on the phone*—then I will never see you or talk with you again. I feel that strongly about it. I've kept my life as pure as I can make it—I've kept away from evil and the bad vibrations that come from being around evil—and I truly believe that man is the devil. If you ever had anything to do with Charlie Manson, I wouldn't want the vibes you would pick up to get around me. Now I know that may not be fair to tell you this, but I'm telling you from my heart. That's the way I am. It's your decision to make, but if you value my friendship at all, you better stay clear of that one."

Others had given me advice, but Dolly was giving me an ultimatum. Say yes to Manson, and kiss her friendship goodbye. As a professional journalist, her words shouldn't have had any effect on me. It was my decision to make. Yet I heard myself say, "Well, Dolly, I guess you've decided for me. I won't do it."

"Now don't say you won't just because I don't want you to," she told me. "You shouldn't do it because *you* shouldn't want to. Why let that evil come anywhere near you?"

"You're right Dolly. I won't even think about it anymore. And besides, your friendship is too important."

Of course I thought about it a lot. But I never interviewed Manson...and I stopped hearing from Dolly. Oh, she continued to send her annual Christmas baskets of jellies, candies, and polished glass and herb-scented balls, but the phone calls ceased. So did her letters, which she had occasionally written until the Manson incident came up. On the Christmas following our last conversation, I sent Dolly a note, thanking her for her basket of goodies and inviting her to lunch when she was next in L.A. Weeks later, I received a large envelope from the "Dollywood Ambassadors" in Pigeon Forge, Tennessee. Inside was a letter that began, "Dear Fan, Thank you for your letter to Dolly Parton. Because of her hectic schedule, we are answering mail for her. The Dolly Parton Fan Club is now Dollywood Ambassadors, and we have added you as a member." Included in the envelope was a picture of Dolly and some brochures about Dollywood and about gifts I might want to purchase, most of them variations of the Christmas basket she had sent.

In 1986, four years after I had passed on Manson, Charlie Rose went to San Quentin Prison and did a television interview with Manson for CBS News *Nightwatch,* for which he won an Emmy Award for Best Interview in 1987. I watched it and wondered if Dolly had as well. I doubt it. Then, in 1988, *Redbook* magazine asked if I would write a profile on Dolly. She agreed and we met in her Los Angeles office. She was dressed in skin-tight jeans, a white tank-top and a faded denim jacket. A white stretch limo waited outside to take us to the restaurant where we had lunch.

We talked about how she looked; how she felt; the problems her TV show was having; her plans to tour in the summer; her new record deal with CBS; her long-distance relationship with her husband Carl; and her ability to juggle the many projects in her life. It was like old times—we just picked up where we had left off six years ago, except for the elephant in the room, which was the fact that I had turned down the Manson interview in favor of her friendship, and yet that friendship no longer existed. After the meal and before dessert, I brought it up.

"It was Manson that turned you away from me, wasn't it?" I asked. "Just the fact that I was even considering it turned you off."

"Yes, it did," Dolly said. "I just had the worst feeling about that. I really think you'd have suffered for that—to see him that close, all that bitterness and insanity. I didn't even want nothing to do with you if you were going to have something to do with him."

Well, I never had anything to do with the evil Charlie Manson, and I no longer hear from Dolly. I'm sorry that I don't see her anymore because I so enjoyed our times together. But I'm even sorrier that I let her convince me not to interview Manson. I don't know if his evil would have rubbed off on me, or if one of his crazy followers would have found out where I lived and blown up my mailbox, but nothing happened to Charlie Rose, other than getting his own nightly talk show, a gig on *60 Minutes*, and the occasional hosting of the *CBS Evening News*. Dolly Parton is a terrific, sensitive, extraordinary artist who has a deserved place in our culture, but I shouldn't have listened to her in this case. I should have followed my own instincts. Once again, being true to yourself is a good lesson to remember.

26. THEY'RE NOT YOUR FRIENDS

And that doubly applies to the seduction of a celebrity friendship.

In the summer of 1984, I flew to Aspen, rented a car, and drove to **Goldie Hawn** and **Kurt Russell's** getaway house in Old Snowmass. Goldie, with her giggle first heard on *Laugh-In,* was truly America's Sweetheart. We loved her in *Cactus Flower, Foul Play, Shampoo, The Sugarland Express,* and *Private Benjamin,* which she also produced. Kurt was her partner in life, a rugged, handsome former athlete who had starred in some big films of his own, like *Silkwood, Escape From New York*, and *The Thing*. They had both been through bad marriages and wanted to keep their romance going without the wedding bells. What kept them attracted to each other were their differences. Kurt was a hunter who once killed a wild boar with a knife. Goldie was a nurturer who followed a spiritual path. Kurt was an outspoken conservative who had little use for the liberal Democrats that Goldie supported. It was a match made in Hollywood heaven.

When I met them for that interview in Aspen, I liked them both. They had wit, energy, opinions, and interesting friends. We hit it off immediately. Goldie wanted to hear about my Japanese wife who practiced herbal healing on our children and Kurt liked to tell me I was full of shit to believe that Jimmy Carter was a better president than Ronald Reagan. Goldie would pronounce "No talking religion or politics at the dinner table," when we sat down to eat together. And then we'd proceed to talk about religion and politics. Kurt was irascible but good-natured. Goldie lit incense sticks and hit ancient bells to set a mood.

When *Playboy* decided to put Goldie on their cover to accompany our interview, I went to the photo shoot in Los Angeles. The photo editor had one shot in mind: Goldie inside a six-foot high round champagne glass, her legs stretched overhead like one of Leroy Neiman's "Femlin" illustrations that appeared in various poses on the Party Joke page. Goldie took one look at that prop and balked. "I'm not getting in that," she said, and headed for the dressing room until they came up with another cover shot.

The problem was, there was no other shot. The editor had mistakenly put all her eggs into this idea. Goldie was "bubbly," and they had a bubble machine ready to bring in the New Year with her inside the glass. That was the standoff when I arrived.

"Can you talk to her?" the photo editor asked. "She wants to know what else we had planned. She thinks we have three different sets, but we don't, we only have this one."

I knocked on her door and heard the ice in her voice when she said, "Come in." This wasn't America's Sweetheart; this was Cruella Deville. Goldie was pissed at how they wanted to portray her. She found it insulting. "Let them get the other sets ready and we'll see what they come up with."

"To do that, Goldie, they'll have to strike the set they prepared. It's all lit and ready to go. Why not shoot a few in the glass and see how it looks before they strike it? It will save time, and what the hell, you might even like what you see."

"You really think I should be the bubbly idiot in a giant champagne glass? Am I always going to be the airhead from *Laugh-In*?"

"You're way more than that," I said. "Which is why you can make it work. And if you don't like it, you won't approve it. No harm done."

Goldie trusted me and agreed. We walked out together, she got into the glass–wearing a white shirt, opened black bow tie, red stiletto heels, and showing a lot of leg–did the shot, and then said, "I don't think we need another set, this should do."

That January 1985 cover is now considered a collectible. Goldie liked it, Kurt liked it, her kids liked it, and we became family friends. She invited my wife and me to her home in Pacific Palisades for dinner and we had them to our home a few months later. It became something we continued to do for the next six years. We also were invited to their annual Christmas party and Goldie even insisted that I bring my wife and two small daughters to their Malibu summerhouse while they were away. Whenever she and Kurt took exotic trips they would share with us the family pictures they took, including ones of Goldie in her birthday suit sunning herself on the deck of a private yacht in the middle of the Mediterranean. In other words, we became close with them. We were two couples who enjoyed each other's company.

Then I was asked to write a cover story about Kurt for *Entertainment Weekly* to promote his film *Backdraft* and everything changed.

It was Kurt's idea to add some color to the article by flying us to lunch in his six-seat twin-engine Cessna from the Santa Monica airport to Oceano, near Pismo Beach. Once we were in the air Kurt decided to give me a flying lesson. "Take the control yoke," he said. I didn't even know it was called a yoke, and he enjoyed my discomfort.

"You're rising at a rate of 500 feet per minute," he laughed. "Look at your altimeter. We've gone from 5,000 to 6,000 feet. You don't want to do that, you want to keep it steady."

The Sierra Madre Mountains were ahead of us and I said I didn't want to crash into them.

"You're above them," he said, "just lower the plane."

"You want me to go down? I don't want to go down. I want to go up, away from those mountains."

Kurt never lost his good humor as I continued to drip with sweat. But eventually, common sense got the best of him and he took back the controls. We had a nice lunch, a good long walk, and I wrote a piece about him based on our conversations.

When the article was published in June I read it with dismay. The editors had decided that I wasn't hard enough on Kurt and added a paragraph toward the front that I didn't write. This is what it said:

"Russell's career has been in need of real heat for some time. Despite his various credits—ranging from the no-nuke message movie *Silkwood* (1983) to the no-brain beefcake fest *Tango & Cash* (1989)—he has long been stuck on the special back burner Hollywood reserves for second-tier leading men. His critical successes, like 1988's *Tequila Sunrise*, have often been box office disappointments. Possibly doubting his drawing power, Universal didn't even put his face on *Backdraft's* poster. But *Backdraft* may change a lot of minds: It took in $15.7 million its first weekend, a record for a non-sequel opening over the Memorial Day holiday, and has remained No. 1 at the box office. Kurt Russell finally has a hit he's proud of."

I cringed when I read that. Nobody likes to be called a "second-tier" actor. I've never called anyone that. I had been upfront with the editors at *EW* that I knew Kurt on a personal level and that we were friends. That's why I was able to give them a story they wouldn't normally get. I flew his plane, for Christ's sake. I didn't set out to hurt him or his feelings. And I didn't. That is, I wouldn't have had they published the article as I had written it. At the very least, they should have shown me their edit and allowed me to make some adjustments.

I didn't call Kurt to explain this because the damage had been done. The magazine had come out. But I figured that I would let him know what happened and apologize to him when we next got together. It was our turn to host them for dinner and I called Goldie to make a date.

She didn't return my call.

I called the following week.

She didn't respond.

I dropped her a note. Still no answer.

"Do you think it's because of the article?" my wife asked.

"I don't think so," I said. "I'm sure he was angry, but we often piss each other off when we get together. I can't dictate what *Entertainment Weekly* is going to publish, even under my byline. It's the nature of the beast. All I can do is stop writing for them." Which I did. But Kurt didn't know that. All Kurt knew was what he read. "Second-tier leading man," must have stuck in his craw.

I didn't know this for sure because I just stopped hearing from them. I could only assume. The other possibility, my wife thought, was that when we spent the weekend at their Malibu house I forgot the code numbers to get in and their security service had to come and ask me for the password, which I remembered. But that would not be a reason to stop talking to us. Or could it be?

A few years went by. Then one day I was talking with Al Pacino, and he said he had met my friends, Goldie and Kurt, at an Oscar event, and he really liked them.

"They're not my friends," I said.

"What happened?" he asked.

"I don't know for sure," I said, telling him what I thought might have happened, but saying that I doubted that Goldie would have shut me out as well. Friends would talk about things that might be hurtful between them. They wouldn't go silent, would they?

"You need to know," Pacino said. "You can't leave it this way. Write to her and say that I told you to write. Ask her why the silence."

So I did. And Goldie replied, saying that she thought we understood each other but that the article I wrote about Kurt didn't present him in a way she recognized, and because he was hurt, she was too. She just thought it best not to talk to me again.

I replied by making a copy of the 17-page article I had written and sending it to her, along with a copy of the magazine article, as I was sure they didn't keep that one. I suggested she read what I wrote, then read what had been printed, and see if she could recognize Kurt in what I had actually written.

Goldie sent me a handwritten letter. She said she was "down on her knees" with her apology. She loved what I had written and so had Kurt. She was just so sorry about the misunderstanding. She later called and invited us to dinner.

On the drive there my wife asked if I was going to make an issue out of what had happened. She knew that I had my principles and that I was still upset that they had thought so little of me that they ignored my attempts to reach them. "What do you think?" I said.

When we sat at their table, Kurt brought it up first, but I stopped him. "Let's have a nice dinner," I said, "and talk about it afterwards." So we sat there—with young Kate, Oliver,

Boston, and Wyatt as well—and made pleasant small talk about what we were all doing or had done in the years that had past. Then we went to their living room and I said what was on my mind. I compared the misunderstanding to a Guy de Maupassant story about the pearl necklace. I could understand how hurt Kurt must have felt when he read that lousy paragraph, but what I could not understand was their complete silence. We had had our differences before, I said, but it didn't stop us from staying friends. If I had hurt him, why hadn't he called me about it? Why hadn't he shown his feisty, fiery side? Why did he take the cowardly way out, by turning off the friendship we had developed over six years? Or was I mistaken thinking what we had *was* a friendship?

And that's when I realized that it wasn't. We lived in different worlds. We came together because we amused them. And when we stopped the amusement, we were cast off. Forgotten. Not thought about again.

When we left that evening Goldie said she looked forward to the next time, but I knew there would be no next time. We had a nice little run with them, but in the end the lesson I learned is that there will always be a professional distance between a journalist and everyone else. No matter how close you might get, you must realize they're not really your friends. It saddened me, and if I hadn't spoken out we'd probably still be exchanging dinners every four months, but I wouldn't have been true to myself and we would have remained in their world of pretend.

27. MY MEDIOCRE GOLF GAME
IS WHERE IT SHOULD BE

On a lighter note, my sense of self was reaffirmed after **Jeff Daniels** explained to me why he quit golf because he got too good at it.

Jeff Daniels might play *Dumb and Dumber* when the money is right and Jim Carrey is up for it, but he is anything but. When his wife Kathleen joined our conversation, she told me that they own five copies of that particular film, though her favorite films of his were *Gettysburg*, *The Purple Rose of Cairo* and *Terms of Endearment*.

It rarely happens that the subject's spouse joins the conversation, but it's a welcome opportunity to get fresh insight that goes beyond the standard publicity bio. Kathleen Daniels filled in some of the details of how they met (working together in their hometown community theater in Chelsea, Michigan) and when they married (she was 20, he 24). I asked him an impromptu question having to do with any embarrassing moments in their relationship and he told me a funny story that I would never have gotten had she not entered the room.

"We rented an RV," he recalled, "and took a family trip from Michigan to Cooperstown, New York to the Baseball Hall of Fame. Pulled into a truck stop in Erie, Pennsylvania, gassed it up, pulled out, going up the highway, forgot my wife. The kids said, 'Where's mom?' I'm going 'Don't do this, I'm driving a building here.' 'She's not here Dad, really.' The next exit was five miles. I got off and turned back. But by then, she had grabbed a 25 year-old guy and said, 'I need you to follow that RV, that's my husband, he forgot me.' They jumped in his Ford Taurus and took off. Well, we'd already come off the highway. They flew by us. I got back to the truck stop; she wasn't there. Now I was thinking some trucker put a gun to her back and took her. So I called the state cops. She went to the next rest area 15 miles away not finding me, so she called the house in Michigan. The house sitter happened to be there. I thought about where she might call and I called home. The house sitter gave me the phone number of the rest area where she was waiting. That was one of the most embarrassing and the most frightening things that ever happened to me."

It was a funny story that I'm sure his three kids have teased him about over the years, and it reminded me of similar scenes in the films *Reservation Road* and *Breakdown* and more recently in an episode from Will Forte's TV show *The Last Man on Earth.*

Besides acting, Daniels is an accomplished musician and golfer and when his wife left us I asked him what gave him more satisfaction, music or golf. I knew that he had put out a few albums and had played guitar on Don Johnson's album "Let it Roll," and had even written about 200 songs since the early Seventies. "150 of them are just crap," he said, "but there's some that are decent. In my quest to continue to raise money for my theater company (The Purple Rose Theater Company that he founded in Chelsea), I had to take the guitar and go out there and do ninety minutes. It's very Harry Chapin/Gordon Lightfoot mixed with patter—some are very funny."

His golf game was more than decent. He regularly shot in the eighties, which is an achievement I've only done twice, but I'm a mediocre golfer who enjoys a nice walk and the occasional par and rare birdie. I know what it's like to chase a score, and most golfers who shoot in the eighties strive to make it into the seventies, to know they're improving. Golfers like me are happy to break 100, and know that breaking 90 is an aberration that shouldn't be taken seriously. But Daniels was in a different category. He took the game seriously enough to take lessons so that he could improve. And when he began to get good he knew that he would have to devote more time to playing and take more lessons to continue to get better. Instead, he achieved his goal of breaking 80 and then quit cold turkey.

"Golfers know what happens when you break 80," he said. "It will be the end of you, because once you break 80, you're supposed to break 80 every time. But you have to work very hard to break 80. You have to go to the range; you have to shoot three rounds a week minimum, plus lessons. Then it became: I shot a 78 yesterday, but today I shot a 79, what the hell's wrong? Well, nothing's wrong. I got tired of being able to hit a perfect seven iron today and not being able to tomorrow. And I had put the guitar down and golf had overtaken that. So I picked the guitar up and once you learn that blues lick, you have it. It's better for me; it's better for the soul."

I took what he said to heart. I learned to play golf with my father, who was always trying to get me to swing in such a way to keep my ball from slicing into the woods. I never listened, of course, and gave the game up when I was sixteen and didn't return to it for thirty years. I found with the new equipment and balls, I could play well enough to keep my shots mostly in the fairway but not score anywhere low enough to be much of a challenge to my golfing partners who were determined, like Daniels, to break 80. But that was fine with me. Especially after Daniels told me that he gave it up because he had gotten good at it. I knew that wouldn't happen to me because I don't take lessons. I don't listen to advice. I just swing away. If I bogey a hole, I'm happy. If I sink a putt outside ten feet, I'll fist bump whoever I'm playing with. If I shoot in the low nineties, I'm ready to email friends on the East Coast to tell them. And if by a miracle I break 90, well, that's a sucker's ploy by the Great Golf God in the Sky, trying to lure me into newer clubs, higher priced balls, and lessons. But I've got Jeff Daniels as my example. He shot a 78...and walked away. I like the game too much to walk away after shooting close to par (which I will never do). So thanks, Jeff. You did me a solid by telling me how you became a blues guitar player.

Something I have no interest in learning.

Know Your Props

28. BE PROP PROUD

I've been to Europe, Africa, New Zealand, Tahiti, South America, Mexico, Canada, and most of the United States, and I found that everyone everywhere watches reruns of *I Love Lucy*. Back in 1976, *Lucy* ran in 77 countries, and more have probably been added to that list today. Lucy Ricardo is probably as well known as anyone, even though **Lucille Ball** died in 1989. That's phenomenal. When I met Lucy 40 years ago, I was aware that I was meeting a legend. What I didn't know was that she was at a place in her life where she didn't care.

Lucille Ball was one of those people who could have gone anywhere in the world and been treated like royalty. Who wouldn't want to host Lucy? She made the world laugh. Just to be in her presence made one special.

But Lucy didn't care.

"I purposely haven't done much traveling around the world," she told me, "because I don't like to go to Australia, to Japan, or anywhere else. I've turned down trips to a lot of places. I'm not that crazy about making appearances someplace. I've been told by the government—including Presidents

Truman and Eisenhower—that it would be a marvelous thing if I would, but I haven't. I appreciate the fact that they see me as a goodwill ambassador for America, and I know why. Because the rest of the world can identify with what we do and they can laugh and forget their troubles, without understanding the language in many instances. We're very physical and you know what I'm doing and the trouble I'm in without understanding every word. The need for release and entertainment of that kind is universal. They can identify with the nonsense. With all the reruns, I know that I babysat for three generations and I love it, I'm very proud of it."

She also didn't care about being a woman in charge, as she was when she became the first woman ever to be president of a major production company.

"I was not a good president," she said. "I was merely filling up space, depending on men who had been with me for many years that I absolutely trusted. When it came to final decisions, I had all of their opinions. Women being president or women being anything, I don't dig it, and I got out of it as soon as I could. It took me seven years of very hard work to get out of big business."

But when I asked her to discuss how her Lucy character evolved, she showed that when it came to crucial final decisions, she didn't need any men to add their opinions; she knew what worked for her.

"When television came along," she said, "the producers of the radio show I was on asked me to be on TV and do whatever I wanted. I didn't know what the hell I wanted; I didn't know what television was. Finally, they decided on a script about a Hollywood couple who live in Bel-Air or Beverly Hills and they have a pool and I said, 'Wait a minute, for the first time I can give you an answer—I *know* I don't want to do this, because I don't think that there's any part of America that would think any Hollywood couple has any problems. I will not touch that script.' That was the best decision I had made. I said I want to do a domestic comedy about a zany, domestic housewife. I want to be lower middle class, so that if I have a fur collar around my suit you can write a whole script about it; then I know I have a problem; then I know I can identify with most of America. The writers then added the age group: the younger and the older married couples. None of us knew each other, except Desi and myself. When we all got together we found out by chance that Bill Frawley ("Fred") loved to sing and dance, Vivian Vance ("Ethel") *loved* to sing and her singing was rahhh, the kind that was just perfect for our show, and she played bad piano; I played four notes on a lousy saxophone. We found out these things as we went along."

Ball had worked with the Marx Brothers in *Room Service* and with the Three Stooges on a few of their movies, but said she learned more from Buster Keaton than either of those zany groups.

"The Marx Brothers scared the bejeezus out of me. They embarrassed me. They were forever doing pranks on the stage. One day we had to go in and out of a lot of doors, and during one of the runs they decided to take their clothes off and they came out and there were fifteen nuns and three priests visiting the set. I must say they took it better than I did.

"As for the Stooges, I didn't learn much from them. You just learned to take it and run, go home and dry yourself off. It was wet all the time. I learned that that's not what I wanted to do: be the butt of somebody's seltzer bottle the rest of my life. I also had to learn how to tip my head so I didn't get it up my nostrils. I learned that much.

"But Buster Keaton took time out at Metro to talk to me about props one day and I loved to work with props. He told me to never, never, never go on stage without checking your props. Before Buster, I had many a scene ruined by improper placement of props, improper usage of the weight of certain things. I learned that I was adept at catching toast in mid-air while I was talking and could do it repeatedly. To this day while the curtain is still down I check where the toaster is. Is the water running? Is the gas on or off? Where are the pots and pans, the towel, the knife? Is the stuff in the refrigerator? Is the stuff ready to go out the door when the kid comes? I am very prop conscious and prop proud. I think it's been the success of many a show that our props worked beautifully. The only time you can't depend on a prop is when you have a lion, a bear, a snake, or a chimpanzee. You can't rely on animals. But then, a lot of people you can't rely on either."

What Buster Keaton impressed upon Lucy further reinforced on me the need to be prepared for any situation. When you are interacting with someone or with an audience, you can't rely on anyone but yourself.

29. BACKUP YOUR EQUIPMENT

As for my own props, I learned that lesson a few years earlier when I was working on my first *Newsday* magazine assignment. I had spent three years in the Peace Corps, then another eight months traveling from West to East Africa, then to India, Kashmir, Nepal, Thailand, Hong Kong and Japan. After I returned to the U.S., I was in New York with fresh eyes and the confidence that I could write entertaining stories if given the chance. I took advantage of once having won a high school essay contest sponsored by *Newsday*, Long Island's leading newspaper, and managed to get a meeting with one of the editors there. He told me that they were about to launch a supplement to the Sunday paper, called *LI,* and suggested that I might want to meet with that editor. I did and the conversation went something like this:

"We're thinking of doing a story on the history of aviation on Long Island. Do you like to do research?"

"Not really, but I know how."

"Do you know anything about aviation?"

"No, but I can learn."

I was being honest and the editor, who was from England, had his doubts, but since I was sent to him from that other editor, he gave me the courtesy of the assignment. I don't think he ever expected to see me again.

The first thing I did was go to the "morgue"—the newspaper's archival library—and started reading everything I could about the subject. It didn't take long to discover that Long Island was considered "the cradle of aviation." There were hundreds of "firsts" that began on the Island, including the first cross-country flight, the first airmail flight, the first flight piloted by a woman, the first "guided missiles," the first transcontinental air race, the first nonstop solo transatlantic flight (Charles Lindbergh's *Spirit of St Louis*), and the first around-the-world flight. The second thing I did was to write letters to everyone I could find who had anything to do with the early years of aviation. I corresponded with Clarence Chamberlin in Florida, who had established a new world's endurance record in 1919 by flying back and forth over Long Island for over 51 hours and just missed out beating Lindbergh across the ocean. He told me to get in touch with **Carl "Slim" Hennicke**, who still lived in Southampton, Long Island and "was there both before and after me and can give you the lowdown on most of us."

Slim, who had founded The Long Island Early Flyers Club and hoped to move all the memorabilia he had collected from his basement to an air museum he had been lobbying for, had a long memory and liked to talk. He had been a mechanic in his early teens and later continued in that capacity for a number of flying aces; he was also a stuntman, barnstormer, unlicensed pilot, and flying instructor. "The early pioneers were my heroes, like some kids had Babe Ruth," he told me when I interviewed him in 1972. "There're only about 200 left and I've kept in touch with many of them."

We sat in his crowded basement among the labyrinth of 2000 books, yellowing magazines, framed pictures, propellers, rudders, joysticks, wings and plaster busts of men like Lindbergh that covered the floor, lined the walls, and overflowed the tables. He told me some of his early barnstorming stories, like the times he walked on the wings of a biplane waving at the crowds below, or hung upside down like a trapeze artist from the bar between the biplane's wheels, or parachuted down reading the Sunday funnies as the crowd roared its approval. He had a story about each piece of memorabilia he had collected and after the first two hours, his wife called him up for lunch. I passed on joining them so that I could go to a nearby diner, take some notes, and check my tape recorder. It was a good thing that I did because I discovered that while the recorder was turning, the batteries were so weak that they didn't pick up our voices. In other words, I had two hours of gibberish.

I replaced the batteries and returned to Slim's house where I proceeded to ask him the same questions he had already answered. He was an old man who loved to tell his stories and didn't seem to notice (or care) that he was repeating himself. This time I was able to get his stories the way he told them. I also learned a very good lesson for all future interviews, and that was to always use two tape recorders and fresh batteries. Sounds simple, but you'd be surprised how many times that backup recorder later became my primary source.

30. USE GOOD BRUSHES

Once I gained an appreciation for my equipment, I remembered advice that **Arthur Singer** gave me about using only the best equipment.

"For bird enthusiasts, the name Arthur Singer is probably as familiar as that of O.J. Simpson for football fans and Beverly Sills for opera buffs."

That's how I began the article I wrote for the April 21, 1974 Sunday edition of the *New York Times*, twenty years before O.J. would be known more infamously for something else. I was so proud to be writing about Arthur Singer because his son Paul was one of my best friends throughout junior and senior high school, and whenever I was at the Singer house in Jericho, Long Island, just a few blocks from where I lived, I watched as his father puffed on his pipe and drew birds from photographs he had taken from his exotic wildlife trips or from conserved owls, hawks and eagles that he borrowed from the Museum of Natural History.

"Artie," as we all called him, was as mild-mannered as Clark Kent in who he was, and as thrilling as Superman in what he did. That Artie was a freelance artist was inspirational and, along with Ted Harris, was a major influence in the direction my life would take. That he took his son's friends seriously and welcomed them into his studio was memorable. I don't remember any other household I visited where the parents would ask, "What have you been up to? What are you reading? What do you think of Nixon and Kennedy? Do you think we might go to war with Russia over the missiles in Cuba? Were you disturbed by *Judgment at Nuremberg*? Did you see the Picasso/Pollack/DeKooning exhibit yet at the Met?" The Singers thrived on conversation, and they expected everyone to contribute, whatever their age.

To a suburban kid like me, seeing an adult working from his house was instructional. My father was in the pharmaceutical business and my friends' parents held similar mundane jobs. Through Artie, I learned at an impressionable age that a man didn't have to spend long hours in traffic going to and from work, or answer to a "boss" or worry about whether or not there would be bonuses or layoffs at the end of the year. If you had any artistic talent, it was possible to stay at home, smoke a pipe, and work at your own pace. In short, Artie gave me an understanding of the freelance life.

But I couldn't draw worth a damn, I had a tin ear for music, and I was clumsy with crafts; however, I seemed to do okay writing for my school paper, so I took a shot at journalism. I entered a statewide essay contest, and my winning article wound up being published in *Newsday*. My parents were proud of me, but they belonged to that generation that believed in withholding praise. The Singers, on the other hand, were overjoyed. I was showing signs of belonging to that lucky minority class called "artists" who might, one day, enjoy the fruits of a freelance life.

When I joined the Peace Corps and got assigned to Ghana, Artie asked me to look into the Ashanti gold weights and, if I could, bring some home for him. His wife, Judy, had illustrated a book about the Ashanti in 1966, and both Singers were thrilled by the happenstance that I was living in Ghana two years later.

Later, when I was just starting out in my career, who better to suggest as a profile to the *New York Times* than Arthur

Singer? His paintings of birds first appeared nationally in *Sports Illustrated* in 1954, he had illustrated a half dozen *Reader's Digest* covers, he drew the birds that appeared in World Book Encyclopedia, and he had spent four years illustrating *Birds of the World*, a coffee table book that sold a half million copies. He then illustrated the *Birds of Europe* and the *Field Guide to North American Birds*, and would soon be commissioned by the U.S. Post Office to draw what would become a one-sheet of stamps of the 50 state birds.

The *Times* article allowed me to ask him about his early life and he told me about how he had begun freelancing while still in high school. He had an avid interest in jazz at the time and through some of his early art work he got to meet and befriend musicians like Cab Calloway and Duke Ellington. At the age of 15 he drew an illustration of Calloway made up entirely of calligraphy, "letters which formed the name of every piece he played in his repertoire. His book agent flipped over it," Singer told me, "and I got a great big $15 for it, which I thought was a fortune. They used it in every theater all across the country. They made huge blowups of it and ran a contest—anyone who got all the names that were on this thing would get in free."

When I asked him about some of his experiences in Africa tracking birds, he told me about a trip to Lake Baringo in Kenya, during which a storm nearly capsized his boat and between the crocodiles in the water and the rock pythons hanging from surrounding trees, he wondered if the egrets and herons he had gone to observe were really worth it. Once on shore, he decided that they were.

"I've taken thousands upon thousands of pictures of birds in zoos and in the wild," he said. "The birds in the wild give me certain information about locality and terrain. The experience of seeing birds is important because it can make a strong impression on you which might eventually turn into a painting or an illustration."

I learned so much from his example, but I also remember something he said as an aside that stuck with me. I was looking at all his paint and watercolor brushes on his desk and asked if it really mattered what material they were made of. "Of course it does," he said. "You must always use the best brushes."

Simple as that. And yet, just as profound, because it applied to everything a professional uses, be it brushes, sketchpads, notepads, pens, typewriters, tape recorders, computers or TV props for use on a sitcom or drama. You should never go cheap when it comes to equipment. Arthur Singer taught me that, just as he taught me about the freelance life.

When Prepared,
Conversation Flows

31. STUDY. STUDY. STUDY

I had an ulterior motive for wanting to interview **Henry Moore**, one of the 20th century's great sculptors. At the time, my girl-friend Hiromi was a teaching assistant at UCLA in the Textile Department while working on her MFA. She had gone from weaving functional pieces as a student in Japan to bursting out into three-dimensional sculptures made of sisal, furniture stuffing, and other natural fibers. Her use of such material was unique and galleries in Tokyo, Los Angeles, Santa Barbara, Chicago and New York offered her one-woman shows. Some of her sea creature-like art covered a wall when completed, twelve feet long by six feet high. Her professors were full of praise for her work but after a while, praise wears thin. To advance as an artist one often needs good critical feedback. I, too, was guilty of saying positive things about her wall hang-ings, but that didn't really help push her to the next level. What she needed was the opinion of someone who would bypass courtesy, replacing it with constructive criticism. She needed to be challenged in ways that would stimulate her.

"Let's go to Europe and I'll interview Henry Moore," I suggested. "Then when we're done talking, he can take a look at slides of your work." That was my bright idea. A gift to her. Moore was an aging giant. What did we have to lose?

"You're crazy," was her response. "Why would he have any interest in my work?"

"Well, first of all, he doesn't know it. Second, you're an artist, too. Third, what's he going to say once we're there, that he won't look at your slides? Of course he will."

She was skeptical, but she did like the idea of a trip to Europe, so I called my *Newsday* editor and suggested Moore. He agreed, as long as he didn't have to pay for the trip. I then did some research to find out where Henry Moore lived and wrote to him requesting an interview. It took some time, but he agreed and said he would be at his summer home in Forte dei Marmi, Italy. It was along the Italian Riviera, not far from the Carrera Mountains, where Michelangelo got much of his marble, and where Moore got his.

"You weren't an art major," Hiromi reminded me as I began making plans.

"That's the beauty of what I do," I said. "I'm always learning new things."

In truth, I wasn't so glib. Moore was a big trial for me. He was one of the world's most important sculptors and I didn't want to bore him with sophomoric questions. My goal was to get him to think about things he hadn't thought about before, if that were possible, so that when I asked him at the end if he would look at Hiromi's work he would be happy to do so. To do this I had to prepare.

I began reading books about Donatello, Michelangelo, Bernini, Rodin, Brancusi and other great sculptors. I read histories of art and wrote down quotes of artists that could lead to interesting conversation with Moore. I became obsessive with my questions, writing them in notebooks and then typing them in an order that I believed would make our talk flow. Knowing that we would want to travel through other countries in Europe before getting to Italy, I planned a route that would involve planes and trains before renting a car when we got to the Italian Riviera. Also knowing how nervous I would be as we approached Forte dei Marmi, I thought that I would benefit by having my questions pasted into a 6x8 inch spiral notebook so I could study them on the train. So I meticulously retyped my questions to fit and numbered them as well. I filled half the notebook with hundreds of questions and all the way from Holland through Belgium and France I studied these questions, over and over.

When we walked into his backyard, Henry Moore was sitting on a garden chair thumbing through the pages of a book of drawings by Jean-Francois Millet. He didn't get up. "Look at some of these drawings," he said straight off. "You know you can judge an artist by his drawings."

"And how many great artists might you discover that way?" I asked.

"Maybe only twenty great draftsmen," he said, listing among them Millet, Rembrandt, Michelangelo, Raphael, Reubens, Seurat, Picasso, Matisse, Degas and himself. "Drawing is the same as form. You're trying to explain or express the shape of something on a flat surface by the science of drawing, which is either using light or shade, or perspective, the two means of representing without making the shape itself. To draw well means that you must understand form. And that's the same with sculpture."

We hadn't even been properly introduced but we were off and running, talking about art. I took out my tape recorder but not my notebook. It didn't seem necessary. I had studied my questions so thoroughly that when it came to do the actual interview I was well prepared and didn't need them. This was a revelation. I always depended on my questions, to be there for me when a conversation lagged. But once Moore and I started talking, we didn't stop for hours, and when we were done I asked if he would take a look at Hiromi's slides and photographs. "I don't really look at students' work," he said.

"She just looks young," I said. "She's a teaching assistant at UCLA. And she's had a few shows."

Moore reluctantly took a look, and then looked again at Hiromi, this time with an enthusiastic smile. "Yes, yes, I see what you're doing," he said. I sat back, letting my tape recorder run, to capture the words of encouragement I knew Hiromi would want preserved. They talked for an hour, and I thought about what a great day we were having. Hiromi was getting some good advice, I learned about the importance of drawing when judging artists, and that going over one's questions repeatedly until they were practically committed to memory was a very valuable thing for an interviewer to do.

32. TRUTH IS A CHANGING COLOR

I had my first great day as an interviewer when I was with a disciple of Henry Moore's some years earlier. Part of it had to do with his gregarious and affable nature, and part of it with the fact that I was a stranger in a strange land and ran all over Accra looking for books to aid my preparation.

I probably learned more about myself in the Peace Corps than anywhere else. It's not surprising, considering that I was fresh out of college, on my own, and my tour happened before the invention of cell phones, computers, the Internet, Facetime, or Skype. America was in a nasty war in Southeast Asia and young men like me were suffering as soldiers, draft dodgers, hypochondriacs, or conscientious objectors. The Peace Corps wasn't a way out of being drafted, but it was a way to stall the local draft board from calling you in. I had first become interested in the Peace Corps when President Kennedy proposed it and, though I was still in high school at its inception, it captured my imagination; I filed it away as something to pursue after college. That the Vietnam War was disturbing our consciousness at the time just added to my pursuit of peace. And Ghana turned out to be a friendly, peaceful place.

After arriving in Ghana, we 35 volunteers traveled to Winneba where our training would take place. Winneba was eye-opening: The con artists were waiting for us at the local bars, where they tried to pass off fake Rolex watches for twenty cedis and a beer. We danced drunkenly in the streets with the townspeople, who powdered our faces with white chalk during the annual deer hunting festival. We heard stories about Sassabonsam, a devilish figure who stopped time for those who caught a glimpse of him after dusk and snapped them back to reality when the sun came up.

At the Specialist Training College I met **Vincent Kofi**, the head of the Art Department. He was a man of girth, with a wide-open personality. He was 46 and had studied at the Royal College of Art in London in the early '50s, where he said he learned more about Africa than he had ever learned as a native. He studied Henry Moore, Jacob Epstein, Ernst Barlach, and Constantin Brancusi, and had an innate sense of himself as an artist. He was good at seeing what others couldn't see, and he "found" his art inside the trunks of trees. Like all sculptors of vision, he looked at his raw material and carved away the excess (in his case, the bark and wood) to find the form hidden within.

On that first day, I was with a group of people visiting his studio, so I didn't get a chance to sit and talk with him one-on-one. But later, on a trip to Kumasi, the capital of the Ashanti region, I learned that Kofi had left Winneba to teach in the Fine Arts Department at the University of Science and Technology there. I went to see him and he took me to a nearby forest where he chose his wood. Then we went to his house where I met his wife and family and we spent a few hours talking about his work. I had heard enough to recognize a good story in him and queried the editor of *African Arts* magazine suggesting Kofi as the subject of a profile. Some months later I got the go-ahead so, after reading as many art books as I could from the University of Ghana, I invited Kofi to my apartment in Accra for an interview. He told me the brand of beer he liked and I borrowed a reel-to-reel tape recorder. When he arrived, his presence filled my living room, much as Pavarotti's presence would when he came to my home in Los Angeles a dozen years later.

I hadn't yet thought of myself as an interviewer. I was a 21-year-old college graduate teaching at the Ghana Institute of Journalism in Accra, and Vincent Kofi was my first professional interview. I can't remember how nervous I must have been before he came to my apartment, but I do recall how easy it was to talk to him, and how wise he was with his responses to my questions. He spoke of the depth he found in people, and trying to match it in his sculptures. He described how each work was a struggle and that he often only slept two hours a night when he was working on a piece. He was always "bargaining" with his material. And his sculptures depicted the plight of the African, who "has been battered around so much that you wonder if this is our lot." He said he was always looking for the truth in his pieces, "and it doesn't matter the subject you're treating."

That's when I asked him what the truth was when it came to art. I've often wondered about that. Art has a way of defining life for us and when we see a work of art that moves us, it's because it has somehow struck a chord; it's not false. But is it "true?" And can there be such a thing as truth derived from a work of art?

"Truth," Kofi said with assurance, "is when you are convinced about something. You might be wrong, but you have your conscience to rely upon. The truth can vary, like the color turquoise: in daylight, it's one color; at night, under artificial light, it's another. Truth depends upon circumstance. It's a reflection of how you sum up things."

He went on to talk about what made an artist a "true" artist ("sensitivity and imagination") and how he had remained true to himself by not selling his sculptures to European institutions because he wanted his work to stay in Africa. He spoke about how he had shows in galleries and in public buildings, but they never got the reaction they did when people saw his carved tree trunks at lorry parks and market places, as they were transported from one city to another. These were the people who "would never enter an exhibition hall," who understood and could relate to his work.

It was an instructive afternoon talking about art and Africa over a half dozen bottles of Club beer and I felt enlightened by this robust man with a big laugh and a great enthusiasm for life. I spent three years living in Ghana, recording my impressions for a book I wrote but never published. I called it *Turquoise*, and gave Kofi credit for showing me that I could write about a country and its people, one that I didn't really know much about, and that it was okay because it was my truth about Africa, a truth quite different from an African's truth, but a truth nonetheless, depending on the light.

33. AFTER YOU CAUSE THEM
TROUBLE, SMILE

Just as I had to school myself about art, I had to do the same about the world of opera when I managed to convince my *Playboy* editor that **Luciano Pavarotti** was a worthy subject for an in-depth interview.

When I heard Luciano Pavarotti for the first time, I knew I had to meet him. I had never heard a voice like that. As a boy I had been obsessed by Mario Lanza, which may seem strange for a kid growing up on the streets of Brooklyn. But when Lanza belted out "Be My Love," I thought if he was addressing any particular woman, that woman was a goner. But I had never actually been to the opera until I finally got to interview Pavarotti in 1982. In preparation, I listened to every album of the great tenors that I could get my hands on: Giuseppe di Stefano, Franco Corelli, Jussi Bjoerling, Carlo Bergonzi, Beniamino Gigli, Enrico Caruso, Placido Domingo, Jose Carreras. None of these wonderful voices came close to the magic of Pavarotti. He had the sweetest, most lyrical, most mesmerizing voice of any of the tenors. I would entertain friends by playing them the same aria by all these tenors and asking which they liked best. I wasn't alone in believing that the greatest voice in my lifetime was that of Luciano Pavarotti.

But when a magazine like *Playboy* agrees to his being one of the dozen annual interviews, it can't be just a paean to his greatness; it must also be critical. And Pavarotti definitely had his critics. There were those who accused him of demeaning his artistry by appearing on talk shows, in TV commercials, and in a movie. Former Metropolitan Opera director Rudolph Bing called it "unnecessary and undignified." Bing also had harsher words, saying, "Seeing that stupid, ugly face every-where I go is getting on my nerves." There were others who criticized the large amounts of money he was paid for concerts. His fellow tenor di Stefano worried about his ambition and excessive publicity. Placido Domingo complained about his appearing on the covers of *Newsweek* and *Time*. Some priggish classical music stores put signs in their windows saying "We Do Not Carry Pavarotti's Greatest Hits."

I spent months following Pavarotti from the MGM back lot where he was filming *Yes, Giorgio* to the opera houses in New York, Chicago, and San Francisco, where he sang to sold out audiences and standing ovations. We covered a lot of territory, geographically and intellectually, including all the criticisms. He believed there was a definite conspiracy among jealous people in his profession to bring him down.

"In Europe, they say fantastic things," he said. "But here they say terrible things. OK, they want to shoot me, then let them shoot me. I am very big! I know why they are shooting, anyway. I know: There is some kind of conspiracy."

I mentioned Domingo's name, but at first he was reluctant to call him out. "I don't want to say any name," he said. But he couldn't help himself. "Every time I am on the cover of an important magazine, he reacts in a certain vein and the newspapers help him. It's something I would *never* do. If I see somebody else on a magazine cover, the first thing I will do is telephone and congratulate him, because I know how difficult our profession is. I will have the envy, of course—but *inside* me. When *Time* was making the interviews of tenors, looking for the most popular talent to be on the cover, I was not the tenor who was being considered. At that time, I thought they wanted to put Domingo on the cover. But during that time many things happened. I began to make recitals. I had a best-selling record. I did television. The writer found my personality interesting and they put me on the cover instead."

He returned to the overall sense that there was a conspiracy against him, and that Domingo was used to fuel the fires between them. "There is a certain kind of conspiracy behind the critics," he said. "There is very, very clearly a conspiracy. And the fact that I am answering them and saying that there is a conspiracy will make them write even worse about me. I don't care. I think it is unjust and I think some important critic should make this point."

It wasn't easy to ask him what he thought of Rudolph Bing's remarks, since I had to repeat them to his face. About it being undignified and unnecessary to appear in *Yes, Giorgio,* Pavarotti countered by saying "It is *very* necessary, because I am intent to enlarge the world of the opera. Mr. Bing wanted to keep the world of the opera small and restricted. This statement makes me think that Mr. Bing is not an intelligent person who follows the times."

That's when I threw out Bing's harsher, more personal criticism about Pavarotti's "stupid, ugly face."

"I don't care what he said!" Pavarotti huffed. "If he thinks I have a stupid, ugly face, it is his problem. I mean, he doesn't have a good face himself. The only reason he is talking like that is because *his* face is not all over. Believe me. With all due respect I have for him as a man of the theater, I think he should take a little more care when he talks."

The criticism had to be answered, and Pavarotti didn't shy from doing that. But he also responded to all my questions and spent a great deal of time talking to me before and after his performances. He even came to my house in Los Angeles to taste my wife's special dumplings. When my two-year old daughter wanted to sing *O Solo Mio* to him, he applauded with delight.

After the interview appeared, I went to see him in *Aida* at the Met in New York. Backstage afterwards he was signing autographs and talking to fans when he saw me. He signaled for me to come to him and when we shook hands he pulled me down to whisper in my ear, "You caused me a great deal of trouble."

I was in his grip and didn't know if the trouble I caused had angered him or not, so I just smiled conspiratorially. And then Pavarotti laughed wholeheartedly. It was our own private joke.

34. SOME CELEBRITIES ARE CAPABLE OF DOING A FAVOR

The importance of preparation was driven home to me when I had to do an emergency interview without benefit of prior research. That nightmare happened when my expected star backed out at the last minute and another was able to put aside his star status and graciously agree to help me on a moment's notice.

I still find this incident hard to believe, because celebrities are pampered people. They have entourages. They have unlisted phone numbers and email addresses. They have layers of people who get between them and their adoring public. They live with expectations of privilege. They're used to having things done for them. I don't want to appear cynical, but it's not often they will go out of their way to do anything for anyone other than a very close friend.

So when I flew to New York in the mid-'80s with a full TV crew to interview Morgan Fairchild and found out that she had come down with laryngitis, I tried not to panic. She was in a Broadway show and we had rented the theater for the morning. The crew got there at 6:00 a.m. to set up on the stage. I was to meet Morgan there at 8:00 a.m. At 7:00 a.m., we heard from her manager with the bad news.

It's one thing when a print interview gets postponed, but quite another when it involves a crew, the cost of the theater rental, and all the plane fares. I had one friend, Joel Siegel, whom I thought might be helpful. Joel and I were college friends, and he went on to become a very visible television movie critic. I hated calling him so early in the morning, but that's what friends are for, right? And though I had awakened him, he went to his Rolodex and started reading out all the names of stars that I might consider. I told him not to bother with any women because we needed someone in an hour, and I doubted that any woman would be willing to go on camera without extensive cosmetic preparation. I also nixed all the really big names because I just couldn't imagine cold calling them and getting a response. But then Joel said, "**Charles Grodin**" and I thought, yes, he seemed approachable. He had costarred with Warren Beatty in *Heaven Can Wait*, with Miss Piggy and Kermit the Frog in *The Great Muppet Caper,* and appeared in *Rosemary's Baby, The Heartbreak Kid*, *Real Life*, and *King Kong*. From his public persona, he seemed like a nice guy.

I called him at 7:15 a.m. When he answered, I apologized for the early morning call. I told him I was in a desperate situation and that Joel Siegel had given me his number. I explained I didn't want to get Joel in trouble, but when we thought about who might be kind and thoughtful and understanding enough to consider coming down to the theater in forty-five minutes to be interviewed on camera, he was the only name we both agreed upon. He listened to my pleading and then said, "Sure, I'll come down. Which theater?"

God bless Charles Grodin, I thought as I hung up and ran over to the theater to see if anyone on the crew might know anything about him. I was really in the dark, not knowing much more than the few movies I had seen, and I had no time to run to a library to find out about him. This was before the Internet, so I couldn't just go to IMDB or Wikipedia and get some quick facts. But no one on the crew knew anything, so all I could do was sit in the back of the theater and try to calm my mind before he arrived.

After I thanked him profusely for showing up, I mentioned that besides Morgan Fairchild I was going to be interviewing Norman Mailer the following week and half-joked that since I hadn't had time to prepare for him, I'd give him a choice between asking him my Morgan Fairchild or Norman Mailer questions. He chose Fairchild and I saw that he was ready to be playful, which was a good sign.

I plunged right in, asking him what it was like working opposite Miss Piggy.

"I'll talk about anything you want," he said with a very straight face, "but asking me to comment about my feelings for her, I'd rather not get into that. It's too personal. As for Kermit, he doesn't like me and I don't like him."

He didn't object to talking about his many appearances on *The Tonight Show* with Johnny Carson, saying that of all the talk shows that one was the "least relaxing." He then compared it with talking to me, saying, "In an interview like this, you're fairly confident no one's going to see it, so you're at ease."

I prefer asking people specific questions that relate directly to them, but with Grodin I had little choice but to ask more generic questions, like: How ambitious were you growing up? Do people recognize you when you're walking in New York? Do you have any siblings? Did you always want to be a star? Which of your films did you most enjoy doing? Did you mind being upstaged by King Kong? How did you get along with Warren Beatty? How do you think you're perceived? Were you a virgin throughout high school? How good an actor do you think you are? What are your greatest fears? What do you want most?

To that last question he responded, "I guess to be powdered down a little bit, because I'll bet I'm shining. Aside from that, what I most want is a Fudgsicle. You can't get Fudgsicles or Creamsicles any more."

His irreverence reflected an understanding that I didn't know much about his personal story and with some of these questions he quipped, "Are these Morgan Fairchild questions?"

He gave me a potential ending when I asked "What would you like to come back as?"

"Morgan Fairchild," he answered.

I could have left it there, but had to laugh. "Pretty sad," I joked. That spurred me to ask him his saddest memory.

"I think today. This has all the potential of one of those."

Grodin was a good sport to do this at the last minute, so early in the morning. Not many celebrities would do what he did. He had done me a solid, and I was forever grateful. At the time, I wished I had been more prepared for him. But in retrospect, had I asked more pointed direct questions, I doubt I could have elicited some of those delightful whimsical answers.

35. SOME CANNOT ARTICULATE

There are times, though, when no matter how much you prepare, if the subject is more known for his silence than his ability to articulate, be warned that there must be a reason.

For jockey **Willie Shoemaker** I had prepared nineteen pages of questions, 407 in all. At the time, he was the greatest living jockey in racing history. When he turned pro in 1949 he won seven races his first week and 219 his first year. The next year he tied with Joe Colmone for most wins, with 388. In 1953 he set a record for most wins, with 485. A year later he won over 30% of his races, the highest percentage for an

American rider in the 20th century. He rode Swaps to victory in the Kentucky Derby in 1955. He won the Derby again in 1959 on Tomy Lee, the year he was elected to the Jockey Hall of Fame at Pimlico. He'd win the Kentucky Derby two more times, on Lucky Debonair in 1965 and Ferdinand in 1986. By 1961 he had ridden 4,000 winners, and before he was done, he more than doubled that. He won 12 stakes races on Spectacular Bid. Sports columnist Jim Murray wrote, "He does with a horse what Rembrandt did with a brush or Ruth with a fastball." Trainer John Russell said he was Joe DiMaggio, Willie Mays and Gordie Howe rolled into one, pound for pound the greatest athlete who ever lived.

Plenty to talk about, right? So why did The Shoe cancel on me on the day I was to meet him in the jockey's locker room at Del Mar? He didn't give me notice the week before, or the night before; he called just as I was getting into my car for the drive down from L.A. "Willie," I said, "You can't do this. I've spent months boning up on you. You're the greatest jockey alive; this is going to be a piece of cake for you. We're just going to talk about your incredible career. It's the first time *Playboy* has ever interviewed a jockey. It's going to reach a huge audience. It will only be good for your sport. Don't pull out like this at the last minute. Give me a chance to give you a chance. Let me come down, let's see how it goes."

Shoemaker relented and I hung up before he had a second round of second thoughts. I probably should have known what was in store, but I just couldn't let him back out. Not when I had spent so many hours filling my head with racing lore. His nickname didn't scare me; it actually made me more determined to break through his silence and get him to reveal himself. I knew he'd be uncomfortable when I brought up his three marriages or some of his controversial rides or how tough it was for his family during the Depression, but though I had to cover such territory, it was really my hope to get into his mind. What was it like to be a truly great jockey? Was he really a greater athlete than the baseball and hockey players he was compared with? I wanted to find out what made Willie Shoemaker run. (Or ride!)

The only problem was that Willie Shoemaker, whose nickname was The Silent Shoe, didn't like to talk. He was polite, courteous, even-tempered. He would listen to my questions and nod his head. He would relive some of his greatest rides as I described them, only to say a few words—a *very* few words—about them.

"You once said that a horse named Olden Times gave you one of your most rewarding rides," I prompted.

"Olden Times was one of my most satisfying rides," he responded. "He was considered a miler, a horse that could only go a mile, and I won a race on him and made him go a mile and three-quarters on the grass. He'd never run on grass before."

This was typical of what I was up against—short, clipped, generic answers. When I asked about the best horse he had ever ridden, he answered "Spectacular Bid."

"What made him great?"

"He ran on all kinds of race tracks all over the country and all kinds of conditions and he won."

This wasn't news, everyone knew that answer. But come on Willie, we're talking about Spectacular Bid! A horse who belonged in the pantheon of great horses like Man o' War, Secretariat, Native Dancer, Affirmed, Citation, and Seattle Slew.

I tried again. "What are the qualities that make a superior horse?"

"Ability to run fast. He's got to be able to outrun everybody else in whatever distance he runs and under whatever conditions. That's about it."

That was it? What about having a smooth stride, greater intelligence, a generous heart, and inherent ability? Yes, he agreed, all of those things as well. But he didn't offer any of them up; I had to continue to prod him. If I tried to get him to discuss what it was like during a race it came out like this:

"Is there a lot of talking and shouting to other riders while you're racing?"

"Some, but not a lot."

"*Sports Illustrated* once reported how you once came from five lengths behind L.C. Cook to his side, shouting, 'Hey, Cookie, you're working awfully hard at that. This is the way it's supposed to be done.' Do you remember that?"

"I said that. I used to do some cute ones like that."

"Do other jockeys talk back to you?"

"The older ones do."

When I tried to get him to talk about tragedy on the racecourse, he could only acknowledge that it happened.

"At Santa Anita once, didn't three horses that you were riding break their legs in the same day?" I asked.

"In one day, yeah."

"Did it make you reassess how you were riding?"

"That kind of got me thinking. It was just coincidence, I'm sure."

There are all kinds of stories having to do with races that were fixed and about the Mob being involved, but whatever Shoemaker knew, he kept to himself.

"You were suspended for misjudging the finish line in the 1957 Kentucky Derby and easing up on Gallant Man, who would have won. A lot of bettors believed you threw the race. Have you ever been involved in a fixed race?"

"Not that I really know of, no."

"Have you ever been approached by anyone in that regard?"

"No, I've never been approached at all, ever."

"Is organized crime involved in racing?"

"If they are, I don't know anything about it. I don't know anybody in organized crime."

"How can races be fixed?

"Guys have been caught holding back their horses."

"What about trainers who have doped horses?"

"I'm sure they've done that too, but most of them get caught sooner or later."

"So how clean is racing today?"

"It's really on the up and up."

This went on for hours. We talked in the locker room and at his home for days. I managed to get him to open up a bit about his childhood and some of his injuries, but in the end I knew the interview would be in the editing. I would have to describe most of the details of his career in my questions because he just didn't have it in him to put them into his answers. I did ask him how he got the nickname "The Silent Shoe," though it seemed obvious from hearing his responses. "I had crooked teeth and I didn't want to open my mouth," he said. "The other reason was that I figured the best way to learn was to listen and not talk. It made life a little easier."

Easier for The Shoe, but not for this journalist who foolishly thought he could crack his silence. The interview never ran in *Playboy* and I learned my lesson. For guys like Willie Shoemaker, no amount of preparation would get him to embellish his life story. His actions spoke louder than his words. I hadn't even noticed his teeth.

With Paul McCarthy before a performance, when he was a struggling artist. I thought that he was my opposite and felt the need to understand him and his art. 1977

Marlon Brando and I sat with our backs against his bungalow. "Conversation keeps people away from one another," he said. "What you're really having in silence is a full and more meaningful conversation." 1978

"I don't want to do this interview," Betty Friedan said. Once again I pleaded with her to continue. "I don't have the patience for this," she said. "It isn't going to do me enough good." 1983

"William Carlos Williams was playing my record as a 33 rpm and it was a 45. So I adjusted it and he heard it the way it was supposed to sound." "That's good," Williams said. "So's my music for your libretto," Ted Harris said, and then he played it for him. 1973

"You really think I should be the bubbly idiot in a giant champagne glass?" Goldie asked. "Am I always going to be the airhead from Laugh-In?" 1985

I watched Arthur Singer draw birds from photographs he had taken from his wildlife trips or from conserved owls, hawks and eagles that he borrowed from the Museum of Natural History. 1987

Henry Moore looking at Hiromi's work. "Yes, yes, I see what you're doing," he said. They talked for an hour. Hiromi was getting some good advice. 1976

Childhood Is The Key

36. EVEN THE FAMOUS WERE KIDS ONCE

There isn't a person alive who didn't have a childhood, but it's easy to forget when you're talking to a Nobel laureate or a Pulitzer Prize winner or someone who has an Oscar, Tony or Grammy on his or her mantelpiece. But no matter how famous or accomplished a person is, if you go back to a person's early developmental years, you may find a wealth of material that could surprise you.

Unless I was doing an interview about a specific subject, I would never leave without asking about those early years. Maybe because my own were rife with humorous and horrific incidents, I assume it's like that with everyone else. Not many of us were blessed with perfect parents, easy-going siblings, protective friends, and non-abusive relationships. Life is a struggle and it starts early. I look at my two-month old grandson screaming his lungs out for no apparent reason and I see how early that struggle begins. When he was five years old, Rodney Dangerfield earned a nickel to kiss a man who kept more nickels in his pocket. Alec Baldwin and Mel Gibson had brothers who liked to engage in bare-knuckle knock down sibling brawls. Most stars have personal or family stories to tell when they were growing up, and such tales can be good icebreakers, as those years are often long ago and far away, and with distance comes perspective.

Lily Tomlin once made a good point when she spoke about being a bit tongue-tied as an adult when she met a childhood idol for the first time and how she had to go back to her own childhood epiphany to remind herself that people are just people.

I've interviewed Tomlin at my office and in her home (which once belonged to W.C. Fields), and spent time with her when she agreed to be interviewed by my then 14-year-old daughter for her high school public access TV show, something Lily surely didn't have to do. When my other daughter, three years younger, gave her a drawing she had done of Tomlin's Edith Ann character, Lily wrote her a nice note and gave her an Edith Ann doll.

Over a wide-ranging conversation, Tomlin told me about the "bad girl" stars, like Beverly Michaels, Dorothy Malone, and Ruby Gentry that influenced her as a child. Then there were the funny, sexy or bohemian stars that she loved as a young woman, like Lana Turner, Bridget Bardot, Audrey Hepburn, Jeanne Moreau, Doris Day, Lucille Ball, and Imogene Coca. All of these women had a powerful effect on Tomlin, and helped her develop into the star she became.

Tomlin has appeared in thirty movies, including her most recent *Grandma* (2015). The best of them—*Nashville, The Late Show, Nine to Five, All of Me, Short Cuts, The Incredible Shrinking Woman, A Prairie Home Companion*–still hold up today. Her two most beloved characters are the child Edith Ann and the phone company operator Ernestine. But none of them define her as much as her one-woman show, *The Search for Signs of Intelligent Life in the Universe*, written by her partner Jane Wagner. That show ran for a year on Broadway (between 1985–86) and on one particular night Katharine Hepburn, Barbra Streisand, and Meryl Streep were in the audience. Had she known they were there, she told me, "I would have had dry mouth. I wouldn't have been able to speak. I would have been too scared, petrified."

But early on, when she felt this same dry mouth anxiety upon meeting some of her childhood idols, she overcame her speech petrification by remembering what she had learned when she was ten. Her mother had embarrassed her in front of company, complaining how skinny and tomboyish she was, and she had found a way to neutralize the pain.

"Very early I went through a realization that my parents had been children," she said. "I'd look at my mother's baby picture, and suddenly I thought that my mother was just like me. So I knew she didn't know anything. Then I thought my teachers were kids too, and I knew they didn't know anything. Then I began to understand that *everybody* had been a child, and I knew that I couldn't rely on them 100 percent."

Throughout my career I've occasionally become tongue-tied when I've met someone famous unexpectedly, like when I happened to be in the same backstage room at the Strasberg Theater with Sophia Loren, who was there to see her son perform, or when I was alone with Michael Jackson at the Sharper Image, both of us shopping for gadgets. It happens. And even when I'm about to interview someone for the first time, I can get the kind of dry mouth Tomlin was talking about. I did with Dolly Parton and with Truman Capote. But then I found my voice and that feeling went away. But it's easy to forget your voice in the face of celebrity, and that's why Lily's lesson about everyone having once been a child is a good lesson to keep.

Lily reminded me that no matter who are you or what heights you've reached, you still put your shoes on one foot at a time (even if you have a butler who holds the shoehorn).

37. WATCH OUT FOR WHIPPING BOYS

James Garner wasn't dealing with shoes when his father remarried a woman who thought young James would look better in a dress.

When we think of Garner, the image of the clever card-sharp cowboy (*Maverick*), or the shrewd private detective (*The Rockford Files*), comes to mind. He was a handsome, winsome, lovable rogue who always came out on top. He appeared in forty movies, but nothing compared to the ten years he put into those two television series, which garnered him *TV Guide's* vote as the Best Dramatic Actor in the history of television. It would be hard to imagine Garner as a serial killer, a la *Dexter,* or a chemistry teacher gone bad (*Breaking Bad*), though he could certainly have played John Hamm's role in *Mad Men*.

He definitely didn't get his easy-going manner from his formative years. His mother died when he was five, and he and his two brothers were split up among relatives. A year later his father married a woman who rivaled Cinderella's stepmother in cruelty and abuse, and the family was reunited when the wicked witch moved in. For Garner the next seven years were pure hell. "My stepmother was a nasty bitch," he told me. "She used to beat the hell out of me particularly. I think it was because I was the most available. My brother Jack, who was two years older than me, was kind of sickly, so she didn't beat on him so much. I've seen people for years just pick on certain people. Directors do that, they find whipping boys."

I had read somewhere that she used to make him wear a dress, which made him uncomfortable when I brought it up. "It was out in the country and we'd be in some little store and I'd just go hide because it would embarrass me terribly," Garner said. "It happened a lot. If I did anything wrong, I'd have to go put on the dress. Then my brothers would tease me and call me Louise and a fight would break out. I was the youngest, but I was pretty tough."

The humiliation came to a head when he turned thirteen and she came at him one time too many. "I fought back. I decked her. I had her on the bed, choking her. My dad and my brother pulled me off of her. I can understand how kids can rebel to the point of murder. I don't agree with it, but I don't know what I'd have done—because she was tough. *Tough.* I'm sure I wouldn't have let go of her until she quit breathing because she'd have killed me if she got up. Then they held me down so she could whip me. But that's the night that broke up the marriage with my dad and her. They started drinking later and...God, I hate to tell this story. I get so upset when I read about how badly people were treated during their childhood. It's just part of growing up."

The psychological scar ran so deep that when Garner was 54 he returned to Oklahoma to appear in a parade in a covered wagon. His brother told him that Wilma, their former stepmother, was working there. "I was actually scared," Garner admitted. "I had said a lot of things about her over the years and she was the type, I figured, who'd take a rifle and blow me right off that covered wagon going down Main Street. That's how mean she was."

This childhood witch had affected the rest of Garner's life. In one sense, she made him strong and independent. "If I wanted something I was going to have it." But she also screwed him up when it came to relationships. "It made me very leery throughout my life. Commitments are very difficult for me. Committing to somebody has always been hard."

If I hadn't brought up that embarrassing dress and reminded him of being called Louise, I never would have understood James Garner's backstory. And though we covered his entire career, nothing he said equaled the power of that nasty bitch Wilma.

38. READ MORE BOOKS

Just as Garner choked his stepmother, **Freddie Prinze, Jr.** had a similar desire to pound someone unconscious when he was twelve.

Prinze, Jr. was ten months old when his 22 year-old father, comedian Freddie Prinze, committed suicide. Growing up an only child with no dad around to teach him how to catch a baseball or throw a football, he created a fantasy world to live in. "Kids would see me out in the field jumping around alongside the *X-Men*," he said. But he often got tired of kids calling him gay because he still played Make-Believe Superhero while the others had moved on to more pre-teen activities, so sometimes he got into fights, including one he never forgot. "It was at one of the few parties I went to in high school. I don't remember why he was mad—he was a bully—but when I walked out of the place he pushed me and I fell down and everybody started laughing. I got up and tried to walk away and he came at me again, so we got into a fight. When he fell on the ground I just kept hitting him until his face wasn't hard anymore. I didn't want to stop beating him until he cried. That's when I stood up and then I started crying too, because I was so upset. And then I ran." He skipped school for a week and when he returned nobody bothered him.

His father's friend was in a couple of Bruce Lee movies and taught him karate and jujitsu, which he practiced for eight years. He also memorized his father's comedy albums. When a friend asked him what he liked to do, he answered, "I make shit up; I dream about being a superhero." "Go act," his friend said, and Prinze, Jr. thought it a good idea. He moved to Los Angeles and became an actor with a little help from his father's former manager. By the time he was 24, he had appeared in *I Know What You Did Last Summer* and became a teen idol.

He was living alone in a house in the San Fernando Valley when I interviewed him. We began in his living room and wound up in his bedroom. What I noticed in both rooms were the empty bookshelves. "Where are your books?" I asked.

"I don't read books," he answered.

"Seriously? I collect first editions and you don't even read?"

"I collect," he said. "Comic books."

"So you *do* read," I smiled. "What're your most valuable comics?"

"I have 2 through 10 *X-Men*, number 16 *X-Men*, 20 through 30 *X-Men*; I have number 11 *Spider-Man*; number 4 *Silver Surfer*, number 4 *Fantastic Four*. The most valuable is number 2 *X-Men*, probably worth a few grand."

I had signed first editions of Joseph Heller's *Catch-22*, Truman Capote's *Other Voices, Other Rooms*, Norman Mailer's *The Naked and the Dead*, J.P. Donleavy's *The Ginger Man*, but there was no sense bringing them up because Freddie would have never heard of them. He read comics and watched cartoons. I also read comics and watched cartoons as a kid; most kids do. And most of us learn to read from comics and advance to books. Prinze, Jr. never advanced. He would eventually marry the actress Sarah Michelle Geller and she would introduce him to the Harry Potter books. I don't know if he read them or just watched the movies, but I suspect he would have been a different actor and would have had a happier childhood if someone had given him *The Catcher in the Rye, Lord of the Flies* or *The Chronicles of Narnia.*

39. A SMOLDERING RAGE CAN FESTER UNDER A SMILING VENEER

Anthony Hopkins also had an unhappy childhood.

I first interviewed him for *Playboy* in 1994 after he won his first Oscar for *Silence of the Lambs* and was knighted by Queen Elizabeth. I wrote about him for two other magazines in 2007 and again in 2009. I also brought him to see Al Pacino in *Salome* in 2006, and afterwards we went backstage where the two actors hugged and praised each other. I've had a few lunches with him at the Peninsula Hotel in Beverly Hills, where we discussed other projects, and we've talked on the phone a number of times. But though he always showed a great enthusiasm whenever we were together, and an even greater zeal after he left the Wadsworth Theater where we saw *Salome*, I had the feeling that underneath his jolly exterior there was a great deal smoldering within. There had to be, of course, for him to so chillingly portray characters like Hitler, Hitchcock, and Hannibal Lecter. Even on the days when we had lunch, I felt there was something "off" about Hopkins. When I looked back at the interviews I did with him, I saw that he had explained himself very clearly and, like James Garner and so many others, his issues all took root in his childhood.

Hopkins was born on the last day of 1937 in Port Talbot, Wales. He had no friends and considered himself a recluse as a child.

"I didn't want to be what I was," he said. "I was an idiot at school. I didn't know what time of day it was. We lived in the rural part of an industrial, steel-working town. When I first went to school I was in a completely alien environment. I can remember the smell of stale milk, drinking straws and wet coats and sitting there absolutely petrified. That feeling stayed with me. The fear stayed with me through my childhood and right through adolescence—that gnawing anxiety that I was freaky, that I wasn't really fitting in anywhere. I wasn't popular at all. I never played with any of the other kids, and I didn't have any friends. I wanted to be left alone all through my school years."

And yet, there was something in him that desperately wanted to be noticed. But as an awkward, "freaky" kid, he said his tactic for standing out was to find a way to be ridiculed and cheered at the same time. "I was in a little school called Bridge Street School and every lunch I could get on the bus and go home, which was about three miles away. But I would never get on the bus; I would run beside it, like an idiot, like the school clown. I was so ill when I got home, it's a wonder I didn't have a heart attack. I was throwing up because I was exhausted. I used to race the school bus, and naturally it would get ahead of me and I'd catch up at the bus stop and kids would say, 'Come on.' I would do things in a weird way, like I wouldn't go to my own birthday parties."

His parents didn't know what to do with him, so they sent him to a boarding school. "I lived away from home from the age of eleven. There would be times when I wouldn't speak to anyone for four weeks. The teachers would slap me about the head, but I still wouldn't speak. The headmaster told my mother and father that there was something wrong with me. In 1953, when I was fourteen, I was reading Trotsky's *History of the Russian Revolution*. I was asked if I was a Communist or a Marxist. I didn't know what they were talking about. The book was taken away from me. Then some of the kids would call me 'Bolshoi, Bolshoi, bolshoi'. I went completely into myself. I thought I would defy them all. That has stayed with me the rest of my life, the thought that I would show them all one day. But that sense of potential failure is still in the back of my mind. I still don't hang around people. I'm not gregarious with anybody."

His school years were pure torture for him. "The British public school system is one of the most insufferable systems of all," he reflected. "It gave me enough rocket fuel to get out and do something different. It pushed me into rage for years. I look back at it now and think it wasn't that something was wrong with me; it was that something was right with me. I may have hurt a few people along the way, but it got me what I wanted."

His father was a temperamental baker who often blew up when loaves of bread were undercooked. "He was a man of colossal energy that didn't go anywhere. He was just spinning his wheels. He was exhausting to be with." His grandfather on his father's side was "hard as nails, confused, frustrated, powerful, a sentimental ogre, and a bit of a tyrant. I styled Hitler after him."

Hopkins was a bit of a tyrant himself, as I discovered when I asked him about his daughter from his first marriage. She changed her name when she decided to give her father's profession a shot. I asked him if he ever considered her a friend. "Oh, yeah. I saw her just recently," he said, "but that's over with as well. I walked out of my first marriage, which was a disaster, and I left my child, Abigail. I wasn't fit for marriage or to bring up a family."

He managed to get Abigail a small part as one of the housemaids in *The Remains of the Day*. After their one scene together was shot, he put his arm around her and told her she looked terrific. But he was also wary of her. "We got close a few years ago," he said, "and she came and stayed with me. She was doing her own numbers, playing some sorts of scenes for herself, trying to impress me, but being manipulative. I said, forget it. I just withdrew. I always withdraw from people. I try not to let people absorb too much of my energy. Once people start latching on to me and try to draw things out of me and control me, I wave them goodbye, sometimes forever, and I won't go back. I don't like being controlled by anyone."

"No exception for your own daughter?" I asked.

"I was quite prepared to go into the wilderness without her. I was prepared not to see her again. It doesn't matter to me, you see. We have to be tough and callous about it all, live our lives. It's a selfish way of looking at it, but I don't have a conscience."

The man is a brilliant actor who feels uncomfortable around other actors, has had problems with directors who aren't as prepared as they should be, and though he has found fame and fortune playing other people, he considers most actors "pretty simpleminded people who just think they're complicated. Actors are nothing. Actors are of no consequence." And just to make sure he included himself in his diatribe he made a point to emphasize that "I'm as phony as everyone else. We're all phony. We're all charlatans, we're all flawed, and we're all liars."

His cynicism ran deep. Beneath his surface, he could be wicked and cruel, like so many of the characters he played. "I've played bright people and monstrous people," he said. "I enjoyed playing Hitler [in *The Bunker*]. I played a man called Lambert Le Roux in *Pravda*. He was like *Jaws*, in the way sharks move. This man knew exactly what price people had, and he knew that everyone had a price. I loved playing that part because he saw through all the bullshit. He knew that contained in each human being is the jungle. That's a pretty bleak look at life, but there is a part that is exciting. Hannibal Lecter also sees the jungle inside each human being; he sees the dark side. It's a nihilistic truth and it's a Nietzschean view of the world. I had no qualms about playing Lecter."

How cold did it get inside Hopkins' heart and soul? I wondered.

"We would all like to be machinelike and have no emotions," he said. "I long for it all the time, have no emotions so that I could make no mistakes and be ice cold. I'd love to be like that. I long to be somebody who is ice cold, brutal, tough and uncompromising. Of course, I'd probably hate myself. But then, all my problems come from arguments with myself."

I was learning more about Hopkins than I had anticipated, and when I thought we had reached into the core of his darkness he gave me the bonus of a mantra he created for himself that he repeated every day, like a meditation: "It's none of my business what people say of me or think of me," he began. "I am what I am and I do what I do for fun and it's all in the game. The wonderful game, the play of life on life itself. Nothing to win, nothing to lose, nothing to win, nothing to prove. No sweat, no big deal. Because of myself I am nothing, and of myself I've been nothing."

40. CLUBFOOT BE DAMNED

Dudley Moore felt like "nothing" for a long time, having been born with a clubfoot. "Humor comes from pain," he said when we talked for an on-camera interview in 1982. "Some of the funniest things in the world to me come from large areas of pain. But I try to forget that and go for it."

Dudley Moore was a very funny, very likable, extraordinarily talented man. He was a classically trained pianist and jazz musician who put out ten albums and toured the world with his Dudley Moore Trio. He was also an improvisational comedian who, along with Peter Cook, Jonathan Miller, and Alan Bennett formed *Beyond the Fringe*, a satirical revue that started in Edinburgh, Scotland and played to sold-out audiences in London and on Broadway. He starred in some blockbuster films, like *Foul Play, 10* (which brought fame to both Bo Derek and Ravel's *Bolero*), *Unfaithfully Yours*, and *Arthur*, (which brought him an Oscar nomination). That he could be as successful as he was with his background is a remarkable story.

His pain was real. He was born with his feet turned inward and, although he had surgery on his left foot, it remained small and his leg withered from the knee down. It became a source of anger, embarrassment, and humiliation. It didn't help that as other boys grew tall, he remained short. He wound up being 5'2" with a clubfoot. Not exactly conducive to winning favor with the opposite sex or shining in any sport. He did his best to hide his handicap, believing "if people knew about it, they would immediately leave the room coughing into airsick bags."

He admitted that he wouldn't ever entirely lose the anger he felt at having a deformity. "I was left in hospital for long periods of time," he said. "My mother fought for me to go to a 'normal' school, which I admired her for. The school was worried that I might break my leg, which was very thin, playing soccer. But it was my mother who said to me, 'There's nothing wrong with you.' Then she would say, 'You can't ride your bicycle to school, but you're totally normal.' So there was this strange polarity. It was either 'You're perfect' or 'You're helpless.' And I felt perfect and helpless. The perfection was there when she said it. But most of the time I felt very humiliated and very frightened. I was teased about it a great deal at school, and that's one of the reasons why I became a clown, to stop them from getting to me. Kids are very cruel about that sort of thing and comedy was a defense against being bullied. Feeling like a piece of shit was not a great advantage in those days, and those days lasted a very long time. In many ways, my leg has been the focus of my inadequacy, a crutch to use as a reason for not doing things. It's taken me a long time to get around it. It's still something that humiliates me—but I've been able to harvest it creatively."

Dudley was very open about discussing this horrible time in his life, and I found that refreshing, even inspiring. When I saw him, he had been through two marriages, with Suzy Kendall and Tuesday Weld, respectively, and was living with Susan Anton, a striking blonde performer who was nine inches taller than he was. He said he had never lost his insecurities about what he deemed his inadequacies, but he had managed to rise above them. "My father, on his deathbed, said to me, 'Don't let anything stand in your way.' Coming from him, who had a miserable life, I took it to heart."

"And now you're the object of Bo Derek's affections," I said.

"I haven't got a body like Tarzan," he joked. "It's very close. I've got all that he's got you know; two nipples and a wee wee. But that's about as far as it goes."

41. CERTAIN MEMORIES ARE BEST FORGOTTEN

Dudley's father was encouraging. Not so **Halle Berry's** dad. He was someone she has tried hard not to think about.

Halle is one of the world's most beautiful women. She was high school prom queen, first runner up in the Miss USA

Pageant, a Bond girl in *Die Another Day,* and No. 1 among *People's 50 Most Beautiful People* in 2003. Yet, when you know her backstory and her miserable childhood, you can better understand the mistakes she made in choosing men who both physically and verbally abused her, cheated on her, and just didn't treat her right. An early boyfriend socked her in the head and she lost 80% of her hearing in one ear. When I asked her about her first husband, baseball player David Justice, she said she didn't want to hear anything he said about her because he was an outright liar. He accused her of always being suspicious of him. And no wonder. She said, "If your husband cheated on you with prostitutes, strippers, every twinkie walking by with a skirt, you'd feel the same way. End of story." She called her second husband, singer-songwriter Eric Benet, the most amazing man she'd ever met, until he cheated on her as well and blamed it on a sexual addiction. Then came French Canadian model Gabriel Aubrey. They had a child together, but the relationship didn't last. When Halle hooked up with French actor Olivier Martinez and wanted to move to France, Aubrey fought her for custody of their daughter and wound up getting into a brawl with Martinez that landed both men in the hospital.

Physical violence has followed Halle Berry all of her life, as she witnessed the way her father treated her mother when she was growing up. Her parents separated when she was four, which was old enough for her to remember what she wished she could forget. "My father was very abusive to my mother. I saw him kick her in the ass. She often had less than pleasant things to say about him. But she always let us know that while he was a shitty husband and beat her up, she tried to separate their relationship from ours. I didn't see him from the time I was four until he came back when I was ten. My mother said, 'I'm going to give it a shot,' because she wanted us to have him in our lives. He lived with us for one year, in 1976, and it was the worst year of my life. He beat on my sister. Never me. We had a toy Maltese, and he threw that dog across the dining room at dinner, and the dog almost bit its tongue off. The blood, and that image—when somebody mentions my father, that's the first thing I think about, that dog flying across the room. I remember crying, 'God, let him leave,' so my life could get back to normal."

But how could life get back to normal, when normal wasn't normal at all. Learning how to fight from her parents, she and her sister fought serious fights, even drawing blood. "Part of me feels we never recovered from the fighting adolescent years," she said. "I moved away from home at such a young age that the relationship never quite repaired itself."

Halle survived those terrible years to win a Golden Globe (*Introducing Dorothy Dandridge*) and an Oscar (*Monster's Ball*). But she could never erase the scars of an abusive childhood, numerous sadistic relationships and three failed marriages. The lens through which she viewed men and relationships was directly related to the father who came in and out of her life as a child. It was a tough lesson for her to learn, and a tough one for her to pass on as well.

42. DON'T FORGET THE SIBLINGS

For James Garner and Halle Berry it was the trauma of an awful stepmother or abusive father that affected how they dealt with people. For **Elizabeth Shue**, it was the shock of losing her brother William that changed her perspective on life. He was 26 when it happened; she was 25. He was a medical student at Rutger's University; she was a few credits shy of graduating from Harvard. A close-knit family (her other brother Andrew would follow her as an actor), they went on a summer vacation to a favorite pond on Block Island, Rhode Island, where they could swing from a rope into the water. She watched in horror as William grabbed the rope, swung out like Tarzan, and fell short of the pond as the rope snapped, impaling him on a broken tree branch.

It's always delicate to ask about such tragedy, but when you're interviewing someone and you're aware that this had happened, how can you avoid it? Talking about the loss of a loved one will always be revealing, but that talk is more often about a parent or grandparent, not a brother or sister.

I traveled to Harvard in 2000 to interview Shue, twelve years after her brother's fatal accident. She had returned to Cambridge for a semester to complete her dual degree requirements in political science and government. She also had a big-budget sci-fi thriller called *The Hollow Man*, costarring Kevin Bacon and directed by Paul Verhoeven to promote. The film that brought her to the public's attention was her harrowing performance opposite Nicolas Cage in *Leaving Las Vegas*. But like her brother Andrew, her perspective on making movies was different from most actors. "My brain was starting to dry up," she told me when we met at the Charles Hotel. "In Hollywood, you're fortunate if you get a role where your brain is engaged, but those experiences are rare. I felt I needed to do more with my life." Andrew dropped acting altogether and got involved with a website for mothers called ClubMom. Both Elizabeth and Andrew named one of their children after their brother William.

He was never far from their thoughts. "His death stripped away what wasn't important," Elizabeth said. "I stopped running away from who I was. I see it as a gift that he gave me."

The other gift she got from his death was "the confidence that therapy would be a good thing for me. That was probably the major turning point in my life, in terms of understanding myself."

Besides the always present thought of why her brother died and not her, she had to come to grips with the fear of someone finding out that she wasn't worthwhile, and the jealousy she felt when her younger brother found fame (he was on *Melrose Place)* before she did. She had to come to an understanding of her competitive nature, and know that it was all right to have such feelings.

I knew this wasn't an event she wanted to relive through conversation, but I knew it would be revealing, so I was careful to approach her tactfully and with sensitivity. Just bringing it up sparked her to go within and to answer without guile or avoidance. And I learned just how important it is to incorporate sibling rivalry, jealousy, and love into any comprehensive understanding of a person's psyche.

43. FATHER KNOWS BEST

Shue's brother's death occurred when she was 25, the same age **Chris O'Donnell** was when he talked about the importance of his experience with his father.

Chris O'Donnell surprised me when he said he was living just three houses down the street from me in Nichols Canyon for the months that he played Robin in *Batman Forever.* He said he even walked his dog in the canyon every day. So how could I never have seen him? I saw him on the set when he was making *Scent of a Woman* with Al Pacino during the few days that I visited Al in New York, but we didn't talk even then. We finally talked after he had appeared in nine films, but before he married his girlfriend, had five kids, and became a TV star (*NCIS: Los Angeles*).

Like Freddie Prinze, Jr., O'Donnell didn't have an answer for the question: What books are you reading? I expected him to mention John Grisham's *The Chamber*, as he was about to star in the adaptation of that novel. But he hadn't read it. "I never read much," he said, "other than school text-books, the newspaper and scripts. Growing up I was a TV junkie: *The Brady Bunch, Green Acres, Laverne and Shirley, Happy Days.* I've got bookshelves, but no books. I've got to get some."

What is it with these guys, I wondered? How do you make it through life without books? They seem to do just fine with television, comics, and now the Internet. But I do believe that non-readers make for poor interview subjects. Their brains just haven't been stimulated with complex ideas.

Chris O'Donnell didn't feel comfortable being interviewed and confessed to fear being considered boring because he didn't want to say anything that might be picked up. "I don't feel that I can talk freely to a journalist," he said when we met at the Four Seasons Hotel in L.A. "I don't try to be completely calculating in everything I say and do, but there's no way I'm going to talk. I feel so violated when I do interviews. I get pissed off with myself after I do one, like I hate myself, why am I doing this? I still don't know why I am."

When I moved to safer grounds, his close-knit family, he returned to the kinds of questions that journalists have asked that make him glad he's got his parents. "You get a lot of ques-tions like, 'What's your philosophy?' And I'm thinking, I'm 25; I don't have a philosophy. I still go to my dad for advice."

Kudos for O'Donnell's honesty. Boo to the fact that he was indeed a boring interview. But I still learned something from him. When you want to get philosophical with someone 25 or younger, ask his mom or dad first.

44. IT DOESN'T HURT TO KNOW
THE PARENTS

Speaking of parents, I got to know rock star **Anthony Kiedis** because I knew his parents.

In 1965 I was a sophomore at UCLA majoring in Political Science, which I later changed to English. The Theater Arts department offered a course on acting and, just for a change of pace, I decided to take it. The teacher paired us off and instructed us to find a two-person one-act play to perform. My partner was Jack Kiedis from Michigan, twelve years my senior. We chose Edward Albee's *The Zoo Story*, about a quiet guy sitting on a park bench reading the newspaper when confronted by an obnoxious guy determined to provoke him into a heinous act. Jack wanted to play the obnoxious guy. We spent weeks rehearsing—on campus, then my apartment, and finally his. Before we got to his place he warned me that there would be a lot of kid's stuff around. He was hesitant to admit to having a wife and child because he preferred the coeds he met on campus to think he was single. Jack had a roving eye and a success rate with the opposite sex disproportionate to his looks. His kid, Tony, seemed wise beyond his age, which was three. His wife, Peggy, seemed to tolerate her wandering husband until one late night when she stumbled upon a photo of him with a sorority girl taken at some party. That was when she came knocking on my door, holding Tony, to ask if I knew anything about it. I said that I didn't, and when I saw him the next day I asked him why he'd left such a picture for his wife to find. He said he had stuck it between the pages of a book and placed it on the top shelf, but it fell down when Peggy was cleaning, and the picture popped out. "But why did you even keep it?" I asked. "I liked the way I looked," he said.

Another time we were in my car on our way to my apartment when he spotted a blonde young woman walking down the street and told me to pull over. We were in traffic on Santa Monica Blvd. and, before I had a chance to slow to a stop, Jack jumped out of the car and walked up to her. I saw him talking to her as I drove on and that night I called to ask him about it. "Who was she?"

"Just some girl," he said.

"Did you know her?"

"No. I just found her attractive."

"What happened?"

"We went back to her place."

"And...?"

"It was great, until her husband came home and caught us in bed. I tried to run out but he grabbed me and threw me down the stairs."

Jack was a revelation to me. I was still a naïve teenager and he was an admitted thief who had served time in Michigan. He stole all his books from libraries and bookstores; stole clothing from department stores; and traded in some of his stolen goods to get cash to pay for the record albums that wouldn't fit easily under his jacket or down his pants.

I lost track of Jack after we graduated and didn't see him again for fifteen years, when I ran into him at a sports club. He told me he had become an actor and had changed his name to Blackie Dammett. He said he had done some TV shows and played a deranged psycho who escapes from a mental institution in *National Lampoon's Class Reunion*. He and Peggy had separated a long time ago, he said, and Tony had become the lead singer of a rock band that was just starting to break out. "You should catch one of their shows," he said. "It's pretty wild. They get naked, and put tube socks over their dicks."

"What's the band's name?" I asked.

"The Red Hot Chili Peppers."

The band broke through, all right. In 2012 they were inducted into the Rock & Roll Hall of Fame. But growing up with Jack/Blackie as your father didn't make it easy on Tony, who went by Anthony when he came into his own. There was a lot of sex, drugs, and repeated attempts at rehab. His close friend and guitarist Hillel Slovak died from a drug overdose.

When Blackie told Peggy that we had met, she got in touch with me when she was visiting her son in Los Angeles, and brought him to our house one evening for dinner. My young daughters were thrilled and Anthony invited us to one of his concerts. Over the years I've interviewed him for different magazines. I didn't have to go through his publicist or record company to get to him because I had his phone number and email. And as I was not only a friend of his parents but also knew what a character his father was, we got into some real intimate shit when we talked.

"My dad had the wrong idea about how to get through life," Anthony said. "His dad was kind of a raging tyrant. My father rebelled against him and wanted to be the opposite. I knew about his thievery. He came up having to survive in such a way that whatever it took, he would take whatever was not bolted to the universe. If he could get away with it, it was all good. So I grew up thinking that's how you do it, you take whatever you can. In the long run that's futile. You're going backwards. You're not gaining, you're losing.

"I got into drugs at a very young age and it was super destructive and almost deadly. My dad included me in his pot-smuggling escapades. He and I were constantly at risk, from age six when I would come to visit and they would be doing giant dope deals out of Topanga. I'd be in the house and there would be piles of drugs and piles of money and piles of people. When I was twelve, we'd fly to Wisconsin with suitcases filled with pot. I guess he thought that I was a good beard. Being seen with a kid defused any criminal suspicions that law enforcement might have. That's a pretty good grift, having a little kid with you while you're doing something illegal. It would be like, 'Oh, that's a father and son; there certainly can't be a hundred pounds of weed in those suitcases.' But he must have thought it was OK. He was willing personally to take the chance with his own life. And he must have felt that whatever happened, I would be OK."

Each time I saw Anthony, we'd talk for hours. He even came three times as a guest to my interview seminar at UCLA. We covered his acid trips when he was in the eighth grade, his relationship with Sonny Bono and Cher, his near-death experiences, his learning to sing, his surfing, yoga, and motorcycling. We also covered the sex he had with his dad's girlfriends, the women he dated, the stories of what it was like when the Chili Peppers toured, and the birth of his son Everly.

We reminisced about a short film his dad made while we were at UCLA. It was about a group of four and five year old kids who hit a homeless man with a bottle and then robbed him. Anthony—then still Tony—was the one who got to break the bottle over the wino's head. It was a trick bottle that cost twelve dollars and we only had one, so it had to be done in one take. I was responsible for making sure Tony knew how to do it. Jack was behind the camera. It went well, and when the film was shown at Royce Hall, Tony sat between his dad and me. He still remembered that night.

I've written about the parents of some of my friends, like the artist Arthur Singer and the meteorologist Sylvio Simplicio, but

Anthony was the first child of a friend that I had written about. And the most famous. A lot of journalists have requested interviews with him, but he doesn't talk to many. But he talks to me because we have this history.

Childhood is the key.

Good Copy Comes From Harnassing Big Egos

45. PHONERS CAN BE REVEALING

Over the years I've learned how to complete an interview over the phone when necessary, but I've never really thought it as effective as being with the person. There is nothing like being able to look a person in the eye after asking a gut-wrenching question. Body language can be as revealing as any spoken answer, and if you aren't able to see the person you're not able to follow up the way you might if you are there. Then again, there's something to be said for not having to get dressed and driving to meet the person you're interviewing, but instead just hooking up by phone in your sweatpants or PJs, with a notepad by your side so you can scribble notes as you talk.

If I've already been with a person and need a few additional responses, then the phone is an easy way to get it done. But if you still need some important answers that didn't get asked when you met, it can be tricky. I once spent a few hours with **Warren Beatty** but left some of the more difficult questions for the end. Then he got a phone call and had to cut our interview short. He didn't like giving out his phone number, but he asked for mine and said he'd call me the next day, which he did. But when I asked him about the IRS coming after him for unpaid taxes, he hemmed and hawed and then said he had to run but would call me back. Of course, he never did. And I learned that the question that most upset people had to do with money and taxes.

But I learned something else when I had to interview **James Ellroy** by phone for a Japanese magazine. Ellroy lived in Kansas and I was in Los Angeles. The magazine didn't want to pay for my airfare, hotel and expenses, so I figured I'd try talking to the writer whose style was "so hard-boiled it scorches the pot," according to *New York* magazine. Elmore Leonard was a fan of Ellroy's writing, believing that "Ellroy's got more energy in his writing than anybody going today. There should be a warning on his *Black Dahlia* that if you read it aloud, you're liable to shatter your wine glasses." Novelist Steve Erickson wrote, "Ellroy has put terror back into American crime fiction—not the Stephen King kind of terror, but the terror that arises from ordinary urban disease."

Ellroy's muscular, pungent prose in books like *The Big Nowhere, L.A. Confidential, White Jazz,* and *American Tabloid* has been compared to jazz great Charlie Parker—peppery, rhythmic and unpredictable. The characters in his novels get thrown out of buildings, get fed shotgun shells and have their lips glued shut, and have their hands submerged in boiling oil. People's faces get blown off, famous real life politicians and mob associates mingle with his fictional people, and characters often carry over from one book to another.

Like a literary Muhammad Ali, he liked to proclaim, "I want to burn crime fiction to the fucking ground. I want to destroy every last bit of niceness and cheap empathy in the American crime novel. All other crime novels are tepid compared to mine. I want to be known as the greatest crime novelist who ever lived! I want to be the American Tolstoy."

When we spoke he liked to spice his conversation with growls and barks, saying outrageous things to promote himself. "There's never been anybody like me in American letters," he said ten minutes into our conversation. I asked him how he felt about criticism. "I've been called a racist, a fascist, an anti-Semite, a homophobe, a misogynist, an anti-Mexican, anti-Communist," he answered. "And there have been people who have just rejected my books on aesthetic grounds as well as political grounds. I get pissed off, grrrrr, but then I forget about it."

Ellroy didn't feel that the system that policed the country was corrupt, but rather that corruption *was* the system. "Keep in mind," he said, "that I write about life in extremis and the hermetically sealed inner world of hepcat jazz musicians, desperate homosexual informants, corrupt D.A's and beat cops."

In *American Tabloid,* he wrote about President Kennedy's assassination, and I asked him if he thought Kennedy deserved to die. "By the laws he lived by, absolutely," Ellroy said. "He betrayed the Mob, he betrayed the Cuban exiles with the Bay of Pigs, he fought with people he shouldn't have fucked with and he paid with his life. If *Tabloid* wasn't anything else, it's really the story of Bobby Kennedy's Oedipal dialogue. Bobby Kennedy had a very strong moral center. He was the only one of the brothers who saw through the Kennedy family mystique. He was the only one who sided with Rose Kennedy emotionally. His going after the Mob is really the act of going after his father and his brother paid the price."

Ellroy had a lot of villains in *American Tabloid*, including F.B.I Director J. Edgar Hoover, Howard Hughes, and Fidel Castro. When I asked him about them he didn't mince words.

"Gay Edgar Hoover is absolutely the premier villain of the American 20th century," he barked. "There's nothing good you can say about him. Parenthetically, he no more went outside in drag than I can flap my arms and fly from Kansas to St. Louis. I don't think he was an active homosexual. I think he and his roommate Clyde were some sort of Victorian homosexual couple who never had sex.

"Howard Hughes was a germaphobic racist, far rightwing, dope-addicted fuckhead, lucid only about half the time. I played him for some real laughs, and he returns in my next book. I've got him shooting codeine into his dick.

"As for The Beard—Fidel Castro: the Bushy Bearded Beatnik Bard of Bilious Bamboozlement—history has exposed him for what he is, a tyrant. He has staying power however, since he's been around since 1955."

Just listening to Ellroy, I began to understand how the *Kirkus Review* called him the comic book Dos Passos of our time. When I brought that up, Ellroy shot back, "I never read Dos Passos. *Kirkus* can suck my dick. Fuck them up the ass with a faggot pit bull with an 18-inch dick and shoot a big load of syphilitic jism up *Kirkus's* ass."

Later in our conversation he said, "I'm an exhibitionist by nature and inclination."

"Really?" I said. "I hadn't noticed."

He said he always knew he was a genius, even when he got caught shoplifting "seven or eight times" out of the hundreds of occasions he did it. When I asked him how many times he was arrested before he became a writer he said "about thirty."

At 27 he was diagnosed with alcohol brain syndrome. "It just meant that I had a psychotic brain rupture when I was coming off of alcohol. It was a brain malfunction where I couldn't think of stuff I wanted to conjure. I was physiologically insane at the moment I had that brain episode."

We talked for a few hours without either of us seeing each other, but with Ellroy I didn't think it mattered. He spoke about his wild youth, his dropping out of high school, his getting discharged from the army soon after he joined it at seventeen, his addiction to booze and drugs, and the unsolved murder of his mother when he was ten and how he hated her at the time. "Her death engendered in me a tremendous curiosity for all things criminal," he said, "specifically Los Angeles and its criminal history of the 1950s. I turned her death into something useful very early on. That's something that a lot of people find odd to hear. The truth is my bereavement was complex and ambiguous."

Ellroy had a lot of backstory and he wasn't reticent about answering whatever I asked him. What I learned was that it was possible to do a noteworthy, quote-worthy interview by phone. But you need a true egotist to make it work.

46. NARCISSISTS DON'T WANT YOUR STORIES

Ray Bradbury had an ego that matched Ellroy's, but there were questions he didn't bother answering if it had nothing to do with him.

Bradbury wrote story after story, book after book, including such gems as *The Martian Chronicles, Fahrenheit 451*, and *The Illustrated Man*, earning him his place in speculative fiction circles as a man of great imagination. He often said that some of his stories were totally original and nothing like anything else that had ever been written, and perhaps he was right. But had he read everything written to make such a claim? And isn't it the critics and readers who should say such things, not the writer?

I interviewed Bradbury in the basement of his Los Angeles house and wound up using different parts of it for *Newsday*, the *L.A. Free Press*, and in *Endangered Species*, my book of interviews with writers. I mention this to point out that Bradbury was a very good interview subject. He loved to talk, he had a lot to say, and he could be both inspiring and motivational. But when the subject wasn't about him or his ideas, he sort of blanked out. Though I have interviewed many narcissists, most leave room for curiosity. Marlon Brando, for instance, was interested in everything I had to say that wasn't related to him because he studied people. Barbra Streisand was interested to hear about my time with Brando when we met a few years after I had interviewed her. But Bradbury turned a deaf ear when I tried to turn our interview into a conversation. He had zero interest in anything I had to say that wasn't related to him or his work.

As long as I stuck to my role as interrogator, he kept to his role as self-promoter. When I asked him about the significance of his 1950 novel, *The Martian Chronicles*, he responded, "I'd like to believe that the astronauts who eventually go there will have read *The Martian Chronicles* and that I may have a part in preventing that future that I worried about when I wrote the book."

When the space program was brought up, he let me know that "NASA called recently and I said, 'Where've you been? You've needed me all these years.' Because they talk too many technical things and they don't talk poetry."

He was disappointed that no one in the Disney organization came to him for advice about their theme park, so he went to see the boss himself. "I went out to see Uncle Walt some years ago. I heard he was going to rebuild Tomorrowland. I said, 'Walt, why don't you call me in and let me help work on it with you?' He said, 'Ray, it's no use. You're a genius and I'm a genius, we'd kill each other the second week.'"

All of these are good quotes. They make good copy. And Bradbury had a headful of such quotes, which is why he was such a good person to interview. I would later learn that he had an anger in him that was unforgiving when he felt he was slighted, as he was when he went to Ireland to work with John Huston on the screenplay for *Moby Dick*. Huston had his own dark side and could often be cruel. When he discovered someone's weakness, he went after it. He preferred to surround himself with people of strength. If he could bring a writer or an actor to tears, he lost any sympathy for them. If they could hold their own, he would pour them another drink and share war stories. When he found out that Bradbury crossed the Atlantic by ship because he had a fear of flying and also refused to drive because he was afraid to be in a speeding car, he lost all respect for the writer. "He's a gifted man," Huston told me, "but a bore beyond description."

Huston's production assistant, Jeanie Sims, thought Bradbury and Huston "were chalk and cheese. John was one of the great eccentrics, the last of the swashbucklers, and Ray was basically a small-town American, exactly the opposite. And it was very easy to prick the bubble of his pride. He had such a big ego; you had to keep pumping it up to work with him. And John wasn't going to do that. He was the one with the needle."

When Bradbury refused to fly with Huston to Paris, that needle began to poke deeply into the writer's confidence. Huston baited him whenever he saw an opening until

Bradbury came close to a nervous breakdown. And when the script was finished, Huston invited him to a dinner that included other guests Truman Capote, Humphrey Bogart, Lauren Bacall, Richard Brooks, and Gina Lollobrigida. Huston brought Bradbury to tears in front of everyone when he stood up and pointed his drink at him and said, "You're the fellow who writes about going to Mars, but you don't fly. How do you write that shit? Don't you find it inconsistent?"

At the end of the evening Huston sat in his limousine when Bradbury approached. He leaned in and punched Huston. Huston said it was too bad that it took Bradbury until the end of his time in Ireland to grow some balls.

Bradbury would get his revenge the only way he knew how, by writing a half-hour TV drama called "Banshee" and a novel, *Green Shadows, White Whale,* both about Huston. But he could never get the humiliation out of his system. More than a dozen years after I had sat with him in his basement, I got in touch with him to see if he'd talk to me for my book about Huston. I knew about what had gone down between them and thought this would be a good opportunity for Bradbury to unleash his demons, but Ray couldn't bring himself to do it. The man who loved to talk about himself refused to open up that particular hornet's nest, exposing the incident when he was made to feel small and weak. Huston might have thought that inconsistent, but true narcissists don't ever want to put themselves in a vulnerable situation where their strengths might be challenged and their weaknesses exposed. And I knew Bradbury had absolutely no interest in hearing me relate Huston's side of what happened in Ireland. He had written it the way he wanted it written and that was the way it would stay.

47. TALK IS CHEAP

Alec Baldwin's anger was more pronounced than Bradbury's when he felt he was being slighted, or if someone as lowly as a journalist had put something over on him.

When I went on the Universal Lot to see an edgy Baldwin for a pre-interview, we spoke in his trailer and he told me all the topics he specifically wanted to avoid. I looked at him forlornly and said, "Alec, you just knocked off half my questions." It didn't matter to him that now I would have to go home and rethink what I could ask him. He was sick of journalists bringing up his temper, his sometimes rude or outrageous public behavior, his relationship with his then-wife Kim Basinger, or some of the turkeys that he had starred in. He felt that he had a lot to say about the country and current events and he preferred to keep the dialogue at a "higher" level.

I could respect that, though I knew what my editor wanted and it wasn't what Alec Baldwin thought about nuclear proliferation or gun control. But since he had asked before we did the interview, I had to respect his request. I went home, put aside the questions I had prepared, and wrote new ones. The next morning I returned to Universal, knocked on his trailer door, and found a more relaxed Baldwin. "You know what I told you yesterday about what not to ask me?" he said. "Forget about it. Ask me anything you want."

"Really?" I said, a smile widening my face. "Great." Luckily I had taken both sets of questions with me and I pulled out the original set. "Let's get down to it."

"With the beating you and Kim took in the media from *The Marrying Man*, were you concerned about how the press would treat you guys for *The Getaway*?" That was one of my questions. "Jeffrey Katzenberg and the Disney executives are powerful people. Was it a mistake for you to be so outspoken against them?" That was another. I also asked him about his courage to have spoken out against Neil Simon, one of the icons in his business, calling him "as deep as a bottle cap." And did he have any regrets for being so outspoken?

Baldwin had no regrets. He answered my questions boldly, saying that whatever he said or however he had behaved, he would not take anything back. "What it boiled down to," he said about the Disney fiasco with *The Marrying Man*, "was that I worked for somebody I didn't like and I told him to kiss my ass. So what? I worked for a bunch of people who didn't have any idea what they were doing. I had very, very cancer-causing, corrosive feelings for a long, long time. But I don't have any regrets about anything. Let's face facts, these people [at Disney] are not making great films. I feel uncomfortable now, because you'll probably print my assessments of them rather than have the balls to make a statement about how this business really works."

So.... I asked him how the business really worked.

"A studio talks to any entertainment magazine, and who is that magazine beholden to? That magazine is dependent upon them for access to feature stories and advertising revenue. These executives say, 'You print this, you put a spin on this,' and I go and say, 'Don't do that.' Who are they beholden to? Whose story is going to get printed? What I learned is, that's the way it is across the board, everywhere. I know personally of three stories about movies that were made by that company which make my movie look like it was a picnic, but you never read about them."

Baldwin was bitter about how he and Kim Basinger were treated and he was angry about how his wife was later treated when she backed out of the film *Boxing Helena*, a case that eventually went to court. He had a lot of anger about how unfair it all seemed and he didn't hold back. Nothing wrong with that; it made for a good interview.

During a break I mentioned to Alec that we had both grown up on Long Island. I told him about how the father of a friend of mine was outed on the front page of *Newsday* as one of the five Mob bosses on the Island and how that had blown my mind, as I knew him in a very different light. Alec got very excited as I spoke about this and said, "This is a movie! We've got to make this. After this interview is over, let's talk some serious business. I'll work with you on it. It's a great story." His enthusiasm seemed real and it was contagious. His movie instincts were a lot more tenable than mine, and when I left him that afternoon I thought there might actually be something to my story of an innocent kid and the Mob boss father of his close friend.

When the May 1994 issue of *Movieline* came out with Baldwin on the cover, I thought the magazine did a good job with the layout and the lead ("The Accidental Actor"), but Alec wasn't very pleased. He called me–at 5:00 a.m.–to let me know. He was on the East Coast, so he didn't realize he was waking me up. He was only thinking about what he had originally said to me when we first met to discuss what he hadn't wanted to talk about. "I specifically told you I didn't want you to write about Kim and *The Marrying Man*, Jeff Katzenberg and Disney. You've got me saying negative shit about people and films I've done and what the hell is that about? What good does it do me? I *told* you I didn't want to go there!" He was enraged, and spewed out more negative shit about how I had deceived him and broke my word. I let him scream because I had no choice; I couldn't get a word in anyway, until he finally paused to catch his breath. Then I said, "Alec, you told me when I came to do the interview to forget about your restrictions and to ask you anything I wanted. Don't you remember that? I had put away my original set of questions and then you said to go ahead and ask them, so I did."

"What the hell was I thinking? I sound terrible. Bitter. This doesn't help me any."

"It's not as bad as you think," I said. "I like that you say what you think."

"I gotta go," he said, miffed that once again the press had somehow screwed him. "It's not what I wanted."

Alec and I never got together to work on that Mob movie idea and I don't know if he remembered telling me to ask him anything, but his ego was large and it was all about him, which is often par for the course when dealing with these guys. But with Alec, I also learned that talk is cheap.

48. GOD BLESS NON SEQUITURS

But athletic accomplishments are not. Especially when you've accomplished something no other athlete has, as **Mark Spitz** did when he won seven gold medals at the 1972 Olympics in Munich, one of the most spectacular individual swimming efforts ever recorded. Unfortunately, that was also the Olympics during which eleven Israeli athletes were gunned down by Palestinian terrorists. Spitz, being Jewish, was given extra security and rushed out of the city. Three years later, I asked him about how that was handled. He said he thought he should write a book about his escape from Munich.

"They had thousands of troopers running around this village of 20,000 athletes," he said. "I was put into a security, eight to ten bodyguards, the whole bit. Then I was ordered by the German government—because they knew I was through swimming, you know–'Get this son of a bitch outta here, take him somewhere out of Munich.' At that point nobody knew what was going on and, being Jewish and them attacking the Israelis, they didn't know what the hell they were going to do, and I was the focus of attention. The way I analyzed it was, if they wanted to come get me they could have. Everybody knew where I was. I was at a speaking engagement with this woman whose husband was killed in that Israeli incident. I was the last speaker, and when I got up the whole joint was crying because of this woman, 'cause they showed the husband being killed and the whole bit. I got up and said, 'If you think I'm shook up, I have a hard act to follow.' I have realized that nobody has ever come and asked me, 'What do you think?' or 'What is your concern?' or 'Weren't you concerned about your life?' or 'What were you going through?' I had done all this jazz in swimming and nobody ever stopped and really asked me. I said nobody really cared what happened to me. They just look at it as though I fled the country to escape to save my own life. I was on radio for a whole hour in Florida where they could call up and ask questions and the whole Jewish population got so shook up. One woman called up and she thought I was supposed to single-handedly take on all of Germany for what had happened when I wasn't even born. What I said was, 'Nobody really cares what I have to do.'"

"What is it that you feel you have to do?" I asked.

"I don't have to do anything," he said.

Mark Spitz was a tough guy to like. You couldn't take away his accomplishments, and he certainly did his best to capitalize on it. He posed in his American flag swimsuit wearing his seven gold medals around his neck for a famous poster. He did a commercial for the milk industry that became controversial when people around the world complained that he was sending the wrong message to children who were lactose intolerant. His celebrated mustache got him a lucrative contract with Schick to promote their shaving products. He was a narcissist, which is not unusual for a top-notch athlete. But he couldn't seem to wrap his head around anything serious other than himself.

He retired from swimming after the '72 Olympics and didn't do much to help promote the sport. When I asked him what it would take to get him back in the pool, he answered, "Money. If I'd be getting $400,000 winner-take-all, yeah, hell, I'd go back and train. Because my time is worth that much."

So many of his responses had to do with how special he was that I had to ask about his ego. "In a room with Bobby Fischer, Jimmy Connors, Muhammad Ali and yourself, who would survive the battle of the egos?"

"Yeah, I could dig that," he said. "That would be cool. I'm a totally satisfied athlete and what I have done speaks for itself. If you want to get into a money competing game, I can hold my own with them, except for Ali."

When I returned to what happened in the '72 Olympics, hoping that he might have some compassionate thoughts for those who lost their lives to terrorists, he responded with this jaw-dropping reflection.

"As I was drying my hair this morning, I was looking in the mirror and thinking, Jesus Christ, you must have been like the most radical son of a bitch when you swam because you had a mustache. How did I get the mustache? In college, we weren't allowed to have facial hair and all that jazz, we were supposed to look like the all-American athlete, right? With short hair and all that crap. When I got through college, I started growing a whole beard, but it kept itching and I got down to just the mustache. I went to the Olympic trials and I was going to shave it off but I never did. I went to the training camp. I went to Munich. I was going to shave it off just before I swam and then I just said screw it, I'm not going to shave it off. I'm swimming great. I broke five world records in the Olympic trials: why shave it off? Now people recognize me because of the mustache and I'm getting it back in spades because I didn't grow it to have it forever. That wasn't my intention. I grew it because it was like, 'cause it was like, I mean, you know, I'd have never, given the opportunity, 'cause the coach didn't want it and all that jazz. I was offered $5000 to shave it off—it got up to $50,000 at one point, and then I turned that into a nice-figured contract with Schick and I never did shave it off. See, I swam in the Olympics as an athlete, not as a circus star. The mustache is an identification factor."

Spitz's agent had called him "The greatest living hero since Lindbergh." Other people, notably the athletes he competed against and most members of the press, had less inflated opinions. The rap on Spitz's life story was that he had been programmed: first by his father, then by his coaches and, after his great success, by his agent and public relations people. Because of the difficulty talking with him, many reporters took to calling a meeting with Spitz a "non-interview." I never felt that way, because even a "non-interview" can be revealing. And I definitely thought that the more Mark Spitz opened his mouth, the more he revealed himself.

When I asked if he rejected the notion that his whole life seemed to be one of guidance, training, grooming and programming, he came through with this:

"Look at anybody who's been successful in something and he's usually been guided—either by himself or by some program. I think where people get lost is they go to college and they say, 'Screw all this stuff, I'm just going to float around and decide what I'm going to do in a year or so.' Those guys are still floating. When they send up capsules into space, if they don't program where the hell to go, they'll just fly all over the goddamn place."

"Do you see yourself as a space capsule?" I asked.

"I think everybody should look at themselves as space capsules, man. If their trajectory is screwed up, then they're going to be screwed up. I see a lot of people who are empty capsules out there, floating around. It's not my fault. I just hope I don't become one of them."

49. DIRECTORS ARE SOMETIMES BETTER ACTORS THAN THEIR STARS

Whereas Spitz was living in the conceited "space capsule" reality of his accomplishments, other narcissists are often living in denial.

I sat down with director **Billy Friedkin** for a TV interview in 1985, when he was promoting *To Live and Die in L.A.* Friedkin's most innovative films were *The French Connection* (1971) and *The Exorcist* (1973). I had watched him direct Al Pacino in *Cruising* in 1979, when gay protestors lined the streets of New York where the film was shot, blowing whistles to disrupt the production. The story was about a detective submerging himself into the S&M underground gay culture as he tried to track down a homophobic killer. That was when I first met Pacino, who said what attracted him to the film was that it interwove the coming together of the cop and the killer. The book it was based on had separate chapters of these two characters. Richard Cox was cast as the killer and he thought it was the break he needed to become a star, or at least to raise his profile to land him future work. But as the movie was shot, Pacino began to have doubts about the direction Friedkin was taking it.

When the film was being edited in Los Angeles, Pacino was concerned enough to fly out to see a rough cut. He didn't tell Friedkin he was coming, so when he got to the editing bay, Friedkin was surprised. "What are you doing here?" he asked his star. "Oh, you know, I was just out here in L.A. so I thought I'd drop by, see what you're doing." "You can't come in like this and see the film," Friedkin said. "It's not ready for you to see." "It's okay," Pacino said, "it's like seeing rushes for me. I thought maybe I could be helpful." "No," Friedkin said. "You can't see it."

Pacino couldn't believe that Friedkin would lock him out, and it confirmed his suspicions that the movie being edited was not the movie he had signed on for. And when the film came out, he understood why Friedkin wouldn't let him in. He had altered the structure of cop and killer, removing most of Richard Cox's scenes and focusing on Pacino's detective. It was unbalanced and not very good.

I knew about this because after Friedkin wouldn't let him see the rough cut, Pacino called me to meet him for lunch at Imperial Gardens, a Japanese restaurant on Sunset Blvd. in West Hollywood. It was raining that day and when I got there, Al was standing by the front door looking forlorn. The restaurant was closed and he had been standing there for twenty minutes. We found another place to eat and he told me what had just happened. He couldn't believe that Friedkin wouldn't show him the cut. He felt filmmaking was a collaborative effort and, in addition to expressing his concerns, Pacino hoped he could bring fresh eyes and a different perspective. He knew that the director had final cut, but he thought that he could be helpful. Friedkin obviously saw it differently. He didn't want his actor to interfere with his process or his vision. He belonged to the Alfred Hitchcock School of Directing. Hitchcock once said, "All actors should be treated like cattle."

So when we sat down for our interview, I asked Friedkin about this incident, wondering why he wouldn't let Pacino see the rough cut. He denied doing that. I was more specific, mentioning that Pacino had flown out from New York without warning him, and just appeared at his editing bay. Friedkin said it never happened. I tried again, saying that I had had lunch with Pacino right afterwards, but Friedkin stuck to his guns. Al had never come to see a rough cut. Friedkin had not barred him from seeing it. It never happened.

I didn't press the matter any further. What was the point? I wasn't there as a prosecutor. If Friedkin wanted to deny what I knew for a fact, then all I could do was doubt everything he said. I had caught him in a lie. I'd seen the look on Pacino's face when I met him in front of that restaurant. It was the look of a beaten, confused, shell-shocked man who didn't understand what had just gone down between him and his director. Pacino was never able to forgive Friedkin. He told me years later that he was on a plane in first class and Friedkin was on the same flight. Friedkin went to greet him and stuck out his hand. Al said he looked down at Friedkin's hand but couldn't shake it.

It's not very often when you catch someone lying *for sure* on camera. I could have kept pushing him, but I didn't. What purpose would it have served if, after presenting more and more details he said, "Oh yeah, now I remember." Or if he just continued to say it never happened. I accepted that he was lying and moved on. But it showed me that directors can also be good actors, and that you can't always believe what people tell you, even when cameras are recording them.

50. SOME LIKE TO GOSSIP

I wouldn't say I caught **Zsa Zsa Gabor** in a lie, but hers was the sort of ego that tended toward bitchiness and high exaggeration.

The most unforgettable thing about the flamboyant Zsa Zsa Gabor was her name. One might find it difficult to name one of her movies, but one could never forget her unique name. "Zsa Zsa" sounded like something a baby on the verge of speaking actual words would say.

She was born in Budapest somewhere between 1917 and 1923 and became Miss Hungary in 1936 somewhere between the ages of 13 and 19. She was also a fencing and Ping Pong champion as a youth. She spoke of her sisters Eva ("a little bitch") and Magda ("the grand dame"), and said they were brought up believing they were members of the privileged class, based on their good looks and proper schooling at a Swiss boarding school. "My father was one of the richest men in Hungary," she said. "He bought me a sable coat for my fifteenth birthday." She allegedly achieved the title of Princess when she married her ninth husband, Prince Frederic von Anhalt in 1986, but some dispute whether he really was who he said he was. But by that time, it didn't really matter. Zsa Zsa might be the original "famous for being famous" celebrity, the forerunner to Paris Hilton and the Kardashians.

Her willingness to talk about her many marriages in her thick accent, calling everyone who spoke to her "dah-link," made her a popular guest on talk shows. She found laughs zinging such one-liners as: "I was a marvelous housekeeper. Every time I leave a man, I keep his house." "I have never hated a man enough to give his diamonds back." "The only place men want depth in a woman is in her décolletage." "You never really know a man until you have divorced him."

She was also a nasty gossip.

Zsa Zsa didn't like Marilyn Monroe, probably because she knew that George Sanders, her third husband (from 1949–54) had "a big affair" with Marilyn. She also knew that Marilyn was a much more talented actress than she was. When I interviewed her she tried to come off as a proper lady who hardly had sex with anyone she didn't marry, though she did slip in that the greatest lover of them all was the Dominican playboy Purfirio Rubirosa, whom she never married, but bedded when George Sanders was cheating on her. "*He* was a lover," she said. "He was oversexed. He had Barbara Hutton, Doris Duke. After Rubirosa, almost nobody was a good lover. But I didn't love him, I loved George, who was not a good lover."

She talked about having an affair with John F. Kennedy when he was a senator, and about being on a plane sitting next to young Jacqueline Bouvier, who spoke about dating him. "She was not very elegant," Zsa Zsa said. "I was a big star then. When the plane landed, Jack was there and when he saw me, he picked me up off the ground, and Jackie saw this. She never spoke to me again. And American men think European women are gold diggers. It's American women who are gold diggers."

But it was the way she spoke about Marilyn that exposed her jealous, gossip-driven nature. "She was a very dull girl," Zsa Zsa said. "She thought if a man who takes her out for dinner didn't sleep with her then something was wrong with her. Just look at her background, it's all about family, and poor girl, she didn't have anything. When George was making *All About Eve* in San Francisco, we had a suite and Marilyn had a room next door. George said, 'Let's make a game of it. Let's see how many men are going to go into her room tonight.' I think it was four. That's a terrible thing to say about somebody the whole country admired, but let's face it, that's who she was. She was really a sex symbol, but not my taste. I'm sure she was gorgeous, but my taste was more distinguished, like Grace Kelly, who was a dear friend of mine. I was with her when she first met Prince Rainier. But she was very unhappy. It wasn't a happy marriage."

Marilyn Monroe died in 1962. Zsa Zsa was badmouthing her twenty years after her death. All I asked her was whether she ever knew Marilyn, and she didn't hold back her vindictive snipes. I thought it was distasteful, but also very revealing of who she was and, in the end, that's what one wants from any interview, Dahlink.

51. DON'T BRAG ABOUT YOUR SUCCESS

Unlike Zsa Zsa, **Jon Voight** was extremely talented, yet he too experienced jealousy. But instead of flaunting his superiority and denigrating his colleagues, he wallowed in a fearful, confusing, philosophical state, juggling an ego that expanded and contracted as he assessed his position in his chosen profession.

He came to my house the same week I received the January 1978 issue of *Writer's Digest* with my mug on the cover. I hadn't expected that. I had written an article about interviewing, but the editor had held it for more than a year, waiting until he had a hook. When *Playboy* published my interview with Barbra Streisand, he thought that was a sufficient coup that deserved a cover story. He had the photographer pose me with my arms folded, standing in front of a poster-size blowup of the *Playboy* issue with Streisand on the cover. I bring this up because I hid the magazine before Voight arrived. I thought at the time that movie stars were on the covers of magazines, not journalists, and it would have been awkward if he saw me on a magazine cover. I felt it could alter the dynamic between us.

Voight was a pretty big star, having appeared in *Midnight Cowboy, Deliverance, The Odessa File* and *Coming Home*. His next film was *The Champ*, and our interview for *Oui* magazine took place at the gym where he was training, subsequently continuing at my house. I watched his intense workouts as he learned to box, and I listened to his diatribes about jealousy and getting older. He thought acting was "magic" and he believed in magic. But he also thought that he was in constant competition with both himself and other actors. "I was in acting class the other night," he said, "and almost killed somebody. I went berserk for no reason, absolutely turned on this guy like a viper. And all those people think I know what I'm doing. He was scared: he looked at me and said, 'What are you doing? What's going on with you?' I tried to explain: 'Well, I'm getting older. I'm jealous. I'm angry. I'm all fucked up, life's passing me by...'"

With the success he was having, I found this a bit overdramatic, but Voight had definite opinions about time and life. "It's a humorous situation, life," he said. "We're all sentenced to life. You know you're going to die; you just don't have any idea why you're here: you can't remember your major experiences past a certain age—there are quite a few traumatizing experiences that you keep trying to go back to and see how you can fix them, and you've forgotten half of them—and then it's over. And somebody says, 'Well, that was life—how did you like it?' And you say, 'Well, I don't know: it was OK. I'd like to be Jesus Christ or Gandhi, but I just had my life.' Christ probably said to himself, 'What a life. Look at this—can you believe it? All this evidence and they're gonna take me instead of *that* bum? What a life!'"

Voight's fame came early, with his first film, playing Joe Buck opposite Dustin Hoffman's Ratso Rizzo in *Midnight Cowboy*. It overwhelmed him and he went into hiding, not wanting to talk to anyone in the media. "Success is a very strange thing," he reflected about that time. "It complicates things. I just didn't know what to do with it. Everybody was asking me questions and paying attention to what I thought. I was frightened of becoming a part of the Establishment, which was a negative thing to me then. My attitude was that everybody should look at everybody equally and that there shouldn't be this glamorization of certain people as opposed to others. But you probably don't know what I'm talking about, you've never been on a magazine cover, you've never been singled out that way. It changes you. It can fuck with your head."

The temptation to correct him was there. He gave me an opening so wide a Mack truck could have driven through it. But I demurred. The interview was about him, and pulling out that issue of *Writer's Digest* would have just complicated matters between us. He might have felt he didn't have to explain himself as much, and what kind of interview would that have been? I wanted him to tell me more about his anger at others in his acting class, about how he would have preferred being Christ or Gandhi if given a choice, and how, when we die, "we go into little capsules, like a gymnasium, which are like airports throughout the universe. And these capsules are roller-derby houses. And that's where we go; we play roller derby. They give you a number, put kneepads on you, and in you go."

I much preferred checking into the trippy mind of Jon Voight than pulling out a magazine cover and saying, "Me too." He continued to talk, off the wall and into my tape recorder, for hours, in long paragraphs that both amused and shocked. I'm convinced he did so because I was able to sublimate my own ego and keep the focus on him.

52. PROVOKE!

One of my favorite early interviews was with a married couple that lived in Bay Shore, Long Island and liked to race cars on the weekend. *Newsday's* Sunday magazine liked to do family profiles of eccentric people, and **Jay and Toni,** with their clashing, competitive egos fit the bill in spades. They didn't hold back when it came to who wore the pants in their household. They both did!

They met on a blind date and when Jay invited Toni to watch him race, she thought she was going to see something exciting. Instead, she saw Jay go once around the track and flip over. "I was disgusted," Toni told me. "All he did was tell me what a good driver he was. I saw him go around once and that was it."

Toni married Jay anyway and became his sharpest critic. "I'm always telling Jay he never passes, he will not go on the outside for nothing," she said as we sat around their kitchen table. My role was simply to egg them on.

So finally Jay got Toni her own race car so she could stop her Monday morning quarterbacking, and see for herself what it was like to go up against other drivers. "Let her find out for herself what it's all about," he said with a glint in his eye. "She's always telling me, 'You shudda went this way, you shudda went that way'—we'll see what happens now. She's gonna get it now."

For Toni's first time in the Ladies Powderpuff Derby, she found that her heart was beating in her left foot; it wouldn't stop knocking. "I was petrified," she admitted.

"I don't like to tell her she does good," Jay said, "because they say you get a big head, but anything she can get in, I'm putting her in, including demolitions."

"I'm putting myself in," Toni said.

"Don't let this go to your head," Jay warned.

"Go to my head! If I wudda listened to you I mighta *been* on my head! You told me to take my foot off the clutch and put it on the brake when I come to the turns. It was the girls who told me, no, you don't do it that way, don't even touch the brake; when you're in second and you let up on the gas you automatically slow down. That's what I did. If I listened to you I wudda been in trouble."

"No you wouldn't have."

"Yes I would."

This argument went on between them for the entire time I was there, recording it all. Jay tried to talk about his triumphs and Toni would bring him down, recalling how he got barred from racing at Freeport after he punched the track owner in the mouth; how he totaled car after car; and how he once went off the track and down into a gulley at 99 mph sideways.

When they slowed down, I asked which of them was the better driver, or who would win if they raced each other, or if they were both in a Demolition Derby, who would knock the other out. They responded like champs, each of them sure they would outdrive or out-smash the other.

"I work all week for the weekend, because I love to race," Jay told me before I left. "I love Toni and she loves me, but it's a different love."

"We're different kinds of people when we're driving," Toni added. "When we're in there, we'll put each other in the wall; after the race we'll apologize."

I was glad I didn't have to apologize to either of them when I wrote about their love of racing and their love for each other, even though I fully understood which of those loves came first. I got to understand this because I wasn't afraid to egg them on. It didn't take much, just a little push here, a bit of sarcasm there. In the end, the piece became part of a trilogy I wrote about the car racing scene on Long Island. Their part was called "For Toni and Jay, Racing is a Family Affair." It got a lot of letters to the editor and I was asked to do another three-part series on the horse-racing scene at Roosevelt Raceway. For that one, I sought out the betting couples that would respond to my provocations by hauling off on each other. And I learned that they're everywhere!

Sex Is Always On The Mind

53. IT'S ABOUT SEX

When I went to interview **Pierce Brosnan** at his home in Malibu for *Cosmopolitan* magazine in 1996, he had lost his first wife to cancer and was living with a woman who was pregnant with their child. I had written about him before, for *Movieline*, and also did a cable TV interview with him, so we knew what to expect from each other. But the editors at *Cosmo* wanted more than Brosnan talking about his past and future wives, his childhood and his movies. They saw him as a handsome, sexy hunk that their readers would not toss out of bed if they were lucky enough to lure him in. Bronson was the new James Bond and that certainly upped his sex IQ. "Get him to open up about sex," I was instructed. "Get him to be as specific as possible."

I have always disliked such instructions. I heard them every time I did a Playboy Cable TV interview ("Don't forget to ask about sex") and, though I never minded discussing the subject when it came up naturally, I didn't like it when a director whispered in my earpiece to remind me, and I didn't care to be told by *Cosmo* how to approach Brosnan. But this is about learning, and I was always learning when it came to writing for magazines. For *Cosmopolitan,* and quite a few other magazines and cable shows, it was always about sex.

To do this, you've really got to make your subject comfortable. You've got to be able to joke about the topic you're hoping to get into and you've got to cover as much other territory as possible before you slip in the sex questions. When we talked about his current relationship with Keely Shaye-Smith, he said that before he met her he was "moving about with the greatest of ease and swiftness, not staying too long in any one place or with any one person. I had relationships. One feels guilt, but one needs to be held. It can be very difficult, because you feel you're betraying your past life and the wife you had. Then you begin to enjoy being footloose."

This was my opening. The sex talk would come once I could get him to talk about the women in between his former wife and his current girlfriend, because it would be indiscreet to discuss those two. "One woman I had a relationship with— the only gift that came from it was Kundalini yoga, which I've stayed with. Then, in the spring of '92, I fell in love with someone who was just toxic. It was a really poisonous relationship. I knew I was on the wrong train to start with, but for maybe nine months, the lust factor got the best of me."

Asked to describe that lust factor, Bronson went Bond on me, which was what *Cosmo* readers were hoping for. "Great sex, like great performances, certainly comes from relaxation. To be free to explore and to do anything you want with and to that person and also allowing it to happen back to you as well. So there's no one person leading the dance. Then it becomes very exciting. There's nothing like great sex. It's poetry. Great sex is when you don't want to wash yourself for the rest of the day. Great sex is when, at the moment of orgasm, you're totally vulnerable. It's an amazing expression of the self—so raw, so animalistic. When you really enter into it and you're secure with your partner, it's the most joyous, luxurious, magnificent experience, and you want to go back and do it again and again and again and again."

I must have shared my own sex stories to get him to speak this freely, but his are what got printed, and when I ran into him walking on a street in Santa Monica a few years later, he remembered what he had told me and said that he still couldn't figure out how I got him to talk so openly about sex.

"It's probably why women are always smiling at you," I joked. "Either that, or trying to smell you to see if you've washed."

54. ENCOURAGE DREAMS OF GIANT PENISES

Sex wasn't such a joyous or magnificent experience for **Lesley Ann Warren,** whose nightmares often included giant penises. She wanted to meet before we spoke on camera, so we arranged to have lunch at La Serre, a fancy French restaurant in Studio City. I knew she was attractive–she played Cinderella when she was eighteen and was nominated for an Oscar as a ditzy gangster's moll in *Victor/Victoria* in 1982, when she was 36–but I wasn't prepared for how stunning she was in person. She exuded an aura that radiated light and sunshine and splendor. I felt like I was having lunch with a beauty queen who wanted to meet *me*!

I also felt like a gambler trying to keep my poker face. I knew the questions I wanted to ask and some of them were of a personal nature. I didn't want to scare her off or make her be on her guard during our lunch, so I refrained from asking her anything at all and just told her stories of my adventures in and out of the interviewing trade.

A few days later, when we met again, there were two cameras ready to record our conversation. We both felt relaxed, having shared that lunch and, after we warmed up discussing some of the roles she had played, and her five Golden Globe nominations, I zeroed in on things I read about her teenage years, when boys began to hover around her.

"When I was twelve I had bosoms and was very voluptuous looking," she candidly told me. "That got a lot of attention. The boys used to talk about me. They were riveted to my body, and it was just horrible. I didn't know how to handle it. I hated my breasts. Hated them!"

That pre-teen pubescence led to her being asked out by older boys, who wanted to get their hands on what she had. "I've always had an inherent submissiveness coupled with an overt sexuality—that's a real attractive package to men," she said.

"I was seventeen when I first had sex and it was horrible. I had a virgin mentality before *and* after I had sex. There was no caring involved, no gentleness. I remember it well. I went home, ran to my bedroom, and just cried and cried. I talked to my parents about it. My dad was disappointed but loving. My mom was pissed off. She was mad. That didn't help at all. I was turned off by sex after that. I used to have nightmares about giant penises—I swear! Which is not to say I didn't have sex, which is a terrible paradox, and it manifested in the kinds of roles I was asked to play: either Cinderella when I was eighteen or a hooker soon after."

As an actress, she always felt vulnerable, as opposed to models, whom she saw as being "perfect. I was intimidated by models. They have a sense about themselves—they exude confidence, whether or not they feel it. I wanted to be like that: so together and invulnerable."

She married a hairdresser named Jon Peters in 1967, had a child with him, and divorced him in 1974, when he began cutting Barbra Streisand's hair and eventually moved in with her. She didn't hide her vulnerability, admitting that she once truly believed in the Cinderella story. "I thought some prince was going to come along and save me. But that didn't happen."

Instead, she learned to overcome her fear of giant penises, even though she had to deal with a lot of big pricks in her business.

55. TAKING A CITY IS BETTER THAN SEX

Some anti-NRA protestors might have considered **Charlton Heston** one of those big pricks, but Heston's take on sex was that he experienced something better during his long career. When my editor at *Movieline* wanted me to do Heston, my first thoughts were not of his movies, but his politics. I associated Heston as a leading force (and four-term president) of the National Rifle Association, and the picture that came to mind was not of Moses parting the Red Sea. Rather, it was of Heston addressing an NRA convention, his rifle-bearing arm raised over his head, warning Al Gore and other anti-gun advocates that if they wanted to disarm him, they would have to take his weapon "from my cold dead hands."

So the idea of meeting this man in person intrigued me. "Heston, yeah, sure," I responded to my editor, "that should be fun."

She caught the glint in my liberal eye and said, "I'm not interested in his politics, I just want him to talk about his movies."

"What fun is that?" I asked, my enthusiasm beginning to simmer.

"He's had an incredible career that's spanned five decades. We're a movie magazine."

"Yeah, but he's in the news as an activist these days, not as much as an actor."

"I can always give the assignment to someone else," she said.

Not a chance! I thought. So, in 2000, I went to see the 77-year-old Heston at his home, with two handlers accompanying him when he came to greet me. It was two years before he was diagnosed with Alzheimer's, and though he walked slowly he seemed to have full use of his speech and memory. The handlers were there to make sure I didn't upset him with my questions. They weren't necessary.

We started out talking about Tim Burton's remake of *Planet of the Apes*, as he had starred in the original in 1968. That somehow segued into how he had a pretty smooth ride from the very beginning of his career when Cecil B. DeMille first saw him on the Paramount lot and immediately cast him as the manager in *The Greatest Show on Earth*. "My second picture won the Academy Award, and I had the leading role," he said. "I'm a great believer in serendipity."

His good luck continued throughout his career, as he appeared in numerous films that had iconic moments. Besides parting the Red Sea in *The Ten Commandments*, he raced a chariot of horses around a Roman racetrack in *Ben Hur*; he played John the Baptist to Max Von Sydow's Jesus in *The Greatest Story Ever Told*; he fell to his knees and cursed God when he saw the Statue of Liberty half buried in sand and realized the planet that had been taken over by apes was his own in *Planet of the Apes*; he painted the ceiling of the Sistine Chapel as Michelangelo in *The Agony and the Ecstasy*; he played a Mexican narcotics agent opposite Orson Welles and Janet Leigh in *Touch of Evil*; he had memorable death scenes in *Antony and Cleopatra, Omega Man* and *Khartoum*; he delivered Marc Antony's famous speech in *Julius Caesar*, he got pissed off at the owner of the pro football team (Cameron Diaz) in *Any Given Sunday* and delivered one of his favorite lines: "I honestly believe that woman would eat her young." And at the end of *Soylent Green,* bloody and beaten, he shouted in futility at the authorities, "Soylent Green is people!"

With so many scenes in his repertoire, I wondered which one stirred him the most. It didn't take him long to come up with the answer. "It was in *El Cid*," he said, "in the scene where his troops take Valencia. We were shooting outside a real 11th-century castle. I led a troop of mounted armored horsemen up the beach. There were at least a thousand people, both inside and outside the gates. They were all screaming 'Cid, Cid, Cid!' I rode through the gate in armor, got off the horse, walked up a 40-foot circular staircase to the top of the wall and turned and watched as they screamed, 'Cid, Cid, Cid!' So I know what it's like to take a city. I really know what it feels like. Better than sex."

56. PORN NEEDS CAREFUL PLANNING

I don't think taking a city would get **David Duchovny's** wood up more than a well-acted porno film featuring a few of his favorite porn stars.

Duchovny once shared a room with John Kennedy Jr. on a class trip to Washington D.C. in 1975, when they were both students at Collegiate Prep School in Manhattan. He studied poetry with Maxine Kumin as an undergrad at Princeton and with Harold Bloom as a grad student at Yale. He had a teaching fellowship and was working toward a doctorate in Modern Literature when a friend introduced him to acting as a way to supplement his income. He left Yale to pursue acting and never looked back.

One might assume that any lesson learned from Duchovny would have something to do with academics, but that is not the case. What I learned from him concerned a baseball bat, therapy, and pornography.

Though I've seen some porn and once interviewed Marilyn Chambers (*Behind the Green Door*), I would consider myself mildly passing through that particular genre. Duchovny, on the other hand, was a serious observer into the seedy side of sideline sex. "Without getting into a discussion about how it demeans women and all that shit," he said when I brought it up, "I like to watch other people fuck. That's the fun part," he explained. "They're doing all the work. My big porn years were the late Eighties. It's like watching sports—it has eras. Was Marilyn Chambers better than Ona Zee? Who knows? The names that will forever be in my pornographic heart are Alicia Monet, Alicia Rio, Amber Lynn, and Ginger Lynn. You know how the movie-going public likes to see Tom Cruise—they like to have a known quantity out there. I was the same way with porn. I was like, 'Who's that nobody? I'm not sure she's good.' Alicia Monet was my favorite. If she only knew how many lonely periods she got me through. I don't think porn stars know how weirdly important they are in people's lives."

Duchovny wasn't only an aficionado of porn stars; he also knew the difference between watching porn in the U.S. and in Canada, where the early seasons of *The X-Files* were shot. "At hotels in Canada you get full porn," he pontificated, "unlike in America, where they cut out all the penetration and private parts, and you just get a shot of the guy from behind, which I don't need to see. When I watched porn, I'd rent three tapes and do reconnaissance work first—I'd fast-forward to see what caught my eye and then I'd catalog it. Then I'd make my choices and go back and watch. But you can't do that in a hotel because the movie won't play again for another eight hours. So if you're masturbating and not just watching, you have to make a decision fast. I had to change my porn-watching habits and commit early. In Vancouver I learned that beyond the initial commitment to the scene where I wanted to get off, I had no control over the moment I got off. Once you go over that edge to an orgasm, you can't pull back. So you give over and then you're at the mercy of the cuts—and all of a sudden you're looking at a guy's sweaty ass and you're coming, and then you're thinking, Oh, my God, I'm questioning my sexuality, because that wasn't half bad."

This was quite a mouthful from Duchovny, and I wondered if he initially got interested in *The X-Files* because he thought it might have been about the porno industry and not extraterrestrials. But I was still a bit flabbergasted thinking about how he would get three porn tapes so he could meticulously plan the outcome of his hand job. That's when I asked him how much time he spent in therapy.

He said six years. "When we were shooting in Vancouver I called him; we did the phone thing," he said. Was he calling to complain about ejaculating over a guy's sweaty ass? Probably, but I didn't ask; I just let him continue. "Each session lasted an hour. I paid for the call, which I didn't think was fair—he should have paid. I'm good on the phone. My view of therapy is that it helps you tell the story of your life to yourself as you're living it, in a way that makes you happier than you might be without it. I don't really believe it's a way of getting to the truth, and I don't believe it can heal you. It teaches you to seize the narrative of your life in a way that makes it better for you. That's what I've gotten out of it. If the greatest artwork in life is the creation of who you are, then it's good to apprentice to a good therapist."

I had always found writing therapeutic, so here again I was learning something from Duchovny. And when I asked him about his fears, he said that after marrying Tea Leoni and thinking of having a family, "My greatest fear is being unable to defend my loved ones." He knew how to use a gun, he said, but didn't have one. However, he did have a baseball bat. "Thirty inches is the best," he informed me. "Thirty-four is a little long because you can't swing it in the doorway."

I, too, had a baseball bat under my bed, but I never thought about swinging it in my doorway. When I got home I told my wife we should rent one of Alicia Monet's films, and then got into a discussion about whether she believed the greatest artwork in life was the creation of yourself. When she saw me attempt to swing my bat in the doorway to our bedroom, she didn't understand when I cursed that it was four inches too long.

"It's Duchovny," I said.

57. DON'T ACT SHOCKED

Listening to what Duchovny said about porn made me think about what I learned when I interviewed **Marilyn Chambers.**

When Playboy Cable said that Marilyn Chambers had agreed to an interview, I had to confess that I had never seen her in action. They got me a copy of *Behind the Green Door* and my wife and I sat together watching this woman getting three men off at the same time while enjoying multiple orgasms of her own. I had to laugh when my wife murmured "Tough job."

When I started thinking about what to ask her, I realized that my questions would be unlike any I had previously considered asking any of the other stars I'd interviewed. Until this assignment I had never even thought about whether French, Italian, American, African or Japanese semen tasted differently. I would never have asked Meryl Streep if she ever fantasized sex with an entire football team. But Marilyn Chambers was given such a fantasy as a birthday gift, so the question was legitimate for her. I wondered what her parents and grandparents thought when they saw her movies. I was curious to learn if the size of the man's penis really mattered to a woman. I thought I could ask her the secret to not choking on a large member. Or find out the Do's and Don'ts regarding anal sex. Was she able to keep sex from getting boring? What were her favorite sex toys? How did she overcome men's erectile dysfunctions, and how hard was it keeping a man hard? Was there such a thing as mental sex that achieved orgasm? How many electric vibrators had she burned through? Did she really own a gun shop in Las Vegas that specialized in machine guns and automatic weapons? Was the Mob involved in the porno industry? How did she lose the 20-carat diamond pussy ring that Sammy Davis Jr. had given her? And what happened to the guy who swallowed it?

Though we had rented a clean, well-lit room at the Hilton Hotel in Universal City to tape, I knew that this was going to be a very dirty interview. How could it not be? She was not just a porn star, but a Porn Queen. Her movies, like *Behind the Green Door, Resurrection of Eve, Insatiable*, and *Up and Coming*, outsold the videocassette sales of Barbra Streisand and Robert Redford films around the world. My director was hoping that she might strip down for the interview, as she had for some of her radio interviews, but that didn't happen. She came dressed in a blue silk blouse and red wool pants. She had a thin gold chain around her neck, a gold bracelet around her wrist, a diamond ring on her finger. Her nails and lips were painted red, and her auburn hair was fluffed like Farrah Fawcett's in her famous swimsuit poster. She looked like she could have posed for the box of Ivory Snow, which, in fact, she once did.

It was a very straightforward conversation that we taped and, if you watched it without the audio, you would think we were talking about the usual things, like her growing up in Westport, Connecticut, being a junior Olympic diver and gymnast, seeing her neighbor Paul Newman driving around in his beat-up VW with a Porsche engine. And we did talk about those things ... for a few minutes, anyway. But if you turned the audio back on, and didn't know what she did for a living, you would have heard a conversation that would have titillated or shocked, depending on your prurient interests.

Among the things I learned from Marilyn Chambers was that, "You can have the most incredible orgasms without ever screwing or touching. It's a mind fuck, but it can be done. I've done it. Laying next to a man and having an orgasm by letting my mind control my body."

And that, "Nobody's ever satisfied with the equipment they come with."

And, "If you can't create suction then it feels like a garage. You have to have suction because that's what gets a guy off. 'Suction, suction, I want suction!' But when you start choking on it, there's a certain breathing technique. You can open your throat, like a sword swallower. It's a certain position. People think that everybody's the same. But everybody's different. Practice makes perfect."

As for vibrators: "They taught me how to have terrific orgasms. Use the kind that plug in. Forget the batteries, God is that frustrating!"

To prevent premature ejaculation: "Apply pressure at the base of the penis."

And when I said I wasn't exactly sure what she meant when she said, "I'm not a fluff girl," she explained: "A fluff girl is somebody who gets a guy up for the scene. A true professional will go in the corner and do it himself. I'm not going to brag, but I usually don't need them."

Oh, and by the way: No, size doesn't matter and Yes, men from different races and countries have different tasting semen.

I did not know a lot of what I heard from this experienced woman and if I had to sum up what I learned in a few words it would be "Don't Act Shocked." Just encourage your subject to talk about her expertise. And when she's done, ask if she's fulfilled a purpose. Here's what Marilyn Chambers answered to that: "What I'm doing has benefitted mankind. I help you visualize your fantasies. That's a very important thing in somebody's love or sex life, because we all have fantasies."

And then she smiled, looked at me with coquettish eyes, and asked, "What's yours?"

58. DON'T GIVE QUAALUDES TO UNDERAGE GIRLS

But of all the conversations I've had dealing with sex, the most troubling was with **Roman Polanski.**

When I went to Poland in the winter of 2009 to promote my novel, *Catch a Fallen Star*, and to serve for the second time as a juror at the Camerimage Film Festival in Lodz, the question most reporters asked me concerned Roman Polanski. At the time, he was under house arrest in Switzerland and the U.S. was trying to have him extradited to stand trial for having sex with a thirteen-year old girl at Jack Nicholson's house in 1977. The question wasn't unexpected, as my publisher had warned me to anticipate such inquiries when I arrived. Polanski is, after all, a very famous Pole. His name has been in and out of the headlines for forty years. Film buffs know him as the director of such films as *Knife in the Water, Repulsion, Rosemary's Baby, Chinatown, The Tenant,* and *The Pianist,* which won him an Academy Award (in absentia). Those who read the newspaper associate him as the husband who lost his pregnant wife, actress Sharon Tate, in a brutal random murder at the hands of the Manson "Family" in 1969. Those who have read his autobiography or other biographies about him know that he lost his mother at the hands of the Nazis in Auschwitz. Tragedy seems to have followed Polanski like a shadow.

Though he lives in Paris and has a vacation home in Gstaad, Switzerland, the Poles see him as one of their own, and most are very forgiving when it comes to his transgressions. Regarding his rape charge, they see the situation differently: True, the girl was a minor, but she was already regularly sexually active with her boyfriend. Her mother allowed her to go off to be photographed by Polanski. The broken Quaalude he gave her was not something she hadn't tried before. The champagne they drank, again, nothing new. Her resistance in Nicholson's hot tub, as they frolicked naked together, was minor—she said "Don't" and he said, "Go into the other room and lie down." And she did.

I interviewed Polanski in his Paris apartment in 1987, while I was doing research for my book about the Huston family. I wanted to talk to him about directing John Huston in *Chinatown,* but also about the "rape" incident, because Anjelica Huston was in Nicholson's house at the time, being Jack's then girlfriend. When the police later came to investigate, they found some cocaine in Anjelica's purse, and in exchange for not pressing charges against her, she had agreed to testify against Polanski. It wasn't one of her better moments, and I wondered how Polanski felt about it.

"I couldn't really blame her for accepting the deal," Polanski told me, "though it left me feeling slightly bitter. From her point of view, she didn't do anything wrong. I thought she did, then...but now I don't."

What made him bitter was that with Anjelica being able to place him at the scene of the alleged crime, it fortified the District Attorney's case against Polanski. The grand jury indicted him on six counts: furnishing a controlled substance to a minor, committing a lewd or lascivious act, having unlawful sexual intercourse, perversion, sodomy, and rape by use of drugs.

Anjelica Huston felt "completely innocent" and confessed that it was extremely hurtful for her. "I felt maligned and ill done," she said. "And the fact that it was printed in newspapers that I was prepared to testify against Roman was the worst part of the whole episode. You don't testify for or against anyone. When you testify you tell the truth, which is what I'd have done. The fact that it was printed in that way made me look not only unattractive but also a sneak."

John Huston admired Polanski's work as a director. He told me, "There was no question, after three days seeing him operate [during *Chinatown*], that here was a really top talent." But when it came to Polanski's fleeing the country before being sentenced on the charges he was indicted for, Huston drew the line. "He did something against the law and he skipped bail. I wish that he hadn't done that." When I asked him if he felt that way even if it meant going to prison, Huston responded, "If necessary, sure. Why not?"

Polanski couldn't fathom going to prison for having what he considered consensual sex with a young, mature girl. "I was incredulous," he said. "I couldn't equate what had happened with rape in any form. It was just sex."

Polanski was generous with his time when I saw him in Paris, and he was friendly and affable when I saw him again in 2007 when he had come to be honored at the Camerimage Film Festival in Poland. He definitely had a "European" take on the joys of sex and couldn't quite grasp the puritanical thinking of the American judicial system.

So, how was I to respond to reporters who wanted to know what I thought about his situation? Should he be sent back in handcuffs to stand before a judge and finally be sentenced, 32 years after the deed? John Huston thought he should have manned up. But Polanski's lawyers felt that their client had been betrayed by the judge, who had agreed to sentence him to time served and then changed his mind the day before Polanski was to stand before him. Polanski felt he had been lied to. He had agreed to be psychoanalyzed in prison for 42 days and to abide by the findings of that analysis. But when that analyst advocated he be released on time served, the judge decided not to abide. So Polanski got on a plane and never looked back.

It was complicated. When I first answered the question in Poland, I mentioned that I had two daughters, and if a 44-year-old man had given one of them a Quaalude and had her wash it down with champagne, then asked her to undress and get into a hot tub to pose for pictures, and then go to another room to have sex, I would not want such a man to escape justice. But wasn't Polanski already punished by his actions? Wasn't he deprived of working in the U.S., of living the Hollywood life? Of ever working in England as well? Didn't he have a teenage daughter with Emmanuelle Seigner (who had married him when she was 18 and he was 51)? And how would he explain himself to her? Wasn't that, too, a form of punishment? Polanski was 76 years old. He had a tragic family history, later had made a mistake and consequently was denied access to the great Hollywood movie-making machinery. For over thirty years his actions had been ignored. But now, with a new District Attorney in Los Angeles, the justice system was coming after him for its pound of flesh.

What did I think should be his fate? I was asked this in Warsaw, in Krakow, and even in Lodz. I hemmed and hawed. I said I believed in justice, but I wasn't sure exactly what that was anymore. The young girl he had sex with was now a woman in her forties. Polanski had paid her a half million dollars from a civil suit. She felt he should be left alone, that he had already paid a dear price for his actions. Polanski found support from fellow filmmakers like Mike Nichols, Woody Allen, Neil Jordan, Martin Scorsese, Pedro Almodovar, and Steven Soderbergh, who joined writers Salman Rushdie and Milan Kundera, and French president Nicolas Sarkozy. They all signed petitions asking that the Swiss courts free him immediately and not turn him "into a martyr of a politico-legal imbroglio that is unworthy of two democracies like Switzerland and the United States."

In the end, I came to the conclusion that there was no "correct" answer. The prosecutors and the judge had made mistakes, just as Polanski had made mistakes in judgment. So, not wanting to offend a nation that idolizes Polanski, I finally told reporters, "I don't know what to say about Roman Polanski, other than to think twice before you give an underage girl a Quaalude before joining her in a Jacuzzi." I continued by bringing it home. "In my novel, there's a scene in which the ten-year-old daughter of my main character is sexually molested by an actor the same age Polanski was when he committed his sexual act. I dealt with the guy by having the mother of the young girl stab him with a penknife and then run him over with her car. He doesn't die, but winds up a cripple.

When he gets out of the hospital, my main character sees him at an outdoor restaurant with a young boy; he sends the boy away and pummels the actor, who was his best friend, knocking him out of his wheelchair. But that's fiction for you. It's nowhere as convoluted as real life."

Find Common Ground

Most of us can remember the early influences of our lives–the books, magazines, essays, poems, movies, and television shows that pushed our brains along a certain path. For me, the magazine was *Mad*, the TV shows were *The Ernie Kovaks Show* and *The Honeymooners,* the essays were often written by Norman Mailer, the poems were by Robert Frost and T.S. Eliot, the books were *The Catcher in the Rye, A Portrait of the Artist as a Young Man, Siddhartha,* and *The Ginger Man*, and the movies were two of Brando's best, *On the Waterfront* and *A Streetcar Named Desire.*

These influences gave me a strong desire to experience the world. I knew from an early age that I wanted to be a writer, and that a writer needed material to write about, and that material is what existed out there in places I didn't yet know. *Mad* magazine gave me a sense of irony and satire. Ernie Kovaks showed me the absurd. Jackie Gleason's Ralph Kramden taught me about reaching beyond one's circumstances, always looking for that brass ring, and never accepting falling short as failure. Mailer wrote essays that were smart, thoughtful, controversial, and tough. Frost articulated the decisions we all face regarding the less-traveled roads. Eliot introduced J. Alfred Prufrock and all his doubts and insecurities leading to making real decisions. Other characters, like Holden Caulfield, saw the phoniness all around him. Stephen Daedalus made the decision to follow his dream and not do what was expected of him. Siddhartha rejected the easy life for one of contemplation. Sebastian Dangerfield refused to let the bank clerks and debt-collectors get in his way. Terry Malloy in *Waterfront* refused to be bullied. And Stanley Kowalski in *Streetcar* was brash and ballsy, shouting in the face of bullshit, yet with an inherent sensitivity for the woman he loved.

In high school I wrote poetry and submitted it to magazines like *The Atlantic, The New Yorker* and *Esquire*. None of them were accepted and all of them got rejection slips that I pinned to a corkboard on my wall. I wasn't being a masochist; those slips only made me more determined. In college I wrote a novel and put it in a drawer because it wasn't good enough, but it didn't make me think of becoming a lawyer or doctor; it served as a reminder that I needed more life experience. Upon graduation I decided against graduate school and joined the Peace Corps, where I wound up being sent to West Africa for three life-changing years.

59. FIGURING OUT LIFE'S PUZZLES

When I interview people, I often get into conversations about influences, but until I sat with **Oliver Stone**, I hadn't met anyone who spoke about the same writers, magazines and films as the ones that meant so much to me. These similarities formed our liberal values and made us highly skeptical about the way things were reported vs. the way things really were.

When Stone told me that he wrote a novel when he was twenty and put it away for thirty years because it wasn't as good as the writers he was trying to emulate—J.P. Donleavy, Norman Mailer, Joseph Conrad and James Joyce—I couldn't help interjecting that I had done the same thing. When he said that he developed a thick skin from all the rejections he kept and filed away, I told him about my corkboard of rejection slips. He understood the need to seek experience and that's why he dropped out of Yale to teach in Vietnam. I went from UCLA to teach in Ghana. What we had in common was a desire to seek experience in order to develop our creativity.

As we walked down the corridor leading to his office, I noticed the walls were lined with framed posters of the 18 movies he had written and/or directed. "If you believed what you were reading in those days," Stone said, "a man had to test himself in life. That was the way I accepted it. I was more interested in knowing more about life, because I was puzzled by life. What drove me was Conrad's concept of something being mysterious out there, something that I had to understand that I had never understood.

"My mind was in search of adventure and experience. Experience was the only way I could authenticate myself, because I grew up in a family where I had certain things given to me, like the Buddha. He grew up sheltered, and his mother and father tried to keep him away from anything ugly for many years. And then one day, by accident, he saw an old man, and he thought that was horrible, because old people had been kept away from him. He went out into the world, and his father went crazy, his father wanted him to inherit the kingdom, to be a prince, to have all the riches, and he walked away from it to follow the path that had come to him. It's a very startling story.

"I'm driven by my own inner drives. I've had failure and success. I've had derision and applause in equal measures. If that happens to you enough in your lifetime, you begin to realize the illusion that it is. It's a ploy. Once you accept that as an illusion, it only becomes about your interior consciousness and achieving what your *you* is. That's all it is, it seems to me."

I could relate to what Stone said because I felt the same way. I had my share of failure and success, with the former far outweighing the latter. But I also learned more from the failures because they challenged me to reevaluate what I was trying to create and whether or not it was worthy. I learned that failure is only crushing when you accept it; otherwise, it's a great motivator. That's when your inner drive kicks in. When you begin to understand what your *you* is.

"If I were to do any honest mathematical assessment of all the efforts I've made in film and in life, most of them would be misses," Stone said. "Many scripts, ideas, and developments went down the tubes. But I learned from the failures. You can find a thousand rejections in my files, and there must have been another 12,000 from phone calls. I've had so much rejection that I don't get bothered too much when somebody turns me down or somebody disses me. What kept me going was my conviction that if I could ever fucking see the daylight, and I was past thirty, that I could become the filmmaker I wanted to be. And what I was learning would come in handy then. And it was true. I'm developing as an artist, but it's certainly a slow go."

I didn't go down the same road as Stone, though we both struggled in our chosen professions. Our family backgrounds were too dissimilar: his parents divorced when he was fourteen and attending boarding school. His father warned him not to trust anyone. His mother took him to a nudist colony. He went from teaching in Vietnam to enlisting in the Army so he could join the war effort. When he returned from Vietnam he dropped acid and got busted for grass, winding up in prison in San Diego for a few weeks before a lawyer could bail him out. Eventually he managed to enroll in film school at NYU and studied with Martin Scorsese. And there, he found his calling.

I used to complain to my parents that they were too normal. I didn't suffer from a broken family. My father once warned me against joining a civil rights protest march in Mississippi, but I ignored him. My mother didn't want me to smoke pot but I managed to convince her to try it. I avoided the draft and would have fled the country before being forced to wear a uniform and learn to shoot innocent people.

I could talk to Stone about my life as he explained his and in the end we found that our conversations went deep—*Movieline* published it over two consecutive issues –because we had enough in common at the outset that we felt comfortable exchanging our life stories. It didn't hurt that I had spent time with some of his heroes, like Norman Mailer, John Huston, J.P. Donleavy and Marlon Brando. It made it that much easier to relate. Especially when we both thought the world of Alfred E. Neuman.

60. JAMES JOYCE MAKES YOU SMARTER
James Franco showed little of the intellect that Oliver Stone displayed, but I was able to discover one writer we had in common.

The few hours I spent with James Franco for a *Movieline* cover story left an impression that he wasn't very bright and somewhat obnoxious. In retrospect, I was wrong about his not being very bright. In the years since we talked, Franco has become something of a Renaissance man. He received B.A. and M.A. degrees from UCLA, Columbia, NYU, Brooklyn College, Warren Wilson College, and is a Ph.D in English candidate at Yale. He taught courses in filmmaking and screenwriting at NYU, USC and at UCLA. He has published a novel, a volume of poetry, and a collection of short stories. He got involved in the avant-garde art scene (including doing something with Paul McCarthy). He had a solo exhibition of his videos, drawings and sculptures at the Clocktower Gallery in New York. He (poorly) cohosted the 2011 Academy Awards show with Anne Hathaway. He appeared in a cult TV show (*Freaks and Geeks*) and starred in a number of intense and well-acted films (including *Howl, 127 Hours, Milk*, and *The Rise of the Planet of the Apes*). He directed a number of short films and a feature docudrama about poet Hart Crane. He made his Broadway debut in John Steinbeck's *Of Mice and Men*. And he and Seth Rogan pissed off the North Korean government in 2014 to the point where sanctions and even war was threatened (*The Interview*).

But that all happened after we talked, when I told him that someone might someday do an in-depth interview with him, but it wouldn't be me. Why not me? Because I found his responses to my questions inane, indifferent, and uninteresting. Many of his answers were not even answers, just a shrug, a smile, and the word "Nah."

I asked him what role challenged him the most in his career. He answered "Nah," and turned his face sideways.

I asked him about his experience appearing in *Spider-Man*. "Nah, don't ask," he answered.

Did he relate to James Dean, whom he had portrayed in a biography and won a Golden Globe for his performance? "Nah, I don't know."

Did he at least learn something from studying Dean? "Keep it real," he said. But that wasn't even his answer. It was what Dean once told Dennis Hopper, who passed on the advice to Franco. When I tried to get him to talk about himself, he said, "As an actor it's probably not to one's benefit to be overexposed. If you want to play different parts, you don't want to reveal too much of your personal life. It's defining."

It was a frustrating interview, trying to get something out of the tight-lipped James Franco. But I remembered that in an earlier published interview with him, the writer noted that he had a copy of James Joyce's *A Portrait of the Artist as a Young Man*. So I asked him about that.

"I've read most of Joyce," he said.

"Including *Ulysses*?" I asked.

"Yeah, and I read *Finnegans Wake*. Or at least some of it."

We didn't go into too much detail about this because the clock was ticking and I had to make sure I asked him about things that most movie magazine readers wanted to know. James Joyce wasn't one of them. But Joyce is a bellwether writer for me. I don't know many actors who have read him. And just that Franco gave *Finnegans Wake* a shot should have simmered my cynicism about his intelligence.

When I think about Freddie Prinze, Jr., who didn't read books, and Chris O'Donnell, who hardly ever read books, and James Franco, who liked to read and write books, I have to conclude that Franco has had the most interesting and diverse career of the three. Franco would most likely get along well with the very fine actress Julianne Moore, who credited books for her career. "It was the experience of reading that made me an actor," Moore has said, "—the feeling of being so enmeshed in a narrative, of feeling like you were inside a book."

So this was a lesson that didn't set in until many years after our interview, but I see it clearly now. Knowledge of James Joyce makes you smarter.

61. PLAY THEIR SPORT

J. P. Donleavy not only had knowledge of James Joyce, he lived in a stone house where Joyce once visited, and he wrote his first book, *The Ginger Man*, borrowing one of the styles Joyce used in *Ulysses*.

When I was teaching at UCLA, I often turned my students on to *The Ginger Man*. Most of them had never heard of Donleavy; as a college student, neither had I, until one of my professors thought I might like his work. I did, and became a lifelong fan. So, when I began doing interviews for *Newsday*, I convinced my editor that Donleavy was a worthy subject. Off I went to his 180 acre Irish estate in Mullingar, an hour's drive north of Dublin. Donleavy was born in the Bronx, but once he started earning money from his books, he moved to Ireland because artists didn't pay taxes on their earnings.

He said the primary creative interest of his youth was art, but he knew he wasn't going to become famous as a painter, so he decided to write *The Ginger Man*, a novel that he felt would do the trick. It did, but it also involved him in litigation for a good part of his life. He sold the novel to Maurice Girodias's Olympia Press in France, which published it in their pornographic Traveller's Companion series. Donleavy was outraged, and defied the contract he had signed by selling the novel to American and British publishers. Girodias sued him. Donleavy subsequently wrote a book about *The History of the Ginger Man,* detailing the labyrinth of legal battles involved with the book. It also gave him the seed for his second novel, *A Singular Man*. "The whole life of litigation and how it affects somebody and the intimidations involved are part of that book," he told me. Though he has written 18 other books and five plays, none captured the public's imagination like *The Ginger Man*.

The book has had numerous printings; the most recent being by Lilliput Press, honoring the 60th anniversary since it first appeared in 1955. Johnny Depp wrote the introduction, saying "There is nothing quite like *The Ginger Man*, an uproarious, pioneering masterpiece; a bedeviled, timeless jewel of scandalous misdeeds, hurled upon a people who, at the time, were psychologically unequipped to receive such a liberating statement that both charmed and repelled in equal measure. Mad, wanton youth at its most honest, brutal, hilarious, evocative and insubordinate best." He correctly pinned the main character, Sebastian Dangerfield, as "the prime candidate for patron saint of incorrigible, debauched but conversely loveable bastards." And he credited the novel as a forerunner to Hunter S. Thompson's *Fear and Loathing in Las Vegas* and Bruce Robinson's *Withnail & I*. Oliver Stone was also a huge fan of the novel and recognized Donleavy as a big influence of his youth.

While Donleavy's characters are often audacious and outrageous, the man himself is soft-spoken and somewhat shy. He told me that Henry Miller was one of his favorite writers. He showed me his study on the second floor and the Hermes portable typewriter he still used. He was proud of his thirty-foot long indoor swimming pool, where he swam each day to keep in shape. "I have to literally train like an athlete, just to keep myself alive," he said. "It's a very debilitating way of life, being an author. Just sitting there is very bad for the body." We talked about De Alfonce tennis, a sport he invented and would write a book about. And we played Ping Pong, a sport in which he excelled.

As we played, he showed me no mercy. He had a wicked wrist-twisting serve that made the Ping Pong ball curve in different directions. It was almost impossible to return until one got used to it, and by that time the score was heavily in his favor. No one likes to lose every game played, but in this case I was glad—in retrospect—I did. As I had bragged a bit about my own table tennis prowess before we started, his victories put a smile on his face and changed his mood from being wary with a journalist to opening up about his writing life. He employed five people who took care of his working farm as he spent half of each day pounding out two or three hundred words. It wasn't easy and it wasn't much fun, he admitted. But it was the price he paid to live in a two-story stone house that felt like a castle, in a place as far from the Bronx as one could conceive. And it afforded him the luxury to continue to probe his extremely fertile and raucous imagination.

"When you're working on a book you don't get any pleasure at all," Donleavy said, as we relaxed in his living room after our games. "It's very grueling writing it; not that it's an implacable grimness, but you're working at it, so you never get a chance to sit down and enjoy it. Words are tough to handle. Each day you're constantly struggling. You wake up and you're trying to find new words. It's an unending business. You very rarely find yourself sitting around and enjoying yourself. For instance, if you take a walk in the rose garden out there, you sometimes catch yourself up a whiff of roses to your nostrils and suddenly you have to remind yourself that that's to be enjoyed.

"I came across something that Franz Kafka wrote about being a writer, that it somehow wrenched you out of the kind of contemporary world that people knew. You unpleasantly had to be torn from this human compatibility that other people enjoy. I think this is, regrettably, true. You can't live like other people. And I don't suppose that any author wants to admit that this is true, finally, because it makes him appear to be such a difficult thing, and people are *always* trying to appear pleasant and acceptable to the world. But I think this is the case whether one likes it or not. It's not a very happy way of life, except that you don't seek other ways of life. I can't describe my life as being particularly unhappy, except that I am aware that this other part of it does exist; that you literally tend to isolate yourself, and you proceed in what appears to be a very unhappy existence. I'm aware that people who have office jobs, working with their associates, it's a pretty bloodcurdling, tough, harsh, debilitating way of life. But other than working cutting grass in Woodlawn Cemetery as a young man, I never had a job."

For a man who has been called a recluse, I credit Ping-Pong for the frank talk that followed, and for a lifelong friendship with one of my writing heroes. So, play their sport. There's no way you can lose.

62. HAVE STORIES TO TRADE

But if you don't know their sport, find something else you might have in common, as I did with **Alex Haley**. What we had in common was the *Playboy* Interview. Haley conducted nine of them before finding his *Roots*. I've done four dozen. We had a very particular profession in common, and a lot to talk about when it came to discussing our adventures in the interview trade.

Haley's failed attempt at profiling Miles Davis in 1961 led to his coming up with the idea of turning it into a question-and-answer, and the *Playboy* Interview was born. He would go on to interview Malcolm X, Martin Luther King, George Lincoln Rockwell, Cassius Clay, Johnny Carson, Melvin Belli and Sammy Davis Jr. before writing two culturally significant books, *The Autobiography of Malcolm X* and *Roots*.

Before we discussed the phenomenal success of those books, we shared what we had in common: doing *Playboy* interviews. When I asked him what he had learned from them he said, "That most people would like to be better understood." I agreed, though not necessarily the case when it came to politicians, who basically wanted to make sure they didn't say anything that might hurt their chances for re-election.

He agreed with me when I said that I had learned that a good interviewer must exhibit a chameleon-like personality, be fully prepared, and have self-confidence. Then he added that an interviewer is really like a surgeon, "You may disagree violently with what that patient believes philosophically, but your job is to perform surgery the best you can." He also felt that an interviewer shouldn't look for any particular answer or quote, "because you'll never find it. It will be something that you will happen upon."

That led to specific examples. When he tried to establish rapport with a recalcitrant Miles Davis he went to the Harlem gym where Davis worked out and watched him go through his boxing routine. "He knew I was there," Haley said, "and one day he came up to me with his hands on his hips and jerked his head toward the ring. The invitation was clear: get in the ring with him or forget any hope of an interview. So I got in the ring, though it didn't last all that long." This reminded me of being with Al Pacino at his home in Sneden's Landing when he was preparing for *Scarface*. He had hired a trainer to work him out at a nearby park and invited me to join him. So I borrowed a pair of his sneakers and wound up doing 30, 50, and 100 yard sprints with him, running at half speed for two miles, and then doing ten standing jumps onto an upturned garbage bin. I could hardly breathe when we finished, but the talk flowed later that day.

With Malcolm X and Johnny Carson, Haley needed to find the right question to unlock their emotions. "I was uptight with Malcolm because he kept going on about the Nation of Islam and his leader, Mr. Elijah Muhammad, and I just asked him to tell me something about his mother. At the time he was up walking and he stopped as if someone had jerked a string to him. He looked at me and I knew that I had touched some button within him. He began to talk again, but more slowly. And when he spoke his voice was up a notch. 'It's funny you'd ask me that,' he said. 'I can remember the kind of dresses she used to wear. They were always faded and gray. And I remember she was always bent over the stove, trying to stretch what little we had.' It was 11:30 at night and that man walked that floor until daybreak and spilling out of him came the first chapter of *The Autobiography of Malcolm X*. And after that night Malcolm was never, ever reluctant to talk."

The same was true with Johnny Carson, he said. "A very collected, cool person, difficult to reach. We were at the Hotel Bel-Air and he was giving his conventional responses, but then we got to talking about his having left Nebraska and that got him to open up. He was in school there and was peripherally running a little radio station—he was everything from general manager to janitor. He told me how he used to spin records and how he would think about wanting to do television shows and a great revelation came to him—that what he wanted to do was not in Nebraska. As he was telling me this he became nostalgic. He began dragging his words, remembering."

I responded to these stories with ones of my own dealing with Barbra Streisand and Henry Fonda. With Streisand, I had to reestablish her trust. Each time I saw her it took nearly an hour for her to warm up to me until finally I convinced her that I wouldn't write anything until we both agreed the interview was finished. With Fonda, he was ill and tight-lipped until I brought up an incident with his son Peter that got him to react heatedly. But it also broke the ice and allowed him to talk more freely about things he had previously repressed.

When Haley first went to interview Cassius Clay, he found the young champion "very cunning. He would do things to put you off as an interviewer. I'd ask him a question and he'd appear to be asleep. This was very disconcerting." Haley found the key in Clay's childhood, about a time when he missed the school bus and wound up running alongside it all the way to school as the kids in the bus cheered. "That taught him something: Always perform—do whatever you do to make people watch you. And that is what he used both in and out of the ring."

For me, the person who was most disconcerting was Elliott Gould, who kept answering my questions with the word "Information," until I broke through by suggesting I come back another day and he insisted we continue.

Haley told me how he once brought Jim Brown and Muhammad Ali (by then he had changed his name from Cassius Clay) together and Brown told Haley that he could outbox Ali "because what Ali doesn't know is how fast I am," and then Ali told Haley, "I would have to win because Jim Brown thinks I don't know how fast he is." So then I told Haley how I once was in Steve Martin's house with Al Pacino and Marty Klein, who managed both of them at the time. Martin and Pacino didn't know each other and to break the ice Klein said, "Larry, you've interviewed both these guys, who's the better interview?"

That led Haley to reminisce about how Martin Luther King Jr. and Malcolm X would each ask him about the other: What did King think about Malcolm and what did Malcolm think about King. And I told Haley how Streisand, Lily Tomlin, and Truman Capote wanted to know what Marlon Brando had to say about them.

The interview Haley was most proud of was the one he did with the head of the American Nazi Party, George Lincoln Rockwell. "Because I learned most about how an interviewer needs to be detached from the subject and even be hospitable to what the subject may say and feel, because your job is to communicate to the reader what that person feels. Rockwell was a graduate of Brown University. He had become a Lieutenant Commander in the Navy. He'd been a jet pilot and commanding officer of a pursuit squad. No matter what you thought, you couldn't be stupid if you'd done those things. He wasn't sure he wanted to do this interview but felt he could use the exposure. He called to ask me a personal question: 'Are you a Jew?' I quickly said, 'No, sir.' Well, when I turned up there was a very shocked set of Nazi people! [*Laughs*] It just never occurred to them that I was black. Rockwell was a darkly handsome, angry man. Very angry. Had on a white shirt with dark trousers. He flung his fingers right in my face, almost on my nose, his face mottled with anger. 'I'm going to tell you right now,' he said, 'we call your kind niggers and we think you should all be shipped to Africa.' Somehow a calm descended on me, right at that moment, and I said to him, 'I've been called nigger before and this time I'm being paid very well for it, so now you go ahead and tell me whatever you've got against us.' And that was how the interview began."

The closest I've come to trying to interview a bigot was with Robert Mitchum, but that happened after I spoke with Haley.

We traded stories about the person whom we were most disappointed with: his was Bishop Pike, who "never answered a single question. He just talked in circles." Mine was Robert De Niro, who didn't want to talk about anything personal, and when he was asked for an opinion, gave contradictory answers to almost every question.

I asked him whom he would not have wanted to interview and he answered Henry Kissinger, "because of the way he speaks in oblique ways. He won't come right out and answer something, because of the innate political strategist that he is." I offered up two people that I had turned down when my editor suggested them: Clint Eastwood and Stephen King. This was before Eastwood had started directing, and his con-servative outlook didn't sound like someone I wanted to spend a lot of time with. (At that time in my career, I could pick and choose whomever I wanted to interview). With King, I knew I would have to read a lot of his work and I tried with *The Stand* and only got halfway through (still, 400 pages!) and just didn't want to spend months reading a half dozen others. As I write this now I think I should have made the effort for both of them.

Haley told me that when he met other interviewers at the Playboy Mansion in Chicago, they would spend time asking each other about the perfect question. "The one question I got out of that," he said, "was if you were talking to a married cou-ple, ask each of them if they remember the first time they ever set eyes on the other. It always evokes a response." I told Haley that I had one stock question I asked, which was: If you could live inside of any painting, which would you choose? (I always thought there was a good book there, showing the painting and the response to it.)

I don't know if trading such stories qualifies as learning experiences, but it was enlightening in its own way. However, the actual lesson came when we began talking about *Roots*. He had done nine years of research about the Afro-American experience from 1750 on, and wasn't sure how to handle it, until he read a book written by a young Jewish girl who wrote it while hiding in an attic in Amsterdam. "The most effective book that came out of the whole Third Reich was *The Diary of Anne Frank*," he said. "So I thought, how can I tell about what happened to millions of Africans? Let me strip it down to one, Kunta Kinte, this little boy that my grandmother had told me about. Let me let him be born on page one, so the reader can watch him come into the world, and then deal with him day after day after day."

Then he explained how he needed the proper atmosphere to write different sections of the book. Haley had spent twenty years in the Coast Guard where he honed his writing skills by penning love letters for fellow sailors. While most writers would probably get nauseous trying to write a book at sea, Haley felt he could "talk" to his characters on board a Norwegian freighter that sailed from Long Beach, California down South America and back. "I wrote the first third of *Roots* on that freighter," he said. "That's what I love about going to sea—you're isolated, you can talk to people by yourself." But his room on the freighter was too comfortable for him to write Kunta Kinte's experience after he was captured and dropped into the hole of the slave ship that brought him to America. So he returned to his apartment in San Francisco and tried imagining what that might have been like. "It was atrocious. I kept throwing the pages out. I felt I had to do something physically to help me better understand what he was going through. So I went to Africa and found a ship called *The African Star*, sailing from Monrovia, Liberia, to Jacksonville, Florida. I got on as a passenger and found that they had cargo with one hatch that wasn't sealed off. It was only half filled with bales of raw rubber, and after dinner I would slip down in that hatch undetected. It was dark, eerie, dank, and I took off my clothing to my underwear and just lay down on my back on these big planks, trying to imagine that I was Kunta on the slave ship. I did this for two nights and caught a good, rousing cold. On the third night I couldn't make myself go down into that hole. Instead, I walked like a zombie to the stern of the ship and stood there. I had my foot up on the bottom rail, hands on the top rail. It was dark, but you could see the iridescence that happens behind a ship. And all my troubles came in on me standing there by myself. All my debts. It seemed I owed everybody I could think of. And I knew that almost everybody I knew was beginning to laugh at me about the book, that I'd never finish it. The publisher wasn't happy; I wasn't either. It was just such a low point in my life. Then a simple thought came to me: all I had to do was step through that rail and drop in the sea and it would be over. I wasn't alarmed; it came almost as a sense of relief. Then I had an experience that I've never had since: I heard people talking who I knew were behind me somewhere, and they were saying things like, 'No, don't do that, you must go on and finish.' And I knew exactly who they were: my grandmother, Chicken George, my great grandfather, Miss Kizzy, her father—the African. They were all the people that I had been writing about. And I had a wrenching sense that I had to get away from the stern of that ship. I turned myself around and went scuttling back amidships like a crab, because I didn't want to go near the rail on either side. I got back to my little room and pitched down head first on my narrow bunk and I cried. I don't think I cried like that since I was a baby. It was a purging. Then I got up about midnight, and went down the hole and lay back down again in my underwear and began to feel, for the first time, not guilty. I made notes like crazy and wrote out what I had scribbled the next morning. And that's how I wrote the section of *Roots* where Kunta is in the slave ship."

Haley was a rare interview for me, the only person I've ever interviewed who was also once an interviewer. It was fun trading stories with him, and that definitely helped open him up. And I learned how dedicated a writer must be to turn a good idea into a great book. I also learned that the drive for realism can lead to suicidal thoughts and long, lonely nights sleeping naked on a wooden plank in the hull of a freighter.

63. DON'T BE AFRAID TO CHALLENGE UP FRONT

Like Haley, I had a major turning point in my life when I found the strength to risk everything and stand up to Barbra Streisand, my first *Playboy* assignment, but publication was delayed because I promised I wouldn't turn it in until we both agreed we were done talking. Consequently, I had time to do another interview for *Playboy* in the interim, this one with **Henry Winkler**. At the time, Winkler was the biggest rage on television, playing The Fonz on the sit-com *Happy Days*. He was so popular that no less an actor than George C. Scott told him to enjoy his success because he might never again get another role as high profile as that one. However, *Playboy* wasn't sure that Winkler was worthy of the full interview treatment, and told me that we could do a smaller ten or twenty question interview with him and, if that seemed promising, extend it to the full blown front-of-the-book interview. That was a challenge to me. I didn't want to do small, hidden interviews for the magazine. I wanted the big ones. Winkler was one of those borderline figures—high public profile, but certainly not iconic like Streisand, or newsworthy like James Earl Ray.

When I went to meet him in his dressing room at Paramount studios, he had just returned from a vacation in Bora Bora and was getting ready to star in his first movie, *Heroes*. I was able to relate to him because he knew one of my best friends when they were both at Yale so we were able to start off smoothly. I could feel his energy as he spoke about transitioning from TV to films, but I felt I had to be honest with him and let him know that the magazine was considering running a smaller interview with him, rather than the regular in-depth *Playboy* Interview. That took some of the wind out of his sails. He wasn't expecting to be reduced in size, not at this peak in his life. He was the highest paid actor on TV; he had just been the King of New Orleans Mardi Gras, with a million people shouting his name as he floated by in his silver-lame 15th Century Venetian costume; and major stars were asking for his autograph for their kids.

"What do I have to do to be the main interview?" he asked me. "Say I fucked Mary Gitler in the fifth grade?"

"That would certainly be a start," I laughed.

"Well, just ask me anything you like, let's make this happen."

Those were magic words. I asked him about the importance of being Fonzie and how his life had changed. We talked about the groupies and the security, the 56,000 letters he received every week, the sensation of feeling God-like, John Travolta on *Welcome Back, Kotter* imitating his Fonzie character, and separating his real self from his fictional self. We discussed the importance and the pitfalls of being Number One, having a greater impact on young men than Al Pacino, Robert De Niro, and Dustin Hoffman combined, not doing commercials and not wearing jeans, marketing his name, and becoming a millionaire. We even covered his sexual fantasies, his childhood, the problems with his father, smoking weed, and attending Yale.

We talked in his dressing room, at his home in Studio City, and on the *Heroes* movie set in Santa Rosa. We smoked a joint after I agreed not to mention it in the interview. And in the end, *Playboy* published the long-form interview in August 1977. The Fonz had proven worthy. And so had I. What we had in common was the conviction that we deserved to be treated front and center and not as a sidebar. And by discussing it openly, our talk became a collaboration that worked to our mutual benefit.

64. DEALING WITH BIG EGOS: FLATTERY WILL GET YOU SOMEWHERE

I had to dig deep into my past to find common ground when I interviewed **Jerry Lewis.** He had said things in *his* past that he didn't want brought up again—like when he once told a reporter that he would rather have had his son returned from Vietnam in a coffin to his coming home addicted to drugs, a devastating remark that no future interviewer could ignore. He was also sick and tired of being asked about his inner connection with muscular dystrophy and why he devoted so much energy each year to put on such a charitable telethon. So that left me with a real dilemma.

The French loved Jerry Lewis more than his own countrymen, though that wasn't always the case. When he teamed with Dean Martin, they made a dynamic duo that brought them wealth and fame. When he made the decision to ditch Dean and go on his own, his fans saw a different side of him. He was no longer the spastic goofball playing off the suave, handsome crooner, but a hardened business person with a huge ego, convinced that he was the soul of their act and could carry on with the same adulation as before. But Lewis without Martin was like Laurel minus Hardy, Costello without Abbott, Groucho missing Harpo and Chico. He didn't exactly disappear. In fact, he became an innovative filmmaker, directing and starring in such classic movies as *The Bell Boy* and *The Nutty Professor*. Nonetheless, he was no longer a media darling, and when he allowed journalists in to profile him, they wrote about his quirkiness, like how he never wore the same sweater twice, or how he once set fire to a toilet. Lewis felt that he was no longer beloved and all actors, especially comic actors, have a need to be loved.

When I met him at his office in Century City he saw me as an antagonist before any words were exchanged. The first thing he did was take a small tape recorder from a drawer, place it on his desk, and let me know that everything he said would be on his recorder as well as mine, so that "when" I misquoted him, he would be able to go to his tape and prove whatever inaccuracies I put out to the public. "I do this," he said, "because I've been fucked by reporters in the past and I don't like getting fucked."

"Not a problem," I responded, though it was certainly an unexpected curve. "Mae West wouldn't let me use a tape recorder because she thought I might fuck her by turning it into a record. I much prefer the accuracy that a recorded conversation provides. I have no intention of twisting your words."

"We'll see about that," he said. Then he got up from his desk, picked up a golf club he kept nearby, walked around to the middle of his large office and started swinging the club. I saw it as a not-so-subtle warning. He was doing his best to intimidate me, and he was starting to succeed.

I knew that I had to change the atmosphere in the room because if one of my questions ticked him off, and if he happened to have the club in his hand when I asked it, he might go beyond a verbal response to deflect his answer. I knew that when there's tension in the room *before* an interview gets underway, it's not going to get better unless the subject can be put at ease. In this case, given the golf club and the negative history with reporters, I felt a time-out was necessary. So I broke character. I stopped being a journalist and turned into a fan.

"You know, Jerry," I said, "when I was a kid I had my tonsils removed and the doctor told me that I should refrain from talking or using my throat for a week or I would be sore and uncomfortable. I was only eight years old and remember how, after the operation, my father wrapped me in a blanket and carried me to his car. When I got home, my parents gave me ice cream and said that I could have all that I wanted, since it would soothe my throat. They also allowed me to recover by letting me watch TV all day, and what I most remember is watching your old Martin & Lewis films and laughing so hard that I was sore for two weeks."

Lewis put down his golf club, returned to his side of the desk, and looked at me in a softer, more benevolent way. I had resorted to flattery of the most blatant kind—*and it worked!* "You know, Larry," he said, using my first name for the first time, in a voice that had no hostility or defiance in it, but was friendly, even kind, "people don't always see me the way I see myself. But I have a feeling we will get along."

That "we" made me a colleague rather than an interrogator in his eyes and it allowed me to ask him whatever questions I had prepared, including the ones about what he said about his son. He didn't deny saying it and still felt that way. He also admitted he had lost a good part of his audience in America after his split with Dean Martin. He wouldn't go into why they split up, nor would he discuss how he became so involved with MD, but he didn't blow smoke out his nose when I asked these things. My little story of how he made me laugh until it hurt when I was a kid changed the entire dynamic. It was a lesson I would use throughout my career: Flattery can turn a frown upside down. And it doesn't cost anything if it also happens to be the truth.

65. MAKE YOUR SCREEN DOORS HALF SOLID & USE A WOOD STRIP AT A DOOR ENTRANCE

I didn't have much in common with **Harrison Ford**, but took advantage of knowing that he had once been a carpenter before becoming an actor. He had come to my house for our interview and I mentioned that I was all thumbs when it came to fixing things. Especially faulty screen doors that never seemed to work properly.

"Probably because the weight of the top and bottom rail is not sufficient to bear the strain put on it by the pneumatic door closing," he said. "Best to go with a solid bottom half. The dogs and kids won't kick it in to start with, and you'll have more meat on that middle rail."

Seemed like he knew what he was talking about, so I tossed him one more. "Why does the hot water in my upstairs bathroom turn cold after a few minutes when it doesn't happen in the downstairs tub?"

"I don't know, man, might be your karma," Ford said.

"But it also happens when my wife goes to bathe," I countered.

"You might be your wife's karma," he answered. Touché Han Solo. Touché!

66. BE PATIENT. BE THOROUGH.
GIVE SOMETHING

Henry Fonda's family karma wasn't all that hot, but he was in a place where he could appreciate small gestures and somehow we managed to find a common bond in our appreciation of primitive art and modern prints.

Fonda's silence was deafening to his family's ears, to the point where his wife Shirlee eagerly agreed to my request to interview him for *Playboy*. He didn't have long to live after the release of his last film, *On Golden Pond*, and when I got to his house in Brentwood, Shirlee took me aside in their kitchen and told me that he had become more recalcitrant than usual and had just clammed up. She was hoping that I could spend enough time with him to get him talking again.

It was the reverse of what I was used to. Most subjects are reluctant to go deep and long, but here I was being asked to take my time and spend as many hours as possible with Tom Joad / Mr. Roberts. I always liked Fonda's work; like Spencer Tracy and Gary Cooper, there was an aura of truth he brought to his roles. From what I had read about him, I knew that he wasn't the best father in the world and that he had had five wives, an indication that he wasn't easy to get along with. But when you saw him in *Twelve Angry Men, the Oxbow-Incident, The Grapes of Wrath,* or *The Lady Eve,* you believed his persona. The curmudgeon that he apparently was in real life was evident in *On Golden Pond*, for which he deservedly received the Academy Award for Best Actor.

He was courteous and gentlemanly when I walked into his living room and introduced myself as he sat in his wheelchair. It soon became obvious that he wasn't comfortable talking about himself, but he had told his wife that he would do this and he was a man of his word. When he made a commitment he kept it, even if it meant appearing as the same character in the same play on Broadway for over 5000 performances, as he did with *Mr. Roberts*. Though he would answer all my questions, it took a while to get him to expand on those answers. He was good for two hours at the most and after each session I would help him out of his wheelchair so he could use the bathroom. By the third day, that simple hands-on act brought us close and he became comfortable with my patience and our conversation.

On the fourth day I brought him a small present, something I had picked up when I was in the Peace Corps. It was a three-inch brass African figure that represented health. It moved him, knowing how his health was failing; yet realizing that no such figure would do any good. The following day he said he had something for me. I figured he was going to give me a jar of honey that he had collected from the bees he kept, or perhaps a bag of apples from his trees. Instead, it was a signed print he had done of a magnifying glass highlighting a page from Steinbeck's *The Grapes of Wrath*. Fonda was an accomplished artist as well as an actor and his work hung in galleries. I told him that it made my gift seem paltry by comparison and that once I had it framed and hung on the wall opposite my desk I would be inspired by it daily.

Each day when I left, Shirlee would walk me to my car and tell me that the memories I was stirring in him were bringing him out of his silence. He was talking more to her and his family and she was grateful that I had been willing to spend so much time with him. I had never before been thanked by a family member for taking such precious time from a dying man and I told her that it was both an honor and a privilege to be allowed into his life. I believe the common appreciation of primitive art, coupled with my patient assistance with his personal needs, gave me the inroad needed to unlock the silence that his wife found so disturbing.

Vincent Kofi was good at seeing what others couldn't see, and "found" his art inside the trunks of trees. He looked at his raw material and carved away the excess to find the form hidden within. 1970

"You caused me a great deal of trouble," Luciano said. And then Pavarotti laughed wholeheartedly. It was our own private joke. 1983

With Anthony Kiedis, age 3, when his dad made a short film with him while we were at UCLA. Anthony had to hit a homeless man with a trick bottle and then rob him. I was responsible for making sure he knew how to do it. 1965

Jon Voight came to my house the same week *Writer's Digest* put me on their January 1978 cover. "Success is a very strange thing," Voight reflected "But you probably don't know what I'm talking about, you've never been on a magazine cover, you've never been singled out that way. It changes you."

When I ran into Pierce Brosnan, he said that he still couldn't figure out how I got him to talk so openly about sex. "It's probably why women are always smiling at you," I joked. "Either that, or trying to smell you to see if you've washed." 1995

The following day Henry Fonda said he had something for me: a signed print he had done of a magnifying glass highlighting a page from Steinbeck's *The Grapes of Wrath*.

Stay In Your Comfort Zone

67. WHAT YOU WEAR MIGHT INFLUENCE
WHAT THEY'LL SAY

Clothing is something rarely considered when discussing tips for a successful celebrity encounter. The rules are different for men and women but, for either sex, appearance is going to influence the first impression a celebrity will have of his or her interrogator. My first celebrity interview was with Mae West, and I wore a tie and sports jacket. I wanted to make a "nice" impression, and also show respect, but I wasn't comfortable. I've never worn a tie or jacket since then, and I used to instruct my UCLA students before our celebrity guest came to class to dress the way they would if they were interviewing our guest at his home and not in our classroom. I didn't ask them to dress up or down, I just wanted them to think about it. And then we could discuss that nonverbal aspect of interviewing the following week.

I first became aware of this issue when I went to Malibu, where **Louise Lasser** had a beach house. She was the star of the cult TV show, *Mary Hartman, Mary Hartman,* was once married to Woody Allen, and her father was the tax attorney and author J.K. Lasser. At the time, she had made headlines when she was arrested for marijuana possession. I was the second reporter to see her after she got out of jail. The first was from the *Wall Street Journal,* and he was just leaving when I arrived. He was wearing a suit and tie; I was wearing jeans and a short sleeve shirt. When she saw me she looked relieved. "That man," she said when he left, "was so stiff. You want to take a walk on the beach? Do you have any grass with you? You can't write about my asking because I'm still on probation and I'll have to kill you."

I thought about why she apparently felt she could talk so openly to me before she actually got to know me, and concluded that it had to do with my casual appearance, especially compared to the suited gentleman who preceded me. So I tested this theory out when I had to interview **Warren Beatty,** one of the world's great Lotharios.

Beatty's reputation for seducing beautiful women was part of his biography. Not being of the opposite sex put me at a disadvantage before I even got to his lair, which was a small two-room suite on the top floor of the Beverly Wilshire Hotel in Beverly Hills. So I decided to wear something that would throw him off balance. I had an African fugu from Ghana that was worn over the head and came down mid-thigh over my jeans. It wasn't a sweatshirt or a shirt, but more like an outfit that musicians who played the talking drums might wear. It was very comfortable, but looked pretty outrageous, especially in the context of Beverly Hills.

When Beatty opened his door and saw me, he looked puzzled. Who was I? What the hell was I wearing? I just smiled and pointed my finger at him and said, "Warren." And that was it. He let me in and we started to talk right away. I had read enough about him to know that he was always wary with the press, that he hardly gave interviews, and that when he did, he never said anything quotable or controversial. But my outfit had disarmed him. He found it amusing. So he felt at ease with me before we even began. It made a difference. And when we were done, he invited me to join him and his then girlfriend, singer Michelle Phillips (from The Mamas and The Papas), for dinner at a nearby restaurant. I told him I'd meet them there, after I went home and changed. Here again, clothing was important, and I was clearly not appropriately attired for dinner with Warren and Michelle.

68. SETTING FREE ONE'S GENUINE PERSONA

While we know the adage that clothes make the man, does makeup make the woman? I was talking to my proofreader, Rita, about how certain celebrities benefit from a good makeup artist. We all have seen pictures of amazing transformations, when ordinary women get the full makeover treatment. But what about those extraordinary women who are instantly recognizable? How important are the creams, blushes, eye and lip liners, and hairstylists for them?

Rita asked me who were the most natural beauties I had interviewed and who were helped by being made up? The naturals came immediately to mind: Kim Basinger, Nicole Kidman, Sophia Loren and Halle Berry. Most of the others were attractive, good-looking women who became gorgeous creatures when plucked and powdered. But was there a lesson here, or just an observation?

"When a woman is all gussied up, people see her differently, so she has a tendency to behave differently," Rita said. "But when she is in her natural state, sans make-up or professional hair-do, I think she actually feels more natural, and is more open and honest. She has dropped her "image" and her genuine persona is set free. For example, when I go to work, with my high heels, nylons, silky slip, pretty blouse and soft wool suit, I feel very feminine and professional and that's exactly how people see me. I am treated with respect and consequently, I act respectfully. I even walk straighter. Yet feeling the swish of my nylons against my slip when I walk is kind of a turn on, a very sexy and sensuous sensation for me. But that 'wanton woman' hides behind the 'business woman,' and no one ever sees her–until I change into my jeans and a T-shirt. Then I subconsciously let myself go, and become the playful girl next door, much more likely to make racy or provocative remarks. If you were to interview me, you would get two different women. Both would be warm and friendly, because that is my nature. But the professional would be guarded, to maintain her image. The girl in jeans would give you a much more interesting interview. She might even shock you with some of her revelations."

This made me think about some of my interviews with female celebrities. Just as I felt most stars were more comfortable with me if I dressed down for them, were some of these women more candid talking to me because they arrived unadorned, without the makeup, heels, hair and jewelry that made them sparkle on the covers of magazines or on the movie screen? By literally letting their hair down, were they more relaxed and open?

When **Cameron Diaz** came to my house, she looked nothing like the cover photo of the March 1997 issue of *Movieline*. In that, you see a young woman with perfect skin and a puffy lower lip lying back with the forefinger of her right hand curled as if inviting you to join her on the divan. She is stunning. You want to run your hand along her smooth cheek. You can understand how they cast her as the woman to knock Jim

Carrey's eyeballs out of their sockets in *The Mask*. And yet, when she entered my house just a few hours after posing for this, she looked nothing like that picture. She had removed all the makeup that was used to make her glamorous. She obviously didn't have an overactive ego, and I felt an immediate rapport with her.

"What appears to be glamour is kind of old," she told me. "My being on the cover of a magazine is the least favorite thing for me. That's the Industry putting its will to work." Indeed. She looked like a half dozen young women that I knew in college. It wasn't her looks which first hit me but her personality. She had a great open mouth smile that turned into a laugh at the slightest provocation.

When **Angelina Jolie** arrived at my door, I saw a not very tall woman in an open black leather jacket and a black T-shirt with a white planet imprint and the words New London, CT below it. Her lips were as full as they were in photos, but her eyes seemed puffy and her eyebrows thin. When I asked her if she saw herself as a beautiful woman, she spoke in a forthright way about her appearance. "I don't like the way I look. I don't think I'm pretty. I'm actually a bit strange-looking." She definitely had a gothic look to her, a look that indicated she didn't give a shit about being glamorous or ethereal. And that made me feel comfortable.

I interviewed **Penelope Cruz** over lunch at the Chateau Marmont in West Hollywood. I found a woman who had her hair combed back, her face scrubbed clean of any traces of makeup, and an ordinariness that just didn't fit with how she appeared on screen and in photos. When I asked her to talk about her face, she said, "I can look completely ugly, like in the movie *Don't Move*. Or I could look good in another character. It can go both ways in very extreme ways. And it can change completely. I'm not a very good liar with my face. It's ironic, because of what I do, it's my job. In life, if I'm pissed off or sad, everyone catches it. And I don't like it, but I don't like to walk around hiding whatever I feel that day." No eyes turned when we were shown to our table. She simply melted into the garden where we dined as if she wasn't world famous or one of the world's great beauties.

What I admired about these three women was that none of them seemed to be hiding what they felt when we talked. We traded stories, some of them intimate; we laughed when relating personal foibles; and when subjects turned serious, they seemed emotional without emoting.

From them I learned that being beautiful was a lot of work and often required a lot of workers, but that it was also okay to let down your hair, remove the makeup and feel "ordinary" and comfortable once in a while. As my proofreader noted, dropping the "image" allows your genuine persona to be set free.

69. PLAY OFF OBSESSIVE BEHAVIOR

Christopher Walken's comfort zone was in the kitchen– an unusual place to conduct an interview unless it's for a cooking show.

For most of the five days I was with Walken, we stood in the kitchen, where he was most comfortable preparing meals, cutting vegetables, and following me around to wipe the space where I had placed my coffee cup. I had not expected this obsessive behavior from Walken. I wasn't even sure if he was aware of it. But he did it so often that it became a game with me. I would ask him a question, take a sip from my cup, walk a few steps and put the cup down again. He would pick up a dishrag, wipe the countertop where my cup had been (even though I had not spilled any coffee), and continue talking. I did this at least a dozen times and he wiped behind me each time until I finally called him on it.

"What are you wiping?" I asked.

"What do you mean?" he queried.

"Do you realize that every time I pick up my cup, you wipe the spot where it was, even though there's nothing to wipe?"

"It's not my kitchen, so...."

"So you're obsessed with cleanliness?"

"It's funny you say that. To me it's an absolute necessity. Everybody should be that way. Cleanliness is a good thing. I'm very clean. I don't like things that aren't cleaned up. But I hardly use soap at all; it makes me feel sticky. I don't like to use soap in my hair—I usually just run it under the water."

"Your hair is one of your trademarks. Wasn't it Anthony Perkins who turned you on to taking good care of your hair so you wouldn't lose it?"

"That was when I left college, when I was 19 and was in a play. He had a great head of hair. He said the reason men go bald, aside from genes, is that as they get older, the scalp gets tight, the blood gets cut off and the follicles die, particularly with stress. He knew a lot about it. He said that women have a layer of lanolin under their skin that men don't have that keeps their scalps loose. He told me what you do is pull your hair forward five minutes a day, and I've done it every morning since. You take your whole scalp and just pull it pretty hard, yank it around. I heard that Kennedy, when he was in the White House, had somebody come in every day and do it for him. He had a great head of hair."

"What other beauty secrets do you have?" I wondered.

"If you've got red eyes from staying up too late you should put warm, wet tea bags on them. It's very soothing."

Walken's quirky mannerisms are manna for mimics. Who doesn't know someone who can do a Christopher Walken impression? From his hilarious *Saturday Night Live* routines as the faux suave Mr. Continental to his inciting Will Ferrell that he's "Gotta Have More Cowbells!" to Annie Hall's psychopathic brother Duane, The Man With the Plan, Batman's nemesis Max Shreck, and *True Romance's* mob boss Vincenzo Coccotti, there's something memorable and imitable about so many of his performances. He talks....with pauses. He can sound robotic. His hair appears to be brushed upwards. He has a distinctive gait. A distinctive voice. A distinctive look. He has been called both creepy and spooky. He prefers the second to the first.

"I hope I'm not creepy," he said when we talked at a house he was renting in Los Angeles. "Creepy is not a mammal. Creepy is like an insect. Spooky is OK. Racehorses get spooked, they're emotional."

When asked to describe himself, he answered, "Unexpectedly conservative. Anybody who gets to know me is surprised. My life is quiet. I like it that way. I'm very sensible and pragmatic. If somebody were to do the story of my life, it would be about my wife and me around the house. It would be like watching paint dry."

After our time in Los Angeles, I flew to New York to continue our interview. I sat in the audience when he hosted *Saturday Night Live*. I also saw how he calmed down his wife Georgianne when she saw fresh blood on their expensive rug, blood that hadn't been there before director Abel Ferrara's visit. "He must have cut his foot before he came," Walken said. "His sock was all bloody." "You know how tough it is to remove bloodstains?" his wife asked. "So we'll be able to point out that this is where director Abel Ferrara bled for his art," Walken smiled.

Walken has been bleeding for his art since he made his first public appearance at the age of three, and says that acting, singing and dancing is the only world he knows, so much so that he jokes that he isn't from Planet Earth but from Planet Show Business. That's his comfort zone. He is unlike any other actor I've known in his fastidious, compulsive ways. He is a terrific cook who could easily have his own cooking show; he has a great sense of humor with a wonderful laugh; he can tell a good story; and when you are with him, it's very easy to forget that he can scare the crap out of you with some of the chilling characters he's played in the movies. I learned to play off his obsessive behavior, and ever since we spoke I've been pulling my hair forward whenever I think of him. I've yet to try the warm tea bags, but I've recommended it to friends who party hearty and could really use the tip.

70. DO THE OPPOSITE

James Spader was also good with advice, though definitely not in his comfort zone, because he said talking about himself made him uncomfortable.

As the subject of an interview, he will be the first to tell you that he's a bad interview. "I don't take pride in that," he will say when you first meet. "I don't have a problem sitting and talking. I'm just not comfortable talking about myself. I don't like the spotlight. It's a dilemma."

We talked in a room at the Beverly Wilshire Hotel in Los Angeles. It was a safe, sterile place for him and it was clear from the start that he was going to keep his emotions in check. The persona he had perfected wasn't going to crack under questioning. But since it was an amusing, if supercilious, persona that would be all right. I was able to learn about his rebellious childhood, his passion for knives, and his appreciation for women, sex, and mind-altering drugs. He found it interesting that actors often lost the distinction between acting and reality when the cameras stopped rolling. "You're supposed to fall in love with somebody when the story calls for it," he said. "That's your job. But what if you do? It's a tricky emotion to play around with. It's so seductive. That's the problem—love is the one emotion actors allow themselves to believe. They'll go off and play a killer but won't allow themselves to believe they're a killer. They don't see that it's the same thing."

I'm not sure if "smarmy" is the exact word to describe the kind of characters James Spader plays, but it's close. It's not when the synonym is "groveling," but it is when it's "unctuous" (as in *smug*), "oily" (as in *slick* or *slippery*), "creepy" (*disturbing, unnerving, unsettling*) or "insinuative." Two of his TV costars, William Shatner (*Boston Legal*) and Camryn Manheim (*The Practice*), described him as "weird," "recalcitrant," "strange and eccentric." Maggie Gyllenhaal, who was the object of his sadomasochistic obsessions in *Secretary*, wondered what he might be like as a human being. He has a particular and unique style of acting that exudes his sense of superiority and high intelligence engulfed in a glowing conviction of self-satisfaction. That's how he comes off in films like *Sex, Lies and Videotape, Bad Influence, True Colors, Secretary*, and *Crash*, and in his three successful TV series: *The Practice, Boston Legal*, and *The Blacklist*. Smug as he might seem, when he's on camera he's mesmerizing. He holds your attention. You wait for how he will deliver his next line. You may think him a pompous ass, but you don't root against him. And that is the mark of a fascinating actor.

When Spader accepted his Emmy for Best Actor for his role as a lawyer in *The Practice*, in keeping with his quirky image, he complimented the women in the audience on their taste in shoes. I thought I might learn something from him about that if I ever found myself tongue-tied in a room of beautiful women or on a stage in front of a huge audience. "If you're at a loss for something to say or trying to engage a woman in a room, compliment her shoes," he told me. "That seems like the best way."

Spader didn't seem like the type who attracted girls by excelling in sports when in high school and he wondered why I thought that athletes were the ones who most succeeded in that department. "Why should it be the quarterback?" he asked. "He's in the locker room with a bunch of guys. He doesn't get laid at all. Football is played in the afternoon. You need a shower afterward. Come on, that doesn't get you laid. If you want to be with girls, go into theater. You're there at night, after school, and it's dark."

Another lesson to take to heart, I thought, though a bit late in my development. But he shared a third lesson as well, which was a good one for up and coming actors who hoped to break out from expectations an audience had of a recurring character they were used to. "How do you keep such a character fresh?" I asked.

"I'll tell you exactly how," he said with authority. "You put him in a set of circumstances, you think about what he might do, and you do the opposite."

He wasn't as "bad" of an interview as he had initially predicted, and he even showed me the knife he carried with him at all times. But perhaps he said more than he meant to, because when I asked him if he had any regrets about our interview his answer highlighted his discomfort: "Just one: that I agreed to do it."

71. NUNS MAKE PRIESTS UNCOMFORTABLE

When **Andrew Greely** agreed to speak to me, I expected to find a man who was comfortable with everyone. He was a celibate priest, novelist, social activist, philanthropist, and Vatican irritant, and had a very positive take on women. In 1993, when Bill Clinton occupied the Oval Office, he told me he would much prefer to see Hillary Clinton in charge. He thought that women should be allowed to enter the priesthood. He wished he could write like a woman. And when asked to describe God, he said She was probably an Irish female comedienne who looked like Jessica Lange or Audrey Hepburn. He understood that men often disliked women and felt it was because men feared them. And he himself admitted to a bit of that fear when he told me he was intimidated by nuns, and was always uncomfortable in their presence.

He was well aware of what his critics had to say about him. A chapter in his autobiography, *Confessions of a Parish Priest*, listed the most common complaints about him: that he wrote too much and never had an unpublished thought; that he was the richest priest in America; that he had serious psychosexual problems; that he wrote pornographic trash; that his novels were puerile potboilers that only sold because of the novelty of a priest writing about sex; and that he was brokenhearted that he was never made a bishop.

I asked him about such criticism and he deflected each one with the smoothness of a man who was very secure with who he was and what he did for a living. He agreed that he had sexual problems, but added that he didn't know anyone who didn't. "It goes with being human," he explained. He said that there were academic scholars who didn't think his novels were trash, and he felt people read them because they were good stories. "One of the great put-downs of my work," he said, "is to say that I'm no Graham Greene, to which I say, 'I suppose that's true, but why need I be? Why is that the criteria? I'm not James Joyce or James Michener either.' Am

I brokenhearted that I'm not a bishop? The day I set the first word on paper I ended any chance of becoming a bishop and I knew what I was doing."

He also believed he knew what he was doing by speaking out against the "psychopaths, sociopaths, antisocial personalities, pederasts, crooks, alcoholics, and incompetents" who were "routinely appointed to the American dioceses." When I asked him if he felt like a lone voice in the wilderness with such remarks he said, "It's bleaker now than when I wrote that." His view was that the Vatican had established too much of a distance between themselves and the laypeople. "The leadership of the Church has lost its nerve," he said. I wonder if he would have altered his opinion of the Vatican with the election of Pope Francis two months before Greeley died in March 2013.

Greeley saw the priesthood more as a job than a calling. "It's like being a high school principal or a psychiatrist; you lose a lot more than you win. And even when you're moderately successful and you're trying to console the bereaved, for example, well, you do a little bit toward easing their pain, but you don't do much. You're dealing with an impossible problem: to ease the pain of loss. You fail at the things that are important."

Since he had experience as an academic, a journalist and a priest, I asked him which one is the most likely to trigger the cardinal sin of envy. "The priesthood is the worst," he said, "because the reward system is so small, you can't help feeling the deprivation; yet envy is such a disgrace to what the priesthood is supposed to be."

Greeley was ordained in 1952 at the age of 24 and spent ten years as an assistant pastor of Christ the King Church in Chicago. He received his Ph.D. in sociology in 1962 and became the senior study director at the National Opinion Research Center in Chicago for four years. He also taught at the University of Chicago for ten years, but was denied tenure in 1973. Without a parish in Chicago, he turned to writing as his pulpit, publishing 120 books, fifty of them novels.

His novels with such titles as *The Cardinal Sins, Ascent into Hell, Virgin and Martyr, Thy Brother's Wife,* and *Fall From Grace* weren't really steamy; they had an audience because of the novelty of a priest writing about what came naturally between a man and a woman. He also believed that equality between the sexes regarding church practices should be natural.

"The Church can't cope with women and women's demands for equal treatment in the Church," he said. "The Church can't conceive of women being priests because they have never been priests and if you make women priests you're going to have to share power, and change the way you do business. It's terribly unjust. But the ordination of women would break up the male clerical monopoly and notably change its culture and orientation."

I had to smile when he told me that he was always uneasy around the nuns at Christ the King Church and remained uneasy with them for the rest of his life. "Nuns don't like priests," he said, "because priests have all the fun. They have good reason for not liking them. We've treated them like cheap help in the Church for ages and ages. They have a lot to be angry about. And there are not very many doing it anymore. It's hopelessly unfair."

As a Jew who didn't think much about how the Church operated, talking to Greeley was educational for me. I had no idea how nuns felt about priests. And I still couldn't wrap my head around the idea of celibacy, though Greeley was fine with it. "I'm the only one I know who holds the positions that celibacy ought to continue and that we ought to ordain women. I also believe in a limited term of service for the priesthood, like the Peace Corps. But I can't get anybody to take that seriously."

Greeley seemed to be a voice in the wilderness, decrying practices that should have been reformed long, long ago. He ordered 1,000 copies of the *Modern Maturity* issue from AARP when our interview appeared. The only other subject that used one of my interviews to showcase his voice was Hugh Hefner. Maybe they had more in common than anyone ever thought. I sure wouldn't be at all surprised if nuns made Hefner uneasy as well.

Eat, Drink, & Try To Be Merry (Because It Don't Mean A Thing!)

72. IF THEY OFFER YOU A DRINK, DON'T MAKE IT SOFT

Henry Fonda gave me a work of art. **Lauren Bacall** gave me a beer. But I had to work for it.

I had gone to see her at the Dakota in Manhattan for my book *The Hustons*. I waited for her in the lobby until she returned from her walk in Central Park and we took the elevator to her apartment. She was very much like her on-screen persona: husky, straightforward, a bit brash, and very sure of herself. You could immediately tell that she was a no-nonsense type woman. And she would have a lot to say about the often nonsense-provoking prankster that was her dear friend John Huston.

But before we got into John, Bogie, *The African Queen* and *Beat the Devil*, we sat in her high-ceilinged living room, with floor to ceiling bookshelves housing what seemed like thousands of books and a rolling ladder to get to those above reach. She asked me how Huston was doing, we traded some hospital stories, and I told her about my trip to Europe where I met with Olivia de Havilland, Edna O'Brien, Suzanne Flon, and Roman Polanski. She had something to say about each of them. But first she played the polite host and offered me something to drink.

I asked for orange juice.

She stared at me as if I were an alien who didn't understand that when a woman like Lauren Bacall asks if you wanted something to drink, she didn't mean orange juice. I could just as well have asked for chocolate milk.

"This isn't a fucking candy store!" she bellowed. That's the appropriate word here. Bellowed. As in, "*This isn't a fucking candy store!*" Words that still ring in my ears whenever anyone asks if I'd like something to drink.

"I'm sorry," I stammered. "I'll have a beer."

I wasn't even sure if asking for a beer was appropriate when Lauren Bacall is extending the offer. I probably should have come up with a fancy single malt Scotch or, at the very least, Jack Daniels. But Bacall seemed satisfied that I wasn't a teetotaler and went to her kitchen to find me a brew. I wiped my brow and filed this lesson away. When someone asks "Drink?" you answer "Whatever you're having." If that doesn't feel appropriate, make it a whiskey. Neat.

73. LET THERE BE DRINK!

If the Bacall lesson was to man up to the bar, the lesson I learned from **Vincent Kofi**, George C. Scott, Ava Gardner, and Truman Capote was to keep it flowing!

Kofi liked beer and easily guzzled six large bottles when we spoke at my apartment in Accra. He didn't need it to loosen up, as he was an enthusiastic, freewheeling spirit who was articulate about his art and had a deep, hardy laugh—and a love of beer.

George C. Scott was a nasty sonofabitch when he drank too much and lost control of his senses. He attacked Ava Gardner more than once, swelling her face when they worked together on John Huston's *The Bible* in Italy; breaking a bottle and pushing its shard edge to her face as he pinned her down with his knees in one of the cottages at the Beverly Hills Hotel; getting thrown in jail in London when he broke into her hotel room and threatened to kill her. "When George was sober," Ava told me, "he was highly intelligent, and God knows a wonderful actor, but when he drank he became crazy and beat women. Afterwards he was apologetic, ashamed, promising it would never happen again. But that's what drunken bullies always say. And never mean." When I talked to Scott at his home in Greenwich, Connecticut, he drank from a pitcher of Bloody Marys and became scarily testy when I brought up those incidents. "I don't talk about Ava," he said. Fortunately, he didn't get violent with me, and the vodka definitely loosened him up to frankly discuss his conservative positions regarding politics and social issues.

Ava Gardner was a famous drinker who was fabled to have drunk most men under the table as she danced flamenco on top of it. Producer Ray Stark confirmed that when he and Huston were pursuing her to appear in *Night of the Iguana*, they took her to a nightclub in Madrid, where they drank into the night and then Huston had had enough and left Stark alone with her, but he couldn't keep up either. "She wore us out," Stark recalled. "I never thought I'd see the day someone could out-drink and outlast John Huston, but Ava was in a class by herself."

She was someone who needed drink to talk to a journalist. She rarely gave interviews and when she did, she couldn't speak when she could see the tape recorder. I had to put it under her coffee table to keep it out of sight, though she knew it was there. She offered me chilled white wine and we polished off a few bottles one afternoon, and a few more when I saw her in Los Angeles. That was after she had had her stroke and wasn't supposed to drink or smoke. But she did both. I don't think wine affected her that much, as she didn't seem much different either way.

As for **Truman Capote,** when he came to be interviewed for Playboy Cable TV at the Drake Hotel in New York, I offered him his favorite vodka, Stolichnaya. He demurred, saying he would just have water. But after an hour, as the questions got more interesting, he said, "I'll have some of that vodka," and poured himself a full glass. No ice, no juice, just straight Stoli. When he finished it, he poured another glass. And when he finished that and we were still filming, he figured he might as well finish the bottle. Capote was an admitted alcoholic and a good example of a happy drunk. His famous quote was: "I'm a homosexual. I'm a drug addict. I'm an alcoholic. I'm a genius." If loose lips truly sunk ships, Capote's lips loosened with each downed glass. His tongue was as sharp as a stiletto, and the more he drank, the deadlier his observations.

So what I learned from being with drinkers is to have their favorite drink available, and let them drink freely. And always sip when they gulp, because someone has to maintain control in an interview, and it always worked out best if it were me.

74. BRING WHATEVER IT TAKES TO MAKE THEM COMFORTABLE

Joan Collins's favorite drink was Crystal champagne. She wouldn't talk without it.

There was a time when Joan Collins hit the celebrity wheel of fortune. She was never a huge movie star herself, being better known for her affairs with them. She looked a bit like Elizabeth Taylor and had a flirtatious way about her that made her interesting. But when she was cast as Alexis Carrington Colby in the TV series *Dynasty* that ran from 1981 to 1989, her bitchy, scheming character captured something we hadn't seen before. She was almost 50 years old, but still hot, so it wasn't just an old nasty dowager she was playing, but rather someone who was imminently fuckable. That she was continually fucking over half the other players in this series (including engaging in some marvelous cat fights with costar and nemesis Linda Evans) made it fun to watch. That Collins was willing to take it all off in *Playboy* at that age made her interview-worthy as well. So I got the assignment.

Joan Collins made her first stage appearance in *A Doll's House* at the age of nine, and attended the Royal Academy of Dramatic Art while still a teenager. She left England to feed her greater ambitions in Hollywood, but after appearing in a few passable films (*The Girl in the Red Velvet Swing*, and *Rally Round the Flag, Boys*), she found herself cast in crime capers, biblical epics, and horror films. But none of her films brought her the international attention that *Dynasty* did. In 1985 it was the #1 show in the United States. Collins was nominated six times for a Golden Globe Award, winning once. She was also nominated for an Emmy as Best Actress in a TV Drama Series.

She was pretty full of herself when she contracted with *Playboy* to be photographed in the nude by the legendary portrait photographer George Hurrell, to be followed by an interview in a separate issue. She was a calculating business woman who was so sure that her appearance in the magazine would boost its circulation that she demanded a cut of any earning above its normal monthly magazine sales. I thought that was pretty ballsy, but the magazine agreed and the sales went through the roof.

Her demands from me were not financial, but rather based on pleasure. Her assistant called two days before I was to see her and said that Joan would like me to bring a bottle of Crystal champagne and a tin of Beluga caviar to our interview. I couldn't help asking what Ms. Collins would bring. "The potatoes," her assistant said.

"Ha," I laughed. "I thought you were going to say, 'Herself.'"

"Better make that two bottles of Crystal," she said.

I didn't know whether she was kidding or reflecting her boss's desires. Was it okay to joke with the assistant of the woman who took no nonsense from anyone on *Dynasty* and had a body worthy of displaying in the raw in a popular men's magazine?

I picked up the champagne for $75 and the caviar for $100 and handed them to the housekeeper when I arrived at Ms. Collins' home in the evening. When she made her appearance, she was dressed as Alexis, with high heels and makeup that hadn't been removed after a day on the set. She was friendly in a queenly sort of way and dug right into the caviar and champagne when it was brought out. After the first hour she excused herself to get into something more comfortable and returned looking less queenly but more real. By our third hour her makeup began to run. I don't think she expected to be talking to me into the night, but I just kept asking questions and she was game to answer them. When the champagne ran out, she asked what happened to the second bottle of Crystal, and I had to confess that I had only brought one, thinking her assistant was joking with me about a second bottle.

"Well, it would have helped," she said, her mascara now running down her cheeks. She was looking increasingly more her age as time progressed.

"Maybe you have a bottle?" I suggested.

"My dear boy, that's expensive champagne. Why would I serve it when *Playboy* should be paying?"

"You're right, Joan," I said. "If you've got another bottle in the fridge, bring it out and I'll pay for it."

"Funny boy," she said. We didn't drink a second bottle and after six hours Joan was exhausted. She looked ten years older and in need of sleep. I thanked her for giving me so much time and she quipped that had I brought the second bottle I might have been there through the morning. I didn't know exactly how to interpret that, but I knew that from then on, if anyone asked me to bring something, I'd go the extra yard.

When Robin Leach's *Lifestyles of the Rich and Famous'* premiered in 1984, at the height of *Dynasty's* popularity, his signature phrase was "Champagne wishes and caviar dreams." I often wondered if he got that from Joan Collins.

75. REAL MEN DO PILATES AND EAT ORGANIC

I also wondered if those crazy looking mug shots of a wild-haired **Nick Nolte** were booze related, because when I saw him, he was more a poster boy for clean living by growing your own...organics.

When most people think of Nick Nolte, I'd bet that one of the first images that come to mind is of his DUI mug shot, where he's looking dopey into the camera wearing a Hawaiian shirt with his hair all askew. Then there'd be images of him as a hunky football player (*North Dallas Forty*), a hard-nosed detective (*48 Hours*), a grizzly-bearded bum (*Down and Out in Beverly Hills),* and Robert Redford's grizzly-bearded walking companion *(A Walk in the Woods).* I doubt anyone imagines Nolte as a guy working Pilates machines in his private gym or walking along his organic garden picking berries off their stems and swallowing them whole.

I certainly didn't expect to see that side of him when I went to interview him about his life and his three latest films: Terrence Malick's *The Thin Red Line,* Paul Schrader's *Affliction,* and Alan Rudoph's *Breakfast of Champions.* I knew about him from what I had read: that he was raised in Nebraska, played baseball, basketball and football in high school and various colleges until his antics got him into trouble with his coaches and with the law. After high school he lived in a whorehouse in Nogales, Mexico, and then joined a commune for five years. During the Sixties, he found a way to make money by selling phony draft cards to college students. The FBI arrested him and he was given 45 years in jail (suspended) and a $75,000 fine. That made him a felon, which got him out of the draft and prevented him from ever voting. He worked as an ironworker, did some modeling, and when he became an actor, critic Pauline Kael called him "the master of the inchoate, the deeply mixed-up." Married and divorced three times, he joined Alcoholics Anonymous when he was 46, but it didn't seem to do him much good. Some of his co-stars said nasty things about him. When Debra Winger worked with him in *Cannery Row,* she said she never knew if his personality was courageous or just stupid. Katharine Hepburn warned him about alcohol abuse during *Grace Quiqley* and Julia Roberts called him disgusting after they made *I Love Trouble.* I was prepared for combat when I arrived at his Malibu estate.

The six acres of land he occupied had six comfortably furnished houses, sprawling gardens, a greenhouse, a tennis court, five dogs, a cat, a caged raven, and an unconnected satellite dish big enough to contact extraterrestrials. For our first meeting, which lasted eight hours, we walked from house to house, picking wild berries from his garden and talking about his keen interest in alternative medicine. "I run around the country hooking up with different doctors and scientists to see what they're doing, to learn why saliva tests are better than blood tests for hormones, to learn more about DNA and how it can signal predisposition for Alzheimer's and heart disease, to understand how protein keeps cellular reconstruction going on. I'm fascinated by all this stuff."

Oh, we talked about all the sensational highlights that brought him to this state of mind and he didn't disappoint with the details. He realized early on that reporters found his wild stories incredulous, so he learned how to pander to their expectations. "I don't think anybody believes me," he said. "Ever since I had to lose my anonymity and become public, there were two things I could do: either totally hide from the experience, or find some way to comfortably exist with it. You can't get anybody to view you the way you want to be viewed. I decided not to struggle with that impossibility. So I basically invented things."

Or not. That was the beauty of Nolte being at peace with himself. He lived the life of a wild man and found respite at home in his organic garden, doing Pilates and talking to New Age doctors about how to live longer and healthier than anyone would have imagined. Real men can fool you every time.

76. HUNGER LEADS TO ADVENTURE

Bruce Willis also lived a raucous life and wasn't particular when it came to choosing between refined sushi or a ham sandwich.

I entered Bruce Willis's life when he was ending his third season on his hit TV series *Moonlighting* and about to start filming his first *Die Hard*, which would catapult him into true stardom. We met in his trailer on the 20th Century Fox lot, where he spent most of his twelve daily hours listening to music, reading books about parenting (he was about to become a father), and wishing he didn't have to put in so much time in character verbally battling his *Moonlighting* costar, Cybill Shepherd. So I provided some relief from his solo act in his trailer. "We can talk about anything, but when we're on set I don't want you talking to Cybill about whatever I might say," he warned.

I hadn't intended on talking to Cybill at all, so I had no problem with this one ground rule. I was more interested in finding out about the wild all-night parties he held when he lived in my canyon that sometimes ended abruptly when the police came. When I asked about that, he answered, "My lifestyle just didn't coincide with the lifestyle of my neighbors."

When I pressed him about his once being arrested, he gave me his side of the story. "We were having a party on Memorial Day, and the police arrived around 10:00 p.m. We were swimming and dancing in the backyard by the pool, and nobody heard the doorbell. By the time I got out of the pool, this one cop was already in my house, and I asked him why he was there. I said, 'I won't talk to you until you get out of my house,' because he didn't have a warrant and I felt invaded. But it just escalated. I was cursing at him and he took offense. 'Why are you saying *fuck* so much?' he said. 'What is this, courtesy class?' I answered. 'This is how I *talk*; I'm from New York.' He said, 'I've arrested more important people than *you*. You think you're going to get away with this?'

"His point was, actors are not above the law. He was thrust into a situation that I'm sure he saw was potentially dangerous.

I had a broken shoulder at the time, and my friends tried to tell him about it. He put the handcuffs on me and cranked my arm up around my back, like you see on TV. I heard it go *snick, snick, snick*—it broke again. And it was chaos. I was yelling in pain, my friends were yelling that I was in pain, and the cop felt threatened, so he called in more cops."

Willis moved out of that house when he was released and found another house in the hills that had its own private canyon. "I had all these fantasies of retribution," he said. "I fantasized this conversation I would have with my neighbors. 'Oh, hi, Mr. Willis. What are those structures down there at the bottom of the canyon, guesthouses?' 'No, they ain't guesthouses.' 'What are they?' '*Speakers.*'"

This was how our conversation began. After he and Cybill Shepherd were called to do a scene (where they seemed overly polite to each other before the cameras rolled), he was given his freedom for a few hours and we left the lot in my Fiat Spider. We were hoping to get to a Japanese restaurant I liked while they were still serving lunch. As we zigzagged our way through traffic with the top down, drivers recognized Willis and spoke to him. I got caught behind a car making a left turn and a van passed us, the driver yelling, "Get another driver, Bruce!"

When I murmured that I didn't think we'd get to the restaurant in time, he said, "Have faith, be positive." But when we arrived, literally two minutes late, the maître d' refused to seat us. I whispered to him, "I'm with Bruce Willis. He's a big TV star. Surely, you can bend your rules." But his star clout was worthless, so we made do with a ham sandwich and a paper bowl of soup at the bakery next door.

"Great sandwich," he said, gobbling it down in four bites. I had extolled the excellence of the sushi and the mastery of the particular Japanese chef next door, and didn't at all enjoy the cup of soup I wound up with at this bakery. But Willis wasn't going to let a maître d' get the best of him, just like he didn't want to give in to the authority of the cops who came to his house. He didn't look at a half-filled glass and see it as half-empty; he saw it as enough to quench his thirst.

"I'm taking life with a lot more humor," he said when I appeared bummed out by the taste of burnt soup in my mouth. "I'm not taking all this shit so seriously. I'm enjoying myself a lot more. I met Glenn Ford at a New Year's Eve party and he said to me, 'Henry Fonda, Bogart, Bob Mitchum—we raised more hell than you guys ever did. We tore this town right up. Just keep laughing, son. It don't mean a thing.'"

Survival Is A Bitch

77. BE WARY OF AN HEIRESS WHO KNOWS HOW TO SHOOT

In 1974 the news story that most obsessed us, perhaps even more than Watergate, was the kidnapping of 19-year-old **Patricia Hearst**, an heir to the Hearst dynasty. She was abducted by the self-proclaimed terrorist organization, the Symbionese Liberation Army, and subsequently transformed into the machine gun carrying Tania. It had all the elements of a great narrative that captivated the nation in the same way O. J. Simpson would twenty years later, when he took off in his white Ford Bronco and eventually stood trial for two murders.

Patty Hearst was living with her boyfriend Steven Weed in an apartment in Berkeley, California when members of the SLA came knocking. They grabbed her and drove off; sending audiotaped messages to radio stations demanding millions of dollars in food donations in exchange for Hearst. The ransom was never met and it may not have mattered, because after nearly two months in captivity Patty decided to join her captors. She released an audiotape letting the world know of her new name and soon after her image was captured by bank surveillance cameras in San Francisco, where she and other members of the SLA threatened to shoot anyone who tried to stop them from robbing the bank.

What happened in those two months to turn the young heiress from a naïve young lady to a radical terrorist? Was it simply her desire to keep them from killing her? Or were they able to convince her that her parents were on the wrong side of history and that power truly belonged to the people? The FBI spent 19 months trying to find her, killing many of the SLA members along the way. There were times when she could have easily escaped, but she was convinced that the police would kill her too. *Newsweek* and *Time* put her on their covers over a dozen times before she was finally captured. During her trial her lawyers built their defense around the fact that she had been brainwashed, but the jury didn't buy it and she was sentenced to seven years in prison. She served two before President Jimmy Carter commuted her. She was later pardoned by President Clinton.

In 1982, before the publication of her book *Every Secret Thing,* I got the assignment to interview her for *Playboy.* It was her first in-depth interview and I knew what a plum assignment it was. Every journalist in America wanted at her. Why did she do what she did once abducted? Did she fall in love with one of the SLA members? Was she raped? Did she worry about getting pregnant? Was she brainwashed? Did she share a communal toothbrush? Did the CIA help set up the SLA as a diversion to get the country's mind off Watergate? How did she manage to evade the law for so long? How much had she changed? What did she and her parents talk about after she resurfaced? Where was her head?

She had married a cop and had a baby girl when I flew to San Mateo to try to unravel the enigma that was Patty

Hearst. She was friendly but wary, and as I brought up things about her captivity and imprisonment that she would have preferred to forget, she often got testy and defensive. I liked her spunk and I wondered at times if I was talking to Patty or Tania. She insisted that Tania had never existed, she had created her to protect herself, and that maybe I wanted to believe in Tania because it was a better story that way.

Our interview was initially conducted over a few days in San Mateo and subsequently at my house in Los Angeles. I did my best to stay friendly, but there were just too many unanswered questions to keep our exchanges civil. There were times she snapped at me, and times I challenged her. Some of our interaction went like this:

"This is the first time I've given an interview with a tape recorder," she said. "I'm always afraid that some jerk will get hold of them and play them on the radio."

I could understand. After all, the last time the public heard her taped voice occurred when she announced her conversion to join her captors. I asked her what she thought of journalists and the media, since she was such a subject of our affection. "I have a very hard time respecting reporters," this granddaughter of William Randolph Hearst said. "That seems like such a sleazy job, chasing people, a pencil and pad in your hand, annoying people. They're so undignified."

"What was going through your mind when they came knocking at your apartment door and whisked you away?" I asked.

"I just remember screaming my head off... I wanted the whole world to hear. It's really hard to describe sheer terror. You just don't comprehend being kidnapped unless it happens to you."

I asked her if she thought her kidnapping was a political act. She responded, "I don't think it's a very political act to kidnap somebody's daughter instead of her father, whom they could just as easily have kidnapped at that point."

Was she forcibly raped?

"I sure was," she said. "And it was humiliating...when you're in a closet, blindfolded...I'm sorry, I don't care what your definition of rape is—I don't care how willing somebody is to do it rather than be killed—that's rape!"

I asked her why she thought so much of the public seemed to have turned against her. She had a theory:

"I think I was very much a distraction from what was going on in Washington. At the time, there was Watergate and we were losing a president quickly. That's another reason why people got so emotional and angry about me. They felt betrayed by the government, by the president—and here *I* was, sticking my tongue out at them. It was just too much. I was a target for a lot of people who were still mad at their kids who were hippies in the Sixties. I came to symbolize a youth rebellion that I wasn't even a part of!"

But she did join the SLA. At least, she said so in her radio recordings. Was she pretending?

"It was a conscious act," she said. "I didn't have to pretend desperately to want them to say, 'Yeah, you can join.' The appropriate SLA line on my conversion was that my parents had been horrible and they were so decadent and I was being rescued from this terrible bourgeois life that I was leading and aren't I the lucky one to have been chosen by them? If you believe this, maybe we can interest you in some swampland in Florida. But people *did* believe it!"

"Still," I prodded, "you *did* join them."

"It would have been crazy *not* to have joined, because they would have just killed me. It would take much more guts to say, 'Never, I'd rather die.' I'm sorry, I'm a coward. I didn't want to die."

"You must know that when you became Tania, you captured the imagination of a lot of people."

"Maybe *you* liked it," she jibed.

"Well," I goaded, "she was a symbol of defiance, liveliness, and anti-establishment at a time when *many* people were feeling that way."

But Hearst would have none of this. "It amazes me to sit here and hear you say that it was a lively image," she challenged. "It was a terribly violent image. It was the result of a violent kidnapping. Tania never really existed except as a fantasy for most people."

What would happen today, I wondered, if a van stopped in front of her and someone stuck a gun in her face and told her to get in?

"I wouldn't," she said without hesitation. "Forget it. I'd rather be dead." And then the anger that had been simmering all along suddenly exploded. "You have a really odd idea about the SLA! You have this romantic notion of what they were like, that it was all one great adventure! You lived it vicariously and it's just too exciting for you and you can hardly control yourself, and it's so disturbing to find out that I don't even think Tania lived except in people's imagination, like yours—and she *still* lives in yours!"

At this point I couldn't help thinking that I had provoked her into showing me Tania; that Tania really did exist. But she took umbrage at such thinking. "Tania was a total invention," she said. "And while you saw a photograph of this person with the machine gun, the rest of the time what you didn't see was me sort of being weepy and meek and not strong or angry at all."

Still, Tania did hold an automatic weapon during one bank robbery, she did pull the trigger and fire off shots to help two SLA members escape from that sporting goods store, and she was in the car when a woman was shot inside a bank in Carmichael, California.

"Did you know then that Emily Harris had killed that woman?"

"Emily said it was an accident because her finger must have slipped on the trigger," Hearst said. "She couldn't have been more than nine feet away with a shotgun going off, and they always used double-ought buck, which isn't exactly bird-shot. It's a shotgun shell with nine pellets in it, and each pellet is the size of a .30 caliber slug. Anybody would get killed from that."

Her response made it obvious to me that Patty Hearst knew guns. Later she would tell me how she wound up becoming the SLA's weapons expert by reading all their weapons manuals and learning how to break a gun down. It wasn't completely new to her—when she was twelve she and her father went duck hunting with .28 gauge shotguns. "There were always guns in the house, always loaded," she would tell me. "My father had a gun in his bedside table and one in his closet and hunting guns all around the house."

I asked her if she still liked to hunt. She said that she did: pigs, deer, and ducks.

"What else would you feel satisfied shooting?" I wondered.

"Oh," she said, "maybe you."

We both smiled, but neither of us thought it funny. And then Patty added, "Every hunter will think I'm right. They'll think, Boy, what a jerk she is to talk to this guy!"

In the end, I could not come to a conclusion about whether I believed she had been brainwashed or whether she had jumped the shark and gone over to the dark side for the misadventure of a lifetime. Her parents had hired a world-renowned lawyer (F. Lee Bailey) and a world-renowned psychiatrist (Jolly West) to prepare her for trial, and since their defense was going to be that she had been psychologically manipulated (i.e. brainwashed), then the hundreds of hours they spent with her might also be considered a form of brainwashing. What I came away believing was that Patty had a strong instinct for survival and would do anything she could to stay alive.

She seemed able to put her ordeal out of mind and return to the life of a privileged heiress, even becoming an actress for some of John Waters' films. But did she hone that acting talent during this ordeal? And seeing how effective it could be, did she carry it through to her life back home, as she faced the Judge in the courtroom? That was something I could never figure out. I don't think even she really knew. So after interrogating her for dozens of hours, writing about her and talking about her on talk shows, I learned that the mind is a very tricky thing to figure out, and it's hard to say what games it will play to survive, whether it be threatened by the SLA or a prison sentence....

78. TRUST YOUR INSTINCT TO REMAIN COOL UNDER PRESSURE

...Or having a gun pointed at you, as once happened to **Sandra Bullock** before she became a movie star. She once worked as a waitress and told me this story.

"I was leaving the place I worked at," she said. "This guy had a gun with an apple on top of it—I think he was pissed at Eve and was taking it out on me. He was really messed up. I couldn't understand a word he said except for 'pussy.' He dragged me into an alley. I had $189 and I certainly wasn't going to give it to him. I told him if he wanted pussy it was going to be dead pussy because he'd have to shoot me. At first I thought about kicking the gun, because I was a dancer, but then I thought, what if it went off in my face? So I thought, if I turned and walked away he might shoot, but he might not hit my spinal cord. That's all I kept thinking. I walked back to the restaurant and I was fine."

Perhaps she learned something about herself that she was able to bring to some of her future roles, staying cool under the pressure of driving a bus rigged with explosives in *Speed*, defying *Gravity*, or becoming *Miss Congeniality*.

79. COURAGE IN THE FACE OF DEATH

A similar occurrence happened to **Farrah Fawcett** in a New York gypsy cab taking her to the theater where she was appearing in *Extremities*. "The driver pulled over, stuck a screwdriver in my face, and demanded all my money," she told me. "I don't usually back down in most situations, and in my mind I'm thinking, If he goes for my face, I'll pull back and kick up at *his* face with my stiletto heels. The screwdriver would get me in the leg, which would hurt but it wouldn't kill me. If he wants to duke it out, my legs are strong. I said, 'Come on, chicken. You going to use it or what? Come on!' He shouted for my money. I said, 'No. If you took me where I wanted to go, I would have. Now do something or let me out because I have to go!' He started screaming, 'Get out! Get out!'"

That incident, and the success of the play, were turning points in Fawcett's life. She proved, both to herself and to others, that she wasn't to be taken lightly, that she was no *Charlie's Angel* airhead. She actually was a tough, resolute woman who figured out how to survive in a town that too often pigeonholed pretty women. Although her bathing suit posters hung on the walls of teenage boys' dorm rooms and bedrooms, her inner beauty surpassed any picture we saw of her.

And when she was diagnosed with a devastating terminal ill-ness in 2006 she fought it for three years with the same fierce determination she showed that gypsy cab driver.

On July 1, 2009, on my way home from her funeral at the Cathedral of Our Lady of the Angels in Los Angeles, I got into a car accident that was entirely my fault. I had been thinking about what had happened after the service, when I was talk-ing in the courtyard with Ryan O'Neal. A well-groomed woman came up to him, and he smiled flirtatiously. "Dad!" she said in reproach. Ryan blushed, apologizing for not recognizing his own daughter Tatum. I blushed as well, embarrassed for both of them. At the time I joked that I once hadn't recognized my 14-year-old daughter at a health spa when she had gotten a new haircut. But this was different. Ryan was there to mourn Farrah, not to use his grief to score with women. That he had unknowingly targeted his 46-year-old daughter made it all the more surreal. Back in my car, the accident cut short my drifting mind and made me realize that the memory of Ryan's behavior might have been the last thoughts of my life.

Farrah Fawcett was unique among the stars I knew. She enjoyed being out of the spotlight, not being chased by fans and photographers. "I never had this burning desire to be an actress," she told me for a *TV Guide* story in 1994. "I didn't study drama, I didn't know the business. I came out here on a lark. I was signed at Screen Gems for $350 a week, then did an Ultra Brite commercial and I started making all this money. I was just going with the flow."

That flow led to her becoming an "overnight" sensation when she appeared on the TV series *Charlie's Angels*, and even more famous when she was the only Angel to leave the show after the first year. She had more serious aspirations, some of which came to fruition when she played an abused wife who set her husband on fire in the TV drama *The Burning Bed*. That earned her both Emmy and Golden Globe nominations. She went on to play complicated women, such as one who hunted Nazis (*The Beate Klaarsfeld Story*), inherited a fortune (*Poor Little Rich Girl* Barbara Hutton), murdered her children for love (*Small Sacrifices*), captured wars and adventures as a *Life* photographer (*Margaret Bourke-White*), was marked for murder (*Murder in Texas*), and practiced law under the threat of death (*Criminal Behavior*).

But it didn't matter how seriously she took her profession, her fans saw her as approachable; many of them couldn't separate the star from the person. "Fame," she acknowledged, "tests and inconveniences you. I didn't like signing autographs when my son was younger and with me, or when I was having a conversation with my mom. It's intrusive and people don't see it. There are just places I can't go anymore. If I stop to sign one autograph, they say, 'Please, we love you,' but if I keep on walking they say, 'We don't care, you're not even a good actress.' Not long ago I was in the ladies room and there was another lady in there. She said, 'Oh my God, it's Farrah Fawcett.' She started weeping, took my hand, kissed it, and then began rubbing it. You're not prepared for that. I'm consciously aware of how it affects my family, my friends and me. Some celebrities may enjoy it but I have a side that I would like to keep private."

She spent more time in her studio painting and sculpting clay than she did before film or TV cameras. She was athletic and played paddle tennis whenever she found a partner. When she learned that I played on Sundays with Al Pacino she invited us to join her and Ryan playing doubles. Al and I were impressed with how well she played—hard and with a competitive spirit. Often when Al and Ryan couldn't play, she and I played singles. We would meet at different courts in Studio City and Culver City. When we took breaks we would talk. She would tell me about the difficulties she had with men or the problems she had with her son Redmond. She would discuss how corporations like Playboy took advantage of her and how she often had to go to court to preserve her self-esteem. She thought that we should work on a book together.

I had written a book of conversations with Al Pacino and invited her to an upcoming book signing I was doing on September 30, 2006. The day before the event she called to tell me a terrible secret she had been keeping, one that would keep us from ever again meeting down at the Culver City courts. "I wanted to go to your book signing tomorrow," she said apologetically, "but a lot has been happening to me. I haven't told anyone, but I've got colon cancer and will start chemo and radiation next week at UCLA. I may lose my hair, but at least I won't have to wear a bag. I was worried about that, but the cancer is in the skin. I asked the doctor, 'Will I be able to play paddle tennis?' I'll be nauseous the first five days of chemo, but I should get better after that."

I don't remember what I said, something stupid and generic probably, but I do recall how she tried to put this terrible news in perspective. "I thought of an opening for our book," she said: "The three words I never wanted to hear: Tumor. Malignant. Anal. Nothing's ever been up my butt."

Over the next three years Farrah fought a battle for her life, one that she knew she couldn't win. But she fought it with dignity, courage, and determination. She didn't roll over and wallow in "Why-me?" pity. Instead, she asked her friend Alana Stewart to film her decline for a documentary that was intended to bring light to her darkness. She wanted to show how debilitating the disease was in hope that it might ignite a spark to raise awareness as well as funds for research. She wanted to use her decline in a positive way.

Some actresses who were as glamorous as Farrah might have preferred that their fans remember them from their beautiful films and posters. But Farrah wanted the world to see how cancer stripped away the façade, how it hollowed the cheeks, burned into the eyes, turned hair wispy and left bodies skeletal.

She had a rare form of anal cancer that she fought with drugs both established and experimental. She fought it on two continents, flying off to Germany for specific laser treatments, and receiving therapy at UCLA Medical Center where, unfortunately, her records were leaked to the tabloids. She fought it in great pain as her friend filmed her struggle. She knew the importance of using her fame to draw attention to this horrible disease, which manifests in so many different forms.

Our government has spent more money fighting unwinnable wars than trying to fight a disease that might actually be defeated if that money were redirected. Cancer was still that unpronounceable word that needed to come out from the shadows. It was not a disease to be ashamed of, but one to be tackled head on. That's what Farrah did and, for those of us who knew her, she gave *us* strength. She wasn't afraid of dying; she had faith that she was going to a better place, where pain and suffering didn't exist.

I asked her about this and she smiled her radiant smile and said, "My idea of heaven is everything that I wish was here. Clouds, time, peaceful and relaxing. Being able to sleep late. Where people are all in white and they're not talking about you behind your back. If they do, then you get to send them back down. I can't wait."

More than a lesson, Farrah was an example of how to overcome the insurmountable with grace and style. She's at the top of my list when I think of profiles in courage.

80. SUCCESS IS FAILURE
TURNED INSIDE OUT

Montel Williams is not far behind. When he called to ask if I'd be willing to work with him on a book regarding his coping mechanisms living with multiple sclerosis, he had only one question for me: What was my opinion of medical marijuana? He wanted to include a chapter about its lifesaving value for him. I told him that I had no problem with anything that helped someone in pain.

And then I had a question for him: "Why me?" A couple of years earlier I had spent a few weeks with him doing an interview for *Playboy*, and we got into some pretty raw, emotional areas. *Playboy* had scheduled it to run a few different times, but other newsmakers kept pushing our interview aside until the editors just abandoned it altogether. That happens occasionally in the world of periodicals, but I was disappointed that this particular interview didn't run, because Montel had a lot to say and I found him to be a complicated and thought-provoking guy. I figured that he must have been disappointed as well and, since he had never seen what I had written, I worried that he may have thought whatever I had given *Playboy* wasn't good enough—which was either a negative reflection on him or on me. Since he had a substantial ego, I assumed he just thought I was the failing party. So now I was curious how he came to ask me to work with him.

"I just remember going places with you that I hadn't gone before," Montel said about our interview. "You were able to bring it out of me. I can't remember crying as much as I did, trying to answer your questions."

Though I have sat through emotional moments with many of the people I've interviewed, Montel had a lot to cry about and was man enough and open enough to allow his emotions to freefall. What he revealed for our unpublished interview was just a prelude to what he would tell me for the book that became *Climbing Higher,* and that was powerful enough to land on the *New York Times* bestseller list for a number of weeks in 2004. He confessed that after being diagnosed with MS, he had a hard time dealing with it. He had made three attempts at suicide before he came to grips with the disease and he described each one in sobbing detail. He went through a divorce, helped some women he had impregnated have abortions, and grappled with being a father to his four children. Throughout his ordeal, he took every prescribed drug available to try to decrease the horrible pain that shot through his feet while taping his daily TV talk show. He found that the legal drugs fogged his brain, while weed went right to the source of the fire he felt in his body. It calmed him without the horrible side effects he got from taking Vicodin, Talwin, Zoloft, Percocet or OxyContin,

Because his publisher (New American Library) wanted the book out at the beginning of the year, I only had five weeks to research and write it—a task I deemed impossible. But Montel had faith in me, even though I couldn't understand why. He hadn't seen the *Playboy* interview I had done, and he may or may not have read some of my other work, but he considered himself a good judge of character. As we discussed the upcoming book over a joint, I told him I was surprised that he had such faith in me, when the only thing we had done previously had resulted in what I considered a failure. He just took a hit and passed it to me, saying, "You'll do fine." I don't recall if he added, "Because success is failure turned inside out," because the stuff he passed me has fogged my memory. But he very well might have, because that's how he saw it. And how I came to see it as well

81. PAY ATTENTION TO DINNER
PARTY STORIES

Nobel Laureate **Dr. Richard Feynman** had a different survival story that he related at a small dinner party that I knew deserved a magazine piece because it was both remarkable and close to life threatening. His friends, the artist Jan de Swart and his wife Ursula hosted the dinner. Feynman told a story of how he had stumbled outside a computer store, hit his head against a wall, and began to lose his mind. "It broke a few little vessels, and they were leaking very slowly, bleeding inside, so that they built up pressure inside my head, and it pushed my brain around out of shape, to make room for the blood. If we hadn't stopped it, I would have gone into a coma and died." Before he had two holes drilled into the side of his head to relieve the pressure, he behaved erratically without realizing it was due to his accident. He put up wrong equations on the blackboard during his lectures and was only corrected when another physics professor noticed. He went to the home of a model he was sketching and after she removed her clothing to pose, he went into another room and fell asleep. When he went to go home he couldn't remember where he parked his car.

I knew a good story when I heard one, and the Sunday magazine editor at the *Los Angeles Times* agreed, so on Feb. 28, 1986, I went to see Feynman at his Cal Tech office and got that story on tape. We also spoke of other things, including his being asked by the government to join a committee investigating the explosion of the Space Shuttle (a problem he solved a few weeks after our talk). He also shared his thoughts on art, literature, publishing, journalism, the Manhattan Project, psychiatry, the human brain vs. machines, hallucinations, his childhood, sports ("I thought I was a sissy") and winning the Nobel Prize in Physics in 1965. He spoke about the puzzles in physics and how he felt that "almost everything is uncertain." When Feynman agreed to write his memoir, *Surely, You're Joking, Mr. Feynman*, he told his publisher, "I'm not going to go on TV, and I'm not going to sign any books." So a signed copy of the book is rare. When I asked him at the dinner party if he would sign my copy, he told me, "I don't sign my book." I apologized for asking, and then he relented and signed it to me. "Not many of these," he smiled.

Feynman was one of the legendary teachers at Cal Tech and had a considerable following among the scientific community. I had jumped at the chance to join that small dinner party and didn't expect to come away with more than a signed book, and I certainly wasn't thinking magazine cover story. But when you're given the opportunity to meet someone like him, you take it, because you never know what might come of it. In this case, I listened to what he said in a relaxed setting, and turned it into an opportunity to meet him on a professional level and probe his brilliant mind with whatever questions I thought would interest us both. Years later, a rare book dealer told me that she had sold a signed first edition of his memoir for $24,000. That got my heart beating until I checked my copy and saw it was a seventh printing. But that didn't really matter, because my dinner and interview with the Albert Einstein of his day enriched my life far more than any first edition would have.

82. GIVE CONTROVERSIAL SUBJECTS ENOUGH ROPE TO SURVIVE...OR HANG THEMSELVES

You could hardly say **Mel Gibson** enriched my life, but he is a survivor in his own right. He displayed little courage when his temper so often got the best of him, and surviving the shit he's put out is something to behold.

Gibson might not reach the rung in Hell where Bill Cosby will reside, but considering all the communities he has offended (gays, Jews, feminists), I'm sure there are many who are sure that if he's right, and there is a Hell, he's already guaranteed a cubicle.

I interviewed Gibson soon after he finished directing and starring in *Braveheart*. That's when he told me he believes in Hell and in a graphic image of the Devil. Since he was convinced there was an afterlife, he said, then Hell had to exist, because there had to be a place for people like Hitler and Pol Pot, and it certainly couldn't be in Heaven, where his mother resided.

As for his description of the Devil, he thought it was "probably worse than anything we can imagine," but he gave it a shot: "The beast with eight tongues and four horns and fire and brimstone."

I've seen such a beast in Nepalese paintings and assumed Gibson had as well. Or maybe he just had visions of what might come if he wasn't a good boy. But then, he also believed that he was going to be with his mother in Heaven. In other words, all that drunken anti-Semitic ranting claiming that "the Jews are responsible for all the wars in the world," all that cursing and threatening to bash his ex-girlfriend Oksana Grigorieva's head in with a baseball bat (that she recorded so the world could hear him at his worst), all that gay bashing where he told the protestors to fuck off, didn't disqualify him from being up there with Jesus, Mother Teresa, and Mother Gibson. At least not in his mind.

I asked him if he thought that the Church should allow women to be priests.

"No," he responded. "I'll get kicked around for saying it, but men and women are just different. They're not equal. Nobody's equal. But women's sensibilities are different."

"Any examples?" I asked.

"I had a female business partner once. Didn't work."

"Why not?"

"She was a cunt."

"And the feminists dare to put you down!"

"Feminists don't like me," he said, "and I don't like them. I don't get their point. I don't know why feminists have it out for me, but that's their problem, not mine."

"What did you so dislike about your former business partner?" I asked, still slightly reeling from what he called her.

"She was more vicious than any guy in business I've ever seen. She thought she needed to overcompensate for the fact that she was a woman. Which is just bullshit. It's like unbelievable ferocity and unreasonableness. Then, when you got to her reason, she'd pull the woman thing on you. She wasn't fair. They don't play fair."

"All women, or just this woman?" I just wanted to give him a chance to get that foot out of his mouth.

"It happens a lot," he said. "They're not coming from the same place at all. There are certain things men will never understand about them. We'll never get it. And you're supposed to be nice to them. Because they can hurt you."

So you have to ask yourself: If Mel Gibson can get through the Pearly Gates, is Hell only reserved for child molesters, serial killers, and Adolph Hitler and not for those who bash gays, Jews and feminists? Are racial slurs, violent threats and homophobia just minor offenses that God will overlook?

Gibson might say that Hell is where those who deny that God created the world in six days and who believe in the theory of evolution reside. He's sure that God created man in his image and that we are not descended from monkeys and apes. "It's bullshit," he told me emphatically. "If it isn't, why are they still around? How come apes aren't people yet? It's a nice theory, but I can't swallow it. There's a big credibility gap. The carbon dating thing that tells you how long something's been around, how accurate is that, really? I've got one of Darwin's books at home and some of that stuff is pretty damn funny."

Gibson's anti-gay comments appeared in a Spanish news-paper. It didn't take long for the gay community in Hollywood to spit on him in protest when he appeared at Mann's Chinese Theater to stick his hands in cement. "They had signs," he said, "they were screaming and frothing at the mouth. Pure hatred. That's when I found out I was a misogynist, a bigot, a racist, a neo-Nazi and a homophobe."

He must have known this before being enshrined in front of the theater, but the memory of it stuck in his craw. When I asked him if he ever considered apologizing for whatever he said, he answered, "I was interviewed on national tele-vision asking me that. I said I'm not apologizing to any-one. I'll apologize when hell freezes over. But I'll say this: it's made me totally paranoid. I've got to learn to keep my mouth shut."

Gibson obviously hasn't learned his lesson, but I learned mine by just letting him talk. Given enough rope he always seems to hang himself. And yet he continues to survive. ...

83. DON'T BEGIN WITH THE SENSATIONAL

Christian Slater, on the other hand, has managed to survive the minefield that was his volatile life after a sobering stint behind bars.

When Slater got out of jail in March 1998, after serving 59 days for booze and drug-related violent misbehavior and resisting arrest, he called to ask if I would consider writing about his experience for *Rolling Stone*. He knew that the media would be all over him for his story and he didn't want to have to tell it more than once. *Rolling Stone* was his magazine of choice and, as I had previously interviewed him for *Playboy* he felt he could trust me to get the story right.

This is what put him behind bars: He was drinking tequila, doing acid and snorting cocaine with Petra Brando and her date, Jacques Petersen, and their friend Michelle Jonas, whom Slater knew. They were partying on the 14th floor apartment of a Los Angeles hi-rise when things got out of control. Slater may or may not have started beating on Jonas, but he definitely got into a fight with Petersen. In his drug-induced state he ran out to the balcony and attempted to throw himself off it when the others grabbed him and got him back into the apartment. A janitor somehow appeared and got kicked in the stomach. When the police arrived, Slater attacked a cop in the stairwell and tried to grab his gun. When he came down from his high, his memory of what had happened was fuzzy. He remembered fighting with Petersen and attempting to fly off the balcony, but had no memory of laying a hand on Jonas.

It wasn't the first time Slater had to be restrained by the police. He had been in trouble twice for drunken driving, in 1988 and 1989. The second time involved a West Hollywood car chase, in which he wound up kicking a cop in the head as he attempted to scale a fence after driving down a dead-end alley. In 1994 police detained him after a Beretta pistol was found in his luggage at JFK airport.

Slater was 29 when this latest incident occurred. He had appeared in 29 movies, including a few like *Heathers, Pump*

Up the Volume, and *True Romance,* where he had been compared to the young Jack Nicholson, his favorite actor. He started acting at the age of seven, when he appeared in a TV soap opera *(One Life to Live)* and at the age of nine, he joined Dick Van Dyke in a nine-month traveling tour of *The Music Man.* At 16 he was acting opposite Sean Connery in the film *The Name of the Rose.* He often seemed to get into trouble and dropped out of high school to pursue his acting career. When I first interviewed him, I listened to his stories and thought that I was sitting with a real-life Holden Caulfield. I suggested that he had a good memoir in him. After the *Rolling Stone* interview (the magazine was eager to get it), he began to think I was right and asked if I wanted to work with him on a book.

I introduced him to playing paddle tennis and we'd talk about it after working up a sweat on the court. Since his latest run-in with the law had garnered so much attention, including an *E! True Hollywood Story* docudrama that reenacted what supposedly happened in that apartment, I believed that he should begin with the sensational and own what happened, and what didn't. Just as Bill Clinton memorably denied having sex with "that woman," I thought Christian should say upfront that he did not pin down the woman's arms with his knees and beat on her face, as was alleged. In Clinton's case, he really did have sex with "that woman." In Slater's, reports of his violent behavior were somewhat exaggerated. "The fight that happened was not between me and the girl at all," he told me. "It was between me and this guy. After the fight, I tried to kill myself by jumping off the balcony. They pulled me back in."

The combination of alcohol and drugs altered his consciousness and made him paranoid. When the police showed up, he scuffled with them, and when he was on the ground he somehow managed to pull a gun from one of the cop's holsters. No shots were fired, no one wound up in the hospital, and no charges of rape or assault among the four people in the apartment were filed. But if you want to bury the incident, you don't resist a cop who has come to take you away, and you definitely don't take his gun.

I knew a good beginning when I heard one, and pulling readers in with his detailed account of what did and did not happen that night would make a riveting Chapter One. What he said for *Rolling Stone* was only the tip of the iceberg and, once I was able to flesh out the story, I knew we'd have no problem finding a publisher.

But just as Rodney Dangerfield looked at his life on the page and realized he didn't want his children to read about his sad, miserable life, Slater read that chapter and didn't feel comfortable having the nightmare of that night as the introduction to his life story. The incident was behind him. Jail was behind him. He had a new girlfriend and a new attitude. He wanted to start over. His life story could wait, he felt. Maybe when it wasn't so raw, maybe then. So we never worked on Chapter Two.

That's where we should have started. Wherever that was. As long as it wasn't what happened in that apartment with those people and those drugs. I might have later convinced him to begin with the sensational, but I should have written the rest of the story first. He had a great story to tell, but I didn't get the chance to tell it because he couldn't see the forest for the trees. When it's your life, the perspective is narrow, and personal survival also applies to legacy.

84. CRYSTALS, KARMA, GHOST ENERGIES AND GUARDIAN SPIRITS ARE RECORDED FACTS

When you know you're going to die, that perspective can actually broaden. **Patrick Swayze** showed me that.

Blame Francis Coppola for keeping Patrick Swayze off the dance floor after the huge success of *Dirty Dancing*. Speaking to Swayze at his five-acre estate that bordered the Angeles National Forest, he told me, "It was not easy to turn down an ungodly amount of money five or six times for *Dirty Dancing 2*, but I remembered something Francis Coppola said when we were doing *The Outsiders*. I had spent a lot of time asking him, Why's he doing this? Why's he shooting that? I wanted to learn because I wanted to direct some day. He took it as me wanting to cover my ass. So he said, 'Patrick, you know, being a dancer... dancers are pretty narcissistic people, they spend their lives looking at themselves in a mirror.' It just blew me away. And it was one of the reasons I became so adamant about keeping dancing out of my life."

Before he died of pancreatic cancer in 2009, Swayze had a wonderful life outside of acting. He had six horses that he could ride into the forest, and a dance studio where he and his wife Lisa could perfect their talents. He was into archery, photography, and surfing, and dabbled in Transcendental Meditation, Nichiren Shoshu chanting, Buddhism, est training and, for a while, Scientology. That's why he was so believable in entering the spirit world in *Ghosts;* he relied on his personal belief in the subject rather than acting tricks to be convincing. And though I'm a bit of a skeptic when it comes to such things, I must admit that after spending the day with Swayze, I learned to tone down my doubts and take some of what he told me to heart.

When I asked him if he had any rituals he went through before doing something risky, rather than rely on stunt doubles for his films, he said, "Lisa and I have a lot of crystals. They're as magical as I decide they are. They've become very important in our lives. The energy that emanates from them is a recorded fact. I believe they give power if you allow them to. I surround myself with them. In *Point Break*, when I had to skydive for the first time, I visualized myself on the ground. Whether or not crystals work, it's the brainwashing aspect that puts you in a very positive head. It helps you connect with that center. I feel that anything you believe is true. If you believe at all in karma, you surround yourself with powerfully positive karma."

I've asked many people if they believed in reincarnation and have often gotten glib responses, like Norman Mailer saying he wasn't sure, which is why he stopped stepping on cockroaches, or Jesse Ventura saying that he hoped to come back as a 38DD bra. But for Swayze, the question was "controversial. I believe I have seen some past lives," he said. "And the things I've gotten from those past lives are part of how I run my life and live my life."

Since he starred in *Ghosts* with Demi Moore and Whoopi Goldberg, and made us all want to believe that the power of love can conquer death, I asked him if he thought ghosts existed. "Do I believe in ghosts?" he repeated. "I believe that the energy that operates our bodies cannot be contained by flesh and bone, that is recorded fact. So what contains it? What keeps it inside this flesh? Why does it not just dissipate in the air? From a physics point of view I believe that we have a spirit."

"And from a personal point of view?" I asked.

"I have had some major blow-away things happen," he answered. "There were times trying to do this surfing for *Point Break* that I thought I was going to die. I think I spent more time on the bottom of the ocean than I did on top of the board. When you're held down for three to six minutes and you finally come up to get a gulp of air, and all you get is the next wave crashing you with a lungful of water, only to be held down again for another five or six minutes—it's the scariest thing I've ever felt in my life. You don't know what's up or down, and you are blacking out. But then I had this feeling of something pulling me up. And I knew something else was looking over me and I felt this energy. I saw crystals in my eyes. And the crystals connected to a man who I knew to be a warrior from a long, long, long time ago. He jumped in front of my face. He was in my eyes telling me which way was up. It was almost like a dream. But I absolutely feel that we have guardians...and that's a big part of the reason for my research into spiritual things and Eastern philosophies."

Swayze was an early environmentalist. He worried about the problems of pollution, greed, and the destruction of the rain forests. He thought that our survival depended on a collective consciousness that could bring the world to its senses. "We all have to have reasons for faith and hope in our lives. Because ultimately that's all we have. The doors in a metaphysical, higher-consciousness way are being opened all over the world right now. It's just a matter if we are going to be willing to educate ourselves and step through them. My fear is from the Saving-the-Earth point of view: Are we capable as a species to unify and get together fast enough to stop the damage we've done? We're not going to do it at the rate we're going, just by passing a few environmental laws, especially with people staying unconscious about the rain forest and the global warming trends. It's going to take a universal consciousness to do it. Do we have that ability? Or are we going to spend more time blaming each other in terms of countries, and trying to kill each other off?"

Sadly, most likely we'll kill each other off, but I'd like to think that the spirit of Patrick, and all the others who believed as he did and have passed into the next world, can turn things around. His was a healthy, positive soul. And he made one hell of a ghost before he departed.

85. OLD ROCK STARS SHOULD
REST ON THEIR LAURELS

Jerry Lee Lewis is another kind of ghost who wasn't as healthy or as positive as Swayze, but one of the few hard rocker survivors.

The week before flying to Dallas to interview Jerry Lee Lewis, he cancelled and rescheduled for San Francisco. He cancelled again a few days before and said to meet him in Memphis. We booked a flight for the third time, only to have him tell us Miami would better suit him. Coordinating a TV crew is tough enough once, but four times? But this was "The Killer," one of the ostensible two "kings" of Rock 'n' Roll (Elvis, of course, being the other). He and some of his illustrious fellow rockers, like Elvis Presley, Chuck Berry, Little Richard, James Brown, Fats Domino, Sam Cooke, Buddy Holly and the Everly Brothers were the first to be inducted into the Rock & Roll Hall of Fame.

Jerry Lee Lewis wet young girls' panties when he kicked back his piano stool, threw back his blonde hair and sang "Whole Lotta Shakin' Goin' On" and "Great Balls of Fire." He set fire to his piano, years before The Who's Pete Townsend smashed his guitar on stage. He was arrested for trying to get into Graceland to see Elvis, while having a gun on his dashboard. He was banned from performing in England after marrying his cousin (his third wife) a day shy of her fourteenth birthday. He "accidentally" shot his bass player in the chest. He checked himself into the Betty Ford Center for drug and alcohol abuse, only to check himself out the next day. He unloaded 50 sewing machines to gullible buyers and quit that job when "Whole Lotta Shakin' Goin' On" started getting radio play. John Lennon kissed his feet when they first met and thanked him for paving the way for The Beatles.

I had 100 questions to ask him and had great expectations that, even if he answered only half of them, it could become memorable. But when he started addressing me as "Killer," I began to wonder if all that rockin' and rollin' had fogged his mind. "I always call people 'Killer,'" he said, "because I can never remember anybody's name." He had given himself the name Killer as a child, he said, and it stuck. So this Killer interrogated that Killer for an interview that should have been a killer, but wasn't.

It wasn't because he toned down his answers to my most sensational questions. Yes, he was arrested for having a gun on his dashboard at the entrance to Graceland, but it was only a derringer and it wasn't loaded. Yes, he shot his bass player, but it happened because someone had given him a loaded .357 Magnum with a hair trigger and he didn't know what a "hairy" trigger meant until it went off. He set fire to his piano because the following act was Chuck Berry, who kept stealing the show with that duck walking guitar playing, so he lit the gasoline bottle of Coke he had brought on stage and, as the flames burned the piano, he passed Berry with the words, "Follow that, Chuck." Kicking away the piano bench happened on stage one night in 1957 when he was trying to find a way to incite the audience. "I did it and they just went crazy. Well, I found me my gimmick then." He said he "hated" singing "Breathless," because "it's such a hard song to sing; it leaves you breathless when you do it. Over the years I kinda got tired. I'd rather do 'Melancholy Baby.'" He didn't care what anybody thought when he married his cousin Myra. "Everybody blackballed me bad. They said I had done the worst thing in the world. They tried to kill me. I just laughed about it. Spell my name right, you know?"

The obituary writers spelled his name right in 1981 when reports circulated that he had died on the operating table from a severe stomach problem. "There was nothing wrong with my stomach," he said. "It was just my hard head that I had a problem with. I took too many aspirins for a headache I had; a whole handful of them, maybe 15 or 20. I didn't know aspirin was bad for you. I just got through drinking three milkshakes and hadn't eaten any other food and the aspirins ate right through my stomach. I thought, 'This is it, the ball game's over.' My stomach just burst open on me, tried to kill me. They had to operate three times and pronounced me dead. But I knew I wasn't gonna die."

The aspirin story was as deep as I could get Jerry Lee to go. Elvis, Buddy Holly, Chuck Berry, John Lennon, cousin Myra, his preacher cousin Jimmy Swaggart, the wild out-of-control Rock 'n' Roll years—these were all stories worthy of insight and elaboration, but they were just not forthcoming. He spoke about them all, but not with eloquence, shock or humor. I guess one shouldn't expect much from a guy who literally took a handful of aspirins to cure a headache.

Would he like to have changed anything if he had a second chance in life? I wondered. Not at all, he said without a moment's hesitation or reflection. "I don't know what I'd change. Even the bad times were good."

Good for him, but not for me. Sometimes the most promising subjects turn out to be a bore, even though he had survived a lot of wild shit.

■ ■ ■

I don't think some of the women who survived bad marriages would agree with Jerry Lee about those bad times being good.

The first time I laid eyes on the woman who would become my wife, I knew I had found my soul mate. She was sitting in a friend's car, and mispronounced my name upon introduction, but I knew instantly she had a purity of soul unlike any woman I had met, and that she would make me a better person. It took her a bit longer to feel mutual sentiments, but after eight years we tied the knot.

So I understand when people I interview tell me how they met the loves of their lives, and how they just knew that their love would last forever. But since so many people I've talked with are actors, I also understand that they live in a world of illusion and delusion, and that frequently presents problems.

Three beautiful and talented women come immediately to mind: Kim Basinger, Angelina Jolie and Nicole Kidman. The men they believed they would be buried next to after a long life of love and happiness were Alec Baldwin, Billy Bob Thornton and Tom Cruise. We all know how each of those turned out, but still, there's a lesson to be learned from listening to how they publicly spoke about them when they were married.

86. WHEN YOU TRULY BELIEVE YOU'VE MET YOUR SOUL MATE, GUESS WHAT? YOU HAVEN'T

In 1991 **Kim Basinger** was promoting *The Marrying Man* that costarred Alec Baldwin. "Alec is one of the most talented actors, one of the greatest musicians, one of the greatest *anything*! He really is a wonderful, wonderful talent."

The film was a flop, but Kim didn't care because, "I met Alec." They got married in 1993. It was Kim's second marriage, and I interviewed her again in 1994. I asked her to distinguish between her two marriages. "The first one was about protection and not seeing clearly," she said. "The second one is about as much clarity as one could have right now. This was about having gone through a lot of things together, having seen the worst and the best parts of each other. This is about being in love and being attracted to this human being, really loving him, who he is." She said that their wedding was the most romantic experience of her life and that Alec was the best kisser. "To me, kissing is the most important part of sexuality," she said. "I love to kiss Alec."

I also interviewed Baldwin that year and he told me that he and Kim were "very interconnected, very aware of each other. Our lives are very intermingled. My wife's the Number One priority. I've never met anyone like her. I look at Kim and I see somebody who could have had a lot more of the riches of this earth if she was more out for herself, if she was more selfish. What I want is for us to have great memories. Our wedding was one. And I know I'll never get married again."

In 1997 I did a third interview with Kim, eighteen months after she had given birth to their daughter, Ireland. I asked her if her love for Alec had changed at all. "It's totally the same," she said. "In a different way. In the same measure I love my nine dogs and my seven cats."

Angelina Jolie met Billy Bob in 1998 when they were making *Pushing Tin* together. She knew immediately that he was different from the previous men in her life. "When I met him," she said, "my first thought was: Oh God, that's the kind of person I was hoping existed. The way he talks to people, the things he laughs at. Even physically, the way he looks, the way he dresses, the smile in his eyes, his sense of humor, and his mind when he talks about his work. I was so happy to have met somebody that made a lot of sense to me. I'm just happy to know he's alive. It's like discovering an author who speaks to you, you think, Thank God, that's exactly what I've been trying to say."

Jolie's eyes lit up when she spoke about him, and she didn't hold back her feelings. "I have never felt truly understood or even physically understood by another human being until recently. He's an *amazing* lover! He knows my body. That release that I was looking for, I finally found [*Laughs*]. Just the way he walks. Fuck! The way his boots look in the closet. The way he looks first thing in the morning, when he's just half-awake and I can jump on him. He's just sexy being who he is. When he's passionate about something and he can't get off the phone. Or he can't stop writing. He was supposed to be somewhere two hours ago but he's in a writing frenzy. Or he's in the studio until four o'clock in the morning. His car used to run out of batteries because when he was in a hotel he used to sit in his car and listen to music and think until he ran the gas and batteries out of his car. That kind of intensity translates in every way, and when it's directed towards you, it's the most amazing feeling in the world."

"Amazing" was a word she used often when referring to Billy Bob. "He's an amazing person. He can't help it, and it could be the thing that will drive him mad. It's hard for him to live in himself some times. We all have a bit of that, but he has it to an extreme. He feels everything. He notices everything. And he can't help but be completely honest. He admires and loves things. He knows every different thing about music, because he admires other musicians, because he knows that note he heard somewhere and he can remember it. Or he knows what he hates. A lot of people aren't very open about that. He feels so much, and he's got so much inside of him, that he needs lots of different outlets. He's a great friend, a wonderful father. I go down in the middle of the night and he plays for me the music he just wrote. We're creating characters. We also remind each other in the middle of the night when we're talking that nothing else matters, that we will go through different physical things, we will go through painful things, through times when we both feel like failures, or when somebody's in danger or sick—that will be life. If we can get through all of that, that will be our success. And to know that we're going to get through that, and we will hold on to each other and make things okay, that's what it's really about."

She was so over the moon with the guy that she wanted to *be* him. "We're flawed, like everybody, but we know what to encourage. We want to be the same kind of person. When you finally love somebody and see somebody you really care about, at that point you feel it's so great that he's on this planet. I don't want me being in his life to make his life less. It's important to me. I want to see his films, to hear his music; I want him to be pure and perfect. I don't want to affect him in a bad way."

She said she had never really known anyone the way she felt she knew him. Surely this was a match made in heaven. "We really know each other. Even in the last few months we've sat up talking about deep, deep things. So I know him even more today. We both want to fight for justice, we both don't like lies, we both can't stand things that are superficial or false or somebody trying to hurt somebody or things that aren't free, that are closing in on you. We both have felt sad and alone a lot in our lives. We feel like there is no end to a certain restlessness in our spirit. It's still hard to believe that maybe we can actually stop each other from going back inside ourselves. We cancel each other out."

I mentioned that the gossip columnists were having a field day predicting how long their marriage would last. She would have none of it. "Are they doing that, really? Still? We didn't have a long drawn-out romance that led to a marriage—we were suddenly married. We're both two of the weirder people in this business, which you'd think they'd say we were perfect for each other. A lot of marriages in this town come and go.

We are an exception to that rule, I believe that. Time will tell. It's upsetting in a way when they attack and insult us, say that we don't love each other, say that it isn't real, or put out rumors of us with other people. But we both are desperately in love and therefore need each other to survive. We've been alone for so long, we finally have actually found our match. It's impossible for anything to happen to us. It's more of a survival thing. Also, if you love somebody you want to make sure they don't want something else—you'd hate to think they're not having something they want. You hope that you're enough, but it's your nightmare that maybe they're not satisfied in their life. For me, there will always be that. I'll be jealous if there's somebody who's around him if I have to go away for a long time and maybe be something I'm not—I may think he needs that and wants that more. I've actually told him if I ever caught him cheating on me, I had some daydream about throwing razor blades on the bed. I know where his sports injuries are. I would take a baseball bat. And he knows that. I wouldn't kill him, because I love his children and they need a dad. [*Laughs*] But I would beat the shit out of him. Absolutely. And her! So any woman who reads this: don't even think about it."

Nicole Kidman was 23 when she married Tom Cruise, against her mother's warning that she was too young and should "Hold on." She told me that marriage changed her. "I trust more," she said. "I didn't really trust before Tom. I love being part of his life. We have a thing where we write each other letters, which I keep in a letterbox. It's pretty romantic. We've grown together as people and we're very secure in our relationship. Before *To Die For* I was frustrated about my career. I hadn't worked for a year. Tom was working all the time, and that was when I really realized how much I loved this man. I was able to go, 'Your career is almost more important than mine.' I never felt that way before. I never wanted to live with somebody. I wanted to be alone, take care of myself. I had this fear of being dependent. But it's fantastic when you feel that no matter what happens, you have your friend and your lover on this path with you. That's what I was always looking for. And when I found it and was able to say, I can love somebody and he's going to love me back and not hurt me—that was a huge thing for me. When I met Tom, it was that thing: this is the person that I've been searching for. That's why I get worried when he goes up in a plane because it makes me think, God, I don't know what I would do if he wasn't in this world."

Kim and Alec had an extremely bitter divorce in 2002. She hasn't remarried, though Baldwin did in 2012. Angelina left Billy Bob in 2002, hooked up with Brad Pitt two years later and had two children with him, making her the mother of six. Before their highly publicized marriage in 2014, she said, "What I've learned from Brad is to be able to have the kind of family whose happiness and well-being comes before your own. We built a family. He is not just the love of my life, he is my family. He has expanded my life in ways I never imagined." She filed for divorce in September 2016, unhappy with his parenting skills (or lack thereof). Tom Cruise left Nicole in 2000 and married Katie Holmes in 2006; she divorced him in 2012. Nicole found another love of her life with country music star Keith Urban, marrying him in 2006.

I'm still with my wife, going on 47 years. But you'll never hear her say I'm "one of the greatest *anything!*" Or that I brought her to life. Or that my career was more important than hers. And I've got no problem with that at all. We're survivors.

And it doesn't matter if you're an heiress, a waitress, a dirty dancer, a writer, a movie star or a hard rocker—surviving is a bitch.

To Get Where You're Going, Know Where You're Coming From

87. TREAT YOUR PLANTS TO BAROQUE MUSIC, AND STAY CLEAR OF FLUFFERS

Jim Carrey, like Robin Williams, first made us laugh before he got serious. He more than held his own on the TV show *In Living Color* playing various strange characters, including the extreme Fire Marshall Bill. He ate up the entire screen when he made his first film, *Ace Ventura, Pet Detective*, and followed that with the more outrageous *The Mask*, and then dumbed himself way down for *Dumb and Dumber*. But once he established that he was a combination of Robin Williams and Andy Kaufman, he settled down to a few more sober-minded films like *The Cable Guy, Liar Liar, The Truman Show* and *Eternal Sunshine of the Spotless Mind*.

He didn't want to do our interview at his home in Brentwood, so instead we met in an empty warehouse in downtown L.A.

He seemed comfortable in the sparse surroundings, a place which made it simpler for him to reflect on both the highs and lows in his life.

Carrey didn't have it easy growing up. When he was 14, he left school in the ninth grade after his father lost his job and the family lost their house. They wound up becoming factory caretakers in Scarborough, Ontario, working as janitors and security guards at a wheel-rim factory, and living in a VW camper.

His father, whom Carrey described as the nicest man imaginable, turned into a bigot when they had to deal with the Jamaican and Indian workers. "My father's generation didn't go to therapists and they didn't have self-help sections to wallow in," he said, recalling how he and his brother also took to bigotry to unleash the frustrations of living a homeless life. "The climate where we were working was a war-like atmosphere. The Jamaicans and Indians all wore daggers and were looking for a fight. It was like prison. I put nasty stuff in the cafeteria microwave, like women's sanitary napkins with ketchup and mushroom soup on them. I just wanted to make trouble. My brother used to beat the hell out of his cleaning machine with a mallet. I punched a couple of holes in the offices and made up some story about how I was carrying the fluffer and it got caught under the door and I tripped and the handle went through the wall. We actually were much happier when we left that place, though we were still homeless."

All during this time Carrey practiced his comedy and when he was 15 he did small shows wherever he could find a stage. "I was doing Tim Conway impressions," he said. "Imitating Don Knotts meeting the Roving Reporter. I put ten minutes of an act together and went to the hard-core downtown crowd. My mother put me in the ultimate leisure suit saying, 'It's what all the boys are wearing.' I went with my father, who was going to run my tapes. I got in there and everybody's grooving on some underground guy doing junkie humor. I got up and started doing Fred Tripolina impressions. The owner of the club started playing sound bites from *Jesus Christ Superstar*, 'Crucify him! Crucify him! Crucify him!' And getting on the microphone backstage saying, 'Totally boring.' And that was my first experience. I walked off stage and didn't go back for two years."

At 17 he was the only one earning money to support his family. When he was able to afford a basement apartment in Toronto, his family moved in with him. "To create a space I hollowed everything out of this tiny closet and I'd lock myself in for hours, writing poems, songs, jokes. Trying to figure out the universe."

By 21 he was living in Los Angeles dreaming of strangling his mother and resenting his manic-depressive father. "I wanted to help them, but I went bankrupt; I lost all my money. That's when I realized that I was mad at my parents. I resented them because of the pressure I felt they put on me to be a star and save their lives. And I just logicked it out. Dad was not ill. He got depressed but he wasn't unfunctionable. He should have been out there doing something, because it wasn't up to his son to take care of his father. Every man has to have a sense of self and taking care of his needs."

He also didn't like the direction his impressions were taking him. He wanted to expand his comedy, take each audience to its limit. At one club he crawled into the baby grand piano and stayed there during the next four acts. "I had a microphone, my feet were sticking out. The comics who went on after me all thought I was an ignoramus for doing it, but it was one of those times where I had left my house saying, 'Tonight is going to be unforgettable.'

"Another time I stood up for two hours in the main room of the Comedy Store because I just wanted something bizarre to happen that night. It was just me singing songs from my childhood. By the end of it this audience didn't want me off stage, they wanted me dead. That's why I understand Andy Kaufman, because he wanted to basically go, 'You thought you were going to come out tonight and have a couple of comfortable drinks; instead you're enraged, there's a big vein bulging at the top of your head, you think you have to defend your wife.' Suddenly it's the biggest night of your life, you'll never forget it.

"One time the guy who wrote *Peggy Sue Got Married* came down to see me at the Comedy Store and here's the moment I looked into the crowd and saw him: I was standing on somebody's table with a broken beer bottle, taunting six guys who had been heckling me all night. Those were the creative days. On nights like that I always went home feeling bad, because I didn't get the 'love.' But, at the same time, realizing that they will never forget me as long as they live."

When he was living in Toronto practicing his routines in that small closet, Carrey wrote himself a mock check for $10 million. He carried that check with him until the day his father died, when he put it in his father's coffin. He no longer needed it as an incentive, as he got a real one for his work in *Dumb and Dumber* that same year.

But Carrey's teen years gave him an awareness of how ephemeral life can be. He knew only too well the fine edge between living in a car versus in a home in Brentwood; between warding off hecklers with a broken beer bottle and cashing ten million dollar checks. "I used to walk around the streets thinking, 'What separates me from that homeless guy?'

It's literally an accident. If you feel your life is worth something or if you have something to lose, you're always wondering when the ax is gonna fall."

At some point we started to talk about how much he appreciated listening to Baroque music. "It's really good for your brain and all your body systems," he said. "They've done studies with plants in different rooms: one without music, one with Rock 'n' Roll, and one with Baroque. The Rock 'n' Roll music ones withered and died a horrible death, which is what you want from Rock 'n' Roll music. The ones without music grew OK. The ones with Baroque grew three times as big as anything and towards the speakers."

I'm not sure who "they" were who did these studies, but the results are not surprising. We've always heard that music soothes the savage soul, but I didn't know that it wasn't just any old classical music, but Baroque music—works by Bach, Corelli, Handel, and Vivaldi–that got plants to try to wrap themselves around the speakers.

Rock 'n' Roll kills plants? That was something new to me. And I learned that one way to buck up your confidence is to write yourself a large check and hope to cash one just like it when the world finally comes around to appreciating your talent. I also learned to appreciate how fine a line there really is between living in a tent or a mansion. But maybe all of this can fall in place if you stay clear of fluffers. I mean, I thought a fluffer was someone connected with the porn industry until Carrey talked about using one as a tool. You just never know what you can glean when you listen to someone's life story.

88. SOMETIMES THE HYPE HOLDS UP
Probably what separated **Cheech Marin** and **Tommy Chong** from homeless guys was their ability to turn the illegal stuff

that dreams are made of into comedies that brought them stoner fame and fortune.

The magic of the movies and television is that we see actors and we feel like we know them. We get comfortable with Bill Cosby from *The Cosby Show* until we read about what a sleazy sonofabitch he turned out to be in real life. We look at "perfect" couples like Kim and Alec, Sean and Madonna, Sean and Charlize, Taylor Swift and her current squeeze, and then we're upset when we find out they weren't so perfect together. It's always been that way. We get lured into the illusion of performance and get smacked with the reality of these actors' lives. Rarely is anyone the way they appear.

And then there's Cheech & Chong. The poster boys for getting high. The movies like *Up in Smoke, Nice Dreams, Things Are Tough All Over*, and *Still Smokin'*. The albums like *Big Bambu* and *Let's Make a New Dope Deal*. They were called the Abbott & Costello of the Dope Generation, though some of their off-the-wall antics put them closer in spirit to The Marx Bros. Were these guys really getting stoned all the time? Or were they smoking lettuce and only acting stoned when performing, be it live, on film or on record.

I got to find out when they came to the Playboy Mansion and sat by the swimming pool in two canvas-backed chairs for a video interview back in the mid-1980s. Before the cameras rolled they asked if I minded if they smoked a joint. Before the dope got them high I asked Tommy Chong, who was eight years older than his partner, what was his first impression of Cheech Marin. "It was the first time I'd ever seen a Mexican," he answered.

Which was the same impression Cheech had of Chong. "He was Chinese, but not Chinese. He was like Mongolian or something with a goatee and a tattoo."

Chong, who was a Chinese-Canadian, met Cheech at his improvisational strip nightclub in Vancouver. "Cheech had this gorgeous lady in a fur coat with him; she'd flown in from L.A. just to see him for that night."

"To tell me to fuck off," Cheech added.

"But I didn't know that," Chong continued. "I thought this guy must have something because I judge a guy by his girls. He might be the funniest looking guy in the world, but if he walks in the room with a knockout, I take notice."

Chong was 18 when he smoked his first joint. Cheech started smoking "much later in life." Tommy had three wives and five children by the time he was forty and, though weed was always around, his kids didn't take to it. He'd ask them, "Why don't you get high? Mellow out." And they'd say no. As for acid, Chong dropped it in 1968, "When it was called 'Try this.' It was a great trip. It was like the heavens exploded in my brain. I saw the reasons for a lot of things. Had I not had my drugs, I'd probably be a very successful roofer in Alberta."

When the studios began to see that their stoned-out characters were box-office, Universal, Paramount and Columbia all vied for their attention. Columbia paid them a half million dollars to listen to three of their ideas and wound up buying one of them. "We just used the idea to make the deal," Cheech laughed, "and then we made a different movie. Then we used the same idea to make another deal. The studios went for it. We called it 'The Deal Idea.' After they went for it, we came up with the real one. It's called 'Revised Edition.'"

"It's called 'Make It Up On the Walk to the House,'" Chong said.

With all the money they were making from their appearances, their albums and their movies, I asked how they were investing it. "I have a non-profit organization that I put all my money into," Cheech said. "It's called Relatives. It's been going on for a long time and it keeps expanding."

"I invested all my money in koi fish," Chong said. "I heard there'd be a market for 'em and then, you know, if all else fails, you can eat 'em."

As they shared a joint and admired the naked Playboy models who swam in the pool behind them, Tommy said that he didn't like to perform stoned because it screwed with his timing, and comedy is all about timing. "You have to be straight to do any kind of humor," he said. "If your timing's off a beat, your whole act can go down the drain. I can't work under any other circumstances but being clear-headed. I'm not one of those natural funny guys. I have to work at it."

I asked if they had any fears and Tommy said, "There's really nothing to be afraid of except the fear of not being happy. That's what keeps a lot of people down, that's what drives them and that's what hurts them. It's just that they're afraid to be happy."

"Beyond the Valley of Fear," Cheech chimed in.

Did either of them worry about success spoiling them? "That's where acid cleans house for you," Chong said. "You eliminate that stuff. Because the hardest thing about being successful is staying happy all the time. The sense of guilt comes in; all these thoughts creep in to keep you unhappy. Like your Rolls Royce got a scratch on it. Or, they're late with your $200,000 check. All those things."

"Which are all bullshit," Cheech said.

"Yeah," Chong said. "I mean, it means nothing, because we can always remember when we never had nothin' except a smile and a story."

89. BRING YOUR OWN TRANSLATOR

Neither Cheech nor Chong had any difficulty speaking English. **Jet Li**, on the other hand, had a wonderful smile, a good life story, and very little English.

Before interviewing the martial arts action hero for *Reader's Digest*, I was told that, though he had an understanding of English, he preferred to speak in Mandarin and he would have a translator with him. I didn't like being at such a disadvantage. I know how translators can tone down provocative talk or turn long responses into short ones. When my book of conversations with Truman Capote was translated into Japanese, my wife, who is Japanese, said that the interview sounded nothing like me. She said that every time I asked a question, it was always prefaced with "Mr. Capote sir." It was far too respectful. I've spoken to people who understood the different languages in which my books were published, and I've learned how different each translation can be.

Luckily, I was teaching at UCLA at the time, so I asked one of my Chinese-American students if she could speak Mandarin. She could, so I hired her to come with me. I figured she would be more impartial than Li's translator.

When we showed up at the Ritz Carlton in Pasadena and Jet Li saw that I had brought my own translator, he decided to speak mostly in English, turning to Mandarin only when he struggled for a word or phrase. He said that he spent two years studying English before he came to the U.S. to work. "But I spent more time learning Buddhism than English because while English can help me find work, Buddhism helps me understand life. And not just this life but also future lives."

Li was eight years old when he left his family to study at the Beijing Amateur Sports School, and within three years he was competing against martial artists twice his age. He credited his coach, Wu Bin, for teaching him well and for providing different teachers from all over China. I asked him if his coach became a father figure to him and he answered in Mandarin, which his translator translated this way: "Yes, but he was difficult. But once I became a champion, it was easier. His strategy was to be more of a disciplinarian with some of the other students, but with me he would say, 'You're pretty good, so you don't have to work as hard.' That made me work even harder."

My student was taking notes during this time and when we were alone she countered some of what his translator had said. According to her notes, what Jet Li actually said regarding the father figure question was: "A very bad father. He was too tough. All my schoolmates hoped he'd die. They hated him so much! When I was young, I hated him a lot, but when you become a champion, you like him. He used different strategies. Some children he had to beat up, and hit them and train them physically and force them, but with students like me, he used sarcasm. For example, the coach would say, 'Oh well, you're already the best, you don't have to practice.' So I felt guilty, and it forced me to train on my own will."

Since I had recorded Li, I was able to check what he said with a Mandarin scholar at UCLA, and he confirmed the accuracy of my student's translation. So I didn't feel anything got lost in translation, thanks to having a very bright young woman on my side.

90. IN ENGLAND, YOU DON'T HAVE TO BE JEWISH EVEN IF YOU ARE

Jet Li came from a Buddhist background and a guilt-driven coach, so he was well prepared to hit Hollywood running and be the best he could be. On the other hand, from an ethnic point of view, **Stephen Frears** neither knew who he was or where he was going until he was an adult.

Midway through my interview with Frears in his office at Sony Studio, we broke for lunch. That's when I checked my tape recorder to make sure the previous hour of talk was recorded and discovered that the recorder hadn't recorded any of our conversation. The machine was broken, and I didn't have a backup. So I had to leave the studio and find an electronics store where I could purchase a new tape recorder and get back in time for our afternoon session. It was harrowing. I learned that I should never forget a second tape recorder—which I knew already, but somehow forgot—when heading out to do verbal battle with someone whose time is precious.

But I also learned something else from Frears, and it was much more interesting. I had always admired his movies: *My Beautiful Laundrette, Prick Up Your Ears, Sammy and Rosie Get Laid, Dangerous Liasons*, and *The Grifters*. They were all sensitive, emotional, and well directed. I had read that his mother was Jewish, and so I thought that perhaps he had a "Jewish" sensibility and asked him about that. His answer surprised me.

"I'm more Jewish now than I was fifteen years ago," he said. "My Jewishness was concealed from me. And it was really only when I was about thirty that I discovered I was Jewish."

As a Jew who grew up in Brooklyn and Long Island, this was incomprehensible to me. I responded to what he said with two words: "That's astounding."

"I married a Jewish woman," Frears told me. "Here [in the U.S.] Jewishness is talked about a lot and it's very visible and articulated. I find that rather liberating. In England there's a

307

sort of silence about it. There're many things in England that are repressed. That's the nature of English society. They just eliminate what they don't like."

We went on to talk about his work, including how he got screwed out of directing *Donnie Brasco* and how he worked with Dustin Hoffman in *Hero*. "Dustin is like a patriarch," he observed. "He just embraces everything. He is very generous and very unselfish. It has something to do with the age he is. It's like a rabbinical thing. He just holds everyone in an extraordinary way."

I thought it interesting that he saw Hoffman's behavior as rabbinical. When he explained how he worked, I realized Frears' attitude towards directing also had rabbinical overtones.

"I don't interfere with performers. I let actors bring their work to the scene; I'm not very good at telling them what they should do. They already know what they should do. I generally think the less I'm saying, the better. The people who make films are very, very clever. The actors are clever, the cameramen, the technicians. I often think the director is the most dispensable person on the set. It may be my timidity, but I think if I stay out of the way things will get done."

Is that a rabbinical approach to directing? Maybe if you're a rabbi. But if you're a Jewish director? Not being very good at telling people what to do is not in the tradition of Wilder, Kubrick, Lubitsch, Polanski, Cukor, Brooks, or Streisand.

Actually, with the exception of Woody Allen, it's practically unheard of! But then, Frears was spared the whole Jewish karma thing growing up, so maybe that's what kept him mellow.

91. TAKE THE DRAWING & RUN!

Then there are some backgrounds that seem inconsistent with a child's final career. Coming from a respectable upper class African-American family (his father was a doctor) doesn't seem the path to playing the blues, but **Miles Davis** was an artist who broke down stereotypes and challenged assumptions.

Interviewing him at his home in Malibu was one of the true perks of my career. I'd been listening to him since I first heard *Kind of Blue* and *Sketches in Spain* even before I was a teenager. Meeting him was on a par with meeting some of the other giant influences in my life, like Norman Mailer, Saul Bellow, J.P. Donleavy and Marlon Brando. *Playboy-on-the-Air*, the cable TV show that tried to duplicate the magazine, had made the arrangements. All I had to do was show up prepared.

My research consisted of listening to every album and CD I could get my hands on, and reading whatever I could find out about him. It didn't feel like research. It felt like a gift. Even knowing that he could be a very recalcitrant interview subject, I wasn't worried. My admiration for him would be so obvious, I figured, that he wouldn't show me the contempt he sometimes showed on stage when he played with his back to the audience.

I was right. He was friendly. He answered all my questions. He kept himself focused by drawing figures with colored markers on a sketchpad and drinking whatever he was drinking. When he wanted to make a particular point he would look up from his pad and emphasize how hearing Dizzy Gillespie, Charlie Parker, Art Blakey, and Sonny Stitt when he was starting out was better than anything he had ever experienced with his clothes on..."or with them off." He would look me in the eye when saying that before I arrived he was thinking about what his life might have been like if he had had no outlet to play or if he had no one to play with: "That would be weird. That would be cause for committing suicide."

When I asked his definition of "jazz" and "the blues," he answered, "I don't like the word jazz. I associate it with being nigger and stuff like that. When you say jazz, right away people think you don't know what you're doing, you're kicking your cousin's ass, beating him up and then you feel sorry for him so you start singing the blues. It don't go like that. When I was at Julliard a woman started with that shit, that black people were down and out....so I held up my hand and said, 'I'm from St. Louis and I wasn't broke and I can play the blues.'"

He left Julliard after eighteen months when he realized that was "long enough to know I wasn't going to play any white music," and because, "I was learning more on 52nd Street." That's where he started playing with Coleman Hawkins and Dizzy Gillespie, whom he considered "like Picasso. When you're around a guy like that, that shit rubs off."

I asked him if it was true that Mick Jagger once came knocking and he slammed the door in his face. He answered, "I had a pretty girl in bed. He wasn't invited. I just said, 'Not tonight.'" He didn't care much for Jagger, Janice Joplin, Jimi Hendrix, Bob Dylan, or Barbra Streisand. "I don't even think about people like that," he shrugged. Richard Pryor and Rodney Dangerfield were his favorite comedians. He felt cartoon music, like soundtrack for Terrytoons and Bugs Bunny, was the hardest music to play because so much of it was sound effects.

Miles was the first *Playboy* Interview, done by Alex Haley, and I remembered how angry he was when it came to race. He leaned more towards the fight back philosophy of Malcolm X than the turn-the-other-cheek beliefs of Martin Luther King Jr. "I don't think like Dr. King was thinking," he told me. "Like Jewish people who just walked to their deaths without fighting, I can't see that. I can't see how a man who's walking down the street and somebody shoots at him, how he can remain non-violent."

I had read that he once said if he had an hour to live, he'd like to spend it strangling a white man, slowly. Did he still feel that way?

"Yes, but I found out I would need more time. Give me a week—it'd be a big bonus!"

He smiled and looked up from his drawing when he said that. I smiled back, wondering what he might be thinking about me, but I wanted to know why he still felt that way, after all his years of fame and fortune. "I've been in a lot of embarrassing situations just on account of I'm black," he said. "And I remember that shit. They take a toll on you. I've got a yellow Ferrari and when I take it for a drive, cops are always stopping me because they don't see many black guys in Malibu driving a yellow Ferrari. Just a block from my house, I pulled out and a cop stopped me for speeding. How could I get up enough speed in a block for him to say I was speeding? I had a pretty Italian girl in the car and I knew she was the reason he pulled me over. I said to the cop, 'You take the bitch and let me go.' He laughed and didn't give me a ticket. Another cop once followed me to my house and asked me whose car is this? I didn't even answer him. So he asked me who I worked for? I didn't answer that one either. It's that kind of shit, you know? I can't walk into a restaurant without looking for the way out. A black person like me, when I walk into a nightclub, I always want to see if I can get out. I don't like that feeling. And I don't like people who make it possible for me to feel bad. I don't think it's fair because I make so many people feel good with my music."

During the three hours we talked, Miles did about a dozen drawings. Before I left he signed two of them to me and I joked that it sure beat being strangled.

On my way home I stopped at a custom art framer to have them framed. That night Miles called me. "Larry," he said in that deep, raspy unmistakable voice, "what'd you do with those drawings I gave you?"

I figured someone must have told him he shouldn't have been so generous with his work, as they were worth thousands of dollars. "They're being framed," I answered.

He laughed. I laughed. I always wondered if he had called to ask for them back and I was glad I had the good sense to have them framed before I brought them home.

92. "BLACK IS BEAUTIFUL IS INSANE"

James Earl Jones could say the same thing about making people feel good with his acting, but he had to overcome some big hurdles to get there.

I spent a long time interviewing Jones and remember thinking that he was nothing like I thought he would be. He's a highly complex man who presents a jovial face, which is actually a mask. He's been through too much to ever be a hale fellow well met. He didn't even talk for long periods of time during his youth because what came out was a ferocious stutter. He believed it started when his Uncle Randy passed out in an epileptic fit and his grandmother told him to fetch a doctor. But the roads were covered in five feet of snow from a blizzard the night before, and by the time he walked a mile to ask a storekeeper to call the doctor, his words were as frozen as the rest of his body.

"Besides having epilepsy," Jones related, "Randy was also a stutterer, and I used to mock him. So I felt maybe the law of retribution happened. Ever since, I have been a stutterer."

It was poetry that allowed him to speak without faltering, and from poetry came acting. Jones's deep, melodious voice is one of the reasons people attend his stage performances. And in film, he's only too aware that it's his heavy bionic breathing voice as Darth Vader that has singled him out. CNN thought so when they had him voice their signature, "This is CNN."

Jones is also a contrary voice when it comes to discussing race. "I fully expected there would be a race war when I left the army (following the Korean War), and I expected to use my military training to help defend people."

Things got complicated for him when he fell in love with a white woman while acting in summer theater, and when I brought it up he corrected me. "I fell in love with an actress," he said. "Why say white? We know she was white, but why say it? My job—then and now—is to try to keep my head above the race bullshit without losing my sense of reality. Racism is not politics, it's very personal. It's a form of profound insanity. And any excessive racial consciousness is also the same breed of insanity. 'Black is Beautiful' is insane. Whenever I list my genetic heritage I use all three anthropological words: Negroid, Caucasoid and Mongoloid."

I brought up a point made by Raymond St. Jaques, that in the myths and legends of outer space there were no black people until Darth Vader, who turned out not to be black, but who sounded black because it was Jones's voice, and that might imply that the only blacks in the galaxy were evil forces. He shrugged it off. "Black actors should exploit that," he said. "We should play Mephistopheles, we should take advantage of all that mythology that black is evil."

Jones was a practical man who understood the giant racial divides in our country and crossed it when it made sense to him and disregarded it when he knew it made no sense. He didn't go softly into the American night and he didn't become an assassin or a sniper after his military training. Instead he used his anger to burn brightly in plays and films like *The Great White Hope, The Emperor Jones, The Iceman Cometh, King Lear, Othello, Paul Robeson,* and *Cry the Beloved Country.* The man who once couldn't put two sentences together smoothly became a strong, independent voice that continues to fly in the face of Spike Lee films and movements like Black Lives Matter. To James Earl Jones it's all "racial public bullshit." He has strong beliefs about electrical fields and holistic medicine and has practiced primal screaming. He's also been a student of mysterious forces, though he never bought into Darth Vader's ability to reach out and make a guy choke without making contact.

"What I learned about mysterious forces was confirmed in *Field of Dreams,*" he said. "When you're dealing with a mysterious force, don't try to explain it. That's what George Lucas knew. You just let it be."

93. ANIMALS PROVOKE TALK

Kim Basinger understands mysterious forces. Her whole life has been a mystery to her. She is close to being agoraphobic. She doesn't feel comfortable in her skin, which is difficult to comprehend, since she has such beautiful skin. She doesn't like appearing in public. She definitely doesn't like speaking in public. But if she's acting, she loses her fears and will commit to allowing an ice cube to slide up her naked body, as Mickey Rourke did to her in *9 ½ Weeks,* or do her Veronica Lake impersonation of the blonde femme fatale in her Oscar-winning performance in *L.A. Confidential.* She could rationalize taking her clothes off in *Playboy* by convincing herself that "we're all born into this word naked. I am what I am. I take a shower every day. And at the time I needed worldwide exposure. I needed a film. And that served as a silent film for me throughout the world. *Playboy* gave me carte blanche: pick the pictures, do the writing, do anything I wanted. It was just meant to happen."

She was always beautiful, but also almost pathologically shy as a child. She believed that if she spoke in public she would lose consciousness, and once when she was called upon to read in class, she actually *did* faint. "I remember the kids laughing. My mother had to call my teachers and say, 'Please don't call on her again in class.' Her parents were raising seven children and when her father saw that she liked to sing, he encouraged her to enter the Junior Miss contest in their hometown of Athens, Georgia. "I said, 'Daddy, I don't know whether I can do this. I might get up there and die.' Then he got this woman to be my accompanist during the rehearsals. I did *My Fair Lady*, the whole cockney accent, then segued right into 'Wouldn't It Be Loverly.' That night when I did it, all I cared about was, 'God, please help me make it through without dying.' And after I did it there was no applause, just silence. Because here I was, a senior in high school, and I never talked at all. Then they stood up and started clapping. I didn't care about the applause; I just wanted to get off the stage. I thought, 'Am I dead? Is it over?' But with all I've accomplished in my life, nothing will ever be as exciting as the night that I finished singing at the Junior Miss contest and did not die."

She couldn't wait to graduate from high school and go to New York to become a model when she was seventeen. But of all her new city experiences, the one that left a lasting impression happened in Central Park when a horse-drawn carriage came clip-clopping by. "I saw the horse fall dead in the street and I never forgot it. Ever since, when I return to New York I can't pass by without looking at those poor horses and going, 'Someday. Someday this will be banned.' In the name of tradition a lot of things happen with animals that are truly barbaric."

She was always drawn to animals, and seeing that horse drop dead sparked the activist side in her, and over the years she has spoken out for animals that can't speak for themselves. "There are so many animal rights issues; I could deplete myself in one week," she said when I asked about it. "I've really had to choose. In the last year (1996) I've been working on a 'Free the Elephants' campaign through the Performing Animal Welfare Society in California. Hopefully we can get these animals out of the traveling shows and circuses. It's all about re-educating the public to redefine the word 'entertainment.'"

When she said that she didn't believe in any animal testing, I brought up the fact that animal research helped lead to the discovery of the AIDS virus. But she was adamant. "There are other ways. You don't have to be an animal rights activist, you just have to care about one word: injustice. What right does man have to use the 'lesser creatures'? Animals are great teachers. They taught me to be the mother I'm becoming, because I've brought up so many animals in my life."

At one point, between the cats, dogs, pet rats, gerbils, birds, and cow, she counted 21 animals living under her roof or on her property. When someone once sent her a video of 36 beagle puppies that were being mistreated at a New Jersey lab, she dropped any fears of being a public figure and turned into Super Activist. "This tape showed the extreme abuse this Huntington Life Sciences Lab was doing experimenting with animals. Now people can speak out, but animals cannot. I know what it is like not to have a voice. I was mortifyingly shy. Words used to strangle me as a kid. Yet I had so much rage when I saw the abuse in this tape. They were going to break the bones of these puppies all for the sake of a drug that had already been tested in Japan and used on humans successfully. I offered to adopt them all. They said fine, come and get them. So I went, with the TV cameras at my back. We marched across their lawn and I was shaking so hard! We knocked on their door and the president of this lab came out and said, 'No, no you won't get the puppies.' So I did an interview right there in front of their building. They then let me through the door, and the president came down and I said, 'Have you seen this tape? I am going to release it to the press unless you let me into your lab.' Well, the upshot was that we got Huntington Life Sciences shut down."

I've interviewed Kim four times over the years. We've talked about all sorts of non-animal related topics, from her failed attempt to buy a town and convert it into a film studio to her estrangement with her brother; from her losing a lawsuit for turning down a film she verbally committed to (*Boxing Helena*) to her fierce protective mothering of her daughter Ireland; and from her great love for her husband Alec Baldwin to her great animosity for her ex-husband Alec Baldwin. But I'm convinced that it was tapping into her strong emotions regarding animal rights that loosened her up and allowed her to continue to be outspoken about other subjects. "Animals have done more for me than anything else, because they let me forget about my fears," she said.

And just in case you're thinking that she's like the Norman Bates character at the end of *Psycho*, sitting in a locked cell contemplating not hurting a fly that landed on his hand, she still has her common sense. When I asked her about taking animal rights to such an extreme, she looked at me like I was the crazy one and said, "All creatures need to be treated with as much respect as human beings. We're all living things.

But when I was living in New York with my baby, the apartments were sometimes full of rats and cockroaches. If one ever jumped on me, let me tell you, that sucker would be dead in about one second! I'm not going to live in a horror movie."

Distinguish Between The Person & The Performer

94. BITTERNESS RUNS DEEP

Actors don't always like each other, but they generally won't tell you that when you're interviewing them. They may bitch about a director once in a while, but they don't like to stir things up among their peers. When Sally Field complained about how Tommy Lee Jones once hurt her by twisting her arm while filming *Back Roads*, I thought good for her to be so bold as to actually tell that story. I'm not talking about reality shows like the *Real Housewives of Wherever*, since part of their appeal is that they go after each other's throats. Forget them, they're not real and they're mostly not worth writing about. I'm thinking more of when I got Al Pacino to say that he thought his performance in *Dog Day Afternoon* was more deserving of the 1976 Best Actor Oscar than Jack Nicholson's in *One Flew Over the Cuckoo's Nest*. Pacino didn't go any farther than that; he didn't say he was a better actor than Nicholson, and he didn't say he didn't like Nicholson; just that he felt his performance was more worthy. The voters of the Academy didn't agree with him, but it was noteworthy to even get that much out of him because it's so rare to hear a comment like that.

So when an actor goes full blown nuts about another actor, to the point of making scandalous, even potentially libelous comments, it's certainly a lesson in how strong and deep jealousy and anger can run. **Harvey Keitel** was the teacher here. He didn't hold back when it came to what he thought about Edward James Olmos, the actor who wound up marrying Lorraine Bracco, his ex-partner and mother of their child. When I went to New York to interview him in 1995, Keitel and Bracco were involved in a nasty custody battle over their ten-year-old daughter.

Keitel maintained that Olmos was accused of child molestation in 1992. He also went public that he knew the 14-year-old victim and her family. According to Keitel, the charges apparently were dropped when the family was paid a large sum of money by Olmos, thereby suggesting that Olmos bought his way out of the molestation charges. Olmos and Bracco denied the charges and the fighting between them and Keitel was vicious.

This wasn't an easy topic to broach but one that had to be addressed. I asked him if he was willing to say what he could about what was going on. He didn't hide behind legalities and instead said, "I will not stifle you in your work, so go ahead and ask what you need to."

Given permission to go into such unsteady and slippery territory, I didn't hesitate; I jumped right in.

"Do you believe that your daughter lives with a possible child molester?" I asked. I figured that was the bottom-line reason he was going all out to win custody of his daughter, so I cut to the chase.

"He has been accused of that, but he denies it," Keitel said.

I then asked him about a statement Olmos made to a *New York* magazine reporter, calling Keitel "vicious and disturbed and out of control." He believed Keitel didn't even want his daughter, but was using the situation "to hurt Lorraine and myself."

"He knows that statement is a lie," Keitel responded. "There is evidence in court that he paid $150,000 to the alleged victim's family, and of a secret agreement that he entered into with the parents of this child who made the allegation of molestation."

Keitel said that he called both the parents of the child and also Lorraine Bracco when he heard about this payment, but none of them would speak to him. That further incensed him, and convinced him that their silence was based on a secret deal. I asked him if he had discussed any suspicions he had with his daughter.

"I'm not going to get into that, except to say that I ensured the safety of my daughter as best I could, given that I do not have custody."

"How did you do that?" I asked.

"As of this moment, there is a court order that prohibits him from being alone with my daughter without adult supervision."

I noted that Lorraine Bracco told a reporter that he was "motivated by jealousy and hate." She had even written a letter to *New York* magazine saying: "Keitel is both a destructive and self-destructive person. His jealousy and hatred at my happiness in my new marriage have reached a new low."

Keitel said he didn't want to comment on his daughter's mother. But when I asked him whether he had confronted Olmos directly, he said that Olmos refused to speak to him. "The time for him to talk to me was before he paid the money and entered into this secret agreement to hide these allegations from me," he said. We concluded this part of our conversation with him declaring, "I have an obligation to protect my daughter, and I'm going to live up to that."

Keitel had his own tough road out of childhood. He admitted to being disoriented as a teenager and left one high school to try a vocational school, but was thrown out of that. So at 17 he joined the Marines, and admitted, "Throughout my life I've had thoughts of killing. I defy anyone to say that they have not thought about killing someone. The exploration of these primordial feelings is what the entire journey is about."

He spent time in Beirut, experienced anti-Semitism, returned to civilian life and got a job as a shoe salesman, and then a court stenographer. When he began having thoughts of re-enlisting in the Marines, he auditioned for a student film at NYU called *Who's That Knocking at My Door?* and got cast by the director, Martin Scorsese. A kinship developed between them and five years later Scorsese cast him along with Robert De Niro in *Mean Streets*. The only killing Keitel would do from then on would be with fake bullets in over fifty films, as he became a regular in Scorsese's films, as well as those of Quentin Tarantino.

When young people approach Keitel to ask for advice, this is what he tells them: "Don't die. Keep struggling." Advice he tells himself when the rage and bitterness run deep.

95. DISTINGUISH BETWEEN THE PERSON & THE PERFORMER

When doing an interview for cable television, you don't have to censor yourself as you might otherwise. I was thinking about this when I knew that **Sid Caesar** had agreed to be interviewed. But it wasn't really a cable issue with Caesar. He was one of the funniest men who had ever appeared on TV, and he didn't need the freedom of cable to make people laugh. But I wondered how far he might go if he had free reign.

He was known to have been a tough taskmaster when he headlined *Your Show of Shows*. Mel Brooks was a writer for him, and Caesar supposedly once hung him out the window during a writer's meeting. One of his funniest bits was as The Professor, where he would be asked questions and answer them in memorably hilarious ways.

So when he came to our studio, which wasn't really a studio but a hotel room, I was prepared to ask him the usual questions about his life and times, which he had written about in his autobiography *Where Have I Been?* And then, once we warmed up, I planned on asking him to respond as The Professor. After all, this was a televised interview, and Caesar was the master at clowning for the camera.

But Caesar would have none of it. He was fine with the serious questions, but when I brought up The Professor, he got angry with me. "How can you ask me to do that?" he snapped. "I'm a professional, not a monkey who can get into character on your demand. I'm not going to do that and you should be professional enough to know better than to ask."

Oy-yoi-yoi! That did not go well. His irritation took me by surprise. I thought he might enjoy doing the bit, getting a chance to perform, and making us all laugh. But Caesar had recently turned sixty when we talked and, though I had assumed that he had ad-libbed his character's quips, I now wondered if it had all been scripted, and asking him to ad-lib when he really needed his writers was a mistake on my part. I hadn't been sensitive to that situation. In addition, asking him to perform without pay was the same as asking him for a freebie. That wasn't very professional of me; I should have known better. The man I was questioning so seriously was not the light-hearted performer who had made me laugh until it hurt.

When I asked him to sign his book, he wrote: "Ask 1 question at a time. Like life, have patience." He didn't accuse me of treating him like a carnival monkey, but the chill was there.

96. COMEDIANS ARE RARELY FUNNY OFF STAGE

People who make their living making other people laugh often aren't very funny when they don't have an audience. There are exceptions—Mel Brooks and Robin Williams come to mind—but I've interviewed enough comedians to know not to expect to be entertained when asking questions, not even when you try to be a straight man for them. Sid Caesar actually got angry when I asked him to be funny. Rodney Dangerfield was downright depressed. Jerry Lewis had a lot of bottled up fury. Robert Klein preferred to be taken seriously, as did Lily Tomlin, Danny DeVito, Kirstie Alley, Carol Burnett and Goldie Hawn. But the multitalented **Steve Martin** was the one who seemed the most businesslike. He sat behind his desk in his office and answered questions in the way I would have expected the CEO of a Fortune 500 company to respond. And this was when he was still rocking out crowds of 20,000 in giant arenas around the country, before his first movie (*The Jerk*) was released.

Comedy Is Not Pretty was the name of one of his record albums. He could have put out a sequel, *Comedy Is Not For Interviews*. "It's hard for me to be funny for fourteen days or however long we're going to do this," he said when I asked if we might get the "wild-and-crazy guy" into our conversation. "I can't disguise my true self that long."

I thought I'd begin with his childhood. "Nobody gives a shit about where I grew up and all that," he said. "It's boring."

Okay, I thought, let's go with what interested him. "The only thing of interest to me is the future," he said.

"How do you see your future?" I asked, desperately trying to get him talking.

"I have no idea, so I can't talk about it."

"Let's get this straight," I said. "You're bored with your past and you can't talk about your future. The present is probably too fleeting, so that leaves us with what? Sex?"

"Actually, I'm reluctant to talk about sex or my girlfriends or ex-girlfriends, because that's *really* your private life."

"No past, no future, no sex. What about politics?"

"I'm not political, because I don't know what's going on."

"So what you're saying is you don't have much to say."

"If I had great things to say, I'd say them onstage or in a movie, or somewhere else."

Where does one go from there? That was how we began our interview. He might have thought we were going to talk for fourteen days, but I was wondering if we would get through fourteen minutes.

When he said that "In an interview, you're talking directly: you're not an artist anymore," I mentioned that there was an art to conversation.

"That's true," he agreed. "I've turned down all other requests for interviews because I want this one to have meaning."

"Which will be quite a feat," I laughed, "since you've put so many restrictions on yourself."

We jibbed and jabbed for a while and then I said, "Let's start over. You're a comedian. This is an interview. To hell with the restrictions. Now, who's the funniest person in America today?"

He answered "Richard Pryor," and we finally found a way to kickstart our interview. It lasted a week, not two weeks, but it never got easier because he refused to be funny. Making audiences laugh was his job. Talking to me in his office, even though it was going to reach a large audience, was not about performing. It was his way of searching for meaning. I gave him the platform and returned over the years to interview him for three other magazines. He never made me laugh once.

97. DON'T WRITE A BOOK IF YOU CAN'T DISCUSS YOUR CLIENTS

I don't think Dolly Parton's manager was searching for meaning when he thought it might be fun to write a book about his life.

After I finished interviewing Dolly for *Playboy*, she asked if she could take a look at the transcript before I edited it. I said that I wasn't comfortable with that; it really wasn't the way these interviews worked. She said she understood and murmured that she just wanted to make sure she hadn't said something that would offend anyone. I didn't think she had. Then she said, "Tell you what. I promise not to insist on any changes. It would just put my mind at peace. And if I said something I might regret, then that's just too bad for me. But at least I'll be prepared."

I still didn't want to give in, but I really liked Dolly, so I compromised: I said after I edited our interview and got back the galleys, I would show it to her. That way, she really couldn't make any changes, but she would get to see it before it was published. She thanked me and when I got the galleys, I called her. She was staying at her manager **Sandy Gallin's** sprawling house in Beverly Hills.

When I got there, I was shown into the living room by Gallin's butler, and marveled at the wealth on display. The furniture was luxurious, the lamps were by Tiffany, and the books on the shelves were leather-bound. I had no idea how rich a personal manager could be, and just being in this home was eye opening. I looked at the pool outside and saw a bearded man in his underwear skipping rope. I figured it was probably Gallin's trainer and walked out to see if I might pry some information out of him about his client.

But I was mistaken. He wasn't a trainer. He was Sandy Gallin. Dolly's manager. And Cher's, Michael Jackson's, Mac Davis's, Joan Rivers's and a dozen other well-known clients. We started to talk and he said, "Dolly loves you."

"She's great," I said. "What about you? Have you ever been interviewed for a magazine?"

"No," he said, "I don't like the limelight. Some of my friends do, like David Geffen and Barry Diller, but I prefer to stay behind the scenes."

"I get it. But if you ever change your mind, I'd love to write a profile about you."

"Don't think so. But let's see how the one with Dolly turns out."

Dolly came down about then and I said goodbye to Gallin. She read through the galleys and asked if she could make just one small change. "When I said I didn't want to become like Elton John," she said, "do you think you can add an *'an'* before his name? So it would say I wouldn't want to become like an Elton John?" If that was the only objection she had to our very long interview, I didn't see the harm in asking the copyeditor if she could accommodate her. So I made the change.

A month after the interview appeared, Sandy Gallin called and said if I still wanted to write about him, he'd be willing to give it a shot. I didn't have an assignment to do him, but I thought that I should take advantage of the opportunity. So I went to see him and we sat by his swimming pool for four hours talking about his life. He had told me that his attention span lasted around four minutes, but once I convinced him to turn off his phone he loosened up. We had one more four-hour session before he realized that he didn't really want to be profiled in a magazine, but a few years later he called again and said he was thinking of writing a book. Would I be interested in writing it?

I returned to his mansion in the hills and we began talking again. He had no problem talking about his childhood and how he got into the entertainment business, but once I started asking about his clients he became cautious. "I can't really talk about Michael Jackson," he said. "He'd kill me. I'll have to ask him if it's okay."

"What about Dolly?" I prompted. "You're closer to her than anyone. You've told me some funny stories already."

"But you can't use them," he said. "It violates the manager/client privilege."

"Is that the case with all the others? Cher? Joan? Mac?"

"How can I talk about any of them? They're my clients."

"How can you write a book about being a manager if you can't talk about the people you manage?"

"I can talk about the deals I've made for them. I can talk about how they became clients and what I saw in them."

"But you won't talk about the thing people would be most interested in reading, insight into their private lives, amusing behind-the-scenes anecdotes. What about someone like Streisand, who is your friend but not your client? Can you talk about her?"

"Barbra? Are you kidding? She'd send her lawyers if she knew I was talking about her."

"So what kind of book did you have in mind?" I asked, somewhat perplexed

"Well, you haven't seen my photo albums," he said. "I have an album for every year since I became a manager. I must have over 10,000 photos. We could choose among them and I could talk about where they were taken. People love to look at pictures."

So I spent a few days looking at Sandy's albums. They were full of stars, studio executives, producers, directors, and other big movers and shakers. Most of them appeared in groups, often in pictures taken at Sandy's outlandish parties. Everyone seemed to be having a grand time. It was fun, looking at all the pictures, even if a high percentage were out of focus, or not taken by a professional photographer. But that's all it was. There was no book there. At least not a book that I could help him with.

Sandy had a great story to tell, but he would never tell it. His problem was that he *could* distinguish between the public and private lives of the performers he managed, and he preferred keeping his friends, not making enemies. And anyone who has managed the careers of so many talented people must certainly have the kind of stories that would not make them happy. If you're going to write your autobiography, you must make sure your knives are sharpened. Otherwise it's going to be a dull book.

98. YOU CAN'T FLY TO THE MOON WHEN YOUR HEART IS SOMEWHERE ELSE

Tony Bennett also once asked me to work with him on a book. And that, too, came to nothing because he also wasn't comfortable separating himself from his public image.

Bing Crosby lived until the age of 74. Frank Sinatra was 87 when he died. Tony Bennett is ninety and is still swinging. Born in Astoria, Queens, in 1926, Bennett has been singing about broken dreams, flying to the moon, going from rags to riches, being lost in the stars, wanting to be around to put on a happy face, and leaving his heart in San Francisco for seven decades now, and wherever he goes, his shows are sold out. His voice, like that of Louis Armstrong and Frank

Sinatra (who used to say Bennett was his favorite singer), is immediately recognizable, and his soft, masculine interpretation of love songs has captured the hearts of millions of listeners. The NBC television special *Tony Bennett: An American Classic* received three Emmys. Clint Eastwood co-produced a PBS *American Masters* documentary about him called *Tony Bennett: The Music Never Ends*. He recently teamed up with Lady Gaga for a CD of old standards, and it's a tossup of who hitched whose wagon to the other's star. But it seemed like Tony took to her like she was Viagra for his soul.

I first interviewed Tony Bennett for *Newsday's* Sunday magazine in 1976. He was fifty, living in Beverly Hills, and married to a wife who sarcastically called him "Tony Benefit." The hairpiece was in place, his voice had that familiar rasp, and he seemed genial and simple. In 1977 Bing Crosby died and an editor at *Newsday* asked me if I could reach Bennett for a comment, which turned into a ghosted column. Tony loved Bing. As the years passed, Bennett's career didn't exactly thrive, but neither did it falter. He was on the road more than 200 nights a year, singing at hotels, nightclubs and music halls. He went through two bitter divorces, suffered through the ever-increasing popularity of music that was absolute dissonance to him, played tennis, painted, dressed well, and grayed his hairpieces as he aged gracefully. When his son Danny convinced him that he needed a makeover, Bennett gave him a shot, and by the early '90's Tony's caricature had appeared on *The Simpsons*, he sang "Unplugged" on MTV, shared a mike with k.d. lang and Elvis Costello. He shared the stage with the Red Hot Chili Peppers at the Grammys, and walked off with two of those awards for his Frank Sinatra and Fred Astaire tributes. *TV Guide* asked me to write about his resurgence and I went to see him again in 1994, eighteen years after we first met. He still had the same two basic interests–singing and painting–still played tennis, had a young girlfriend, but his divorces gave him a subtext. There was some bitterness about those failed marriages, and it showed when I brought them up; he dismissed them as quickly and painlessly as he could. But you could see it in his eyes, and hear it when he sang certain songs. His public face, however, was of the aging swinger, the crooner who could hold an audience with the songs he sang. For the world to see, Bennett was forever stepping out with his baby.

At a recording studio in West Hollywood, I watched as Bennett put the finishing touches on his next CD. He would listen to the playback of his songs, sitting perfectly still, like a well tailored Buddha in a plaid sports jacket, floral tie, and shiny black moccasins. Occasionally he would jot a note in his sketchpad, which he mostly used to make quick sketches of people in restaurants or at airports.

After that article appeared, I got a call from Danny Bennett, the architect of his father's resurgence. He wanted me to meet with Tony to discuss writing a book. When Tony and I subsequently met at the Peninsula Hotel in Beverly Hills, he told me that he wasn't all that keen on doing a memoir; it was Danny's idea. What Tony really wanted to get out was a book of his paintings and watercolors to go along with the retro-spectives being given him by the Butler Museum in Ohio and the Smithsonian in Washington D.C. Nonetheless, we started talking, and continued talking over the next few months at my home, at the hotel, over sushi at a Japanese restaurant, and at a recording studio in West Hollywood. I even flew up to San Francisco for a weekend at Tony's request, but when I arrived, he had forgotten I was coming.

"But you told me to come," I said.

"I did?"

"You said you wanted to talk during the day, before your performances."

"I did? I must have forgot."

"Well, I'm here," I said. "We can talk around your schedule."

"I'm all booked up," he said. "I don't have the time."

"Tony, you're the one who asked me to work with you. Let's make some time."

"I can't," he said. "We'll just have to find another time."

"Well, since I'm here, maybe Ralph will talk to me." Ralph Sharon was Bennett's musical arranger and pianist. He had been with him for 35 years. "Sure, talk to Ralph," Tony said.

Some of what Sharon told me had hints of fascinating material. Tony hated the Beatles, he said, but his kids loved them. He disliked Barbra Streisand because he believed she stole a lot of his material. He didn't get along with Mel Tormé because Tormé once put him down on a radio show in Australia. Though he professed to love Frank Sinatra, Sharon believed they had a very "tricky" relationship. "Tony would never admit this, but between me and you, during the years Sinatra has not been that supportive. But Tony's always saying, 'I'm his close friend.' I can remember working engagements when we would get a call saying 'Sinatra's coming,' and Tony would get very excited and then he wouldn't show up. This happened several times and each time Tony would be very upset." The same was true of Elvis Presley's manager, Colonel Tom Parker, who promised to bring "a whole bunch of people" to Tony's show at the Las Vegas Hilton and nobody came.

Tony also resented the word "comeback" and was angry with Danny for using it, because Tony felt that he never stopped working. But he didn't leave his record company, Columbia, in 1972 by choice, according to Sharon: "They axed him." As for Bennett's temper, it could be "explosive" and was usually connected to something going wrong with a show. "He is a compulsive worrier," Sharon told me. "I've never met anybody that insecure." The worst thing you could say to him was to compliment his performance. "He'd say, 'I don't want to be rated.' It's even bad to say to him, 'Tony, that was good.' It's like a superstition with him."

Once Tony went to see a psychiatrist to ask for help. The shrink told him, "Help you? When I got problems, I listen to Tony Bennett records." Bennett thanked him and walked out.

He also tried to walk out on the mob. Early in his career Tony had a big hit with the song "Because of You," but couldn't immediately follow it up. The deejays at the record stations were losing interest in him. But Tony had a manager who had some connections and they found him a song, got some good-fellas to make sure it got radio air time, and all Tony owed was a percentage of his take...forever. According to Sharon–who said Tony told him this–Tony wanted out of his deal with these crime guys but didn't know how to do it. When the police came to him and said they knew about his deal and that he should go tell them he wanted out, Tony went but was told he had to keep paying. Eventually he worked out a figure and bought his way out from under.

Regarding his family, Tony never spoke about his father, thought his brother was a "wastrel," and believed that his mother died in pain and the doctors treated her badly.

Much of what Sharon had told me I expected to bring up with Tony, but after San Francisco I didn't see him again. It was probably just as well. During the hours of conversations we had had, I saw how repetitive he could be. He had a set number of stories that he would tell and retell. Some of these stories I had heard twenty years earlier: how he had worked as an elevator man at the Park Sheraton; in a grocery store; as a messenger for the Associated Press; and as a singing waiter before he got a chance to prove himself in 1949, when Pearl Bailey made him a production singer in her Greenwich Village revue. Bob Hope saw him, asked him to sing in his show at the Paramount Theater and suggested that he change his name from Benedetto to Bennett. Rarely did he embellish or go into depth, and at one point he told me his only real regret was that he wasn't as intelligent as he'd liked to be. But I knew that his life as a postwar nightclub crooner was filled with stories of getting high, making it with admiring women, making deals with the mob, struggling with the wife back home, being a distant dad, and fighting off a thing called Rock 'n' Roll. All I had to do was get him to open up and the book would practically write itself.

The only problem was, Tony didn't want to talk about the infidelities, the drugs and booze, the underworld, his two failed marriages or his neglect of his children. He didn't even want to knock the groups his kids liked but which he disdained. And when he saw where some of my questions were going, he shrugged them off and said he didn't really want to get into all that. He had hoped he could fill the book with innocent anecdotes of the road and how "I Left My Heart in San Francisco" served as his passport around the world. But he found that when he left his heart behind, he flew to the moon on wings of neglect and despair.

At the time, one of his ex-wives was talking about doing a book about him and that's why he was even giving thought to doing a book himself. But after five or six sessions, he decided to back off. He told Danny he didn't want to do an in-depth book, and instead he found a publisher who would put out his drawings, which was all he ever wanted in the first place.

The lessons learned from my time with Tony Bennett were these: A) Talk to the people who know him best, like Ralph Sharon. B) Don't fly to another city for an appointment without reconfirming the day before. C) When the motivation to write a book is to counter a vindictive ex-wife's going public, the motivation wanes if the ex-wife is silenced. D) Appreciate *The Autobiography of Benventuo Cellini*. Cellini was a goldsmith and a sculptor during the Italian Renaissance, a contemporary of Da Vinci and Michelangelo. When Bennett said that he liked to read biographies, I asked him which was his favorite and he said this one. He turned me on to a great read.

99. THE TYPECAST APPRECIATE
BEING TAKEN SERIOUSLY

I don't know if Bennett ever read **Shelley Winters'** autobiography, but I'm sure he would have enjoyed it if he had. Winters was often the butt of racy jokes when she appeared on talk shows, but she was far more than a punch line, which I learned while preparing for her, and she was the only person I've interviewed who thanked me for that preparation.

Winters' movie career spanned six decades beginning with *A Double Life* in 1947 and ending with *Jury Duty* in 1995. She won two Best Supporting Actress Oscars: one for playing opposite Montgomery Clift in *A Place in the Sun* in 1951 and the other as Anne Frank's mother in *The Diary of Anne Frank* in 1959. Some of her other memorable films include *The Night of the Hunter, Lolita, Harper, Alfie, A Patch of Blue, The Greatest Story Ever Told, The Poseidon Adventure, The Tenant*, and *Next Stop, Greenwich Village*. She shared screen time with Paul Newman, Sidney Poitier,

Michael Caine, Robert Mitchum, John Garfield, Alan Ladd, Harry Belafonte, Farley Granger, and Burt Lancaster. She shared a room with Marilyn Monroe. She shared a bed with Marlon Brando, Elvis Presley, Howard Hughes, Burt Lancaster, Errol Flynn, William Holden, and Adlai Stevenson. She married four times, including two stormy marriages, one to Vittorio Gassman, the other to Anthony Franciosa,

If she had listened to her father, she would never have become an actress. He was a pattern maker for men's clothing, and when she was a child, he was falsely convicted of arson, and spent a year in prison. Because he didn't think acting was a reputable or honorable profession, Shelley had to sneak out of the house to attend drama school at night. When her dad saw his teenage daughter doing "a very innocent striptease" in a theater, he jumped on stage and dragged her off. She left home afterwards and they didn't talk for a year.

She had lived a full and glamorous life by the time I sat down with her in 1983. She was 63 and had most recently appeared in *Fanny Hill* with Oliver Reed. I asked her about her relationships and marriages, her friendship with Marilyn Monroe and her early death, as well as the various ways she herself had died in movies–stabbed, shot, strangled, smothered, drowned, overdosed, run over, cast into outer space. I was also interested in discussing her involvement in the Civil Rights Movement, her stormy relationship with her father, her psychoanalysis, her friendship with President John F. Kennedy, and her attempt to adopt an Israeli orphan. We also covered her being exploited on talk shows as a sex object, her having an abortion as a teenager, her smashing a sandwich in the face of the Atlanta Falcon's owner for his racist comments, and her slapping Frank Sinatra, calling him a "skinny, no-talent, stupid Hoboken bastard."

She didn't shy away from any of my questions and towards the end she actually thanked me for taking her seriously. "I'm very glad that this interview has taken the note it has because when I get on talk shows the host presses that button and I automatically become the village idiot. I just respond to that kind of thing—the middle-age blonde bimbo—and that's not interesting anymore."

I agreed. I've never found role-playing that interesting unless it was with a Muppet or a Sesame Street character. I've always tried to go beyond the stereotype to discover the person beneath. With Shelley Winters, that person was far more interesting than the character she so often presented when confronted by late night talk show hosts who encouraged her to play the dumb blonde she never was.

When Writing A Biography, The Roshomon Effect Is Real

100. THE SICK BED CAN WORK IN
YOUR FAVOR

John Huston used to smoke–*and inhale*–five cigars a day, until his lungs filled up or closed down or just said, 'Hey old man, what the fuck do you think you're doing? You ever want to breathe again, you'd better straighten out!' By the time I got to him he was pretty good at coughing through a day and a few years later, when the interview we did turned into a book project about his family, he was a certified oxygen tank carrier. It bothered him, but it didn't slow him down. He still traveled between Mexico and Los Angeles, and he continued to work on scripts and make movies. At his memorial, Jack Nicholson quipped that someone should consider putting a stake through his chest to make sure he rested in peace.

The Hustons was a book I didn't know I could write. There was just so much subject matter. John's parents, Rhea and

Walter, were born in the early 1880s and they lived rich, adventurous, documented lives. John was born in 1907 and, as the artist Jan de Swart once said to him, "You must be Methuselah." John had five wives, three children, and dozens of mistresses, most of whom were worthy of individual books. Once I got into the research, I made a list of all the people I would need to talk to and went after the oldest first. John was among them, and I had to make sure I got everything he could remember on tape quickly; those oxygen tanks by his side were a constant reminder of our limited time.

Quickly stretched out to be eighteen months, which might seem like enough time to capture a man's memories. But Huston had been an amateur boxer, fiction writer, screen-writer, director, WWII documentarian, actor, gambler, lover, hypnotist, and raconteur, so those months flew by, espe-cially when his health failed and he wound up in the hospital for a week or two. On such occasions, he would call and tell me to come while he recovered; he hated being bored, and there was no place that bored him more than hospitals. So I would bring my questions and tape recorder and we would talk between his treatments. And regularly, the doctor would come in and smack his back hard to help him clear his lungs. A lifetime of smoking meant those lungs would never clear, but this procedure loosened whatever phlegm was sit-ting on his chest and enabled him to breathe slightly more comfortably.

Although I witnessed this many times, I wasn't prepared to do that myself. But one day when he was staying at some-one's house, just he and his caretaker/companion Maricela, I found myself in a position that was both awkward and terrify-ing. We had been talking about his mother, always a difficult subject for him, as they had had an adversarial relationship.

Suddenly, he went into one of his coughing convulsions. I waited patiently for it to end, but this time it didn't. He just coughed and coughed and it kept getting worse. His face reddened and it appeared he was going to pass out. I went looking for Maricela, who was nowhere to be found. In a panic, I kept calling her name, going from room to room. Then I returned to the living room to be with John. He was still in the throes of this coughing fit and I thought that I had no choice but to go behind him and start smacking his back. I feared that I might hurt him, or that I might even kill him, but I looked at him and said, "John, I'm going to smack your back the way the doctor did in the hospital. I'm not sure it will help, but I don't know what else to do for you." He motioned with his hand and kept coughing, completely out of breath and unable to talk. I think he was motioning for me to go ahead, and just as I pulled back my hand, Maricela came running in from wherever she had been and did the smacking for me.

It took five or ten minutes for John to get his breath back. He was exhausted, as if he had gone five rounds in the ring against a professional boxer a third his age. I sat quietly by his side. Maricela left to get him some water. "I don't think we can continue today," he finally whispered.

"No, I don't think we should," I said. "But I just want to sit here with you for a while, to make sure you're all right."

So we sat a while and when his breathing returned to whatever was normal for a man with severe emphysema, he started talking about his mother again, as if nothing had happened. I turned on the tape recorder and we spent a few more hours going back into his past. He wasn't a man who wasted time, and if he was able to speak, he spoke.

There were more times like this, not as dramatic, but still serious, and I realized that it was important for John to get down as much of his story that he hadn't previously told in his own book. His time in hospitals and his illnesses at home were actually made less difficult and less wasteful when he could be probed with questions that stirred his memory.

101. BROKEN HEARTS WARM THE HEART

My task was to talk to all the people he knew and had worked with and check their memories with his. One of those people touched my heart when she told me of the love she had for Huston and how that love was lost.

Olivia de Havilland is one of those actors defined by the word *class*. At 25 she acted opposite Errol Flynn in such films as *Captain Blood* and *The Adventures of Robin Hood*, and achieved stardom as Melanie in *Gone With the Wind*. She had a sound sense of who she was and didn't like it if someone tried to take advantage of her. She was the first actor to challenge the studio's seven-year contract system that basically enslaved actors to the studio they signed with, prohibiting them to work for other studios without permission, and then at a considerable financial loss. It was her contention that seven years meant seven calendar years; the studios maintained that it meant seven working years. Two courts agreed with her and the California Supreme Court declined to review the favorable decisions of those lower courts. She had single-handedly defeated The Hollywood studio system.

She began her romance with John Huston in 1941, when she was cast in his second film, *In This Our Life*. When I met with her in Paris in 1987, she vividly recalled what happened between them. "John had a largeness of spirit that was wonderful. I loved his conversations. He was always full of ideas and reactions. And he was very articulate. He knew a great deal about all the things I cared about. He knew a lot about painting; he had read a great deal. All of that to me was immensely exciting. It was a powerful coming together of two people when our relationship began in November and December of 1941, when we shot *In This Our Life*. The idea was that as soon as John could get a divorce, we would get married, but so many destructive things happened."

One of the things that happened was that Huston's wife, Lesley, had had a nervous breakdown, and de Havilland insisted that he return to care for her. Another thing that happened was that Huston was also having an affair with his *Maltese Falcon* star, Mary Astor. And that wasn't all. De Havilland remembered picking up the newspapers and reading about his adventures with other women as well.

"He had no self-discipline," she said, but she still loved him. She had had affairs with other tall, lanky men like Flynn, Howard Hughes, and Jimmy Stewart, but Huston was the one who had captured her heart. When he left her for Marietta Fitzgerald, she was heartbroken. "I must say I felt hatred for John for a long time," she confessed more than four decades later. "He saw me at a party when I was about to do *To Each His Own* in 1946 and he began his pursuit again. But I had simply been through too much. I didn't really trust him anymore."

She may not have trusted him, but she wasn't able to forget him. Twenty-two years later, in 1968, she ran into him at the Beverly Hills Hotel and he invited her to visit him at his St. Clerans estate in Ireland. She was then separated from her husband, so she accepted his invitation. When she arrived, Huston gave her a grand tour of his domain and she was struck by how the décor was so in tune with her tastes. Though it had been 26 years since they were together, she realized that the fire had not completely gone out of her heart. She still loved the bastard. She still cried about him when telling this story.

"Then he took me to a room in which he painted and showed me his various canvases," she said. "There was a painting of his housekeeper, Betty, who had just greeted me, and she was stark naked, eating an apple and lying on the floor. That's when I realized the affront of his asking me to come stay at St. Clerans. I couldn't wait to leave."

When she and Marietta Tree met in 1976, they shared their Huston stories. Marietta (who changed her last name from Fitzgerald when she married Ronald Tree, an English Member of Parliament), said she had a fantasy that when John was old, sick and poverty-stricken, he turned to her. Olivia said hers was, "He's on his deathbed and he calls for me!"

After my trip to Paris I told Huston that I had been with Olivia. "You must have been quite a guy," I teased. "Olivia de Havilland is still crying over you 45 years later."

John wasn't one who liked to kiss and tell, but his sly smile and warm eyes said enough. He was a year and a half away from his deathbed and I was sure that he would have been happy to have both those women by his side.

102. IT'S OK TO BE INCREDULOUS

Another classy woman who had worked with John was **Katharine Hepburn**. When I arrived at her Manhattan town house on E. 59th Street, she didn't come to the door to let me in. Instead, she shouted from above, "Door's open!" Upon entering her living room, I found her foot was in a cast and propped up on an ottoman. "Some stupid fall," she explained. It was 1987, and she was 80 years old. She had the shakes and the stammer that impersonators loved to mimic, but she was sharp and could cut to the chase in an instant.

We began to discuss movies, and I asked her why great books rarely made great films. But she took me to task. "I don't agree with that concept at all," she said. "Look at what John did with *The Maltese Falcon, The African Queen, The Man Who Would Be King,* all wonderful books and equally wonderful films. Look at *Mildred Pierce, Gone With the Wind, The Bridge on the River Kwai, Lawrence of Arabia, Wuthering Heights, Lolita, Doctor Zhivago, To Kill a Mockingbird, Brighton Rock, The Godfather.* All quite good films, and all very fine books. So I beg to differ with you."

I had been thinking more of books like *Breakfast at Tiffany's, Portnoy's Complaint, Ulysses, Ana Karenina, Huck Finn,* and *The Catcher in the Rye,* which J.D. Salinger would never permit to be adapted because he didn't trust it could be done well. But she was right to disagree with me, and to make a solid justification of films that translated very well from their source books.

Then when I asked her which of her own films she most enjoyed watching, I didn't believe it when she told me she never watched them. After all, if you had gone to Africa to make a movie with Humphrey Bogart, directed by John Huston, and you had to fight off insects, snakes, cannibalism, and charging elephants, wouldn't you be curious to see the results?

But I didn't want to call her a liar. Instead, I just said, "You're kidding, right? That's unbelievable. Surely you must have seen *The African Queen? The Philadelphia Story? The Lion in Winter? Guess Who's Coming to Dinner? Bringing Up Baby? Adam's Rib?*"

"Afraid not," she said. "One is self-conscious about oneself. I don't think it's ever a source of great joy."

When I returned to Los Angeles I went to see Huston who asked about his beloved Katie. "She never saw your film," I said. "Can you believe that? I can't, but that's what she said. Never saw *The African Queen*. Or any of her other films."

"If Katie said it, I believe it. She wouldn't have said otherwise," Huston said. Apparently he recognized that everyone has their own unique eccentricities, and if John could accept her word, so could I. But this encounter with Katharine Hepburn drove home the point that we are all different, in both behavior and viewpoint.

103. THE RASHOMON EFFECT IS REAL

That point can best be illustrated when it came to filming *The Misfits*.

What do you do when someone tells you a story about what they saw on a movie set and when you go to check it out, another person tells you the story differently? And what if that happens repeatedly, with every witness giving a different version? Who do you believe?

What if the observers happen to be a famous playwright, a high-placed movie studio executive, the producer, the director, the assistant director, the production manager, and the director's closest assistant? Such was the case when I interviewed each of these people about a particular scene shot in the scorching heat of Reno, Nevada during the making of *The Misfits*. In the scene, Montgomery Clift was in a phone booth talking to his mother.

Max Youngstein, United Artist's vice-president and director of advertising and publicity, said he watched Clift sink to his knees in that phone booth as Huston kept telling him to do it again. "John was shaking his finger at him as if it was a whip, and Clift just crouched down like he was getting clobbered, which he was, verbally. It was very cruel of John, the way he treated Monty, who was practically crying from his abuse. I've never forgotten it."

Sounds pretty authentic, right? Youngstein was there, and Huston's behavior left a lasting impression on him. But then I asked **Arthur Miller**, who wrote the screenplay, and was also present that day. "I don't recall that at all," he said, when I related Youngstein's story. "John shot it in one take. He certainly wasn't castigating Clift or down beating him with his finger. Monty was just a tortured soul." **Tommy Shaw**, Huston's trustworthy assistant director, remembered "a few" takes but no finger pointing. "When Monty started to get small in that phone booth it was just his reaction to what he was saying. It's called acting. John respected Monty during *The Misfits*. It was only later, when he played *Freud*, after John learned about Monty's sexual persuasion, when he began to treat him badly." Production manager **Doc Erickson** remembered something about how Clift and Marilyn Monroe went off on their own before that scene was shot, something no one else recalled, though **Frank Taylor**, the film's producer, considered Clift and Monroe "psychic twins. They recognized disaster in each other's faces." And **Angela Allen,** Huston's script girl who kept careful notes of every scene, reminded me that they were shooting each day in nearly 100 degree heat, and people were sinking in their chairs from the heat, "not from John's finger." Actress **Suzanne Flon**, who appeared in Huston's *Moulin Rouge*, was visiting the set and described Clift as "walking near his shoes, as we say in French. He was very touching." When I asked Huston about directing Clift, he acknowledged, "He was a mess, but I don't believe he fell to his knees from anything I said. Clark Gable had a bad back, a slipped disc; Monty would slap him on purpose. Gable didn't have much use for him. But it wasn't Clift who made filming

The Misfits an ordeal; it was Marilyn Monroe. She was always trying to wake up or go to sleep."

So, how does one write about a scene where so many people have different versions of what went down? Did Huston chastise Clift to tears? Did he make him do the scene over and over again? Or did he get the shot he wanted in one, two, or three takes? Was he cruel or just professional? Did he contribute to Clift's "walking near his shoes" in depression or was that just the way Clift was at the time?

Whenever I confronted Huston with different versions of the same story, he always told me, to "go with the better story." If one is writing fiction, that's really good advice. But when your aim is historical accuracy, having so many versions makes it difficult for a writer. What I learned after hearing such diverse eyewitness stories is that people see and remember things differently. It's called the *Rashomon Effect*—contradictory interpretations of the same event. It's not a matter of right or wrong, it's one of perspective and memory. The solution, really, is to tell all sides and let the reader or viewer choose what makes the most sense.

104. "GREAT" IS A SUBJECTIVE WORD

Jeff Bridges's memory didn't match his eagerness to tell me about his time with Huston.

Bridges is a wonderful actor. There is a smoothness about his acting that allows him to play a variety of likeable characters. He doesn't exude that touch of evil that some actors do, like Robert De Niro, so he is far more likely to seem open if you met him in a hotel bar at a film festival. In 1971, John Huston cast him in *Fat City*, a movie that dealt with the down-and-out, unglamorous world of small-town boxing. Bridges was 22 and eager to work with a director like Huston, who had once been an amateur boxer.

When I was researching my book I contacted Bridges and he was quick to reply. Of course he'd talk to me about working with Huston, he said. "I've got so many great stories." That's always music to a biographer's ears. We arranged to meet for lunch at The Ivy Restaurant in Santa Monica. Everyone who had ever worked with or knew Huston had stories about him and I looked forward to his.

Bridges was on time, friendly, and hungry. *Fat City,* starring Stacy Keach as the beaten down but ever hopeful boxer, was shot in Stockton, California, but Bridges had to fly to Madrid to meet with Huston about playing the part of the young boxer. "It was one of the most unusual interviews I ever had," Bridges recalled. "He wanted to meet me at the Prado. The night before, I had met this girl in the lobby of the hotel and we had a great night. Drank too much, ate too much. But I woke up the next morning feeling strange. I had been food poisoned. Didn't even get laid! And that's when I had my interview with Huston, as this sickness came on. He showed me all his favorite paintings and never once spoke about the movie. And all the time I was praying that I wouldn't puke on him."

He laughed at the memory. I thought it was a good prelude to the "great" stories he was going to share about Huston, who had quite a roguish reputation. But Jeff Bridges was a disappointment. He remembered his own wild night before meeting Huston, and he recalled John talking to him about some thrilling paintings at the Prado Museum, but when I pressed him for those "great" stories, all he could come up with was how Huston would tease him about getting into the ring, and how in one boxing scene he got cut and bled. He also recalled how he and Stacy Keach had to shoot a scene in a seedy room where guys were playing cards at 2:00 a.m. "John was there with his oxygen tank and looked like he was asleep or dead. Everybody thought he was in a trance, receiving messages from God knows where. All of a sudden his eyes bolted open and he knew how he wanted to shoot the scene. Seeing him in such a feeble way and then having him spring to life like that with a great idea, it was memorable."

Bridges ate his salmon, his salad, and his dessert without further elaborating on what it was like to appear in *Fat City*, which Muhammad Ali would later say captured the boxing life the way it really was. Jeff had promised me great stories and didn't deliver on his promise. But he beamed when he remembered that wild night before meeting Huston, and grinned from ear to ear when recalling how he was cast without ever talking to John about the film itself. I tried to stir his memory, to ask about how Huston directed, what it was like to work with Keach, anything really to get more out of him, but it wasn't to be. I got those few sentences, paid the check, and waved goodbye after the valet brought him his car.

105. ANGER FUELS CONVERSATION

Some might say that the tale of Huston coming out of a trance at 2:00 a.m. with the inspiration as to how to shoot a scene was a "great" story, but I don't think so. It's a good story, or has the potential for being a good story, but it needed embellishment. Great stories are ones that provide new insight, have detail, and memorable quotes. They can be as short as two words, as in Goethe's last words before dying: "More light!"

To demonstrate a great story—one that reveals insight about Huston—I'll turn to another one of Huston's colleagues, the Irish novelist **Edna O'Brien**, who was asked by Huston to work on adapting A. E. Ellis's *The Rack*. It was about a young man's tortured treatment for tuberculosis in a Swiss sanatorium. She wrote a draft and Huston asked her to fly to see him in Puerto Vallarta to discuss a rewrite. Before they got down to business, O'Brien had one request. "John," she asked, "please don't ever shout at me." She had heard about how he behaved with other writers and didn't want their collaboration to become an ordeal. "John was really a cowboy who wished he was an intellectual," she told me.

When Huston was pleased with what a writer wrote he would be full of praise, but when he didn't like something he would wonder aloud if the writer had ever read a script. "He could be so fucking condescending," O'Brien said. "I had read scripts. I had written some as well. But he totally flummoxed me. My character and my talent just collapses under that kind of psychological pressure."

She appreciated that Huston never talked behind her back, but always directly to her. But she didn't appreciate what he had to say. "He just tore me apart," she recalled. "For two hours he just totally slaughtered me in a way that is unforgivable."

She called it Huston's "brain torture," and accused him of mixing up personal cruelty with work. It had to do, she believed, with his "murderous feeling toward women," and told him "What you're doing to me is awful. You're just trying to kill me."

When she said this to him, Huston told her that women had caused the biggest unhappiness in his life. O'Brien responded that was true for women about men. But she began to sense that she reminded him of his mother. "My theory is that a lot of his cruelty to me was also made worse by self-hatred and guilt." Though she continued to work on the script, the atmosphere was filled with tension. After three horrid months, she was ready to leave. Huston came to visit her and when he saw three withering roses in her room he said, "Which of these do you think you are, honey?" O'Brien pointed to the most collapsing rose. "No, you do yourself an injustice," Huston said. "I think you're that one." He pointed to the second most withered rose. "He thought it was funny," 'O'Brien said, "but it wasn't funny at all."

She left Puerto Vallarta leaving behind a script that would never be turned into a movie, and a belief that Huston was truly a monster. "If he was just a straight monster nobody would have bothered with him," she said. "It was his unpredictability that was so fascinating. He once told me that he hated physical cowardice. Well, he went into the physical terror zones, but not the psychological ones. In many ways, for all the bravura, he was a lost man. Alone, coughing, in that white shirt, looking at television at 4:00 a.m., you wondered what went on in there."

Now compare her detail with Bridges memory of Huston sitting as if in a trance. O'Brien fills in the blanks. She went up against the beast and came away beaten, but she certainly was articulate about who she thought Huston was. And whether she was right or wrong about him, her anger fueled a great story.

106. DON'T PISS OFF THE SECRET SERVICE

While "great" is a subjective word, the word I learned *not* to use when I went to interview First Lady **Nancy Reagan** was "fight."

Nancy Regan's father, Dr. Loyal Davis, was a good friend with John Huston's father, Walter Huston. When I began my research for *The Hustons*, I made a list of anyone still living who knew Walter Huston, who died in 1950. It was a longer list than I had presumed, and included Josh Logan, who directed him on stage in *Knickerbocker Holiday;* Gene Tierney, who costarred with him in *Dragonwyck*; and Loretta Young, who appeared with him in *The Ruling Voice*. I also noted other actors who might have known him, like Lillian Gish, Evelyn Keyes, Katharine Hepburn, Olivia de Havilland, Bette Davis, Ava Gardner, Burgess Meredith, Claire Trevor, Jane Wyman, Eli Wallach, James Whitmore, Mary Wicke, and Gregory Peck.

Nancy Reagan was the First Lady when I wrote to her at the White House. I didn't really expect to hear back, but Walter Huston was a very special man in her life. She was a child when they began visiting him in his vacation house in Running Springs, and Walter would bring out a movie camera and encourage her to act for him. His encouragements—and contacts—were instrumental in Nancy becoming an actress, and she never forgot it. Her secretary got in touch with me and said I could see her at the Beverly Wilshire Hotel when she next came to Los Angeles.

On the appointed day I was given her suite number and took the elevator up to the ninth floor. I expected to see security guards when I got out, but the hallway was empty and I knew something was wrong. I went back to the front desk and was told that she was staying in the newer section of the hotel. I ran through the hotel, crossed over to the other building, took the elevator up, and was met by the Secret Service men who were there to protect her. They walked me to her suite and told me that she was running a little late and that my scheduled hour would have to be reduced to twenty minutes. "No, that won't work," I protested. "We have a lot of ground to cover. This is not about politics; it's personal. She *wants* to talk about her 'Uncle Walter.' I'll fight for that hour."

The two Secret Service men bristled when I used the word "fight." I saw how their backs straightened, and one of them put his hand inside his jacket and I thought, uh-oh, he's reaching for his gun. They didn't know why I was there or what I wanted to talk to her about. They had no idea who 'Uncle Walter' was. And when I said it was personal, for all they knew I was some lunatic who somehow managed to finagle my way into her personal space. Following that with the word *fight* was all they needed to hear to restrain me if I made any funny move.

Before they could frisk me though, the First Lady appeared and walked over to me with a smile on her face. Her personal photographer captured the moment we shook hands, and she nodded at her security that everything was okay. They backed off as we sat down to talk. The twenty minutes went by very fast and when her assistant interrupted to remind her of her schedule, Nancy waved her off. I was asking her to remember a special time in her life, when she and her family would spend their summers with Walter and Nan Huston at their mountaintop home. "Uncle Walter was a very special, happy man," she told me. "He was very, very even-tempered. We had great times. We'd walk up the hill from the house where he had a barbeque and a telescope; we'd look at the stars. We'd swim and play tennis. In the evenings we would sit in front of the fire and Uncle Walter would read Shakespeare to us. I sat mesmerized."

It was a time of innocence and of family, a time long ago and far away. She became emotional remembering those times and continued to tell me about them for an hour. I didn't have to "fight" for that hour, though every once in a while I looked over by the door where the Secret Service men stood and raised my eyebrows at them when they looked my way. I couldn't help it. It felt like some small victory in the face of power.

But had the First Lady not appeared when she did, I might never have had the chance to sit with her, because those guys were on the verge of escorting me out. So the lesson I took away from this incident was: Don't piss off the Secret Service.

107. ACTORS DON'T NECESSARILY UNDERSTAND WHAT THEY DO

The actor who was most pissed off with Huston's direction, or lack thereof, was **Brad Dourif**.

The first time I saw *Wise Blood*, based on Flannery O'Conner's novella, starring Brad Dourif and Harry Dean Stanton, I didn't know Huston had directed it. It was on a premiere movie channel and I turned it on after the credits had rolled, but soon got caught up in the strangeness of the characters. Dourif plays Hazel Motes, a guy who starts his own street church, preaching against the idea of God; Stanton plays a blind preacher, who isn't really blind. It was a strange and original film and the acting was so believable. Dourif's crazed passion delivered the same kind of open-eyed amazement as Robert De Niro's wise guy character in *Mean Streets*. These are films for a particular audience; they're not made for those who prefer blockbusters or films with happy endings. You don't leave the theater with a bounce in your step after you see *Wise Blood*. But you do come away knowing you've discovered a remarkable young actor you probably had never seen before.

When I went to Palm Springs to talk to Dourif for my Huston book, I was particularly eager to understand how Huston managed to get such a performance out of him. Huston was one of the best directors of adaptations. He loved good literature and good writers and that's why he did so well with the works of authors like Herman Melville, Rudyard Kipling, Tennessee Williams, Carson McCullers, James Joyce, and Flannery O'Conner. But when I asked Dourif about Huston's direction, he told me that Huston didn't direct him, which had pissed him off at the time.

"I didn't know what John wanted," Dourif said. "I thought the film aimed at redemption in the end, but John felt the opposite. I thought I was playing my character too much on edge, mainly because I didn't know how I should play him, and when I went to John to ask for his direction, he backed off and just said I should do what I was doing. But what was I doing? I wasn't even sure about how my character reacted to Harry Dean's character. I thought I should have laughed him off and not taken him so seriously. But that's not the way it played. It was all very confusing for me."

When I told Huston what Dourif had said, he seemed surprised. "He was just so spot on, I didn't want to interfere with what he had come up with. I just left him alone. I couldn't have improved on his performance."

Producer Michael Fitzgerald told me, "It was the best performance of Dourif's life." He had seen the conflict between the actor and the director and admired Huston for understanding Dourif's insecurities and letting him work them out on his own. "John operated on reaction rather than action," Fitzgerald said. "When an actor gave him something right, he grabbed it."

"I hated every minute," Dourif said. "He never let on how he felt. He just let me be. That can be tough for an actor."

It can also work, if the director is savvy enough to know when not to give direction. Huston was that kind of director. Dourif may not have consciously been that kind of an actor. But he certainly delivered the performance of his life.

Those Damn Publicists

108. GET THEIR PHONE NUMBERS

Publicists have a schizophrenic job, always trying to please their clients, while promoting them to journalists; often making promises to both that simply can't be kept. And representing up-and-coming artists is much different than representing stars. In the first case, publicists are paid to help promote people the media may not yet be interested in; in the second, they are paid to keep the media at bay from people they *are* interested in. That's why there is such give-and-take between them and the media. I usually get along well with publicists, but I've had my share of run-ins with them that had me cursing under my breath, and making me wonder if the celebrity knew what an asshole his gatekeeper was.

When I was trying to get **Frank Sinatra** to sit for an interview, I had to go through his publicist, Lee Solters, who kept promising an answer for years. It got to the point where I decided to call Sinatra's lawyer, to see if he might get me an answer. His lawyer passed on my request to Solters, who called me. "You think you can go around me to get to Frank," he said. "Good luck with that." I never got to Sinatra.

When I interviewed **Cher** for *Newsday's* Sunday magazine, the art director spread her photo over two pages, but that wasn't good enough for her publicist, who called me screaming that Cher wasn't on the cover. I kept trying to explain that I had nothing to do with whom they chose for their covers but he wasn't hearing me. He just kept yelling until I finally hung up on him.

With **Charlton Heston**, his publicist insisted that she sit near him during the interview. I insisted that she didn't. We compromised and she sat in a corner of the room out of my eyesight. The same thing happened with **Barbara Walters**, who wanted her publicist around to make sure I didn't ask her about facelifts or anything else that might embarrass her. **Halle Berry's** publicist also wanted to sit in to protect her client from bringing up her husband's sex addiction as his reason for cheating on her. When I said I was uncomfortable with her around, she sat on the stairs within earshot and popped out when I brought up the forbidden subject.

After my initial meeting with **Barbra Streisand,** she had instructed me to call her publicist to set up a time for us to begin our interview. I said I'd rather not have to deal with her publicist and asked her for her direct line. The request threw her for a moment and I could see the difficulty in her face, wondering whether or not to give me her number, wondering if I was the kind of guy who might call her unexpectedly after our business was done, forcing her to change her number. But she scrawled her number on a tiny strip of paper and I never had to deal with her publicist again.

It might have been the early hour of my interview with **Meryl Streep** that kept me from remembering this simple lesson. I was told that our interview would take place while she was in makeup, before going on set at Universal Studios to act opposite Goldie Hawn and Bruce Willis in the silly comedy *Death Becomes Her*. Streep was playing a woman who has drunk a magic potion that would allow her to live forever, even when her neck gets twisted grotesquely. I was there at dawn as Streep sat in the makeup chair having latex applied to her neck. As she had to be absolutely still, she answered my questions by looking at my reflection in the mirror in front of her. I looked back at her reflection, as it was the only way to see her eyes. It wasn't exactly the most intimate way to conduct an interview, but when you have a chance to spend time with Meryl Streep, you take what you can get. And when reporters and photographers from the *New York Times*, *Vogue* and *Premiere* are all waiting their turns to talk to her or put her on their covers, along with Willis and Hawn, an hour alone with Streep and her makeup person might even seem a luxury.

She is as close to a national treasure as we have among our artists. She has the ability to get into the skin of whomever she portrays and make that character real. Her accents are flawless, her intensity is faultless, and she is just as charming and disarming in person as she is on screen, whether she's playing a Pole in *Sophie's Choice*, a Dane in *Out of Africa*, or an Aussie in *Cry in the Dark*.

I didn't know that the hour I was given with her was going to be the only time I would have. I thought it was understood that there would be other times for us to do an in-depth piece, so I wasn't in a hurry to ask all my questions. We started out talking about the nature of interviews and publicity, eased into why she chose this particular comedy to do, and what she thought of her costars. I then brought her back in time to her early movie influences (Marlon Brando and Sandra Dee), her childhood ambitions, the singing lessons she took when she was twelve, her being a cheerleader and homecoming queen in high school, and the freedom she felt when she went to Vassar and later to Yale. We touched on the influence Joe Papp had in her life and what it was like to work with Woody Allen, Robert De Niro and Jack Nicholson. We talked about winning Oscars and how women were still discriminated against in Hollywood. What we didn't discuss, because it wasn't a subject I wanted to pass off lightly, was the serious two-year relationship she had had with her *Deer Hunter* costar, John Cazales.

Al Pacino, who was close to Cazales, told me about the incredible love he had seen between them, and how devastated Streep was when Cazales died of lung cancer in 1978. I thought that an interview with Streep that didn't mention Cazales would be incomplete, so when my hour with her was up and she had to go work, I asked when we could continue our talk. She said, "Let's finish tomorrow." I said fine. But then, as I stood in that makeup room by myself, I realized that I didn't have any contacts for her. The interview had been set up by the magazine. Streep wanted to talk the next day and I would need a pass onto the studio as well as a specific time. I called my editor as soon as I got home, but she said she didn't have any direct contact for Streep; it had been arranged through the studio's publicity department. I tried calling there, but no one knew anything about it. When I said, "Meryl wants to see me tomorrow," they said, "We'll get back to you."

But no one did. And when I called the next day, I couldn't get anyone to talk to me. As far as anyone there was concerned, I'd gotten my hour with Meryl and that was more than some of the other journalists were getting. I couldn't expect Streep to call me and say, "Hey, Larry, we never touched on my love affair with John Cazales, when are you coming back?" So, I had to make do with what I had. Because it was Meryl Streep, *Movieline* put her face on the cover. But I wasn't happy with the interview, because it wasn't cover worthy.

I should have asked her for her phone number.

109. DO WHATEVER YOU CAN TO BYPASS THE PUBLICIST

I wasn't happy with my interview with **Jake Gyllenhaal** either and should have gotten his phone number as well, but he would have never given it up. At the time, he was promoting that dog of a film, *Prince of Persia*. "Has to be done fast," my *American Way* editor said, "but I think you're the one who can do it." I appreciated his confidence and contacted the actor's publicist in New York to see about scheduling a time. I got back an email suggesting Friday, two days away, from 9:40 to 10 a.m. at the Disney Studios.

I emailed back, suggesting Friday, from 9:40 to noon, and then maybe we could break for lunch together, and continue for a few more hours in the afternoon or evening. Apparently she didn't think much of my suggestion and got in touch with my editor saying I was causing trouble.

"Take the 20 minutes," my editor said. "You'll figure out a way to extend it."

Normally I would agree. But the start time they gave me–9:40 a.m.–indicated that they were being very precise, and that Gyllenhaal must be on a press junket type schedule, talking to a new reporter every 20 minutes. In 20 minutes, what are you going to get? By the time you're introduced and make small talk about the weather, ask for a bottle of water or some coffee, get settled into the couch, and congratulate him on his new picture, you've eaten up half your time. Then what? Bore down to the nitty-gritty and ask about the rumors that he might be gay and then ask him to explain his breakup with Reese Witherspoon?

Actually, those last two questions would never have been asked, because the publicist made sure that I knew that such personal questions were verboten. Jake's a bit sensitive about the gay rumors ever since he kissed Heath Ledger in *Brokeback Mountain,* she warned. And his relationships with his past two girlfriends (Kirsten Dunst, then Reese) weren't topics he wanted to discuss publicly.

When Robert Downey Jr. was working with Jake in *Zodiac,* he called Gyllenhaal a "total badass. He's nice, all right, but he's also wet, dark, and wild."

Wet, dark, and wild. Intriguing. How wet? How dark? How wild? What does "wet" even mean? And if Jake was dark, was he going to reveal that side of him in a 20-minute interview? I didn't think so. That left wild. If he had any wild stories to share, I'd like to hear them.

I arrived at the Disney building ten minutes early and Jake came ten minutes late. For the 20 minutes I waited, I dealt with two different publicists. The first one, Anne, came in and said that someone would probably be sitting in with us, and I said no, that wouldn't work. I was blunt. She was a bit taken aback. Then another came, Chrissy, and I said the same thing. She started to tell me that there were things that were not to be brought up and I said I knew and that I wouldn't bring them up unless there was a publicist in the room with us, in which case I would bring them up. This caused a bit of panic in her eyes and she said he'd be coming soon, and would I wait outside the room because when Jake arrived he'd like to get comfortable before I came in.

Comfortable? This was a 20-minute interview. "He's 30 years old," I said. "He's just a person, like you and me." But okay, I was already making waves and I knew better, so I went to the other room to wait. Jake appeared with his handler, a blonde woman who accompanied us into the room. I'm not sure if she was his personal publicist or his manager or maybe even his aunt, but she certainly was there to protect him. Then she left and, before we even sat down, I asked Jake if he lived in the same canyon where I lived and he answered yes.

But that innocent query set off a chain reaction of unplanned questions and answers about our neighborhood. "I live next door to David Hockney," Jake said. That triggered a few minutes of art talk and I knew my plans to ask a set number of questions (32 to be exact) had gone to hell. Though we were getting along, I knew one or all of those three women were going to be popping their heads in pretty soon and I was going to be shuffled out. So I had to glance down at my prepared questions and mentally kiss off a bunch of them. We only had another ten minutes and there were some things I felt were critical to address. There was the new movie, of course. But also, since Jake had never talked about his feelings for Heath Ledger since Ledger's death, I wanted to go there. I wasn't sure if I'd get anything out of him, but I had to ask.

"A year ago *Entertainment Weekly* spoke to a lot of people for a piece about Heath Ledger," I said. "The screenwriter, producer, and cinematographer of *Brokeback Mountain* all talked. You were conspicuously absent. Are you uncomfortable remembering him in public?"

"Yes," Gyllenhaal answered hesitantly. "*Brokeback* was painful. But also fulfilling. Anytime you go into pain I don't think you necessarily want to go back. But the results were worth it; the response was huge. Walking through any kind of pain is usually worth it. All those other people—as close as we all became making that movie—it didn't extend much farther than that, so that experience of work could be easily talked about for publications. What Heath and I shared publicly, the experience we had, the press and publicity we did, it was already shared. What we shared as friends, though I respect the interest that so many people have in the mourning and grieving process and how it feels to other people, I feel like... and I don't mean this in an unkind way... but I don't think it's anybody's business but his and mine. So in that sense, if I was really to respect him... and also the way he felt about his life and his private life and what he cared about, because he was a deeply caring and loving human being, with all the other things that came with it too, every time anybody asks me any question about him, it would be like he was sitting next to me and I know he would roll his eyes, because that's the way he was. It's between us."

It wasn't exactly tear jerking or confessional, but you could feel the anguish in his words. I was confident that what he said was as far and as deep and as sincere as he could go for a print interview.

I looked at my watch and could hear the seconds tick away in my head. In the next few minutes I asked him about his love of J.D. Salinger's work; the envy/jealousy and competitive feelings he had for his older sister Maggie; his desire to direct; and his secular Bar Mitzvah. Then his publicists entered the room for the third time. I knew my sands of time were up, so I threw in the obligatory question about *Prince of Persia*.

"Are you going to go the Nic Cage/Robert Downey Jr. / Angelina Jolie/Johnny Depp route, into higher profile, bigger budgeted action/adventure films now?"

"With this movie we set up the potential for something more or bigger," he said. "I saw it as a strange mix of *Star Wars* and *Indiana Jones*. Also, I watched Errol Flynn's 1938

Robin Hood over and over again when I was making this movie. He was my age when he made that. The seriousness which he took the absurdities and the humor he had is what I would compare it to."

"I'm just about out of here, Jake," I said. "Just wanted to ask you about what Robert Downey Jr. meant when he called you a badass: wet, dark and wild. I don't know what wet means, but dark and wild? How dark does it get for you? How wild?"

"Robert is a great seer," Jake answered. "He sees things that I can't necessarily see about myself, and I don't think I should, probably. I think what he meant by dark, at least what he and I share, is that I'm not afraid of the darkness. I'm not afraid of the wildness of things. I do fear them, but I feel I have the bravery to go into them."

"Spoken like a true Jedi warrior."

"Well, that's the quote! And wet means definitely slippery. And also, if I think about the way Robert speaks—because sometimes I have to translate him, as we all do—but I get him inherently. Whenever we come together, we recognize the awe and massiveness of this ocean of stuff we all live in, when he says wet it means I'm in the water, which I'm down with."

I still wasn't sure what all that ocean stuff meant, but I had already gone over my allotted 20 minutes and there were other people in the room.

"So Jake," I said as I stood, "if you were in my position and had to write a 2000 word profile based on a 20 minute conversation in a sterile corporate room, how would you approach it?"

"I would accept the situation for what it was, and then I would hope that the opportunity—if I was interested in the person I was talking to—would come again in a more natural environment. I learned accepting what you have is what you have."

"I've always had a problem with that," I said.

"Of course," Jake laughed, "all you get is 20 minutes!"

I took out my camera and said, "Let's take a picture together."

"No pictures," his blonde wrangler said authoritatively. I handed her my camera anyway and said, "Why are you speaking for him?" Then I looked at Gyllenhaal and asked, "Jake, do you mind?"

"I don't mind," he said.

"Oh boy, you're trouble," the blonde said.

"I may be trouble," I said, "but it's nothing the Prince of Persia can't handle."

Publicists. They're just doing their job. But sometimes, their job stinks. And it's their client who suffers. If you can get around them, by all means, do so. If you can finagle a phone number from your subject, congratulate yourself on a job that will be much improved. Otherwise, as Jake said, accept what you have is what you have.

Writers Rarely Disappoint

Though some writers have achieved fame and popularity while avoiding interviews or any contact with the press (J.D. Salinger, Thomas Pynchon, Harper Lee, J.M. Coetzee, Cormac McCarthy), most writers like to talk, and it's often because they have something to say. Isn't that why they're writers? They also like to be challenged. Writing is a solitary profession, so when the opportunity comes to promote a book or reach a wider audience, writers take advantage of putting a face and a voice to their words. Whether it's asking them how they write, where they find their ideas, what they think of other writers, whether or not they've had Nobel dreams, Freudian-worthy terrors or Oedipal hallucinations, writers I've known and interviewed rarely back away from responding—and sometimes, occasionally, shocking. That's why I've always jumped at the chance to spend time with a writer—especially if it's one whose work I've admired.

110. A KISS IS STILL A KISS

Allen Ginsberg was the most recognizable, often the most controversial, poet of his time. He was at the center of the Beat Generation, along with his pals Jack Kerouac, Neal Cassady and William Burroughs. He wrote the Beat national anthem, *Howl* (which began: *"I saw the best minds of my generation destroyed by madness"*), and shared his most personal revelations in *Kaddish* (which dealt with his mother's actual madness). He was crowned May King in Prague in 1965. He was a character in Kerouac's *On the Road*, and the subject of a dozen biographies and seven films. Among the actors who portrayed him were John Turturro, Daniel Radcliffe, and James Franco.

I read *Howl* and *Kaddish* in their City Lights editions as a teenager, around the time I read *On the Road*, *Naked Lunch* and *Tropic of Cancer*. They had an effect. They made me want to travel, not just to see the world but also to *experience* the world. This was The Sixties, and if you wanted to experiment with sex and drugs among people who spoke different languages, Ginsberg was a guiding light. He was worthy of the crown the Czech students placed on his head as they paraded him through their streets. And he was certainly worthy of a cable TV interview, where he could read freely from his work and say whatever he wanted without being edited or sanitized. Ginsberg was a free spirit, one of the very few poets in America who actually earned a living from his poetry. His openness also had an element of shock, of which he was well aware and quite proud.

An hour into our three-hour conversation at a bookstore in Laguna Beach, I asked him, "You described an arousing night you spent with Neal Cassady in 1946 in your poem 'Many Loves.' He wanted to please you and you said you made a mistake. What was the mistake?"

"I'm glad you were aroused," Ginsberg said, "but you're isolating only one moment of the poem." He then read the section of the poem where he and Cassady were about to have sex, deciding who would be in the dominant position. "The mistake," he said when he finished reading, "was that instead of playing some kind of game trying to get him to blow me, I went and blew him instead, and so from then on our roles were set."

This wasn't an exchange you'd expect to see on a late night interview with Ginsberg, but for a cable show, it was compelling. And the conversation continued in its revelations and intimacy.

His father was also a poet, and I asked him how he reacted when *Howl* was published, as Ginsberg came out publicly about private matters.

"That was very difficult," he said. "That was the big barrier, because when I wrote *Howl* I wasn't intending to publish it. I didn't write it as a poem, just as a piece of writing for my own pleasure. I wanted to write something where I could say what I was really thinking, rather than poetry. From that point of view I thought I couldn't publish this. I didn't want to shove my ass in my father's face: *'Who got fucked in the ass by handsome sailors and screamed with joy.'* I didn't want him to read that, because given our relationship that would be quite embarrassing. We never talked about sex seriously and certainly there was some subliminal erotic thing going on between us, which I shouldn't touch on lightly. Very strongly so. Without him knowing it. So it really would have disturbed him a great deal. But when he saw it, he said it showed a lot of energy and invention and explosiveness and youthful feelings. He didn't like the language, the dirty words, didn't think they were necessary, but he recognized that the whole thing had a flow and a power that maybe the language was a part of and so within a decade we were giving readings together at his poetry club, the Poetry Society of America. So he got over it, and I got over it."

Ginsberg had a more difficult time overcoming the guilt, sadness and confusion of his mother's mental illness. After he sent *Howl* to her at the mental hospital, he went to see her. "She hadn't recognized me about a half year before when I visited. She thought I was a spy, actually. It was very disturbing—I wept. It seemed like the farthest limit of dehumanization and illness and madness, that she couldn't remember me. My mother was really mad. Before we put her in the hospital, she thought people were walking up and down the apartment lobby with poison gas to spray at her. Some people were hanging around the bus station across the street spying on her. And my grandmother was climbing up on the fire escape with old clothes on to spray poisons on her. It was really very difficult. She had many shock treatments. Insulin shock, Metrazol, and electroshock, thirty or forty each. She had a lobotomy."

Talking about this, even years later, still had an effect on Ginsberg, but he didn't hold back when asked about it. "Would you say your childhood was cut short by your mother's mental illness?" I asked.

"Yes, I think so. I didn't get mother love, and that's always been a kind of grief. It's been a dominant motif in whatever I've done. I had to take care of my mother basically, and so I got sick of taking care of women. It was just too much trouble, too horrifying a task at that time. Probably alienated me from women's bodies and smells and situations and blood."

"And yet," I continued, "you've said that you've had wet dreams about everybody in your family."

"That's probably common, don't you think?"

"Not really."

"Maybe not all people remember such dreams."

"Of having incest with all the members of one's family?" I knew we were spinning on all cylinders now. Ginsberg was as blunt and honest as anyone I had ever interviewed.

"Sure," he said, convinced that he wasn't alone, or even in a minority, when it came to dreaming about shtupping family members, "fathers, mothers, sisters, brothers, aunts, uncles...trucks, grasses, earth. When I was about eight I had a dream about rubbing up against the hood of a large truck and having some sort of orgasmic reaction. The imagination knows no limits. That's the essential nature of our humanity, that it's unlimited imagination and dreams. The world of dreams is notorious for adventuring into areas that are forbidden in the conscious life, including incest and all other taboos. That's where we experience the breaking of taboos. I doubt that I'm very different than anybody else. I just remember my dreams. This is my nature and I can't apologize for that. I gather from your question that you're surprised?"

"I guess I just don't remember wanting to make love with my father," I said.

"Not wanting, actually *doing* it! Actually doing it is not wanting."

"In your mind?"

"No, in dreams, dreams, dreams, actual 3-D dreams! I think almost everybody has this. Maybe not so pronounced as the homosexual incest, but certainly heterosexual incest is common. Making it with your mother. It might be that heterosexual incest is more common than homosexual, but I'll bet it's universal. According to Freud it's between ages five and ten when you probably have more erotic dreams."

I thought this might make a good segue to Kerouac. "As a student of Freud, you must have some interesting thoughts on Jack Kerouac's relationship with his mother," I asked.

"It was interesting," he said. "They would get drunk together and speak the most foul language I've ever heard between them. She didn't like any of his friends. She particularly didn't like bearded Jews, but she also didn't like Burroughs, or Jack's wife or his girlfriends. Jack was close with a painter, a strong, good woman, and his mother once pulled him aside and said, 'I don't trust her, she's a witch; I saw her sharpening knives against the candles.' She didn't like it that I was gay. At one time Jack said his mother was absolutely crazy like mine, but he didn't want to throw her to the dogs of eternity as he said I had. So he put up with shocking things. I still remember it, great phrase: Dogs of eternity. But he paid the price of his own life by staying with her."

I wondered what Ginsberg thought of Truman Capote's remark about the way Kerouac wrote, with a roll of paper fed into his typewriter, so there were no page breaks. Capote said on a TV program, "That's not writing, that's typewriting."

"It was a witticism that he pronounced on television," Ginsberg said. "Kerouac liked Capote's prose but he saw him as an insignificant little faggot twit for saying a thing like that, and I did too. I thought that was really beneath Capote's dignity to be attacking another writer like that. It was undeserved. There's an alcohol downer in that remark. It's a slob's remark. I heard from a faggot friend that I slept with, who used to have some gay luncheons with Truman Capote and Andy Warhol, that Capote actually liked Kerouac's prose and was a little ashamed of becoming famous for that remark. Although, like Kerouac, Capote drank so much and downed so many pills and was such a hysteric, it was probably hard for him to reverse it publicly. It was a cheap shot. Kerouac was a more important writer and a greater prose artist than Capote. Capote is still a 19th century naiveté and Kerouac is 20th century open forum post-Pound, post-Stein, post-Joyce. Capote as a stylist wasn't as advanced as that. He didn't have any idea why Kerouac was writing spontaneous rhapsody and he didn't have any grasp of the Zen Japanese Buddhist Tibetan Chinese origins of that kind of style. So Capote's remark is relatively shallow. But it was funny; nobody can deny its humor."

Having called Capote an "insignificant little faggot twit," I wondered what Ginsberg thought of T.S. Eliot, whose poems like "The Waste Land" and "The Love Song of J. Alfred Prufrock" had a strong influence on modern poetry.

"Oh, he's a very great second-rate poet," Ginsberg said, adding, "Incidentally, Eliot, the acme of respectability, was writing this fantastic obscene poem called 'King Bolo,' which he only sent to friends in letters. It has never been published, but it was full of Jew boys, assholes, kikes, pricks, and cunts. Probably Eliot's greatest work."

I didn't know about this obscene work of Eliot's, but some years later Eliot's wife would allow sections of it to be published in *Inventions of the March Hare: Poems 1909–1917*. I was glad to learn about it from Ginsberg. I also learned from him that the poet William Carlos Williams edited some of Ginsberg's early work, much as Ezra Pound had done to T.S. Eliot's.

"William Carlos Williams went through my first book and separated out what he thought were bad, inert poems from the ones that he thought were active," Ginsberg told me. "Once he pointed it out, it was obvious and clarified my own awareness. He took about a hundred pages of poetry and boiled them down to forty."

Though Ginsberg would always be associated with being a Beat poet, he was a significant figure during the hippie Sixties, and even appeared in a film about Bob Dylan. But it was what the Beats stood for that stayed with him, and he was very clear about it when I asked him if there was a Beat creed.

"Yes," he said. It is "that reason is a necessary quality of human mercy. That generosity, charm and majesty are our original nature, rather than dog-eat-dog competition and rivalry. That beauty has permanent value for the young. That sexuality is open. That art is a hopeful way of being lyrical in the springtime. That politicians should learn to practice meditation in order to ground themselves and be in good relation to their own fantasies. That the sacred heart makes sense, although the pope might be a bastard or even Satan, as Blake said."

"Was the practice of meditation a key to get to the sacred heart?" I pressed on. "And how much does breathing come into it?"

"When you pay attention to your breath going out into the air and dissolving and then not pay attention to the in-breath, you'll find that your mind wanders and that your attention strays into memory, fantasy, planning for the future. The traditional practice is to acknowledge your thoughts and then bring your attention back to the breath until it dissolves. This is a method of writing poetry also. By observing the rising and flowering and dissolution of thought forms, you actually see poems rise in your head and dissolve. Simply a beginning, middle and end. All it requires is to copy down what you thought. It's like a big bubble that dissolves."

So here was Allen Ginsberg being filmed in a bookstore, espousing on the skeletons in his closet, his take on the poets and writers of his time, and the shape of things to come. He was convinced that the CIA had assassinated President Kennedy, and that the Mafia was involved in the dumping of nuclear waste. When I asked how corrupt he thought America was, he didn't hold back.

"America's completely polluted," he said. "Just think of how many species of animals we've killed. The first thing we did when we landed on this continent was spread smallpox and venereal disease and kill the natives. They started with the American Indians, they're still doing it in the Amazon with the Amazon Indians. Then you bring in the priests to convince them that their native consciousness is not appropriate and that they should worship some kind of *deus ex machina* from outside. The Catholic priests act as fronts for the bandits and murderers who kill everybody and take their land and make treaties, then break the treaties for the next hundred years. They say to the Indian, you can have this land, but they take it away a hundred years later after oil is discovered on it. All of us immigrants who came here don't have any ownership of the land, yet we grabbed it, and we're treating it with neither courtesy nor discretion. It's really a shame that we're polluting the entire planet."

"How would Allen Ginsberg have changed things if he ruled the country?" I asked him.

"If I were president I would start a large scale person-to-person exchange so that we get to know the Russians and Chinese and whoever it is we're supposed to be enemies of. Send a million college kids down to Nicaragua to exchange information and do a little work, instead of arming the *contras* to create a giant battlefield, wrecking the landmass of Central America. I'd do the same with Russia: take the cost of a couple of battleships or bombs and use it to send a million American girls and boys over there to hang around in Siberia, get high with the Russian kids, exchange information. I'd have people-to-people communication rather than the way it is now, with our politicians who haven't mastered their own aggression or paranoia."

Ginsberg's passions and emotions were apparent throughout the hours that we talked and continued when I drove with him to the airport afterwards. He didn't need a camera crew to capture what he had to say about how the earth was being destroyed. "You've got to realize that if you dump shit in your own well, you're going to get dysentery," he said in the car. "You can't poison your own nest, you can't piss in your own bed. You wind up shitting in your mother's face. Mother Nature."

When we got to John Wayne Airport, which is in the conservative heart of Orange County, I accompanied Ginsberg inside, where we said goodbye. But instead of shaking my hand he leaned forward and kissed me on the lips. One more surprise! And a shock to his fellow travelers who caught the moment. And though I had never been kissed by a bearded poet before, I learned that a kiss is still a kiss. Just one of many lessons from the man who saw the best minds of his post-war generation destroyed by madness and who, during the Vietnam War-protesting Sixties, coined the phrase "Flower power." Allen Ginsberg showed generations of beatniks, hippies, yuppies, and flower children that an artist could rage against the system and not sacrifice his soul.

111. THE DEFINITION OF A MASTERPIECE

Truman Capote, on the other hand, was willing to sacrifice his soul for the dignity of his art, even though Ginsberg criticized him for attacking Kerouac. I don't agree with Ginsberg about Kerouac being a greater prose artist than Capote, but that's a literary matter of opinion. Capote sacrificed his career when he attempted to write *Answered Prayers*, an unfinished novel some considered would have been the definitive portrait of high society in America at the end of the 20th century.

I can't think of anyone who amused me more than Truman Capote. He could put a smile on my face within five minutes of meeting, and he could turn that smile into a laugh or a guffaw or just wide-eyed disbelief within ten. He was a wonderful writer who wrote a few memorable books like *Breakfast at Tiffany's* and *In Cold Blood*. He was also a much-invited guest on late night talk shows because he was a hysterical raconteur (when he was semi-sober), with a quick wit and a comic's timing. He knew everybody and had intimate stories about the most wide-ranging celebrities, from Greta Garbo, Marilyn Monroe, and Elvis Presley to Jean Cocteau, Andre Gide, and Mick Jagger. He implied affairs with Adlai Stevenson, Errol Flynn and Montgomery Clift. He claimed to be the only person to have known Jack and Robert Kennedy and their respective assassins, Lee Harvey Oswald and Sirhan Sirhan. He kept a journal with a list of 4000 people he *dis*liked. He considered all literature—novels, essays, biographies, and short stories—as gossip. "It's so obvious," he said. "Look at *Gulliver's Travels*, he was commenting on the society of his time. *Alice in Wonderland* is gossip. If you start to examine it, we get into incestuous gossip, then into the gossip of adults raping children. Lewis Carroll turned out to be a total monster."

Among contemporary writers, he liked some, like Vladimir Nabokov, Willa Cather, Carson McCullers, John Cheever, E.M. Forster, and Gabriel Garcia Marquez, but found Thomas Pynchon, John Updike, Joyce Carol Oates, Donald Barthelme, Jack Kerouac, and Joseph Heller unreadable. But of all the writers of his generation, the one he most feuded with was Gore Vidal.

When Vidal heard that NAL was going to publish my book of conversations with Capote, he had his lawyer contact my publisher, threatening to sue if they printed anything Capote had said that was defamatory about Vidal. Vidal had already sued Capote for a million dollars over his telling a journalist why the Kennedys had turned against Vidal, and the threat was enough to get a few choice paragraphs excised from my book. When I asked Capote what had happened between them before these remarks, he said he had no idea. "Gore and I were sort of friends when we were teenagers," he told me. "Sort of like at MGM, Judy Garland and Lana Turner were friends as teenagers. And one day I had lunch with Gore and Tennessee Williams and I said something that nobody can remember. But whatever it was that I said, Gore flew into a complete rage. I've never seen anybody so angry, and from that day onward, it was a feud that he fueled, not me, because I never paid any attention to it and I never knew what started it and I never knew what it was about. And I still don't. But Gore has an obsession about me. He's just paranoid and jealous and goes off the deep end. You see, Gore has never written anything that anybody will remember ten years from its last paperback edition. Gore has never written a masterpiece. Now, even J.D. Salinger has written a masterpiece of a kind. Flannery O'Conner wrote a masterpiece or two. Hemingway did. Faulkner did. F. Scott Fitzgerald did. Norman Mailer never has. We could go on and on, but he has not done the one essential thing: he has not written an unforgettable book or a book that was the turning point in either his or anybody else's life. Without that, it doesn't matter how much he does or what he does."

I learned a lot about high society and the difference between the rich and the rest of us from Truman. He said, "The real difference is that rich people serve such marvelous vegetables. Delicious little tiny vegetables. Little fresh-born things scarcely out of the earth. Little baby corn, little baby peas, little lambs that have been *ripped* out of their mothers' wombs. That's the real difference. All of their vegetables and their meats are so incredibly fresh and unborn."

But it's how he described a masterpiece as not only being unforgettable but also being a turning point in the writer or reader's life that has stuck with me. It's a good barometer when looking at my bookshelves and reflecting on the books I've read.

112. SOME DREAM OF NOBEL HEIGHTS

One of those unforgettable books, **Joseph Heller's** *Catch-22,* was a turning point in my life. I was sixteen when I was introduced to Yossarian, Milo, Hungry Joe, Major Major, and the rest of the crazy, bizarre characters that Heller created for his WWII novel. I had a summer job working at a pharmaceutical warehouse, boxing various drugs and sundry items that were shipped out to drugstores around the country. It was boring, unfulfilling work that robots could—and eventually would—do better, and the only thing I looked forward to was the fifteen-minute coffee break and the thirty-minute lunch break each day. That's when I would sneak away from the other workers and read a few pages of *Catch-22*, which always made me laugh (at least until the last fifty pages, when it stopped being funny). I credit the book with saving that summer for me, and for giving me a perspective on war that would affect me five years later when the draft was calling and I became a conscientious objector.

I told Heller this little appreciation when I met him for lunch at the Polo Lounge of the Beverly Hills Hotel, and he didn't seem to give a damn. *Catch-22* wasn't an initial success and it took a few years before it became a cult classic, selling over ten million in paperback. He had originally called it *Catch-18* and only changed it because Leon Uris had beaten him to print with his book, *Mila 18*. What a difference a number makes!

Heller was more interested in discussing his new book, *Something Happened*, a novel Kurt Vonnegut said dealt with "unrelieved misery." It was about corporate life and began: "I get the willies when I see closed doors."

Heller believed that the first sentence of a book sets the tone for what follows and he told me that the opening line that got his juices going actually became the start of the second section in the finished book. That sentence was: "In the office in which I work there are five people of whom I am afraid."

"That line brings with it the type of company," he said, "the fact it's a large company. That's there's only five people of whom he's afraid means he's got a pretty high executive position, because if you're low down there'd be 3,500 people you'd be afraid of, and if he's an executive, then he's old enough to be married and have children. So that line brings to it a suggestion of other possibilities."

Once we started talking about writing, I learned how Heller saw what he did. "To me," he said, "writing is largely a matter of memorizing. I will have in mind what I want to write, often to the extent of language, phrases and sentence structure. I walk from where I live to where I write, and by the time I get there I know most of what I'm going to do in the next two hours. And when I finish I'll have a very good idea of what I want to do the next work session."

He said he had an easier time memorizing what he wanted to write with the second novel because there were a lot fewer characters than in the first one. "*Catch-22* had 44 named characters and a vast number of episodes, so it became necessary to put things down in order. At that time I had a desk blotter that I ruled into parallel columns and horizontal boxes, putting a character and the name at the top of each column. In the left I had a series of events. I tried to keep from having anachronisms from occurring, and to make sure where each character was."

It's always interesting to get a writer to talk about his influences, and it's of particular interest when the writer has written a major book, one for the ages. With *Something Happened*, which may or may not go down as "major" (though it did go straight to the top of the bestseller lists), Heller said the structural model he had in mind was William Faulkner's *Absalom, Absalom!* For *Catch-22*, which has been ranked number seven on Modern Library's list of the 100 best novels of the 20th century, Heller was influenced by the "random and free use of coincidence, the use of street language, and the flippancy and impertinence that you find in Louis-Ferdinand Celine's *Journey to the End of Night*. I don't think I could have gotten the idea for *Catch-22* if I had not read Celine's work. And, to a lesser extent, Nabokov's *Laughter in the Dark* and Evelyn Waugh."

We spoke of the writers he favored (Salinger, Pynchon, and Donleavy) and his hopes of writing a few more books so he could be in the running for a Nobel Prize in Literature, but what I learned from Joseph Heller was how he wrote in his head before he got to his desk, and how a French novelist turned a switch on inside his brain to allow *Catch-22* to come forth.

113. DON'T TAKE NO FOR A FINAL ANSWER

Heller wrote ten books but was overlooked by the Nobel committee year after year, but according to **Saul Bellow,** who went to Stockholm to pick up his prize in 1976, it was not all it's cracked up to be.

I spent years trying to convince my editors at *Playboy* to let me interview Bellow. When they finally said yes, I spent more time trying to get Bellow to agree. I had written to him with my request, but his secretary wrote back saying he was getting over an illness (fish poisoning) and wasn't up for it. I wrote him again a few months later, saying that I hope he had sufficiently recovered and might make himself available to talk. This time his secretary claimed that he was trying to finish a novel and just didn't have the time. I tried a third time a year later and he agreed, probably figuring I wasn't going to leave him alone till he said yes.

That's when it was *Playboy's* turn to say no. They wanted him when I originally reached out to him, but the editors had changed their minds when I told them that he had finally agreed. I was shocked. Bellow was the most valued, most awarded and, by most critics' account, America's greatest living writer. How could the magazine *not* want him?

I had been reading Bellow since high school, when I first discovered *Henderson the Rain King.* What a brilliant book. A man going off to deepest Africa to find an answer to the incessant voice within him whispering "I want." We all "want" something out of life. Bellow wanted to be a great writer. Each of his books raised his level until he perched at the very top of the great American novelists. A 1965 *Book Week* poll of novelists and critics found Bellow to have written the "most distinguished fiction of the 1945–1965 period." Of the six best novels written in those postwar years, three were by Bellow. One of them, *The Adventures of Augie March*, would later be declared The Great American Novel by Martin Amis in *The Atlantic.* With three National Book Awards, a Pulitzer Prize, a Gold Medal for the Novel, the National Institute of Arts and Letters Award, The Friends of Literature Fiction Award, The Prix International, the Croix de Chevalier, and the Nobel Prize, no writer has ever been more honored.

And my editors didn't want him?

How was that even possible?

OK, I got it, the demographics were against him. *Playboy* appealed to young males and young males were more interested in athletes, sex and rock stars than highly prized novelists. But *Playboy* had a reputation for interviewing some of the biggest people in their fields of expertise. Albert Schweitzer, Fidel Castro, Salvador Dali, Stephen Hawking, Steve Jobs, even the head of the KKK, George Lincoln Rockwell, and Hitler's chief architect, Albert Speer, were subjects. How could I tell Saul Bellow that the magazine was no longer interested in him?

I couldn't. I wouldn't. He was too important a figure in our culture to be rejected without an explanation. Since I had none, I decided it should come from the top. So I bypassed the editor I dealt with for interviews and wrote a note to the editorial director of the magazine. I said that the decision to cancel the previously assigned interview with him should come from him, on his letterhead. We owed him at least this courtesy.

I got a note back to go ahead and do the interview!

So I flew to Boston and met Bellow at his office on the sixth floor of Boston University's Department of Theology. There were three black filing cabinets, one wall of books, and four cardboard boxes on the worn purple carpet. It felt like the office of a cheap detective.

We covered a lot of ground that day. He opined on Franz Kafka, Jesus Christ, Marilyn Monroe, his contemporaries, the sexual revolution, Reichian therapy, AIDS, high vs. low art, anti-Semitism, terrorism, immortality, the relevance of novelists, liberating the English language, his childhood illnesses, his mother's early death, his father's abusive behavior, and his five marriages.

When the interview was published in the May 1997 issue, *Playboy* called it a "landmark" on their PLAYBILL page. This is how it was previewed: "Saul Bellow is a literary colossus who isn't known for keeping his opinions to himself. Labeled a conservative in recent years, Bellow nevertheless transformed American letters with his novels *The Adventures of Augie March, Henderson the Rain King* and *Herzog.* He may be America's greatest living writer. On the eve of the release of his novella *The Actual,* Bellow met with Lawrence Grobel for a landmark *Playboy Interview.* Bellow heaps scorn on Truman Capote, reflects on Freud and Trotsky, and has choice words about God, wives and judges."

The interview received a lot of media attention. The *New York Post's* Liz Smith headlined her syndicated column "Saul Bellows His Bile." The *Playboy* editors submitted it in the non-fiction category for the American Magazine Awards for that year—the first time they had used an interview and not a standard article for that classification. And when they published a book called *The Bedside Playboy,* Bellow was the only interview included in that compilation.

Of all of Bellow's remarks, the one that received the most attention had to do with what he said about his Nobel Prize, which he won in 1976. He wasn't overly impressed with the honor and said that he was "very careful to see that it didn't affect my life too much." He pointed out that many deserving writers like Marcel Proust, Leo Tolstoy, and James Joyce never won the Prize. He resented that because of the Prize people expected more from him. "They feel you are a public functionary," he said, "that you have to produce a certain amount of cultural shrubbery on God's little acre." When I mentioned that a lot of writers would like to be in such a position, including **Norman Mailer**, he threw out one of his sharpest quips, "I'd give it to him...if he had anything to trade."

114. WIN TWO NOBEL PRIZES

Mailer would not have taken kindly to Bellow's remark, even though he confessed ambivalence about the possibility of winning the Nobel Prize seven years before Bellow got it. He spent the opening pages of *The Prisoner of Sex* describing how his name was about to be announced as the 1969 laureate (which went to Samuel Beckett), worried that it "would have incarcerated him into larger paralyses. Each time there was a change of government in Canberra or Pakistan, some poor reporter would have his name on a list of notables to be called for a statement. Committees and charity dinners, satellite awards and subsidiary distinctions would have an outsize lust to list him."

Mailer sounded like he was channeling **Dr. Richard Feynman,** who told me that his 1965 Nobel Prize in Physics was "one of the miseries of my life. I wouldn't say that my physics wasn't up to the prize, but I'm not up to it on a human side." Feynman went on to complain about how annoying it was to have everyone ask for his opinion because they figured a Nobel laureate must know all the answers. He said he used to enjoy going to talk to high school physics students, but he stopped getting invited after the Prize, because students figured he was too important to say yes. And when he did visit a high school, it wasn't just the physics club that turned out, but the entire school came to a halt to see what the Nobel Prize winner had to say. "I was a kid fooling around in my pajamas," he said, "working on the floor with paper and pencil and I cooked something up. Does that make me a great wise *schmaltz* that everybody should see? It's a distortion. I'm looked at differently. It's a pain in the ass!"

But **Linus Pauling,** who won his first Nobel Prize in Chemistry in 1954 and his second for his contributions to world peace in 1962, felt differently. He wasn't sure he'd be honored for the first one because, while he had made a large number of discoveries, there wasn't any particular one that he thought might be singled out. "The committee got around that problem by saying that it was given to me for my research on the nature of the chemical bond and its application to the elucidation of the structure of complex substances," he said. Since he estimated that half of the 300 papers he had published could be referred to in those terms, he allowed himself to be "pleased" with the recognition. But it was the second Nobel that made him really happy. "I felt it was sort of a sacrifice for me to give hundreds of lectures about nuclear war and radioactive fallout, but I was doing it largely as a matter of doing my duty as a citizen, not because I liked spending the time on that. I preferred doing scientific research and teaching." And then he gave a broad and contented smile, noting, "In the *Guinness Book of Records,* it says I have the championship. Two other people have received two Nobel Prizes: Madame Curie shared one with her husband and received one full one; then [American physicist] John Bardeen received a third of a prize twice. I'm the only one to have received two complete Nobel Prizes."

So if you really want to clear yourself from the clutter of whatever true or false humility you may have for such exalted recognition and instead walk tall through God's Little Acre, win two of those suckers. Modesty be damned!

115. BETTER TO BE DUMB THAN STUPID

Norman Mailer may have been overlooked for the Nobel Prize, but he did receive two Pulitzers (for *The Executioner's Song* and *The Armies of the Night*) and a National Book Award (also for *The Armies of the Night*). His first novel, *The Naked* *and the Dead*, published when he was 25, was another of Modern Library's 100 Best Novels in the English language. His early success led to his alienation, which he called a 20th century condition. He believed from the very start that a writer of the largest dimension can alter the nerves and marrow of a nation and was determined to be that kind of writer.

"He was the most transparently ambitious writer of his era," Charles McGrath wrote in a *New York Times* obituary after Mailer's death of acute renal failure in November 2007, "seeing himself in competition not just with his contemporaries but with the likes of Tolstoy and Dostoevsky."

I interviewed him a few times in the 1980s and a few months before he died, and I enjoyed challenging him on some of his ideas. I once asked him if he still obsessed about being the Number One writer in America. He answered, "You could have writers who are first in the people's mind, but I don't know if that has any literary value. If you had an election tomorrow there would probably be five of us who would be in contention, and you could have a runoff. The results wouldn't matter because each of us would walk away thinking, 'I was the best.' I don't think it's important. But if there was an election and somebody else won, I'd be annoyed."

It was always interesting listening to him hold forth on subjects ranging from architecture and technology to the evils of plastic and advertising to the yin/yang of lust, masturbation and the pleasures of head butting.

"I've never taken myself so seriously as to speak of Mailer's Law of this or that," he said during our last conversation, "but I finally have one. It's Mailer's Law of Architectural Precedence in American Universities. Go to any university in the country and you have no problem determining the order in which the buildings were erected on that campus. The more atrocious the architecture, the newer the building. If the building next to you is less atrocious than the one you're in, it was built before. The oldest building on the campus is invariably the nicest. That says something about creativity going out of life."

The loss of creatively was a constant theme for Mailer. He placed technology firmly on the side of the devil. He was a great admirer of many of the novelists who preceded him, like William Faulkner, John Steinbeck, Thomas Wolfe, F. Scott Fitzgerald, and Ernest Hemingway. But he didn't think writing mattered as much in the 21st century.

"Hemingway and Faulkner between them captured profound elements in the American soul," he said. "At that time, reading was the most profound way to deepen your knowledge of existence. So writers were respected more. They were more important. We're moving from writing into electronic circuitry, television, and computers. Print, as such, is going to disappear. There is a point where the act of reading a book may become a rare luxury, equal to eating Russian caviar. People now read off computer screens. It's as if the very sensuous qualities of reading are being taken away from us. In other words, reading's become an effort, equal to, say, having a pair of uncomfortable plastic earphones on, the sort they give you in an airplane, where it hurts your ears and your head and the sound's not very good. So you've got to work for the movie that you're seeing."

I often think about Mailer and I can only imagine what he would have to say about the state of our political parties in 2016, when the Republican presidential front-runners were Donald Trump and Ted Cruz, and the Democrats saw a surge of interest in Bernie Sanders over Hillary Clinton. Mailer would have had a field day with those potential candidates, as he did when he wrote about Richard Nixon, George McGovern,

Jack and Robert Kennedy, and the two Bushes. Mailer himself once ran for public office, but he lost his bid to become mayor of New York in 1969. I'm glad, because he would only have become frustrated trying to get through some of his beliefs, and it was far more important for him to write novels like *The Executioner's Song, Ancient Evenings, Harlot's Ghost,* and *The Castle in the Forest,* and profiles of John F. Kennedy, Marilyn Monroe, Pablo Picasso, Muhammad Ali, Lee Harvey Oswald, Madonna, and Jesus Christ. Who knows if any of them would have been written had he become mayor? He probably would have tried to become governor next, and maybe, in his wildest cannabis-induced dreams, made a run for the presidency. Trying to imagine Norman Mailer as president almost seems absurd, until one compares him to a Trump or Cruz. Mailer had better ideas than banning Muslims from entering the U.S. or closing down the government to oppose universal health care.

If Mailer had ever held office he thought he could raise money by taxing plastics and advertising, both of which, he believed, were cancerous to our society.

"One of my most fundamental beliefs is that the government has the right to tax people," he expounded, "but we have a right to say what we're taxed on. I'd love to lead the crusade to tax the hell out of plastic. It would make it too expensive for them to make that crap any more. So it would tend to disappear. Where plastic was indispensable it would still remain, because people would just pay the tax on it. If the only decent fishing rods or skis were made out of plastic, we would pay a little more.

"Another thing I'd absolutely be for is, we're just surrounded with meretriciousness and mendacity in every aspect of our immediate life. So I'd opt for taking away the tax deduction from advertising and let those businesses that need to advertise pay for the privilege, because what they're selling is not their product but a pile of horseshit. They're attaching values that have nothing to do with the product. It's attached to the entertainment that they give you on TV, which is mediocre entertainment at best. So why should that go into the price of a product? Why do we need to have the three major automobile manufacturers all advertising like crazy when we know they're all equally mediocre? Does it really matter? Is there any American who doesn't know that Ford, Chrysler and General Motors products are all on the same level every year? That finally you're gonna pick it for the paint job? Why do you have to have a helicopter drop a car on top of a mountain peak? The millions that are spent on that, for what? To increase the price of the product? So, take away the tax deductions in advertising. You say that'll put a lot of people out of work? Well, great. They'll have to scuffle."

One institution he wasn't very good at was marriage, which he tried six times. He once spent seventeen days under psychiatric observation in Bellevue for stabbing his second wife at a party. No wonder he called himself one of the most wicked spirits in American life.

"One of my favorite remarks," he told me, "is that the only time you ever do anything with great energy is when the best and worst motives in you are both involved at the same time. Or let's say the most love-filled and the most hate-filled motives are engaged at the same moment. Lust is a perfect example of that. When one feels and makes lust for a woman, it's precisely because the love we feel for her and the hate we feel for her are both being fully expressed. And those would-be sexual relations really come from just one side or another of oneself being expressed."

He also had a strong belief that masturbation crippled people and led to insanity.

"The tendency of masturbation is insanity," he said. "In the same way that the tendency of driving 90 mph in a slow speed zone is a crash up. It doesn't mean it's going to happen. But you can't cheat life. There's no objective correlative in masturbation. It encourages one's fantasy life in the weakest fashion possible. It's a release, in the sense it keeps people from something worse happening to them. But to see masturbation as something marvelous and part of a healthy sex life is dubious in the extreme. The tendency for masturbation nine times out of ten is to push people further and further into loneliness and into a fundamental sense of defeat about not getting what they really want sexually."

Sex and violence were the subjects of many of his books and articles, and even though he once literally knocked heads with Gore Vidal, Vidal said of him, "Of all my contemporaries, I retain the greatest affection for Norman as a force and as an artist. He is a man whose faults, though many, add *to,* rather than subtract from, the sum of his natural achievements."

"I head-butt with a lot of people," Mailer said when I brought it up. "People have the wrong idea about it. It isn't that you head-butt and somebody drops. For me, it's a touch of affection. You just butt heads once lightly. It wasn't lightly with Vidal though. But it's always fair for one writer to butt another in the head. Writers have hard heads. The hardest head you'll ever encounter will be a writer's head. It's just like an erect phallus."

Mailer's take on the human condition was unique, entertaining, and often profound. He had an opinion about everything. One of his "takes" was distinguishing between dumb and stupid people.

"I love to keep complacent people off balance," he said. "I can't bear their complacency. Stupidity brings out violence in me, because I consider stupidity a choice. There's a great difference between people who are stupid and people who are dumb. People who are dumb have been injured and there's something soft and tender about their brain. If it's permanent, it's touching, it's pathetic. People who are stupid made one wise decision in their lives, because if you're stupid and you remain stupid, people have to come to you, have to deal with you; you're the center of a great many energy transactions that you haven't earned. If you can take the abuse, it's a way of life. But it's a way of life that poisons everything around you. So stupid people bring out my most unpleasant reactions and emotions. I will needle stupid people to the best of my ability."

I had never given much thought to the difference between dumb and stupid, probably because the dictionary defines them similarly. But Mailer was looking at "dumb" as being naturally limited, and "stupid" as being foolish *by choice*, opting to remain ignorant rather than strive to increase learning and knowledge. But he says stupid people have made one wise decision, and I find that confusing. It seems more likely he meant to say the choice for ignorance was one *irresponsible* decision, but I can't speak for him. The important thing is that I get what he's saying, that stupid people are ignorant, and he liked to needle them. His parsing of dumb and stupid is one of the lessons that I took away from hanging out with Norman Mailer. Of course, I can't ignore his thoughts on masturbation, because it makes me wonder if all the people I've known who have, at one time or another, called me "insane" might have known something about me that I would have preferred to keep to myself.

116. FOLLOW YOUR DREAM

Though writers like to talk about anything, sex is more often reserved for their writing. When I interviewed playwright **Neil Simon** for Playboy cable, however, I knew such talk had to be broached, and I thought perhaps his loss of virginity with a prostitute at the age of 19 was the way to go. But it wasn't much of a learning experience for him. He said his brother took him to a whorehouse and he just wanted to get it over with and get out of there. But it gave him material that he used in one of his plays (*Biloxi Blues*).

But I did learn a lesson interviewing Simon—perhaps the most successful playwright in the American theater. Almost half of his 35 plays were named "Best Play" of their seasons, among them *Barefoot in the Park, The Odd Couple, Plaza Suite, The Prisoner of Second Avenue, The Sunshine Boys, California Suite, Chapter Two, Brighton Beach Memoirs, Biloxi Blues, Broadway Bound,* and *Lost in Yonkers*. He's won three Tony Awards, a Pulitzer Prize, and has had a Broadway theater named after him. When he's not preparing a play he's writing a movie (twenty-five of those) or his memoirs.

But it was how he came to write his first play where the lesson lay. He had been writing successfully for some of the biggest stars of television—Jackie Gleason, Sid Caesar, Phil Silvers—but when he wanted to break into film he was told he didn't have the background.

"I felt if I stayed in television I wouldn't get past the point of situation comedy," he said when we met at an empty theater in Los Angeles in 1985. "Maybe I might branch off and write a film. I was as well known and well paid a writer as Mel Brooks or Larry Gelbart, but when I was with the William Morris office—they were my agents—I would go to them and say, 'I want to do a film, can you get one for me?' They would say, 'No, you have no experience.' So it was Catch-22: you couldn't write a movie unless you had already written one. So I said, 'I see how it works now, I've got to do it myself.' But I didn't know anybody on the West Coast, I had no ins to break into film, so I thought I'd be better off writing a play, because I liked the theater more. So I spent three years writing *Come Blow Your Horn*."

He began writing that play in 1958 when he was still writing for the *Bilko* show and then *The Garry Moore Show.* "Those shows, especially the *Bilko* show, were enormously demanding. We worked six days a week and sometimes at night. So to try to write a play and having no experience—I didn't know how to get actors on or off the stage—it was different than it was working in television. The craft of the theater had escaped me at that point and I had to learn it. That's what took three years."

It also took twenty drafts. "I rewrote it from beginning to end, without a single word of earlier drafts in some of the later versions. I just didn't believe in myself. I kept saying, 'This isn't good enough. It's not right.' That doesn't mean I believed I could make it better, but I felt I had to try. Those twenty versions were shown to at least twenty different major producers in New York, all of whom were interested in it but none of them wanted to produce it. But each of them gave me a hint about what was wrong, so I picked up a little here and there. It was the equivalent to three years of college. Then I was also saved by the fact that I couldn't get it produced on Broadway. Had I gotten it on Broadway it would have failed and that would have been the end of it and I'd have been writing on a sit-com for the rest of my life. What happened was, since I couldn't get a producer, the agent I had, Helen Harvey, suggested I try it out in summer stock somewhere. The fear was if that didn't work it was the last you ever heard of it. But there was about 40% of the play that was good enough for Broadway and 60% that needed rewriting, so I had the advantage of seeing it in front of an audience every night, seeing what worked and what didn't. Then we took six months off and I rewrote it again. Tried it in Philadelphia and it was a big hit."

But seeing it out of town and opening on Broadway were very different experiences. "It was torturous. After *Come Blow Your Horn,* I said I'd never write another play because I can't go through this. My mouth was drier than the Sahara Desert. I couldn't talk, the actors seemed eighty miles away when I was standing in the back of the theater, and my heart was pounding. I said, 'My life depends on this night. If I fail, and fail real big, I'll have to creep away in the night and go someplace else to try and make my living.' I was fortunate that that did not happen to me, even though I was also fortunate in not being an overwhelming success, because that would make your second attempt unbearable. How would you live up to that? So I was in the middle of the road. But there were enough people who started to come and talk about it that it subsidized me for the next two plays. I was able to write the musical *Little Me* and after that, *Barefoot in the Park.*"

19 plays and 22 years later he won the New York Drama Critics Circle Award for *Brighton Beach Memoirs,* and though it only took him four months to write, it took him three times as long to conceive as it did his first play. "It took nine years from the inception of the idea," he said. "It was a big breakthrough for me. Not because it was autobiographical, but it was the first time I wrote a tapestry play. I said to myself in writing it that there are seven characters; I am going to make each one of them the star of the play. So the audience watching can

pick up any person in the play and identify and say, yes, that's what this is about."

Simon found it easier to write plays in Los Angeles than in New York because L.A. was less distracting, which might also be a lesson for playwrights. But for me, the lesson was in the number of times he rewrote *Come Blow Your Horn*, because that was a lesson in dedication and craft. You don't become successful overnight, and even when you hit it big with your first play, it can still take you nine years to figure out your twentieth.

117. PASS ON THE LIMO

Elmore Leonard wasn't an overnight success, but his dedication to his craft earned him the sobriquet the "Dickens of Detroit" by *Time* magazine. *Newsweek* put him on its cover in 1985 and called him "The best American crime writer of crime fiction alive, possibly the best we ever had."

Leonard didn't hang out with a lot of crooks, other than the ones that were in his head. His novels were so full of such sharply drawn criminals that a reader might surmise that he had spent time incarcerated among con artists, pimps, sex offenders, murderers, thieves, embezzlers and bombers. He had their mannerisms and dialogue down. He knew how they walked, what they carried, and how they could out-psych their victims.

When I went to see him at his home in Bloomfield Village, Michigan, his fiction had fooled me into expectations of a fast-talking detective-type with piercing eyes and a high sense of skepticism. Instead there was this gentle, soft-spoken medium build milquetoast of a man wearing chinos, a denim shirt and glasses. How did Leonard learn to write the westerns and the crime novels that made him such a popular writer? This is what he told me:

After he graduated from college in 1950, he got a job as an office boy at an ad agency. "I decided then that if I was going to write I should go about it in a professional way; pick a genre to learn how to write," he said. "So I chose westerns because of movies like *Stagecoach, The Plainsman, My Darling Clementine,* and *Red River.* Westerns were popular in the Fifties and western stories were in all the better magazines, like *Saturday Evening Post* and *Colliers,* and the pulps were still alive. And I subscribed to *Arizona Highways* because of the illustrations. If I needed to write about a canyon, I'd go through the magazine and find one and describe it. It was better than being there."

John Ford, Howard Hawks and Cecil B. DeMille's films inspired him, but he still needed to learn how to handle dialogue, description, and plotting. That's when he graduated to Ernest Hemingway's work. "Hemingway's *For Whom the Bell Tolls* showed me how to write westerns, because it was a western, in a way. They're out in the mountains with horses, with people speaking Spanish; it could be a border story. I noticed the way Hemingway used his senses; he had everything going at once. He made it look easy, because on so many of his pages there was a lot of white space; very often his dialogue went straight down the page and it wasn't more than a couple inches wide. You didn't see dialogue anywhere else—the serious novelists seemed reluctant to use dialogue. And yet he used it so effectively, and he said so much, there was more there than the words themselves. So I began to study him very closely in construction, in his describing a person, what he described and what he didn't. In contrast to writers who describe someone's face in such detail—the wide-set eyes, narrow chin—things that you immediately forget. I started to put him on my typewriter to see what it looked like.

Do a paragraph of Hemingway as it appears and then write the next paragraph myself."

What Leonard discovered was that Hemingway was "too serious" for him. "I realized that I didn't share Hemingway's attitudes at all about himself or myself," he said. "So then I began to read people like Mark Harris, who wrote *Bang the Drum Slowly*. And Kurt Vonnegut, Richard Bissell, to see that you didn't have to be that serious, you could have a little more fun with it." And then he discovered George Higgins's *The Friends of Eddie Coyle*. "It's the best crime book there is," Leonard said. "It loosened me up. I decided to be freer with the language, use more obscenities, get into scenes quicker without setting the scene. I noticed how he opened scenes with people talking before you knew where you were or even before you knew who they are. I liked the way that worked."

Once he could afford it, Leonard hired an assistant to do a lot of the legwork when it came to investigating crimes and criminals. When I asked him what con men, killers and burglars might have in common, he was quick to respond, "They're all lazy. They don't want to work; they don't want to do it the hard way. They don't want to have to learn how to do anything. It's like being a drunk: if you devoted all this effort that you do to drinking to some worthwhile effort, it could be worth money."

When it came to the nitty-gritty of crime work, breaking into houses or buildings, blowing things up, Leonard found answers in books. Researching *Freaky Deaky* he needed to know how to make a bomb, and a Detroit cop turned him on to the *Anarchist Cookbook*. "It's full of drawings and diagrams of how to put together bombs, booby traps, pipe bombs. I liked that a lot." For one scene he wanted to know how to open a drawer and set off a bomb. For that he sent away for a booklet that showed him how to make C-4 plastique using materials easily accessible at the hardware store. When writing *Bandits*, he learned about lock picking from another pamphlet, *Locks and Lockpicking.* "It's all in there."

"Early on I got a good idea of what I could do and what I couldn't," Leonard said when discussing his writing. "Based on that, I try to move the story with as much dialogue as possible and concentrate on the characters. I don't write effectively in the traditional manner of narrative writing, in telling a story with language, with my words. I don't have enough words to do that, so in lieu of that I approach it from the standpoint of the characters. I'm not sure of my ability to describe what's going on; to me it's more interesting to let the characters do it—that way, you not only find out what's going on, but you also learn something about the character. You're doing two things at once. I'm not good at imagery, similes, and metaphors. If they're not good, they're very, very distracting. I said that to Joyce Carol Oates once and she said, 'Well, so much for Shakespeare.' But Raymond Chandler's tarantula on a piece of angel food cake—that kind of metaphor distracts you from the story. You're picturing the metaphor and you are away from the story."

When students approach him for advice Leonard tells them to read. "That's the best way to learn how to write," he says. "The book that really grabbed me was Ira Levin's *Rosemary's Baby.* Not knowing what it was about, I couldn't believe it. At writer's conferences I say, Just break down and outline *Rosemary's Baby* and that's how you write a book."

So that's how Leonard learned to be a fantastically successful writer. But what did I learn from him? That it's important to know your strengths and trust your imagination. Oh, and this, which he said to me as I left his house: "Write for as much money as the market will bear, and if a limo is ever offered to take you to a business meeting, refuse it, because you may want to walk out of the meeting and you won't have any transportation." I already knew about the money, but had never given thought to the limo. I learned that from Leonard. And at a bookstore at the airport narrowly squeezed among the Elmore Leonard paperbacks I found a copy of Ira Levin's *Rosemary Baby.* Read it on the plane.

118. TREAT EVERYONE AS EQUALS

It was **James A. Michener** who emphasized the importance of a writer being paid. He once wrote me a long letter about it, believing that it was what separated the professionals from the wannabes. Michener, like Leonard, cultivated his strengths (storytelling) and accepted his weaknesses. "I know my deficiencies better than most of my critics," he said. "I don't use words as well as Philip Roth. I don't use social structures as well as Joyce Carol Oates. I don't have the quality of touch that Robert Penn Warren has. I do not begin to project myself into the life of another to the degree of somebody like Mailer or Capote, John Cheever, or even Updike. I am not very competent in dealing with sexuality. And I'm not very good at plotting; it doesn't interest me at all. I could end my books anywhere and start anywhere. I am giving a kaleidoscopic view, not a psychological one. I understand narrative. I'm a teller of stories. I've learned how to do that, and I can do it so that people get a feeling of meaning out of it."

Over a period of seventeen years, I visited with James A. Michener many times, seeing him in Florida, Maine, New York, California, and Texas. He had an overabundance of extraordinary experiences from his worldwide travels and research for the sixty or so books he wrote, and his memory was intact right up until his death in October 1997. He was, first and foremost, a teacher. He taught in high school, college, and graduate schools and the first question he asked people was about their education. I found him to be so stimulating, inspiring and encouraging, I was prompted to share his views in my own book, *Conversations With Michener.*

He didn't start writing books until he was forty, and that first book—*Tales of the South Pacific*—won the Pulitzer Prize in 1948. He was well organized and once he decided on a subject (usually a country, like Poland, Spain, Israel, Mexico, or Afghanistan; a state, like Texas, Hawaii or Alaska; or a geographical area, like the South Pacific, Caribbean, Chesapeake, or Space), he methodically broke down the way to present it. His doorstop novels, usually ranging between 600 and 1000 pages long, always covered at least three of five "arbitrary subjects" which he studied intensely before building a story around them. He explained it to me like this: "One would always be the geography, geology, anthropology or botany. One would be an intellectual field like religion, literature, philosophical understandings or history–something with content. The other three could be very arbitrary. In *Texas,* I was deeply into the cattle industry and oil, but also border troubles. What I followed for *Mexico* was bullfighting, mining, and the fact that at the end of the Civil War there were a lot of southerners who were fed up with the north, especially with General Grant, who was such a son of a bitch. In the case of *Chesapeake*, it was railroads, banking, and the history of the church. If you do that vertically for four or five subjects you get a structure that is just so concrete, you know what was happening: that during the Depression corn was selling at a giveaway price; that railroads had decided not to go to Denver; that shipping was tied up because of French-British antagonism. You begin to see ramifications and structures. Never have I picked all five subjects. I don't think I have ever done better than three. But with that in place, you begin to fill in."

We first met in 1981 at his office in Juno, Florida. I sat behind his desk, which consisted of a wooden door on top of two two-drawer filing cabinets, while he sat in a rocking chair. In the summer of 1983 I was with him at the Athenaeum Inn before he delivered the commencement address at Cal Tech in Pasadena. I sat across from him at a table honoring him on his 85th birthday at the J. Pierpont Morgan Library in Manhattan in 1992. In the fall of 1994, after the death of his wife Mari, I sat next to him on his couch in Austin, Texas as we watched *Jeopardy* after an eight-hour marathon conversation, and I sat by his side the next day at a dialysis clinic as he was treated for his failing kidneys. In February 1997 I sat with him in his backyard the day after his being feted on his 90th birthday by the University of Texas, where 350 well wishers came to shake his hand and applaud the publication of his final book, *A Century of Sonnets.* The guests included Lady Bird Johnson, two former governors, three university presidents, and many of the professional people he knew. "I know what it was about," he said, his voice frail, but his mind sharp. "People feel if they're going to get aboard the bandwagon, they'd better do it now. I'm growing older and the other guys aren't here anymore."

We became very close over the years, and I learned a lot about him on all sorts of subjects. He learned to write by rewriting the ending of *The Iliad* so that the Trojans won. He studied the way Arnold Bennett and Samuel Butler structured their novels *The Old Wives' Tale* and *Vanity Fair,* respectively. He read all of Balzac at the age of 14. He began to understand the Southern mentality when he was arrested for vagrancy as a wayward teenager. He met President Calvin Coolidge in the White House in 1924. He worked in an amusement park and saw the seedy side of how con men worked the crowds. He learned sailing in Scotland, and bullfighting in Spain. He learned to love islands from visiting the Outer Hebrides, and he learned to build a stereo system in 1934. He memorized the Beethoven String Quartets and taught himself form and structure by understanding the music of Mozart, Mahler, Stravinsky, Brahms, Sibelius, and Schoenberg. Opera also figured into his development and he could discourse on all the great tenors. His early travels to Colorado were a revelation for him, as he discovered the Spanish, French and "liberal free-swinging" components, and wound up leading the fight for Mexican rights. As an educator, he was invited to the White House by Eleanor Roosevelt in 1939, and met the president after dinner. World War II and the Navy changed his life. He survived plane crashes, defended homosexuals who were court martialed, and made the decision to write about the islands where he served in the South Pacific. And that was the foundation of his first book.

When I first went to interview him, he thought we could get through my questions in a day. I knew that would be impossible, as I had prepared over 500 questions to ask him, and assumed at least another 500 would come up as we talked. That eight-hour day stretched into 40 hours over five days, and that was just the beginning.

But of all the things he said and all the hours of conversation we taped, my fondest memory of the man was how he responded to my then eight-year-old daughter Hana. I had taken my family with me to Maine in July 1992, where Michener and his wife Mari were staying at the time. The plan was for me to spend a few days talking to Jim while my wife and two daughters explored Brunswick and its surroundings. On our last day together I brought my family to meet him and the first thing Hana said to him was, "I'm a writer too." Michener took a genuine interest in her declaration and asked what she had written. Hana reached into her pocket and pulled out a miniature two-inch book, which she had filled with her stories and drawings about a seal named Simon. Michener took the book and began reading it when the phone rang. It was a call he was expecting and he excused himself to answer it. When he returned, he said that the University of Texas had just accepted his terms for a new school in the creative arts, which he would fund with an initial $15 million donation. "Looks like I'll have to make do with whatever I can earn from future books," he said, proud that he could do this for the university. Michener had already donated much of his $60 million art collection to the university and to the James A. Michener Art Museum in Doylestown, Pennsylvania; this was his last big philanthropic donation. It was a cause for celebration. But before any cheers could be offered, Michener sat back down next to Hana, picked up her little book, and finished reading what she had written.

"This is a really good story," he said. "Everybody is happy in the end."

"I know," Hana said. "Thank you for reading it."

"And thank you for letting me read it," he said.

Hana beamed and when Michener leaned down she put her arms around him and kissed his cheek. "Now that," he said, also beaming, "is as good as any new school with my name on it."

I would write about this for *Reader's Digest*, a publication that supported Michener early in his career. It was a very cute, touching moment. But it was also a moment to remember when it comes to how to deal with people. Michener was always extremely gracious and very encouraging—to me, my family, and all who came in contact with him. He treated everyone as if they could enrich his life. And often they did. Even a little girl who showed him her hand printed story and crayon drawings of a seal named Simon.

119. NO MATTER HOW HARD YOU WORK, THERE'S ALWAYS SOMEONE WHO WORKS HARDER

Both Michener and Leonard averaged a book a year over the course of their careers, but compared to **Joyce Carol Oates** they might be considered slackers. Oates has averaged more than three a year over the last half century. Truman Capote dismissed her because he couldn't believe a writer could have as many ideas in her head as she does. I'm in awe of her.

I first interviewed her at her house in Princeton in 1993, when her novel *What I Lived For* was about to come out. That was 77 books ago! Since then, she has published 31 novels, 17 books of short stories, 8 novellas, 7 works of nonfiction, 6 young adult books, 4 collections of her plays, 3 children's books, and one book of poetry. And that's just in the last 23 years. She's been publishing since 1963, and that was thirty years and 62 books before I met her. And those figures don't include the 22 books of anthologies in which she appears. No wonder Truman Capote shuddered when he heard her name. Capote wrote twelve books in his lifetime. Oates might be at 150 before I finish writing this!

It's rare to see such obsession in any of the arts, but writing is unlike drawing, singing, sculpting or boxing. It's the least tactile of the arts and the most cerebral. A writer can spend a day trying to turn a phrase in just such a way, or move a storyline along another few pages. And when a work is finished, an entire imaginary world has been created, born from the writer's mind. It's not a profession without its perils; writers are notorious for drinking and drugging to ease the mental pain or stimulate the imagination. That's why it's not surprising when a writer goes over the edge; yet the suicides of many great writers remain a shock to the cultural grid. Consider the loss of Ernest Hemingway, Virginia Woolf, Sylvia Plath, Yukio Mishima, Yasunari Kawabata, Raymond Chandler, Hunter Thompson, Hart Crane, Jerzy Kosinski, William Inge, John Kennedy Toole, Kurt Vonnegut, Jack London, John Berryman, Richard Brautigan, and David Foster Wallace. All died by their own hands. What often seems to drive such writers to take their lives is a realization that their best work is behind them. That makes a writer like Joyce Carol Oates all the more remarkable

When I asked her about her compulsion to write she said that while she loved to write she also felt frustrated and dissatisfied. "A whole day can go by and I feel I haven't accomplished anything," she said. Considering her output, those days must be few and far between. "I don't want to emphasize any morbidity or pathology in speaking of compulsion, but compulsion does account for virtually any achievement. People don't know how hard I work. You have to have a driving, almost feverish energy. It's demonic. If you don't have the will and you're not hungry and you're not almost compulsive about it, you can't succeed. You can't be a normal, happy, contented person and be a great novelist. You've got to be a little crazy."

She acknowledged her own craziness when she told me that she couldn't stop taking notes. "I've actually been writing while I'm being introduced to give a talk." Which *is* pretty crazy considering that for most people, public speaking is a dread equivalent to death. After saying this, she added, "I really begrudge the hours that I have to go to sleep, because sleep is a waste of human energy. When I travel sometimes I just don't sleep at all. A chaotic rush of images keeps me awake all night."

These images often get written down. Before she writes each novel, she fills notebooks with the backstory of her main characters. She showed me some of these notebooks and I realized that for every novel she publishes, there's another book that never appears, and that's all about what happened to her characters *before* they enter the world between hardcovers. I know about taking notes and making outlines, but not filling up enough pages for a complete book before writing that book! That was a revelation. Her compulsion, her obsessiveness, is kind of insane. But when you're this kind of writer, the kind who considers writing more important than family, friends, sleep, vacations, and walks in the woods, it's not uncommon. Genius works on a whole different level of consciousness. When James Joyce could barely see because of his failing sight, he wrote in crayon. Oates writes before being introduced on stage.

Here is what Joyce taught me about my profession: That there are writers and there are Writers. That Writing is a deadly serious business for writers who see it as the highest of callings. That you have to be more than a little crazy to push through the frustrations and dissatisfactions of your day-to-day output.

Joyce Carol Oates is one of those writers. Not that she would ever be faced with running out of ideas—the woman is a phenomenon in that way. She continues to write at the highest level, and her books have been receiving increasingly better reviews as she ages. She is now 77. Philip Roth stopped writing at 80, and he had an admirable run. Joyce will probably find a way to send back notes from the Other Side, as Truman Capote spins in his grave.

Patty Hearst said her alter-ego Tania may still live in my imagination, but definitely not hers. 1982

I interviewed Mel Gibson in his office, with the sword and axe from Braveheart within reach. We talked about heaven and hell and where he might end up. 1995

With First Lady Nancy Reagan at the Beverly Wilshire Hotel. Before the Secret Service could frisk me, the First Lady appeared. Her personal photographer captured the moment. 1987.

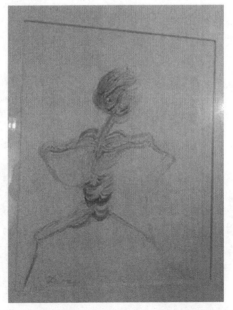

Miles Davis kept himself focused by drawing figures with colored markers on a sketchpad. Before I left he signed two of them to me. That night Miles called. "Larry," he said in his raspy voice, "what'd you do with those drawings I gave you?" 1985

I can't think of anyone who amused me more than Truman Capote. 1982

"Now that," said Michener as my daughters kissed him, "is as good as any new school with my name on it." 1992

XVIII

120. BEAUTY IS WHEN YOU TEAR ABOUT IT

In the summer of 1969 I was visiting my parents in Jericho, Long Island, when an old school friend drove by with her roommate from Cranbrook Academy of Arts in Michigan. I was only in the States for that weekend and was getting ready to go to Europe before returning to Ghana, where I was teaching in the Peace Corps. But something I had never experienced before happened when my friend Eileen stopped her car and introduced me to the beautiful Japanese woman sitting next to her. "This is **Hiromi**," Eileen said. "Larry's one of my oldest friends," she said to Hiromi.

"Hello, Lolly," Hiromi said.

That's all she said, but I was struck dumb. I smiled at her and asked Eileen if she was visiting her parents and then said I'd stop by. I borrowed my mother's car and drove in a trance the three blocks to Eileen's house. I had fallen in love. At first sight.

Until that moment, I didn't believe that such a thing could happen. I thought it was a movie fabrication. You didn't just look at a person and say, "She's the one." But that's what happened. I looked at Hiromi, heard how my mispronounced name rolled off her tongue, and knew—not thought, but *knew*—that this woman had a purity of soul unlike any woman I had met or would ever meet, and that she would make me a better person. I knew that I had met my soul mate.

She didn't know this. Didn't have clue what was on my mind when I asked if I could join them the next day in the city. There was a party in a downtown loft and I watched how she glided through the room, talking to people, and smiling at me when she turned my way. I had no desire to talk to strangers; I only had eyes for her. When I suggested we take a walk outside, she thought a late night walk in downtown Manhattan was a splendid idea. When we saw a woman abandon her child in front of a police station, we brought the child inside and were both shocked by seeing so many other abandoned children wailing for their mothers. It was an unusual moment to share and brought us closer.

I had to leave two days after meeting Hiromi and did what I could to let her know how I was feeling. I gave her an African necklace made of crushed glass beads, a hand-painted leather bracelet that I had brought back to give my sister, and a note that said I wanted to stay in touch.

Which is what we did. While I was in Europe she decided to visit her sister who was in Spain and then meet me in Madrid. We spent ten days together getting to know each other. I returned to Ghana and she to Michigan to finish her schooling. We wrote letters for a year and when my tour was up I traveled to Japan, where she had returned to work on her art. I met her parents, who were not happy to see that her "friend" was a *gaijin*.

Her work had grown from small sisal sculptures to three-dimensional works that reached twelve and fifteen feet in length. She was offered a solo show at a gallery in Tokyo and I knew my presence would interfere with her preparation. But before I left I asked her what it would take to get her to live with me in New York. She said she couldn't plan that far ahead. "What if I wrote an article about you for a crafts magazine?" I asked. "If they publish it, would you come?"

She thought my suggestion was absurd. She was not known in her field yet. She was just starting out. No magazine would be interested in an artist at the beginning of her career.

"So, is that a yes then?" I asked.

"It can't happen," she said.

"But what if it did? Would you come?"

"Yes," she said. "I would come. But...."

That's all I needed to hear. I had only written one published article, the one about the sculptor Vincent Kofi for *African Arts* magazine. But I was confident that I could find a craft magazine that might be interested in Hiromi's highly original work, especially since she had a gallery behind her. So I bought a tape recorder and started asking her how she did what she did, where she got her ideas from, and what was in her mind as she worked on such a large scale making objects that looked like giant sea creatures or intricate webs.

1975

In her broken English she explained how she had gone from being a traditionally trained weaver to an abstract textile artist. "I like working with my materials," she said, "because I can move with rope and sisal and straw. I don't feel I'm used by the loom; I feel I must also be created as I create. Weaving by loom is two-dimensional; it doesn't fascinate me as much. When I work I like to feel I'm part of what I'm doing. That's why I work in three dimensions—I feel my pieces; they take shape in my hands; I mold them, twist them, almost like a potter touching clay. I sew and crochet and tie my rope in such a way as to feel what comes out is an extension of me, another arm, another body. I can stand apart and look at it, and at the same time feel I'm looking at myself. It's not really 'art' for me, it's just....me. What I do is what I am, my work gives me shape."

I asked her how much nature had influenced her work.

"I grew up very close to nature," she said. "I used to make a toy when I was a child, from bamboo shoots...because I had to. I couldn't buy any plastic toys, so I had to invent the toys. When I was hungry, I used to get the bamboo skin and put salted plum in it and bite it. I used to go to the fields and pick flowers and I saw little snakes...I can make a picture in my mind. I appreciate that. Nature influences my work...I want to get into it...not just look. I want people to feel my work doesn't belong to anywhere. When I look at a shell in my hand I say, 'Wow! This is beautiful color.' And I look at the shape...that feeling from nature...it just...I have to create something for myself, too."

Then I asked her about beauty. What did beauty mean to her?

"To me," she said, "Beauty is when you tear about it. I look to create a certain sadness in my work. My work is very visual; I look to create movement, emotional movement, in what I do."

I listened to her speak and felt my own emotional movement about her. Hiromi was as beautiful as anything she created. Looking at her work, looking at her, brought tears to my eyes, and when I returned to the States I wrote about her for *Craft Horizons* magazine. She had given me a definition of beauty. Keats wrote, "A thing of beauty is a joy forever." And through Hiromi I saw how beauty had come into my life, making it a joy that has lasted 47 years and counting. In other words: Forever. Which makes this my favorite lesson. Because through her I have learned more about goodness, kindness, thoughtfulness, and selflessness than I had ever known before. That's why I married her, and how I became a better person. And when I stray, which is often, I only have to look at her to remember where my compass should point.

I just follow my tears.

Acknowledgments

The lessons in this book stem from what I learned from talking to these people for interviews and articles that appeared in *The N.Y. Times, Newsday, Playboy, Rolling Stone, Movieline, Premiere, Cosmopolitan, Redbook, Oui, Hollywood Life, TV Guide, Reader's Digest, Writer's Digest, Modern Maturity, AARP, The Saturday Evening Post*, the Playboy Channel, and for my books of conversations with Truman Capote, Marlon Brando, James A. Michener, Al Pacino, and Ava Gardner and my books *Signing In, Climbing Higher*, and *The Hustons*. I'd like to acknowledge all the editors I've worked with over the years and the agents who have helped me along the way. I'm also indebted to my friend Paul Singer, who came up with some good ideas for the front and back covers, and Ellen Shapiro, who designed them. Then there's my faithful proofreader and sounding board, Rita Settimo, who puts my grammar to shame. And my wife Hiromi, and my daughters Maya and Hana—who have listened to versions of these lessons and could probably point to many I've forgotten.

Lawrence Grobel (lawrencegrobel.com) is a novelist, journalist, biographer, poet and teacher. Five of his 25 books have been singled out as Best Books of the Year by *Publisher's Weekly* and many have appeared on Best Seller lists. He is the recipient of a National Endowment for the Arts Fellowship for his fiction. PEN gave his *Conversations with Capote* a Special Achievement Award. The French Society of Film Critics awarded his *Al Pacino* their Prix Litteraire as the Best International Book of 2008. James A. Michener called his biography, *The Hustons*, "A masterpiece." His *The Art of the Interview* is used as a text in many journalism schools. *Writer's Digest* called him "a legend among journalists." Joyce Carol Oates dubbed him "The Mozart of Interviewers" and *Playboy* singled him out as "The Interviewer's Interviewer" after publishing his interviews with Barbra Streisand, Dolly Parton, Henry Fonda and Marlon Brando. He has written for dozens of magazines and has been a Contributing Editor for *Playboy*, *Movieline*, *World* (New Zealand), and *Trendy* (Poland). He served in the Peace Corps, teaching at the Ghana Institute of Journalism; created the M.F.A. in Professional Writing for Antioch University; and taught in the English Department at UCLA for ten years. He has appeared on CNN, *The Today Show, Good Morning America, The Charlie Rose Show* and in two documentaries, *Salinger* and Al Pacino's *Wilde Salome*. His books can be found at Amazon.com. He is married to the artist Hiromi Oda and they have two daughters.

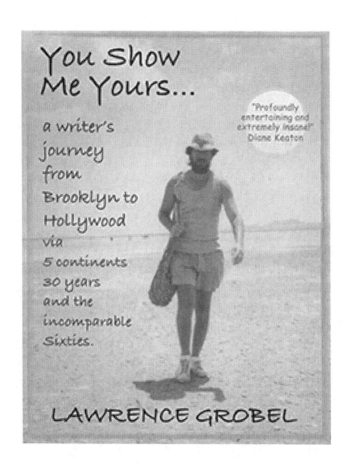

You Show
Me Yours...

"Profoundly
entertaining and
extremely insane!"
Diane Keaton

a writer's
journey
from
Brooklyn to
Hollywood
via
5 continents
30 years
and the
incomparable
Sixties.

LAWRENCE GROBEL

An Excerpt:

You Show Me Yours

A WRITER'S JOURNEY FROM BROOKLYN TO HOLLYWOOD VIA **5** CONTI-
NENTS, **30** YEARS, AND THE INCOMPARABLE SIXTIES

the introduction of the memoir

Lawrence Grobel

Introduction

Stories are all we have. We each possess them. Hundreds. Thousands. The stories of our lives. The stories of those who have been part of our lives. And, depending on who we tell them to, people might be amused, enlightened or offended. Sometimes they can relate, and sometimes they may be stimulated to match a story with one of their own. As I began interviewing people, I found my early stories useful. I didn't just go in and start asking celebrities questions—instead, I'd try to bring them out by relating incidents in my past. That's how I've been able to do what I do—I told them mine, they told me theirs. It's an ancient technique.

Truman Capote told me how he informed Brando about his miserable childhood and his drunken mother who used to lock him in a hotel room and disappear for hours. Brando told Capote his mother was also an alcoholic and he used to have to fetch her from bars and bring her home. When Capote's article appeared, his own stories were left out, and Brando felt cheated. To get Capote to tell me how he got Brando to talk, I first told him about my experiences with Brando on his island in Tahiti. I'd tell Brando my stories as we walked around the island and he would tell me some of his. I would interrupt his stories to say I'd prefer to wait until we were taping, and he would say not to worry, he'd repeat them. But of course I knew that a repeated tale is never as lively as a fresh one, so

I wound up telling Brando my stories for three days, until he was ready to let me turn on the tape recorder.

Dolly Parton liked to share ghost stories, especially after I mentioned that I had served in the Peace Corps and lived in West Africa for three years. She wanted to hear all about the witches who turned into fireballs in the forests, about dead people who came back and talked to friends but couldn't be touched. And about the fetish priestess ceremony I had witnessed in a place called Larteh.

Al Pacino laughed at my prankster stories with my friend Sal, the crazy things we did during high school. It reminded him of the things he did with his friend Cliffy, who once stole a city bus and took him on a wild ride. Goldie Hawn related to the sibling rivalry between my sister and me and opened up about her family. Kurt Russell never forgot the time eight policemen came to my house with a search warrant thinking I was running a child pornography ring. He often used it as an example why we should never give up our right to bear arms, because we were dealing with a fascist police state which might one day force us to defend ourselves against them. Bridget Fonda saw one of the five prints her grandfather Henry had given me and was moved to ask for stories about him. In return, she gave me what she remembered. Alec Baldwin once got excited over a story I told him about how I used to pick up my friend Alexandria at her house and make like I was taking her on a date, when what I did was drive her to the train station so she could sneak into Harlem to visit her boyfriend. When I later found out that her father was mob connected and he had her followed, Alec thought it had the potential for a movie and embellished it with tales of his own childhood.

When I met Henry Moore in Italy I told him a story about how I once went to a gallery of a performance artist and wound up buying the artist herself, who came to live with me for a week. Moore had a hard time with this and went into his theories of what art was... and wasn't.

Chris O'Donnell, before he married and became a father of four, was reluctant to talk about his girlfriend, until I told him how I had lived with mine for eight years before we decided to get married. He also didn't want to talk about the kinds of things he did with girls when he was a teenager, so I told him that my daughter was then a teenager and I knew only too well the kinds of things I wanted to protect her from. Because O'Donnell was then just 25 and not used to revealing himself, he was a particularly difficult interview, and so I resorted to telling him about my travels through Africa, India, and the Orient after I left the Peace Corps; about seeing the Tyson-Spinks fight at the Playboy Mansion with nearly a hundred famous faces, none of whom had time to make a bet, it was over so fast; about collecting first editions; and about spending nine months interviewing Barbra Streisand for *Playboy*. My travels led him to reflect on what he might have missed out on, having turned professional at 18; the Tyson fight brought out his enthusiasm for sports; collecting books turned into a discussion that he'd never really read any books for pleasure and was more influenced by television; and dealing with Streisand for so long left him speechless, he just couldn't imagine talking about himself to anyone for more than a few hours, and even that was a struggle. But in the end, because we had so many subjects to cover by just trading stories, he gave far more than even he thought he had in him. It also didn't hurt that he knew Al Pacino had become one of my closest friends, since he first achieved recognition when he appeared with Pacino in *Scent of a Woman*.

Connections have proved important in doing what I do. I first got to know Pacino because he had read my conversation with Brando and agreed to be interviewed by "the guy who did Brando." Robert De Niro agreed to be interviewed for *Playboy's* 35th anniversary issue because Pacino had told him he could trust me (as it turned out, he wasn't at all happy with what appeared, and let me know it at Pacino's 50th birthday party). Patty Hearst gave me her first major interview after we spent a morning in Hugh Hefner's grotto Jacuzzi, smoothly set up by Christie Hefner. Sandy Gallin, Michael Jackson and Dolly Parton's manager, paid me by the hour to record his life story after he saw how I had handled Dolly, and then offered me a job to help develop the film branch of his company. Ava Gardner called me from London to ask if I'd help write her memoirs, because "If you're good enough for John Huston, you're good enough for me." Huston had given me his address books and told all who knew him to "Just tell the truth" when I came to interview them for the biography I was writing of his family. The timing wasn't right concerning Ava, but it was when Montel Williams asked me to work with him on his memoir of having to live with MS, and Lawrence Schiller did the same for his memoir of photographing Marilyn Monroe. James A. Michener agreed to a book-length interview because of the ones I had done with Capote and Brando. I don't know why Jesse Ventura agreed to talk to me after he became governor of Minnesota or why Bob Knight let me fly to Indiana to interview him after he was fired as head basketball coach by the university, but they did. Ventura's controversial remarks and Knight's scary behavior garnered more media attention than anyone could have predicted...and I had stories that TV and radio talk show hosts wanted to hear.

What I discovered as I continued interviewing people was that while I was there to talk about their lives, what kept us talking were the stories we shared. Celebrities liked to hear stories about other celebrities, especially those who were even more famous than they were. So after I interviewed Marlon Brando I found myself telling Brando stories to Lily Tomlin, Katharine Hepburn, Luciano Pavarotti, Kim Basinger, Robert Evans, James Spader, Harvey Keitel, Christopher Walken, and Oliver Stone. Saul Bellow was amused by stories about Jack Nicholson; Halle Berry and Joyce Carol Oates liked to hear about Al Pacino. Even Barbra Streisand liked to sit around a kitchen table and hear the latest stories about people she knew. So I would entertain them. I would tell the stories of my life, and stories of the lives of their peers. They would listen and respond with stories they had or heard. And I would go home and write about these stories in my journal, which began to grow like kudzu, a ground covering that multiplies rapidly. Over the years I found that I was writing more in my journal than I was for the books and journalism I was doing. People would often ask me why I've never written a book about my life. My first answer was that although I've spent a good deal of my professional life around the rich and the famous, I've always been in the background. My second answer was that I was just too young. But I'm not that young anymore. So perhaps it's time to tell my stories. The ones that got me from Brooklyn to Long Island to Los Angeles to Ghana and around the world, and the ones that found their way into my journal, which I didn't start keeping until I met Barbra Streisand. I've worried about telling some of these stories, but I just keep remembering what Truman Capote said when I asked him about writing about the high society people he knew. "Who did they think I was anyway?" he asked. "I'm not a court jester. I'm a writer."

I remember once sitting with Al Pacino in the backyard of his rented house in Beverly Hills. He was telling me that he'd turned down doing *60 Minutes* because Mike Wallace was going to be the interviewer, and Al didn't quite trust what Wallace might ask him.

"Couldn't you ask for someone else?" I suggested.

"No, I wouldn't do that; that would be insulting to Mike."

"Brando thought Wallace was a sadist," I said.

"Marlon thought a lot of people were. He thought that of Francis Coppola. He thought that of Charlie Chaplin. Here we are, talking about Brando as if he were still around. When he's been gone for a while now."

"We would never have become friends without him," I said.

But that's for later... another story. Always, another story.

Praise For Lawrence Grobel's Other Books

THE HUSTONS: "A Masterpiece" (James A. Michener). "Extensive and fascinating" (*New York Times*). "Brilliant" (Connie Martinson). "The best book of the year" (J.P. Donleavy). "A feast of a book" (*The New Republic*). "Reads like a romantic, exciting and compelling novel"(*The Atlanta Journal-Constitution*). "Dazzlingly complex" (*Datebook*). "A tremendous spellbinder" (Kirkus Reviews). "The work to which all future biographers and critics must turn" (*Daily News*).

CATCH A FALLEN STAR: "...keeps the reader in suspense from the first cannon shot to the finale in this perceptive understanding of the illusion and the reality of the movie capital of the world."

–*DZIENNIK,* 5 Star Review

BEGIN AGAIN FINNEGAN: "...engrossing, energetic, and masterful in its control and its gallery of characters." –Obie Award winning playwright Adrienne Kennedy

YOU SHOW ME YOURS: "Profoundly entertaining and extremely insane!"

–Diane Keaton

427

CONVERSATIONS WITH CAPOTE: "A wonderfully outrageous read...fearless candor about practically everything–and everyone–on Earth....the most entertaining glitz of the season."

–The Denver Post.

CONVERSATIONS WITH BRANDO: "Fascinating...Brando remains one of the century's truly remarkable and intriguing characters. Grobel painstakingly nurtures his sometimes obstinate subject into a state of openness...As interesting as the interview itself is the commentary Grobel provides...A must purchase (*Booklist*). "You got me!"(Marlon Brando)

AL PACINO In Conversation with Lawrence Grobel: "Journalist Grobel, who literally wrote the book on interviewing, puts his talents on full display...giving the reader as much insight into interviewing style as into the legendary actor...Part of the book's draw is witnessing the two become closer as the years go by...making for increasingly engaging and illuminating reading."

—Publisher's Weekly Starred Review

CLIMBING HIGHER with Montel Williams: "An absolutely riveting read."

–N. Y. Post

THE ART OF THE INTERVIEW: Lessons from a Master of the Craft: "Grobel gives readers the equivalent of a master class in this thoroughly entertaining treatise on one of the toughest tasks in journalism.... An invaluable resource for aspiring journalists, the book also satisfies the voyeuristic desires of a celebrity obsessed culture by raising the curtain on the idiosyncratic demands of stars and by putting the reader in the interviewer's chair....*The Art of the Interview* is an overstuffed treat, full of anecdotes, advice from other top writers and the kind of commiserating stories about difficult editors, hellish assignments and prickly stars that will seize the attention of both professional interviewers and their audiences."

–Publisher's Weekly

ABOVE THE LINE: CONVERSATIONS ABOUT THE MOVIES: "This book satisfies on every level. I ate my copy and feel very full" (Steve Martin). "A diverse and lively collection, the highest art of the interview" (Joyce Carol Oates).

ENDANGERED SPECIES: Writers Talk About Their Craft, Their Visions, Their Lives: "As an interviewer Larry's all the things Joyce Carol Oates has said he is: prepared, adaptable, and graced with the intelligence needed to shoot the breeze and elicit intriguing responses from uncommonly gifted and often uncommonly suspicious subjects."

–Robert Towne

Made in the USA
Lexington, KY
26 October 2018